Organizational Ethics in the Compliance Context

Organizational Ethics in the Compliance Context

John Abbott Worthley

Health Administration Press · *Chicago, Illinois*

03 02 01 00 99   5 4 3 2 1

Library of Congress Cataloging-in-Publication Data

Worthley, John Abbott.
    Organizational ethics in the compliance context / John Abbott Worthley.
      p.   cm.
    Includes bibliographical references.
    ISBN 1-56793-110-3 (alk. paper)
    1. Health services administration—Moral and ethical aspects.   2. Medical care—Law and legislation—United States.   I. Title.
    RA394.W679   1999
    174'.2—dc21
                                                99-28710
                                                 CIP

The paper used in this publication meets the minimum requirements of American National Standard for Information Sciences—Permanence of Paper for Printed Library Materials, ANSI Z39.48–1984. ∞ ™

Health Administration Press
A division of the Foundation
   of the American College of
   Healthcare Executives
One North Franklin Street
Chicago, IL 60606-3491
312/424-2800

Contents

PREFACE

THIS BOOK is designed to help build bridges that link the interests and insights of healthcare managers and lawyers with those of ethicists. Although the focus is on healthcare organizations, the concepts and cases are equally applicable to all modern organizations. In the healthcare field specifically, as George Khushf articulates in his article that accompanies Chapter one, bioethicists have recognized that clinical ethics unfolds within organizational contexts. They are, therefore, seeking to learn more about organizational realities and dynamics. Healthcare administrators and attorneys, on the other hand, face intensifying Joint Commission on Accreditation of Healthcare Organizations (Joint Commission) requirements for rigor in attending to the ethical dimension of their organizations as well as compelling government pressures to be in compliance with regulatory, legal, and ethical standards. Therefore they are seeking to learn more about the nature of healthcare ethics. Bioethicists search for ways to bring organizational insight to their ethics interests; healthcare executives and legal counselors look for ways to bring ethics insights—required by regulatory guidelines—to their compliance and accreditation challenges. Drawing from the wisdom of both groups, the following chapters are offered to further the mutual interests of the two groups and to facilitate dialogue and interaction.

For helping me realize the need for a bridge to link these quests I owe special thanks to Emil Moschella, J.D., legal counsel at Blue Cross Blue Shield of New Jersey; Susan Goold, M.D., bioethics professor at the University of Michigan Medical School; and John Griffith,

M.B.A., Fellow of the American College of Healthcare Executives. Emil introduced me to the nature and urgency of the compliance reality in healthcare today, and Susan linked me with bioethicists who are seeking organizational expertise. John, an eminent healthcare scholar and practitioner, introduced me to Susan by recommending to her *The Ethics of the Ordinary in Healthcare* (also published by HAP). They were the bridge builders who enabled me to attempt to construct the spans found in this book, and I am grateful to them.

For facilitating my research I want to thank the Medical School of the University of Illinois and the library staff—particularly Anne Koehler—of Indiana University. For setting me straight on so many aspects of organizational life I proudly acknowledge the experience, intelligence, and kindness of my graduate students over the years.

This volume is a companion to *The Ethics of the Ordinary*. Although that book has been gratifyingly successful, the long-term usefulness of the book depends on insights and skills in dealing with the organizational context within which professional power—the focus of *The Ethics of the Ordinary*—is exercised. Chapter five of that book, "Ethics and Accountability: Dealing With Controls," probes organizational influence over individual behavior. The present book expands broadly on that reflection. In addition, this volume complements Scott Withrow's *Managing Healthcare Compliance* (Chicago: Health Administration Press 1999), which is a detailed handbook for the compliance issue.

Amazingly, little literature exists in the field of healthcare organizational ethics specifically; that which is available tends to address only topical issues such as fiduciary duties, codes of ethics, and resource allocation. Although the field of business ethics is more developed, it too has tended to move toward issues and cases rather than concepts and comprehensiveness. Therefore, I draw from the fields of organizational theory and behavior as well as management and bioethics, and attempt a merger in the conviction that mutual enrichment will result. Healthcare managers benefit from the conceptual insight and theory of bioethicists; bioethicists benefit from the practical insight and realism of healthcare managers and organization behaviorists.

This writing, then, offers an overall framework for probing organizational ethics. As with my former book the effort may be disappointing to some because it too seeks to emphasize ordinary and routine reality more than the grand and glamorous aspects, and to be rigorously practical and descriptively reflective rather than normative and prescriptive. Therefore, the following chapters examine healthcare organizational ethics in the compelling context of Joint Commission requirements and the current governmental and legal emphasis on organizational compliance with regulatory and ethical standards. The intent is to enhance under-standing of the dimensions of healthcare organizational ethics while facilitating development of skills for "doing" it.

Each chapter is anchored in a case based at one of my favorite places: the mythical St. Serena's Healthcare Corporation. Through the cases we meet many of St. Serena's staff and come to learn about this organization's efforts at compliance and ethics. Fundamental concepts are then presented and their application is illustrated by reference to the case. Previously published articles drawn from journals such as *Harvard Business Review*, *Journal of Clinical Ethics*, and *Health and Human Services Administration* are included to offer more in-depth conceptual insight. An annotated bibliography of some of the better literature available concludes each chapter. Chapters one through three build a conceptual framework that is applied in the topical Chapters four through eight. A concluding chapter revisits the framework.

As complex corporations and the healthcare field specifically con-tinue to evolve toward new horizons, the field of organizational ethics poses a paramount challenge for managers and ethicists alike. I hope that what you are about to read helps you to meet that challenge, and that you find the reading to be fun as well as stimulating.

1

THE NATURE OF HEALTHCARE ORGANIZATIONAL ETHICS

ORGANIZATIONAL ETHICS in healthcare has been tagged by the American Hospital Association (AHA) as a "growing movement" in its formative stages.[1] Although the pressure of governmental compliance measures is undoubtedly the major catalyst for this movement, other developments in healthcare are also contributing to the current organizational attention to ethics. Rovner, for example, cites the intensity of conflict between cost and quality in the managed care environment, the competition of values involved in the wave of mergers and acquisitions, and the relentless march of new technology as factors in the current rise of concern about organizational ethics.[2] Taking a managerial choice perspective, Weaver, Trevino, and Cochran contend that pro-action—not just reaction—on the part of executives has also been a factor in this phenomenon.[3]

In the face of this movement, healthcare organizations and bioethicists alike are struggling to figure out what constitutes organizational ethics and how to respond. In the words of health ethicist Leonard Weber, "no one has a very clear understanding of what organizational ethics is all about."[4] The problem, as George Khushf well articulates in the article attached to this chapter, is that very little has been written on the subject, and few organizations have experience beyond the traditional realm of bioethics. This book enters that void.

Business management literature, mostly uninformed by bioethics, is rich in analyses relevant to healthcare organizational ethics.[5] Bioethics literature, mostly uninformed by management theory, is rich in concepts applicable to organizational dynamics.[6] Drawing from and merging these well-developed fields, this first chapter sets a framework for probing the nature of organizational ethics in healthcare.

Some work[7] with a focus on organizational ethics has appeared in the healthcare management field, but such research has tended to be issue-specific and anecdotal more than comprehensive and conceptual. Lacking is a solid conceptual framework through which to develop practical and theoretical insight on the nature of organizational ethics and on approaches to effectively dealing with the ethical dimension of the healthcare organization. Fundamental questions need to be raised and probed if healthcare organizations are to adequately respond to, for example, judicial incentives, federal sentencing guidelines, and Joint Commission on Accreditation of Healthcare Organizations (Joint Commission) directions.

What, for example, does the phrase "healthcare ethics" imply? What elements of a healthcare organization have an ethical dimension? What constitutes ethical behavior by corporate entities? And, by the way, what are the differences among individual/professional ethics, clinical ethics, and organizational ethics? Furthermore, what relationship does the notion of organizational ethics have to compliance standards and programs, Joint Commission requirements, and ethics committees? Once we get a handle on these questions, we must decide how healthcare institutions can professionally approach and manage the ethical dimension of their organizations.

The case that follows and the articles that accompany the commentary will allow us to construct a prism through which our discussion of these and related questions may be illuminated.

CASE STUDY

Case One: Organizational Compliance or Ethical Misbehavior?

The written policies of St. Serena's Hospital are in full compliance with Joint Commission standards. With regard to medical records, for example, no more than 50 percent of patient records are to be delinquent, that is, not completed by the attending physician within 30 days of patient discharge. Joint Commission accreditation policy states that a "Type I" deficiency recommendation results when failure to meet this standard is discovered during the periodic Joint Commission survey.

In reality, maintaining this policy and Joint Commission standard is a bit complicated. Although the attending physician is the responsible authority for *completing* patient records, department directors are responsible for *managing* the records, including ensuring compliance with policies and standards. Responsibility is split. The physicians, who are focused on actual patient care, often leave record completion until "they have time." In addition, a new computer system at St. Serena's has not yet corrected chronic medical record problems in record tracking, record inaccuracy, and misplaced files. In practice, delinquency of medical records is often, perhaps usually, above the 50 percent target. The organization traditionally uses the incentive of a Joint Commission inspection to spend extra time completing sufficient records in the weeks prior to the survey team arrival.

This year installation of the new computer system has made this last-minute compliance tradition much more difficult. Among the department directors concerned about compliance with the policy and Joint Commission standards is Inga, a highly regarded, fast-track career hospital administrator. She arrived at St. Serena's just two months ago and has been trying to deal with inherited deficiencies ever since her arrival. In her previous positions units had always received the highest Joint Commission ratings under her management.

With increased competition St. Serena's is emphasizing achievement of a high Joint Commission rating. Inga's boss, vice president Vinny, has stressed its importance to all department directors: "Whatever it takes," he declares, "St. Serena's will continue its rating as the preeminent medical center in the region." Other department directors under the same pressure have told Inga that in a pinch they have used the computer system's problems as a positive factor: "Files are often missing because of tardy inputting, so we simply remove enough files to meet the 50 percent standard. In due time they will all be completed and the glitches in the system remedied to facilitate compliance with the standards in the future." Good managers like themselves, they reasoned, should not be embarrassed—and the organization should not be penalized—because physicians delay completing patient records. Eventually the physicians will get the message. "In the meantime we must protect the good rating and image of the hospital. Besides, all hospitals do things like this to deal with Joint Commission inspections in a realistic manner."

Convinced that this short-term action would lead to good long-term solutions and that the well-being of St. Serena's (and her own career) needed to be safeguarded, Inga removes some records from the system in a way that is very unlikely to be noticed. Her department and the entire hospital receive an outstanding rating from the Joint

Commission. After the inspection Inga reenters all records and institutes procedures to facilitate better routine adherence to the 50 percent deficiency standard.

Inga's record-removing action was implemented by her subordinate supervisors; one of these supervisors, Nancy, was uncomfortable with what was being done. Nancy considered refusing to cooperate in the maneuver but worried about what such resistance might do to her career at the hospital. She is now considering anonymously informing the Joint Commission.

Questions for Discussion:

1. What should Nancy do? Why? Were she to become aware of the federal whistle-blowing *(qui tam)* program financial incentives, would she be more likely to report the matter? Would federal investigators tend to view the whole matter as an endemic pattern at St. Serena's worthy of intensive investigation?
2. Is the case a matter of "organizational ethics," or is it simply an issue of the professional ethics of Inga and others?
3. Is St. Serena's a compliant organization? Is it an ethical organization? What, if anything, is the difference?
4. What constitutes a compliant organization? What constitutes an ethical organization?
5. Distinguish the micro from the macro aspects of the situation.
6. How does individual professional ethics interplay with organizational ethics in this case?
7. What could be done to improve the organizational ethics of St. Serena's Hospital?
8. Who is responsible for the organizational ethics of a healthcare organization like St. Serena's?
9. Ethically speaking, how important is the value of organizational well-being in situations like those presented in the case? Does an administrator have an ethical responsibility to protect that well-being?

COMMENTARY

Sound reflection, as contrasted with a seat-of-the-pants response, on these kinds of questions requires a basic conceptual foundation. The seemingly simple notion of "healthcare ethics" is a good place to start.

Healthcare Ethics

Traditionally, healthcare ethics has been understood as clinical ethics. Erich Loewy's recently republished and widely used *Textbook of Healthcare Ethics*,[8] for example, is focused nearly exclusively on clinical matters as is Monagle's and Thomasma's new edition of *Health Care Ethics*.[9] What are the ethical issues regarding organ transplants, terminal illness, pregnancy problems, and the like? This has typically been the kind of focal question posed in healthcare ethics discussions.

In recent years the notion of healthcare ethics has evolved from a nearly exclusive interest in clinical issues to more concern about the behavior of individual healthcare professionals in clinical situations. Questions about the ethical obligations of a physician, a nurse, and even a nutritionist or a pharmacist have now become more prominent.[10] My own book, *The Ethics of the Ordinary in Healthcare*, pushed the margin a bit further by including healthcare administrators in its probe of the ethical implications of the power wielded by individual healthcare professionals.

Most recently, both bioethicists and ethicists interested in professional behavior have recognized the over-arching significance of the ethical "climate of the organization" for both clinical and professional ethics. As Brodeur puts it:[11]

> Bioethical problems have dominated the ethical concerns of hospitals and other health care institutions for the past 25 years. The termination of treatment, autonomy, informed consent, advance directives, and issues of reproduction have occupied center stage. In the late 1980s, many institutions began to recognize and address many other ethical issues that focused on business practices, corporate ethics, and managed care concerns.

This perception of the organizational dimension of the concept of healthcare ethics has emerged largely from bioethicists who view it as a logical expansion of the clinical ethics field. In 1994 Reiser argued that healthcare ethicists should expand their academic and clinical efforts to "encompass issues of institutional life and policy."[12] Agreeing, Robert Lyman Potter of the Midwest Bioethics Center argued that organizational ethics is the new frontier of clinical ethics[13]:

> I recommend shifting the boundaries from the clinical to the corporate arena, and argue for adopting a set of behaviors for creating an ethical corporate culture that values ethics in decision making with the same importance as clinical data, financial concerns, and legal issues.

At the same time, healthcare social workers were coming to a similar conclusion: "We propose understanding that clinical ethics are

Figure 1.1 Elements of Healthcare Ethics

embedded in relationships produced by organizational structures."[14] Figure 1.1 depicts these relationships.

In George Khushf's analysis this new perception can be attributed to the experience of healthcare ethics committees in major health organizations over the past decade. These committees, he has found, discovered that their work required them to address administrative and organizational aspects of the clinical issues referred to them. He suggests that now bioethicists need to explore how the notion of healthcare ethics can be given "an institutional presence."[15]

Others view organizational ethics as different from but interdependent with clinical ethics rather than as an expansion of clinical ethics; they see the concept of healthcare ethics as a merger of the clinical with the organizational. The Joint Commission's Paul Schyve distinguishes the patient-provider relationship from the customer-supplier relationship: "The former relationship is governed by 'clinical' ethics, and the latter relationship is governed by 'business' ethics. But these two relationships and their ethical dimensions are not independent."[16] Similarly, management professor Lynn Paine argues that the influence of organizational factors on individual behavior is considerable and important implications for the concept of ethics exist—implications that have been vigorously noted by federal compliance investigators and judges.[17]

In effect, in healthcare today the ethics question has evolved from what is ethical in medical care to what constitutes an ethical healthcare organization, the former being included in the latter. Our understanding of the concept of healthcare ethics is maturing. Figure 1.2 attempts to portray that evolution.

The Ethics of the Ordinary reflected that process of conceptual development. The text emphasized the organizational and administrative

Figure 1.2   Aspects of Healthcare Ethics

realities that healthcare professionals face within clinical conditions; its cases concerned administering informed consent, admitting patients, addressing unprofessional behavior, bending the rules, and so forth. But *Ethics of the Ordinary* focused on the individual healthcare professional, limiting reflection on organizational influences to a single chapter. This book now expands that focus to highlight the organizational context within which healthcare professionals work.

So, how do all these comments relate to the situation at St. Serena's? How does the case help clarify the concept of healthcare ethics? On one level, the case suggests a relationship between the clinical and the organizational in healthcare ethics. The situation begins in the clinical setting with physicians treating patients. The treatment includes physician responsibility for recording patient history, protocols applied, tests conducted, medications prescribed, and so forth; yet the organizational process to provide, maintain, and support the clinical care merges with the clinical process of delivering healthcare. The organizational and the clinical aspects are inter-related and perhaps interdependent, as are the duties of the manager and the clinician. Are organizational processes of record keeping facilitating or impeding the relationship between the manager and clinician? Is healthcare ethics a matter of what the physician does in treating the patient, what the physician does in recording (or delaying recording) the treatment, what the managers do in processing the records, how the managers deal with record-keeping standards, Joint Commission standard-setting and inspection procedures, or all of the above? Is healthcare ethics in the case of St. Serena's a matter of the clinical or of the managerial, or is it an organizational reality that includes both?

On a second level, the St. Serena's case involves both the individual and the organization and questions whether healthcare ethics is a matter of one or the other, or both. The case may be about Inga's manipulation of the accreditation process, the physicians' failure to attend to the record dimension of clinical care, or the organization's structures that make it difficult for both parties and its culture that permits—perhaps even encourages—deception? Reflection on St. Serena's might help clarify just what healthcare ethics is supposed to be about.

On a third level we might note the presumably good intentions of the physicians who are trying to serve all the patients well instead of "wasting" their skills on paperwork, and of Inga who is trying to keep a hospital that provides such good care to so many people operating efficiently and effectively. The seeming insufficiency of their good intentions may suggest an organizational obligation to help. It also suggests that the nature of healthcare ethics might be more complicated than meets the eye.

Analyzing cases like St. Serena's is especially important because of the difficulty healthcare professionals and ethicists alike have experienced in conceptualizing, clarifying, and articulating what constitutes "organizational ethics" in healthcare today. As Reiser observes, the efforts of healthcare organizations to understand their ethical dimension have been "episodic and lack the comprehensiveness needed to deal with the complex issues they now must face."[18] Potter remarks that a consensus is yet to develop on what constitutes an ethical healthcare organization. To accomplish this, he argues, healthcare professionals will need to weave a new field of corporate healthcare ethics and struggle to discern its working assumptions.[19] For example, is the St. Serena's situation a case about the professional ethics of Inga and Nancy, or a case about the ethics of St. Serena's Medical Center? If it is about the organization's ethics, what does that entail? And how does a healthcare professional manage ethically in the midst of confounding realities such as described in the case? Some further conceptual distinctions can be helpful in addressing such questions and in clarifying the notion of organizational ethics in healthcare.

Organizational Ethics

In an early issue of the *Cambridge Quarterly of Healthcare Ethics*—a journal that has expressed a largely clinical view of healthcare ethics—Thompson described ethics in healthcare as a focus on "the ethical problems created or significantly shaped by the institutional setting in which they occur."[20] Certainly the situation at St. Serena's was significantly shaped by the institutional setting. Izraeli and Schwartz, on the other hand, drawing from the Federal Sentencing Guidelines (discussed

Figure 1.3 Elements of Organization Ethics

below), see organization ethics as the behavior of the organization's agents, that is, its managers and professionals.[21] To them it seems to be more an outcome than a setting, though they would acknowledge the influence of the setting on the outcome. Undeniably, the behaviors of the physicians, Inga, and Nancy at St. Serena's have something to do with the organization's ethics.

Potter gives a proactive spin to the concept[22]: "I will define organizational ethics as the intentional use of values to guide the decisions of a system." Organizational ethics involves, he argues, all the activities of the organization, including the clinical patient-provider relationship and the commercial consumer-provider relationship. What values at St. Serena's guided the physicians' tardy record keeping, Inga's record maneuvering, and Nancy's contemplated reporting? Were those values individual or organizational? Were they intentional or instinctive? Did St. Serena's do anything to nurture or discourage those values? Were those efforts cosmetic or substantively effective? Does St. Serena's seem to have considered organizational ethics more as a clinical and not so much as a commercial/managerial matter? Schyve suggests the importance of viewing organizational ethics with both a clinical and a commercial lens[23]: "Separating business ethics from clinical ethics in practice . . . is unlikely to serve the best interest of either the patient or healthcare organization or of those who are trying to resolve the ethical challenges in healthcare." Figure 1.3 suggests this relationship.

Business guru Bowen McCoy also sees organization ethics in terms of the totality of organizational activity. He emphasizes the idea of "shared values" and the practical aspect of having a process for consciously developing values consensus and dealing with conflict of values.[24] At St. Serena's we might inquire whether the physicians and administrators shared the same values, and whether there was an explicit (overt) or implicit (subtle) process for dealing with the tension between values such as organizational well-being, patient well-being, and honesty. Could it be that the physicians shared Inga's value of organizational well-being but just did not realize the effect of late record keeping because no mechanisms existed to get them "into the loop"? Could it be that Inga shares the value of honesty with everyone else but was blinded by the organizational culture that seemed to emphasize organizational well-being above all else? Or were these values simply not shared by all because St. Serena's had not established an organizational process for clarifying and inculcating values?

The idea that organizational ethics are related to the totality of organizational activity is shared by Frank Navran of the Ethics Resource Center. He views organizational ethics as a spectrum extending from compliance with external and internal regulations, policies, and procedures to maintainance of both organizational and universal values.[25] In practice, asserts Lee Raiola of Harvard Pilgrim Health Care—one of few healthcare organizations with considerable experience in attempting to do organizational ethics—organizational ethics is about corporate conflicts of responsibility, conflicts between and among different policies, different values, and different rules.[26] Is such a spectrum of organizational activity, within a reality of conflict, what we see unfolding at St. Serena's?

Finally, Chambliss seems to define organization ethics as fundamentally a matter of power, that is, of the real influence organizations have over individual behavior. Drawing from Coleman's classic analysis of the modern organization as a new "moral actor,"[27] Chambliss sees organizational ethics in terms of a displacement of morality from the level of individual choice to the level of intraorganizational dynamics[28]: "With the growth of organizational actors, we see the decline of individual morality, not so much because people 'don't care' but because it doesn't matter if they do." Healthcare organizations, he finds, present opportunities for setting aside individual responsibility; organizational ethics should be attending to this reality. With this lens for understanding, Chambliss would undoubtedly analyze Inga's behavior, and probably that of the physicians and other managers, in the same vein that he analyzes the situation of the nurse in general: "The organization allows her to do things that she may believe wrong, in the belief that 'that's how things work,' 'others know better than I,' or 'it's a big place so how can I know the whole story?' "[29] Awareness of this is a first step toward developing structures and processes that help healthcare organizations to be moral agents instead of immoral agents. Has St. Serena's institutionally failed in this regard?

Individual Versus Professional Versus Organizational Ethics

Clarification of the difference among, and relationship of, personal, professional, and organizational ethics can help our reflection. The

St. Serena's case is a stark example of the implosion of individual ethics with professional and organizational ethics. An insightful study of nursing ethics some years ago made the point with utmost clarity[30]:

> The hospital nurse finds herself constrained in various and occasionally conflicting ways by the hospital (which employs her), the physician (with whom she works), the client (for whom she provides care), and the nursing profession (to which she belongs). To what extent can she be her own person—be ethically autonomous—in these circumstances?

A similar point could be made at St. Serena's about the physicians, Inga, and Nancy. They are individual healthcare providers, but they exercise their skills as members of a profession and of an organization.

Each of us brings our particular individual and personal ethics into our professional positions. A code of personal ethics reflects moral development from childhood, which is the subject of Lawrence Kohlberg's famous theory of stages of moral development.[31] But the notion of professional ethics focuses on a group of people instead of just one individual. The notion of professional ethics reflects development of the consensus values of the profession and, consequently, is broader than the notion of personal ethics; but it is also derived from the specific perspective of a particular profession and reflects its own special interests. Personal ethics relates to the way we live; professional ethics relates more to the way we work. For this reason many commentators distinguish morality from ethics; the former is principles of personal life and the latter is actions in professional life.

And, finally, we must address corporate ethics. Organizations consist of individual people, therefore corporate ethics encompasses many personal ethics; they consist of many groups, therefore corporate ethics also encompasses many professional ethics. Organizational ethics is complex and this complexity is a hallmark of the nature of organizational ethics. Such complexity largely revolves around values. Personal values enter professional realms where consensus values are derived. Personal and professional values enter the corporate arena where another set of values emerges. The inevitable result is the harsh reality of conflict in which the personal values of one individual come against the personal values of another, where the professional values of one group confront the professional values of another group, and where both personal and professional values confront the values of the corporation. Figure 1.4 indicates the relationship.

The situation at St. Serena's unfolds these relationships. Individual physicians undoubtedly value responsiveness to patients over efficient completion of paperwork; Inga probably appreciates cost savings, managerial efficiency, and organizational well-being more than the needs

Figure 1.4   Components of Organization Ethics

of patients she seldom sees; and Nancy seems to have a clear sense of the value of honesty but perhaps not as clear a sense of corporate well-being. Physicians as a group focus more on the value of patient health and loyalty to one another; managers as a group focus more on the value of corporate health and loyalty. The organization as a whole naturally values its own survival and well-being and the needs of the corporation more than the needs of an individual. The perspective of each gives them clarity on some important values and cloudiness on other important values. We could well ask as federal compliance investigators and judges seem to be doing whether the organization of St. Serena is doing anything, either formally or informally, to help the physicians remember the importance of paperwork, Joint Commission standards, and the corporation's well-being; to help Inga and the other managers remember the priority of patient care and the importance of honesty; and to help Nancy remember the importance of the corporation. Does the corporation merely leave the values issue up to each individual and professional group, and hope that everyone remembers all the values that are important or does it have a sense of organizational ethics and take steps to develop that sense in its individual constituents?

The significance of these distinctions and questions is raised by Thompson from an ethical theory perspective and by Chambliss from a practical sociological perspective. "Principles from individual ethics often distort institutional ethics," writes Thompson. Ethical problems of the organization, he claims, are not the same as ethical problems that face professional groups and individuals. Even when they are similar, he argues, "the ethical principles by which we should resolve them are likely to be quite different."[32]

Chambliss finds that in reality most ethical problems in today's healthcare systems are "structurally created." As he sees it, the clash of group values (such as nurses versus physicians versus managers) is more apparent than the clash of individual values and it takes place in an organizational setting. Healthcare professionals work in a particular hospital or small group practice or other organization with its own customs and constraints. According to Chambliss, individuals work under professional obligations with real peers who pressure, support, and ask for help. "To pretend that someone is good or bad apart from settings that allow or prevent their acting is abstraction in the worst sense and pragmatically foolish."[33] He therefore calls on bioethicists to move healthcare ethics from a formal individualism to a broader "organizational awareness." Would such an awareness help us better understand, as Jones and Ryan contend,[34] why good people do bad things in organizational settings? Would it help us understand why compliance problems persist? Would that advice help St. Serena's? Does it suggest that Inga's behavior is not solely a matter of her personal morality, and that Nancy's decision should not be based solely on her personal ethics? Does this suggest that the organization is and should be involved in the ethics of the behavior of its individual members and groups?

Micro Versus Macro

Ethicists typically have preferred to deal with major issues, and in healthcare those issues have largely involved the provider-patient relationship. At St. Serena's, presumably, the situation was temporary and no one was hurt. So what is the big deal? Is this situation really a matter of ethics? The conceptual distinction between microethics and macroethics can help discernment.

Ethicists have regularly employed this concept to help clarify the nature of the issue, but the concept has been used differently by different commentators. Bioethicists have traditionally used the distinction to separate organizational matters as the "macro" dimension of ethics from patient-provider matters as the "micro" dimension. The macro dimension refers to broad, general issues involving the organization as moral agent, and the micro dimension refers to case-specific clinical matters involving the healthcare professional as moral agent. The emphasis in bioethics has tended to be this micro dimension: "Bioethical language has made moral debates more abstract (by continually referring to general principles), rights-driven, individualistic, and centered on discrete cases"[35] (see Figure 1.5).

Thompson has expanded use of the concept to highlight organizational matters more clearly. He describes microethics as concerned with provider-patient relations, and macroethics as concerned with structures of society as a whole (such as national healthcare policy). Left out, he maintains, has been the "middle range of intermediary associations of

Figure 1.5   Dimensions of Healthcare Ethics

Traditional Bioethics Construct

Macro	Micro
↓	↓
Organizational Issues	Patient-Provider Issues

Figure 1.6   Dimensions of Healthcare Ethics

Thompsonian Construct

Macro	Middle	Micro
↓	↓	↓
Social Policy Issues	Organizational Matters	Individual Issues

which institutions are the most durable and influential."[36] Using the conceptual distinction this way, organizational ethics falls between the micro and macro realities at the point at which they intersect. We might call that point "middlethics." Figure 1.6 depicts these distinctions.

Employing the micro-macro concept historically, some observe that the earliest paradigm of healthcare ethics—in the Hippocratic Oath—focused on the micro dimension of the practitioner, in the latter half of the twentieth century the paradigm was expanded to include the macro dimension of broad patient-rights policies, and "in the last two decades, this paradigm of professionals' obligations and patients' rights has further expanded to include the healthcare organization's obligation to respect patients' rights."[37]

Others have viewed the micro-macro concept differently. Farmer distinguishes a practical micro focus from a philosophical macro focus, arguing that ethics discussions—whether concerned with specific practitioner-patient cases or broad policy matters—tend to be pragmatically rather than philosophically oriented.[38] Fox agrees. He calls this orientation myopic, and agrees that it makes ethics discourse a matter of technique rather than a critical interchange.[39] These authors cite the likes of Bertrand Russell, who would contend that healthcare ethics needs to be more macro and studied not for the sake of definite answers but rather for illumination of the questions that should be asked. "Questions enlarge our conception of what is possible, enrich our intellectual imagination and diminish the dogmatic assurance which closes the mind against speculation."[40] Therefore, should we focus on

Figure 1.7 Approaches to Healthcare Ethics

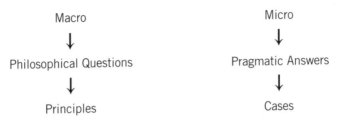

Figure 1.8 Dimensions of Healthcare Ethics

Worthley Construct

	Micro	Middle	Macro
Headliners			
Humdrummers			

raising questions instead of producing solutions in the St. Serena's case? We might respond that healthcare ethics requires a balance as suggested in Figure 1.7.

Finally, in my previous book I used the macro-micro concept to distinguish the "big issue" ethics reality from the "seemingly trivial" realities.[41] I termed the latter "administrative ethics" as opposed to "bioethics." In my analysis, healthcare ethics has concentrated on the grand and redoubtable issues—what I term the macro dimension—regardless of whether these issues involved clinical patient-provider matters or organizational and policy matters. Intense and compelling scenarios have dominated the ethics agenda. Ordinary, routine realities of daily healthcare—what I term the micro dimension—have been largely absent from the agenda of healthcare ethics discourse.

Perhaps a clearer way of presenting this distinction would be to conceptualize and distinguish "headline" issues from "humdrum" issues in healthcare. Clearly healthcare ethics has highlighted headliners and neglected the humdrum. Chambliss describes the situation well: "So much of conventional debate about medical and nursing ethics is inadequate: the frame shift of routinization has bracketed out a vast array of moral difficulties."[42] The routine and humdrum seem to be treated as ethically "trivial," whether they concern social policy, organizational, or individual issues. Figure 1.8 depicts these distinctions in a matrix format that suggests six categories of healthcare ethics realities.

Figure 1.9   Facets of Organizational Ethics

	Headline Matters	Humdrum Matters
Dogma		
Development		
Dilemma		

The striking result of this de-emphasis of the routine and humdrum reality in healthcare is articulated by both McCoy and Chambliss: "Real moral dilemmas are ambiguous, and many of us hike right through them, unaware that they exist," writes McCoy.[43] "The great ethical danger, I think," stresses Chambliss, "is not that when faced with an important decision one makes the wrong choice, but rather that one never realizes that one is facing a decision at all."[44]

Is this the case at St. Serena's? What could be more "ethically humdrum" than record keeping!? Is the physicians' behavior regarding patient records viewed as such a routine matter that all ethical implications are "bracketed out"? Do only headliner issues—like those involving a dying patient—get on the agenda of the St. Serena's ethics committee? Does Inga ponder any ethical aspect of her action or does she see it simply as a routine micro matter? Is St. Serena's a headline case or a humdrum one?

This book attempts to emphasize the routine, humdrum, and micro dimension of organizational ethics in healthcare—the dimension that includes realities like the physicians' daily record keeping at St. Serena's and the often subtle ways that healthcare managers like Inga deal with actors like the Joint Commission. These realities form patterns that are the focus of much judicial and investigatory compliance attention.

The Three Ds

The nature of organizational ethics is multifaceted and those facets can be clarified through the concept of the three Ds: dogma, development, and dilemma—each of which can have either a headline or humdrum focus (see Figure 1.9).

Dogma.

One facet of healthcare ethics obviously concerns laws, regulations, standards, principles, and rules. Some are *clearly* significant, others may *seem* trivial. But they constitute dogma, and violation of them raises questions of ethics, compliance, and accreditation. The government has given the healthcare industry all sorts of dogmas. The Joint Commission provides standards. Organizations establish rules, some of which are written and overt and others of which are unwritten and subtle. Is the St. Serena's case about ethical dogma and about Joint Commission standards and principles of honesty?

Development.

A second facet of healthcare ethics concerns matters for which dogma does not yet exist but about which rules, standards, and so forth, are developing. Currently major issues in managed care are being addressed toward establishing standards and rules, as are seemingly minor issues like accepting small gifts. In these situations some ambiguity exists until the process of designing rules is completed. Is this the situation at St. Serena's, that is, is it a matter of the organization developing information management rules for the physicians and for Inga?

Dilemma.

A third facet of healthcare ethics concerns matters for which dogma exists but in which different dogmas conflict. Again, these conflicts can concern seemingly trivial things like completing paperwork or major matters like Joint Commission standards, blatant deception, and organizational survival. Is dilemma what the St. Serena's case is about? Are the physicians caught between professional rules about patient care and organizational rules about completing patient records? Is Inga caught between managerial principles of organizational well-being and personal principles of integrity? Is Nancy similarly caught between organizational rules of loyalty, personal/family rules about job survival, and personal principles of honesty? Is this a case about which dogma with which to comply? Is it about clarifying dogma organizationally, or is it about organizationally developing guidelines and rules precisely for the kind of complicated situation involved?

The Joint Commission

The Joint Commission has recently enlivened the notion of organizational ethics by introducing "organization ethics" standards (i.e., "dogma") in its accreditation process. Since 1992 standards in the "Patient Rights" section of the accreditation manuals have required healthcare organizations to have a mechanism for consideration of ethical issues arising in the care of patients and to provide ethics training to staff. In 1995 the Joint Commission recognized a wider scope of organization ethics issues, titled this standards section "Patient Rights and Organization Ethics," and began developing standards that require a broadening range of organization ethics issues to be addressed.

Beginning that year, all Joint Commission accrediting standards manuals—including those for ambulatory care, behavioral healthcare, healthcare networks, home care, hospitals, long-term care, and pathology and laboratory services—included a standard requiring each institution to operate "according to a code of ethical behavior."[45] The overview of this section of standards states: "The goal of the patient rights and organization ethics function is to help improve patient outcomes by respecting each patient's rights and conducting business relationships with patients and the public in an ethical manner."[46] According to a senior vice president of the Joint Commission, this emphasis on organization ethics comprising both clinical and business matters will increase.[47]

In this era of intensifying organizational competition in the healthcare industry, Joint Commission accreditation is critical for marketing strategies. The Joint Commission's concern for organizational ethics is therefore a compelling reality to which healthcare organizations will need to respond with increasing rigor and specificity. The Joint Commission's understanding of what constitutes organization ethics is evolving, and healthcare organizations will need to keep abreast of that development.[48] Is St. Serena's keeping abreast? Is the marketing implication of Joint Commission accreditation a key to the St. Serena's case? Should the record-keeping behavior of the St. Serena's physicians and of managers like Inga be subject to Joint Commission scrutiny? What could Nancy do besides turn to the Joint Commission?

Compliance.

Preceding the Joint Commission's attention to organization ethics was the 1991 Federal Sentencing Commission's issuance of guidelines that has resulted in the concept of "compliance" becoming one of the most visible and "buzzword" notions in corporate America. More recently the Health Insurance Portability and Accountability Act of 1997 has combined with the Federal Sentencing Guidelines "to send a sobering chill down the spines of healthcare providers" with the result that compliance in healthcare has become "one of the most popular, fretted-over and discussed words in our industry."[49] What is this "compliance" thing?[50]

The Federal Sentencing Commission began as a straightforward effort to establish uniformity in the penalties given to offenders of federal law and regulations. However, the commission came up with a creative approach to its task—the old carrot and stick method—and in doing so has had a major effect on the practical nature of organizational ethics. The stick part of the approach is the penalty of significant monetary fines and prison terms for violations of federal standards such as those promulgated in healthcare regulations. Multimillion-dollar fines are now routinely assessed, thus providing a clear incentive for organizations to ensure that their corporate behavior is in compliance with federal standards. A key part of this stick approach is the *qui tam* provision, through which investigators encourage potential whistle-blowers (such as Nancy at St. Serena's) by offering a percentage of any eventual financial fine or settlement.

But the profound effect of the Guidelines stems from the carrot aspect: the Guidelines provide for major leniency in sentences (up to 95-percent reductions) if the convicted organization had established an effective compliance program—meaning an organizational process to prevent, detect, and report unethical behavior—*prior* to the violation. Moreover, the Guidelines specify elements considered essential to an effective compliance program, and these include a code of ethics, ethics training, ongoing monitoring, and enforcement mechanisms.[51] Because of the enormous economic incentive the result has been the creation or enhancement of compliance and ethics programs in thousands of corporations.[52] Judges have been fairly consistent in basing the extent of leniency on the extent of organizational efforts; therefore corporations are tending to move beyond mere legal compliance programs to more comprehensive approaches to ethics management because such efforts are rewarded in court. Judges are agreeing with Paine and others that "managers who define ethics as legal compliance are implicitly endorsing a code of moral mediocrity for their organizations."[53]

For example, incidents of "fraud and abuse" happen even when sound compliance programs are in place; because of this judges inquire about organizational efforts to deal with root causes such as an overemphasis on economic and competitive values. Consequently, with such financial and judicial incentives healthcare organizations are well-advised to develop a sophisticated understanding of the nature of organizational ethics and of tangible means of nurturing it. The up-to-date article on compliance that is attached to this chapter provides a solid foundation for that pursuit.

In the case of St. Serena's, is it relevant to know whether the hospital has a compliance program in place? We could consider the case as a matter of "fraud and abuse." Would a sentencing judge wonder whether the compliance program was working? Does it matter whether Nancy has any internal mechanism for reporting the deception she witnessed? Is there anything St. Serena's could do to prevent and detect the behavior of the physicians and of Inga?

However, even if such mechanisms were in place, fraud and abuse still happened. The judge is thus likely to ask whether St. Serena's has done anything such as values-clarification training to address the root causes of the deception. Should such things be part of an organizational compliance or ethics program at the hospital?

The development of the compliance context through the Federal Sentencing Guidelines as well as the evolution of Joint Commission standards through the accreditation process clearly point to the conclusion that organizational ethics in healthcare today must be a program of action, not just a pulpit of preaching. Organizational ethics is about what healthcare institutions *do* in the face of a reality that is ethically complicated and challenging. As Potter suggests, greater clarity in organizational ethics will be acquired gradually by experience in doing, rather than just talking about, organizational ethics. The following readings and subsequent chapters might help us figure out how to get on with the task.

Notes

1. Rovner, J. 1998. "Organizational Ethics: It's Your Move." *Health System Leader* 5 (1): 4.

2. Ibid., 7.

3. Weaver, G., L. Trevino, and P. Cochran. 1999. "Corporate Ethics Programs As Control Factors." *Academy of Management Journal* 42 (1): 41.

4. Weber, L. 1997. "Taking on Organizational Ethics." *Health Progress* 78 (3): 20.

5. See, for example, Vallance, E. 1995. *Business Ethics At Work*. New York: Cambridge University Press; Aguilar, F. 1994. *Managing Corporate Ethics*. New York: Oxford University Press; Clark, R., and A. Lattal. 1993. *Workplace Ethics*. Lanham, MD: Rowman and Littlefield; Donaldson, T., and P. Werhane. 1993. *Ethical Issues in Business*. Englewood Cliffs, NJ: Prentice-Hall; Nash, L. 1990. *Good Intentions Aside*. Boston: Harvard Business School Press; and Andrews, K. (ed.). 1989. *Ethics in Practice: Managing the Moral Corporation*. Boston: Harvard Business School Press, just to cite a few of the numerous sources available.

6. See, for example, Monagle, J., and D. Thomasma. 1998. *Healthcare Ethics*. Gaithersburg, MD: Aspen Publishers; Loewy, E. 1996. *Textbook of Healthcare Ethics*. New York: Plenum Press; Arras, J., and B. Steinbock. 1995. *Ethical Issues in Modern Medicine*. Mountain View, CA: Mayfield; Glasser, J. 1994. *Three Realms of Ethics*. Kansas City, MO: Sheed & Ward; Beauchamp, T., and J. Childress. 1989. *Principles of Biomedical Ethics*. New York: Oxford University Press; Jonsen, A., M. Siegler, and W. Winslade. 1988. *Clinical Ethics*. New York: Macmillan; and Veatch, R. 1981. *A Theory of Medical Ethics*. New York: Basic Books, just to cite a few.

7. Notably, Chambliss, D. 1996. *Beyond Caring*. Chicago: University of Chicago Press; Darr, K. 1995. *Ethics in Health Services*. New York: Praeger; and Griffith, J. 1993. *The Moral Challenges of Healthcare Management*. Chicago: Health Administration Press, among others. In addition, the journals, *Health Ethics Committee (HEC) Forum* and *Bioethics Forum* have, over the years, published pieces related to organizational ethics issues.

8. Loewy, E. 1996. *Textbook of Healthcare Ethics*. New York: Plenum Press.

9. Monagle, J., and D. Thomasma. 1998. *Health Care Ethics*. Gaithersburg, MD: Aspen Publishers.

10. See, for example, the discussion of "physician responsibility" in Jonsen, A., M. Siegler, and W. Winslade. 1982. *Clinical Ethics*. New York: Macmillan; the treatise on nurses in Chambliss, *Beyond Caring*; as well as Taylor, C. 1997. "Everyday Nursing Concerns: Unique? Trivial? Or Essential to Healthcare Ethics?" *HEC Forum* 9 (1): 68–84; and Mandel, E., and J. Worthley. 1986. "Skeletons in the Hospital Closet Revisited." *Nutritional Support Services* (Feb): 44–46.

11. Brodeur, D. 1998. "Health Care Institutional Ethics: Broader Than Clinical Ethics." In *Health Care Ethics*, edited by J. Monagle and D. Thomasma, 497. Gaithersburg, MD: Aspen Publishers.

12. Reiser, S. 1994. "The Ethical Life of Health Care Organizations." *Hastings Center Report* 24 (6): 35.

13. Potter, R. 1996. "From Clinical Ethics to Organizational Ethics: The Second Stage of the Evolution of Bioethics." *Bioethics Forum* 12 (2): 4.

14. Walsh-Bowers, R., A. Rositer, and I. Prilleltensky. 1996. "The Personal is the Organizational in the Ethics of Hospital Social Workers." *Ethics and Behavior* 6 (4): 331.

15. Khushf, G. 1997. "Administrative and Organizational Ethics." *HEC Forum* 9 (4): 301–302.

16. Schyve, P. 1996. "Patient Rights and Organization Ethics: The Joint Commission Perspective." *Bioethics Forum* 12 (2): 14–15.

17. Paine, L. 1994. "Managing for Organizational Integrity." *Harvard Business Review* (Mar/Apr): 103.

18. Reiser, "The Ethical Life of Health Care Organizations," 28.

19. Potter, "From Clinical Ethics to Organizational Ethics," 8.

20. Thompson, D. 1992. "Hospital Ethics." *Cambridge Quarterly of Healthcare Ethics* 1 (3): 203.

21. Izraeli, D., and M. Schwartz. 1998. "What Can We Learn From the U.S. Federal Sentencing Guidelines for Organizational Ethics?" *Journal of Business Ethics* 17 (4): 1046.

22. Potter, "From Clinical Ethics to Organizational Ethics," 4, 6, 8.

23. Schyve, "Patient Rights and Organization Ethics," 19.

24. McCoy, B. 1997. "The Parable of the Sadhu." *Harvard Business Review* (May/June): 59.

25. Navran, F. quoted in J. Rovner, *op. cit.*, 6.

26. Raiola, L. quoted in J. Rovner, *op. cit.*, 6.

27. Coleman, J. 1974. *Power and the Structure of Society*. New York: Norton.

28. Chambliss, *Beyond Caring*, 151.

29. Ibid., 177.

30. Benjamin, M., and J. Curtis. 1981. *Ethics in Nursing*, 23. New York: Oxford.

31. Kohlberg, L. 1976. "Moral Stages and Moralization." In *Moral Development and Behavior*, edited by T. Lickona, 31–53. New York: Holt, Rinehart & Winston.

32. Thompson, "Hospital Ethics," 203.

33. Chambliss, *Beyond Caring*, 117, 182–83.

34. Jones, T., and L. Ryan. 1998. "The Effect of Organizational Forces on Individual Morality." *Business Ethics Quarterly* 8 (3): 445.

35. Chambliss, *Beyond Caring*, 4.

36. Thompson, "Hospital Ethics," 203.

37. Schyve, "Patient Rights and Organizational Ethics," 14.

38. Farmer, D. 1998. "Against Myopia: Public Administration and Ethics." *Journal of Public Affairs Education* 4 (1): 33.

39. Fox, C. 1994. "The Use of Philosophy in Administrative Ethics." In *Handbook of Administrative Ethics*, edited by T. Cooper, 83–105. New York: Marcel Dekker.

40. Russell, B. 1959. *The Problems of Philosophy*, 161. Oxford, UK: Oxford University Press.

41. Worthley, J. 1997. *The Ethics of the Ordinary in Healthcare*, 2–3. Chicago: Health Administration Press.

42. Chambliss, *Beyond Caring*, 58–59.

43. McCoy, "The Parable of the Sadhu," 57.

44. Chambliss, *Beyond Caring*, 59.

45. Joint Commission on Accreditation of Healthcare Organizations. 1996. *Comprehensive Accreditation Manuals*. Oakbrook, IL: JCAHO.

46. *Ibid.*, 35.

47. Schyve, "Patient Rights and Organizational Ethics," 17.

48. Indicative of this evolution is the recently published *Ethical Issues and Patient Rights Across the Continuum of Care*. (1998. Oakbrook, IL: Joint Commission on Accreditation of Healthcare Organizations.)

49. Batts, C. 1998. "Making Ethics an Organizational Priority." *Healthcare Forum Journal* 41 (1): 40.

50. See Withrow, S. 1999. *Managing Healthcare Compliance*. Chicago: Health Administration Press for a comprehensive handbook on the subject.

51. Kaplan, J., L. Dakin, and M. Smolin. 1993. "Living With the Organizational Sentencing Guidelines." *California Management Review* 36 (1): 138–42.

52. Izraeli, D., and M. Schwartz. 1998. "What Can We Learn from the Federal Sentencing Guidelines for Organizational Ethics?" *Journal of Business Ethics* 17 (4): 1046ff. See also Gunn, J., E. Goldfarb, and J. Showalter. 1998. "Creating a Corporate Compliance Program." *Health Progress* 79 (3): 60–63.

53. Paine, L. 1994. "Managing for Organizational Integrity." *Harvard Business Review*. (Mar/Apr): 107.

READINGS

The following readings—one from a bioethics field journal and the other from a business ethics periodical—offer two different perspectives on the nature of organizational ethics. George Khushf, a bioethicist, offers a pioneering statement on the current stage of the journey of medical ethics. His article is both inviting and illuminating in its sense of the nature of organizational ethics. In focusing on the need to improve clinical ethics analysis, he argues that healthcare organization ethics needs to be better understood and probed. He sees healthcare ethics as an emerging "new field of reflection" on how to give ethics an "institutional presence"—a notion dear to the hearts of compliance officers and federal judges. Khushf suggests ten areas to be essential aspects of organizational ethics in healthcare today.

Driscoll, Hoffman, and Murphy, practicing management analysts, focus on the issue of "compliance" and suggest that organizational ethics is largely a matter of rigorous management control systems and practical mechanisms. Theirs is the most current and comprehensive essay on the compliance reality facing healthcare today. The authors provide both a conceptual and practical grasp of what is required to be "in compliance." Stressing that compliance and ethics are more a management than a legal challenge, they describe and illustrate specific managerial mechanisms and measures. Note how they argue that ethics and compliance go hand in hand in a developed organizational ethics program, and that compliance systems give practical teeth to ethical principles.

What would George Khushf have to say to St. Serena's? And Driscoll and company?

Administrative and Organizational Ethics

George Khushf*

Bruce Jennings recently commented on an impasse in bioethics and in political theory more generally.[1] Attempts at addressing ethics and public policy are too often framed by polar alternatives, neither of which is sufficient for addressing the problems confronting society. Either one looks to the individual or to the state; either the market or government. Missing from the discussion has been a broader account of civic society and those mid-level institutions that provide a third way, mediating overly individualist or statist solutions. He called for increased reflection and focus on this third way.

In a more practical manner, Dennis Thompson has made this same point with his call for a hospital ethics. As with Jennings, he notes that:

*Reprinted with permission from HEC Forum 9 (4): 299–309. Copyright 1997 Kluwer Academic Publishers. George Khushf is bioethics professor at the University of South Carolina, Columbia.

Ethics (both as an academic discipline and as concrete practice) has tended to focus on either relations among individuals [referred to as micro-ethics] or on the structures of society as a whole [referred to as macro-ethics], not on that middle range of intermediary associations of which institutions are the most durable and influential.[2; 203]

Thompson has argued that this dichotomy of micro- and macro-ethics has led to a distortion of ethics for institutions, since they require a different type of reflection, one which is responsive to the way organizations such as hospitals uniquely frame issues. Although he only hints at the ways such an institututional ethic differs from the other two approaches, he points to the importance of group decision making, complex interprofessional interests, and administrative involvement as relevant considerations. He also advances an expanded role for healthcare ethics committees (HECs) as a way of addressing these organizational concerns.

This approach to ethics committees as a form of institutional ethics is important. In practice, HECs are doing something unique at hospitals, something that was not really present before they came into existence. They give an institutional presence to ethical reflection, and they involve structures and dynamics that are different from traditional professional ethics.[3] However, it has taken some time to appreciate their unique contribution. At first, the focus of HECs was directed almost exclusively toward the classical macro- and micro-ethical issues. Although in their practice they concretely embodied that "third way" of institutional ethics, this was not made clear in conscious reflection. Instead, through case consultation and early educational activities, HECs considered problems that were understood in micro-ethical, individually oriented terms; for example, issues in withholding and withdrawing of treatment, advance directives, interprofessional relations, etc.[4] The methods used were taken from the general bioethics literature, and they were not made responsive to the unique demands of institutions. It is as if it did not matter whether the questions about the withdrawing of treatment were asked about a patient at home, in a long-term care institution, a Catholic hospital, or an academic medical center.

Gradually the body of literature on HECs matured. Indeed, *HEC Forum* played a role in that development. As people increasingly reflected on the HECs themselves and not just on the traditional medical ethical problems, new concerns came into focus. At first they were very practical. Who should be on the HEC?[5–7] How can prospective and retrospective case consultation be best addressed?[8–10] What educational activities should HECs be involved in?[11, 12] What policies should be addressed as a part of the policy review function of committees?[13] How can one evaluate the effectiveness of the committee?[14] With whom should the interests of the committee be aligned: the patient, the healthcare team, the institution, or community?[15–18] Should the HEC be understood as an administrative or clinical/staff committee?[19–21] Increasingly people came to see that there were important ethical issues behind these questions, issues involving administrative decision making at hospitals, fair representation on committees, and the ways institutional policies frame the more traditional ethical questions about treatment, confidentiality, patient best interest, etc. HECs were thus not simply a way of responding to micro-ethical problems and controversies; they were themselves controversial, involving in their own constitution and functioning important values that were related to the ethical life of the institutions they served. As HECs reflected on themselves, a broader administrative and organizational ethic came into view.

Just as the scope and character of institutional ethics became apparent, structural changes in the healthcare sector made the need for such an ethic more urgent. Again it is helpful to briefly review recent developments in this area. When HECs first emerged, many of the issues they addressed were raised by new medical technologies. [Here I focus on the need that required HECs, not on their precedents or the precedents for consultation; for a fuller treatment of the history, see references 4 and 22.] Perhaps the most important issue (and still the one most often addressed in case consultation) was related to limitation of life-sustaining treatment.[4] Decision making was largely in the hands of physicians, and the coupling of medical paternalism with a technological imperative interfered with reasonable end-of-life decision making. Through case-consultation, HECs were able to provide physicians at hospitals (where most of the controversial treatment decisions took place) with a sense of the developing legal and moral consensus regarding the role of patient autonomy in decision making about treatment, thus placing a check on some medical paternalism. The ethical reflection thus focused on interaction between two individuals, physician and patient (or patient surrogate). For most people involved in HECs, it was still assumed that clinical decisions were insulated from mechanisms of payment and from institutional policy. The issues addressed by HECs were thus rarely tied to broader administrative or organizational concerns. To the degree that ethical issues in clinical decision making were separated from institutional concerns, the rubrics of a micro-ethic seemed appropriate. Recently, however, with the rise of managed care, one can no longer assume such a neat line between clinical and administrative jurisdictions. To address properly ethical problems, one must thus address administrative and organizational issues together with more traditional clinical ones.

In response to the convoluted incentives to overtreat that were found in indemnity based, fee-for-service medicine, integrated networks have developed, which have established mechanisms to decrease utilization and control costs.[23, 24] Among such mechanisms are capitation, withholding funds and bonus arrangements, the use of generalist gatekeepers, and profiling that is sometimes linked to credentialing for closed networks. Hospitals are purchasing physician plans to lock up referral lines and obtain the leverage to pass on their financial incentives to physicians. Larger networks that serve as insurers are purchasing the hospitals. Throughout this extensive consolidation of healthcare delivery systems, there is an integration of payment and provision, such that administrative and organizational policies are increasingly influencing clinical decision making. Often this development is understood in terms of a move from professionalism to an entrepreneurially oriented medicine, and the resultant conflicts of interest are flagged as gross violations of ethical ideals.[25] However, although there are definite problems, this interpretation is far too simple. Behind conflicts of interest one often finds conflicts of obligation, with the introduction of new obligations to patient populations that involve limits on marginally beneficial treatments and thus a modification of former obligations to unqualifiedly advance an individual patient's interest.[2, 23, 26] As population and community interests are integrated with traditional professional ideals, there is a modification of the factors that influence clinical practice, such that institutional policy needs to be accounted for in responding to traditional problems such as withholding treatment. There are also new problems that result from the shift of authority from clinical professionals to administrators. In this context, it becomes increasingly important to ask how ethics can be given an institutional presence.

In sum, there are structural transformations in the healthcare sector that make institutions much more important in the delivery of healthcare, and which demand an ethic that is responsive to the administrative and organizational concerns. At the same time, there is a mature literature, primarily on HECs, that has become sensitive to institutional concerns and is available to respond to this new need. Between micro- and macro-ethics (we could call this an "inter-ethics"), and responsive to developments in the healthcare sector, a new field of reflection is emerging which provides a genuine third way. This is not individual oriented, nor is it directed toward governmental structures and policies, although it considers these dimensions. It focuses on mid-level institutions and draws on multiple overlapping senses of community. This emergent domain will be the focus of a new, regular feature of *HEC Forum* titled "Administrative and Organizational Ethics." Before it became fashionable to address "civil society" and the mid-level of the institutions in healthcare, this journal worked intuitively with the concept. It was anticipated in the journal's subtitle, *An Interprofessional Journal on Health Care Institutions' Ethical and Legal Issues.* HECs are one way of giving institutional presence to ethical reflection, and they have been and will continue to remain a central focus of this journal. However, it is also important to ask about other ways in which the ethical life of an institution can be cultivated. What role does a mission or values statement play in promoting an ethical climate or culture? How can administrators be guided in their formation of policy? Here there is a natural extension from the policy review function of HECs to a more explicit (perhaps even proactive) concern with policy formation and the ethical guidelines that can direct administrators and institutions. Taking the journal subtitle as our cue, this new section will consider the full range of issues related to institutional ethics. We thus welcome submissions in the areas of administrative and organizational ethics for healthcare institutions.

Among the topics we will look for in future submissions are the following.

1. *Ethics for hospital administrators*: Clinical practice is increasingly influenced by administrative decisions and policies. However, administrators often have responsibilities to boards or a community that are in some tension with the responsibilities of clinicians; they may be more directed by a business or market rather than a professional ethic, and there may have been little or no ethics training in their education. We hope to receive contributions that consider the administrator at the juncture of business and professional ethics, and explore the options for ethics education and reflection that may inform administrative decisions. This may include case rounds for administrators,[27, 28] their inclusion and role in HECs,[4] or the possible role for a separate administrative review.[29, 30] We welcome both theoretical reflection on the nature of administrative ethics, as well as practical accounts of the mechanics or experiences that result in administrative involvement in ethical reflection.

2. *Missions and values statements for healthcare institutions*: Presumably, there is a difference between for-profit and not-for-profit institutions, with the latter having a mission and values that warrant their privileged tax status. However, economic pressures and structural changes in healthcare are eliminating the differences.[31] This raises the question of the role that institutional mission and values can and do play in directing concrete practice and policy. Some organizations have found ways to give values statements a major role in directing matters such as recruiting of personnel and decision making, while others have

given little weight to such statements.[32] To further explore these issues, we welcome essays that consider the ways institutions can embody their vision and values in the face of outside economic and social pressures. We are also interested in the types of mission statements that have been developed, the reasons why they have been formulated, and the ways they inform decision making and policy.

3. *Religious healthcare institutions and "deep values"*: Many healthcare institutions are religiously affiliated, but it is not clear what role religious values should have in the provision of healthcare in our pluralistic society. Robert Veatch has argued that cultural and religious pluralism should be extended to a rich pluralism in healthcare itself, with "deep values" regarding human good and well-being directing the ways in which physicians interact with patients and institutions frame such clinical encounters.[33] Others, such as Erich Loewy, seek more directly to sustain a secular basis for all healthcare, and they object to a role religious values may play, especially if those values would direct the deliberations of an institutional ethics committee.[34] We welcome essays that consider the role of "deep values" in healthcare institutions. We are interested in general ethical reflection that considers the role such values should play, and practical accounts of the ways in which they should, can, or do (not) direct concrete clinical and administrative actions. What does it mean for a religious institution to sustain its integrity? How should such an institution relate to people and other institutions that do not share its values? What role should an HEC play at such an institution?

4. *Ethics in hospital accreditation*: External pressures are now placed on healthcare institutions to address ethical concerns, with the most notable example being the Joint Commission guidelines on patient rights and organizational ethics.[35] It is very likely that such external pressures will increase, and institutions will need assistance in satisfying them. We thus welcome essays that reflect on the external guidelines and provide helpful information on how to satisfy requirements. Where is the Joint Commission likely to move in the future, and what new considerations are likely to be introduced? What questions are asked when a hospital is being reviewed, and how should they be answered? Further, we are interested in essays that critically evaluate the appropriateness of the ways in which hospitals are evaluated, and welcome suggestions for alternative formulations of guidelines and review mechanisms.

5. *Guidelines for policy formation and review*: One of the three central functions of HECs is policy review, and several publications have provided examples of the types of policies that can be written.[13] Helpful sample policies have been published in this journal. However, relatively little has been written on the effectiveness of such policies,

and on the role they play in configuring administrative and clinical decisions. There has also been little summarizing of the types of policies that can be written, and the ways such policies function. Further, who should be involved in the writing of what policies (e.g., nursing policies, administrative policies, etc.)? We welcome essays that address these topics.

6. *Managed care ethics*: Much has been written on the ethics of managed care, but very little addresses this from the perspective of an institutional ethic. Generally, the literature on this topic works with a micro-ethic, largely focusing on the role of financial incentives in the physician-patient relation. While this perspective is important, it does not sufficiently account for administrative and organizational concerns. We welcome submissions that consider managed care organizations (MCOs), addressing the values that do or should direct them. What mechanisms are available to assist MCO administrators in ethical decision making? How should institutions review the behavior of physicians involved in an MCO, or address conflicts of interest that may be introduced by the mechanisms of cost-control they introduce? What advice can be given to a healthcare worker or institution negotiating a contract with an MCO? How should the ethical issues be understood from the perspective of an administrative and organizational ethic?

7. *Topics in organizational ethics*: When making his case for a hospital ethic, Dennis Thompson used two examples, confidentiality and patient best interest.[2] These are not normally considered topics in organizational ethics. However, Thompson's point was that these traditional issues need to be understood differently when considering them from an institutional perspective. He then attempted to show how traditional notions of confidentiality and advancing patient interest need to be modified. We would welcome similar reflections on the ways in which traditional topics in clinical ethics need to be re-evaluated from an institutional perspective. For example, how do or should institutional values configure the ways in which treatment decisions are addressed or informed consent is understood?[33] In addition to these reassessments of traditional topics, we also welcome submissions on topics more directly in organizational ethics, topics such as advertising, re-engineering, and personnel evaluation, just to name a few.

8. *External influence on institutional structure and values*: Institutional policies frame clinical encounters, but they do not do so in a vacuum. The institutions are themselves conditioned by broader socio-economic pressures and regulatory policies.[23-25] How do these external pressures and regulations assist or hinder the ethical life of healthcare institutions? What can be done to resist the factors that harm institutional

values? What government regulations should be rewritten or eliminated? We welcome essays that explore such traditionally macro-ethical issues or topics from an institutional perspective.

9. *The role of HECs in addressing institutional ethics*: The central focus of this journal has been on HECs. To what degree are they sufficient or insufficient for addressing institutional ethical concerns? Are there other committees (e.g., administrative) that should be developed to complement traditional HECs? How should alternative institutional ethical mechanisms be related to the consultation, education, and policy review functions associated with HECs? We welcome submissions that explore these issues.

10. *The scope and character of administrative and organizational ethics*: Finally, I hope this announcement and call for papers will itself be taken as a contribution to delineating the nature and scope of administrative and organizational ethics in healthcare. As such, it will be regarded as a proposal open for dispute, to be revised and critically evaluated. Similarly, it will not be regarded as a final statement on the focus of this section.

What topics should be discussed that are not included in this call? Is the characterization of traditional bioethics in terms of micro- and macro-ethics appropriate, and is there a distinct third way (an inter-ethic)? How does or should administrative and organizational ethics relate historically and substantively to the development of HECs and to the structural transformations taking place in the healthcare sector? We welcome critical discussion of the way in which this topic should be understood and discussion best advanced, so that those working in healthcare institutions can be best served in their attempt to promote an ethical culture and life.

References

1. Jennings, B. 1997. "Health as a Civic Problem: Bioethics and the Theory of Civic Society." Presented at the Ninth Annual Bioethics Summer Retreat, Hilton Head Island, SC, 14 June.

2. Thompson, D. F. 1992. "Hospital Ethics." *Cambridge Quarterly of Healthcare Ethics* 3: 203–10.

3. Blake, D. C. 1992. "The Hospital Ethics Committee and Moral Authority." *HEC Forum* 4 (5): 295–98.

4. Heitmann, E. 1995. "Institutional Ethics Committees: Local Perspective on Ethical Issues in Medicine." In *Society's Choices: Social and Ethical Decision Making in Biomedicine*, edited by R. E. Bulger, E. M. Bobby, and H. V. Fineberg, 409–31. Washington, D. C.: National Academy Press.

5. Smith, M. L., and D. Burleigh. 1991. "Pastoral Care Representation on the Hospital Ethics Committee." *HEC Forum* 3 (5): 269–76.

6. White, B. 1991. "Should an Institution's Risk Manager/Lawyer Serve as HEC Members? Yes." *HEC Forum* 3 (2): 87–89.

7. Gottlieb, L. E. 1991. "Should an Institution's Risk Manager/Lawyer Serve as HEC Members? No." *HEC Forum* 3 (2): 91–93.

8. Fletcher, J., A. Jonsen, and N. Quist (eds.). 1989. *Ethics Consultation in Health Care.* Chicago: Health Administration Press.

9. Wear, S., et al. 1990. "The Development of an Ethics Consultation Service." *HEC Forum* 2: 75–87.

10. McCarrick, P. M. 1993. "Scope Note 23: Bioethics Consultation." *Kennedy Institute of Ethics Journal* 3 (4): 433–51.

11. Rawlins, T. D., and J. G. Bradley. 1990. "Planning for Hospital Ethics Committees: Meeting the Needs of the Professional Staff." *HEC Forum* 2 (6): 361–74.

12. Slomka, J. 1994. "The Ethics Committee: Providing Education for Itself and Others." *HEC Forum* 6 (1): 31–38.

13. Monagle, J. F., and D. C. Thomasma. 1996. *Medical Ethics: Policies, Protocols, Guidelines and Programs.* Gaithersburg, MD: Aspen Publishers.

14. Wilson, R. F., et al. 1993. "HECs: Are They Evaluating Their Performance?" *HEC Forum* 5 (1): 1–34.

15. Spece, R. G. 1992. "Should HECs Be Designed Primarily to Assist the Health Care Team and Institution Rather than the Patient? Yes." *HEC Forum* 4 (3): 199–203.

16. Meyer, H. B. P. 1992. "Should HECs be Designed Primarily to Assist the Health Care Team and Institution Rather than the Patient? No." *HEC Forum* 4 (3): 205–208.

17. Weber, L. 1994. "Do HECs Have a Responsibility to the Non-Medical Community Rather Than Only to the Institution, Physician, and Patient? Yes." *HEC Forum* 6 (2): 117–18.

18. Mueller, M. J. 1994. "Do HECs Have a Responsibility to the Non-Medical Community Rather Than Only to the Institution, Physician, and Patient? No." *HEC Forum* 6 (2): 119–20.

19. Wolf, J. S. 1993. "Should HECs Report to the Medical Staff Rather Than to the Administration, Board of Trustees, or Other Administrative Office? Yes." *HEC Forum* 5 (2): 115–17.

20. DeBlois, J. 1993. "Should HECs Report to the Medical Staff Rather Than to the Administration, Board of Trustees, or Other Administrative Office? No." *HEC Forum* 5 (2): 118–19.

21. Blake, D. C. 1992. "The Hospital Ethics Committee and Moral Authority." *HEC Forum* 4 (5): 295–98.

22. Fletcher, J. C., N. Quist, and A. R. Jonsen. 1989. "Ethics Consultation in Health Care: Rationale and History." In *Ethics Consultation in Health Care,* edited by J. C. Fletcher, A. R. Jonsen, and N. Quist, 1–15. Chicago: Health Administration Press.

23. Morreim, H. 1995. *Balancing Act, The New Medical Ethics of Medicine's New Economics.* Washington, D. C.: Georgetown University Press.

24. Rodwin, M. A. 1993. *Medicine, Money, and Morals.* Oxford: Oxford University Press

25. Relman, A. S. 1992. "What Market Values Are Doing to Medicine." *The Atlantic Monthly* (Mar): 99–106.

26. Khushf, G. P., and R. Gifford. 1999. "Understanding, Assessing, and Managing Conflicts of Interest." In *Clinical Ethics in Surgery*, edited by L. McCullough, J. W. Jones, and B. A. Brody. Oxford, UK: Oxford University Press.

27. Reiser, S. J. 1994. "The Ethical Life of Health Care Organizations." *Hastings Center Report* 24 (6): 28–35.

28. Reiser, S. J. 1991. "Administrative Case Rounds: Institutional Policies and Leaders Cast in a Different Light." *Journal of the American Medical Association* 16 (15): 2127–28.

29. Schneider-O'Connell, A. 1995. "A Corporate Ethics Committee in the Making." *HEC Forum* 7 (4): 264–72.

30. Hofmann, P. B. 1995. "Response to 'Institutional Morality, Authority, and Ethics Committees: How Far Should Respect for Institutional Morality Go?' " (see E. Loewy, *CQ* Vol. 3, No. 4). *Cambridge Quarterly of Health Care Ethics* 4: 98–99.

31. Relman, A. S. 1991. "Shattuck Lecture—The Health Care Industry: Where Is It Taking Us?" *The New England Journal of Medicine* 325 (12): 854–59.

32. Mckibbin, S. 1995. "The Soul of a Corporation." *Hospitals and Health Networks* 69 (10): 20–24.

33. Veatch, R. 1995. "Abandoning Informed Consent." *Hastings Center Report* 25 (2): 5–12.

34. Loewy, E. 1994. "Institutional Morality, Authority, and Ethics Committees: How Far Should Respect for Institutional Morality Go?" *Cambridge Quarterly of Healthcare Ethics* 3 (4): 98–99.

35. Joint Commission on Accreditation of Healthcare Organizations. 1995. *1995 Accreditation Manual for Hospitals.* Oakbrook Terrace, IL: JCAHO.

Business Ethics and Compliance:
What Management Is Doing and Why

Dawn-Marie Driscoll, W. Michael
Hoffman, and Joseph E. Murphy*

How does the public prevent large organizations from engaging in misconduct that can cause extensive damage to communities, consumers, and investors? The obvious answers—government regulation, private lawsuits, aggressive investigative reporters—might be wrong in an era when the marketplace is more likely to influence behavior.

*Copyright 1998 Center for Business Ethics at Bentley College, Waltham, Massachusetts. Published by Blackwell Publishers. Reprinted with permission. Dawn-Marie Driscoll is president of Driscoll Associates. W. Michael Hoffman is executive director of the Center for Business Ethics at Bentley College. Joseph E. Murphy is executive vice-president of Compliance Legal Systems Group.

But there is a solution that can work. Companies are being called upon to adopt compliance and ethics programs to police their own conduct and are being expected to take steps to prevent and detect misconduct before the harm occurs. These programs, in their mature form, amount to a management commitment to implement effective methods to address potential wrongdoing.

In this article we will describe what is causing companies and other organizations to take these steps and what it is that managers are doing. We will address the trends in this area and suggest how the public can obtain the greatest benefit from this development.

What Is Causing Organizations to Implement Compliance and Ethics Programs?

Companies and organizations did not get religion overnight. It took both carrots and sticks to motivate managers, On the "stick" (or threat) side of the picture, there has been a steady increase in the use of criminal laws and penalties to punish business misconduct. With each new story of corruption or misconduct, legislatures and regulators responded with new laws and regulations prohibiting activities that in the past were accepted as norms of the marketplace.

Because of new penalties, companies are increasingly worried about employee wrongdoing, particularly since a recent study suggested that due to workplace pressure, nearly half of all U.S. workers admitted to taking unethical or illegal actions in the past year (see article by Petry, Mujica, and Vickery[†]).

What might seem like rather minor ethical infractions—inside and outside the office—are crimes today. For example, if you make up symptoms so that your insurance company will pay for a doctor's visit (18 U.S.C. 1347) or eavesdrop on someone's cordless telephone conversation and then tell what you heard (18 U.S.C. 2511), you could face five years in jail. Taking a confidential list of names and telephone numbers of your firm's clients to a new job will cost you ten (18 U.S.C. 1832); characterizing a loan from your parents as a gift when describing the source of a down payment on a mortgage application could land you 30 years in jail (18 U.S.C. 1041).

But jail might not be the end of it. Employee actions can also cause the bottom line to take a big hit, thanks to punitive damage awards

---

[†]*Petry, E., A. Mujica, and D. Vickery. 1998. "Sources and Consequences of Workplace Pressure."* Business and Society Review *99 (1): 25–30.*

in civil cases, so-called civil penalties, and other remedies that serve as constraints on business conduct.

The amount of criminal penalties seems to go up with each new wave of enforcement activity. Statutory penalties are increasing and creative prosecutors are finding ways to interpret existing laws to expand the amounts of penalties. Not to be outdone, regulatory agencies are also using financial penalties to punish companies that should have corrected pervasive wrongdoing, as drugmaker Astra USA discovered when it settled with the U.S. Equal Employment Opportunity Commission (EEOC) in 1998 for over $10 million, the largest amount paid in a sexual harassment case brought by the EEOC.

The use of nonfinancial penalties such as probation has also caused distress for company managers. When Consolidated Edison of New York agreed to probationary oversight by a monitor as part of its guilty plea in 1994, managers may not have anticipated that three years of detailed reports to the court would lay out numerous stories of disgruntled employees, threats, and a corporate culture marked by poor morale and complaints.

But penalties imposed by government and the legal system are not the entire story—the penalties of the marketplace also serve as powerful motivators. Companies whose reputations are sullied are then punished through the loss of consumer confidence. In the capital markets, investor dissatisfaction as a result of expensive legal entanglement can cause a company's securities to lose value and can result in the company becoming a likely acquisition target or bankruptcy casualty. The recruitment of talented personnel also suffers when companies cross the line and are publicly shamed. For example, Prudential Insurance found that one aftershock of its fraudulent sales practices scandal was the loss of many high-producing sales agents, further hurting its revenues.

The stick of penalties and lost marketplace confidence has not, however, been the only driver of internal programs to prevent and detect wrongdoing. In the United States, the watershed event was the adoption, in November 1991, of the Federal Sentencing Guidelines for Organizations.[1]

Under the Sentencing Guidelines, organizations convicted of federal crimes face a mandatory system of stiff fines and tough probation conditions. Rather than rely on the discretion of individual trial judges, this new system uses a mathematical formula that assigns points to various factors, often causing substantial increases in penalties. For example, companies whose offenses included such aggravating factors as having senior managers involved in an offense could see fines escalating into the hundreds of millions of dollars.

The Sentencing Guidelines were not just an exercise in mathematical sentencing formulas, however. What some might characterize as a social experiment in the control of organizations allowed a company to dramatically reduce penalties if it took steps such as voluntarily disclosing violations, cooperating with investigations, and having in place, before the offense occurred, "an effective system to prevent and detect violations."[2] If a firm had such a program and self-reported, it could escape almost all of the penalty and it would not face a mandatory compliance program.

The lure of the carrot has not been limited to reduction of fines— some companies have avoided prosecution completely, and have been rewarded as good corporate citizens for the voluntary disclosure of violations. Agencies and prosecutors have stated that they will take the existence of compliance programs into account in deciding whether to prosecute a company, a far more important benefit than a reduction in fines after prosecution, trial, and conviction for an offense.

Diligent management efforts to prevent misconduct and ensure that employees conduct themselves properly have also been paying dividends to companies in litigation outside of the criminal context. For example, in the United States, a company program to prevent and react to allegations of sexual harassment can be invoked as a defense in hostile work environment cases. In other civil cases in which the risk of punitive damages is great, some courts have viewed management diligence as a sound basis to reject claims for monetary punishments.

A "due diligence" defense, which has been part of the legal system in a number of countries outside of the United States, has offered a reward to companies that are diligent in preventing misconduct, including protecting members of the board of directors from individual liability. In 1996 this concept was accepted indirectly by Delaware's influential chancery court, long a leader in the development of corporate law. In the case of In Re Caremark,[3] shareholders alleged that the board of directors breached its fiduciary duty of care to Caremark by failing to adequately supervise the conduct of its employees and to institute corrective action. Caremark, a medical services company, had been subjected to government investigations and indictments and eventually paid $250 million in fines, reimbursements, and other penalties.

The Caremark case is a good news/bad news decision. The good news is that the court, in effect, exonerated the board of directors, finding that both prior to and during the government's investigation of the company the board had acted diligently, setting up ethics and compliance-reporting systems. The bad news is that the court issued a stern warning to other boards, stressing that directors could, at least in theory, face liability for failure to have such a program if improprieties then developed in the company.

Caremark has caught the attention of company managers and directors, a wake-up call that the standard for liability has changed. The prior standard was a one-way street of information flow up to the board. Absent cause of suspicion, directors were entitled to rely on the honesty and integrity of their subordinates and to do no more. Now, with the development of the Sentencing Guidelines and the Caremark language (the board has a "responsibility to assure that appropriate information and reporting systems are established by management"), ignorance is no defense. The information flow is a two-way street and the board is affirmatively required to probe and ask questions. Directors must be alert for red flags such as improper use of company assets, pressures on profit margins or revenues, and ethical complacency in the company.[4]

Chancellor William T. Allen, the author of the Caremark opinion, may not have anticipated that it would become a household word among ethics and compliance experts. As he said to a gathering of corporate directors,

> Advisors go to boards and they say, 'Look at this opinion. You'd better have a special session. You'd better do this, you'd better do that.' Frankly, I think lawyers (and I don't mean to be a traitor to my profession) have a little bit of an interest in whipping up excitement about these things.[5]

Yet even Allen was forced to admit the rules of the corporate governance game have changed, warning directors that they must recognize the moment when action is called for, often in opposition to their former loyalty to management. "That's the difficult moment," he said. "It's a moment that some structural protections can help you with. That is, being informed, having the right kind of information."[6]

Diligent compliance programs and clear codes of ethics have internal benefits to organizations, such as protecting them from being a victim of employee wrongdoing. For example, several financial services companies have been devastated by improper currency trading, security pricing errors, and inadequate credit controls. While employee wrongdoing may never be eliminated entirely, a program of training, controls, and audits may help detect transgressions at an early stage.

A model from the mutual fund industry provides a useful example for others. When Invesco Funds Group fired John Kaweske for violating its rules regarding personal trading, the press, Congress, the Securities Exchange Commission (SEC), and the rest of the industry took notice. Fund advisers manage over $4 trillion for over 65 million shareholders; therefore, trust and integrity are key ingredients in the success of the

American mutual fund industry, as they are in many other product and service lines. The SEC invited the Investment Company Institute (ICI) to make recommendations regarding personal trading of fund managers and other investment personnel. In response, the ICI convened a special task force, which ultimately laid out six clear and vigorous recommendations regarding fund codes of ethics and compliance, a "best practice model" for the industry. Two years later, an overwhelming majority of fund complexes reported they had implemented the panel's recommendations.[7]

A company's compliance and ethics efforts—and the good reputation those efforts protect—can be a valuable marketing tool for alert managers, particularly when they are seeking to do business with top companies. Under the influence of the Sentencing Guidelines, blue-chip companies are becoming more aware of the diligence needed to avoid legal and ethical pitfalls. One increasing concern for these companies is the nature of the companies they choose as partners. Whether the issue is the labor practices of suppliers, independent sales representatives who mistreat customers, or due diligence related to a potential merger or acquisition, leading companies are more carefully examining the practices of their potential business partners. Companies targeting those industry leaders will have a substantial advantage in the marketplace if they have compliance diligence programs that apply the same high standards as their corporate customers.

Finally, maintaining employee morale and the ability to recruit new talent are positive results of demonstrating a firm commitment to conducting business according to ethical standards. Nicholas G. Moore, chairman and chief executive officer of the national accounting firm of Coopers and Lybrand, calls this benefit "glue" in explaining his commitment to a comprehensive ethics initiative:

> We have 70,000 people at Coopers and Lybrand worldwide. We didn't want our people crawling out on a limb ignoring the sawing noises behind them. 'Ethics' may seem soft. But Coopers and Lybrand views it as a 'hard' concept. Ethics values are the glue that holds widespread organizations together.[8]

According to Harry Britt, manager of Ethics and Business Conduct at Coopers and Lybrand, six new developments convinced the leadership of the firm to redesign its former ethics initiatives: organization changes that further decentralized the staff worldwide; expansion into new lines of business without specific industry codes to cover all client activities; the increasing diversity of the background and experiences of its workforce; a desire to keep pace with the standards of excellence of the business community; a commitment to follow the advice its professionals give to its own clients regarding ethics and compliance; and the promulgation of the Sentencing Guidelines.[9]

In fact, few organizations need to be convinced about the myriad of reasons to establish ethics and compliance programs today. William E. Giffin, vice president of the Office of Ethics and Business Practices at Sears, Roebuck, and Company, sums up succinctly the three categories of companies with such programs: "Companies that have had a problem, companies that are having a problem, and companies that will have a problem."[10]

The Implications of the Development of Large Organizations

There is a profound reason for this focus on organizational misconduct as the twentieth century has witnessed the development of global-scale organizations in international markets. All segments of the economy and society—the production of goods, provision of services, healthcare—operate on a scale that invites consolidation and expansion among participants.

At the same time, the aggregation of power that comes with expansion has magnified the potential of these expanded organizations to cause harm to society and themselves. Organizations that employ tens of thousands of employees, produce lethal materials, and play highly visible roles in the economy can cause tremendous dislocation in complex modern societies. A release of toxic materials in Bhopal, Ecuador, or Alaska is newsworthy around the world.

When harm and publicity occur on this scale, public opinion shifts, regarding post-wrongdoing remedies as unacceptable. Yet it is the nature (and limitation) of most legal systems to impose remedies and punish behavior after events warranting attention have taken place. Not surprisingly, then, society's focus has moved from a reactive litigation-based approach to one that intervenes to prevent harm or to detect it at an early stage, but without crippling the productive engines of society.

Taken from this perspective, new developments in the ethics and compliance area are the logical product of this global trend, requiring that organizations, whose very raison d'etre is to marshal human resources to specific ends, include the prevention of wrongdoing within their own business objectives.

The "Ethics Versus Compliance" Side Show

No review of compliance and ethics programs in companies could proceed far without noting an area of commotion in this field, a polite disagreement over what is the "right" approach: ethics or compliance programs.

From the ethicist's perspective, compliance is a very limited endeavor, mostly the domain of lawyers. Compliance programs exist to tell employees about the law and to prevent violations of law. Employees are motivated to do the right thing by a fear of being caught, but such programs are inherently limited and rarely help employees resolve those situations involving right and wrong that are not covered by the law. Organizations must develop the ethical commitment and expertise of their employees. Educational efforts must be initiated to encourage employees to accept their shared responsibilities to uphold the ethical culture of the organization and to use appropriate ethical reasoning in making business decisions.

Keith Darcy, former ethics consultant with Prudential Securities, describes compliance-only programs as punitive and rudimentary: "If the only thing we do is reside in the rules-based, compliance-based legal focus, I don't think we necessarily challenge our organizations to revise and grow," Darcy says.[11] In short, compliance-only programs do not fully engage the moral dimension of the employees—a dimension that must be put into play to gain the employee buy-in necessary for program success.

Compliance-only advocates may view an "ethics" approach as an ephemeral exercise, likely to waste managers' time by pursuing moral hairsplitting exercises, leaving them unschooled in the legal requirements that will determine the fate of the company in legal proceedings. They will observe that executives' moral pronouncements are likely to evaporate against the force of business necessity. They may also question the legitimacy of having corporations instructing individual employees on moral issues.

While there is room for debate about the nature of right and wrong and the role of law in society, the real issue is not whether an "ethics" orientation or a "compliance" focus is preferable. The important goal of any program should be to reduce the risk of misconduct in the organization. Such a focus requires an examination of the use and abuse of power and policy in these organizations and a determination of the steps and systems best designed to intervene before harm is inflicted.

Experience suggests that good ethics programs and good compliance programs are interdependent; each is incomplete without the other. A good compliance program must emphasize values and moral responsibility, because this increases the program's effectiveness among employees. A good ethics program must help employees to know and obey the law if it is to have any relevance to the company in its actual environment.

Training in the law or training in ethics will be equally ineffective without full organizational commitment to the program, and each one will be useless if it is presented without the essential infrastructure to ensure that managers have the necessary support mechanisms and strategies to make the program work.

The Evolving Standard for the Good Citizen Organization

Compliance and ethics programs are not a new phenomenon. Long before the Sentencing Guidelines appeared, lawyers talked to employees about what the law required, and some companies invited outside speakers to address employees about business ethics.

One retailing chain's primitive code was a business card with five "do's and don'ts" on one side and the telephone number of the general counsel on the other side. For the most part, there seemed to be little interest in measuring the program's effects on employees and the organization's conduct.

In the years leading up to the Sentencing Guidelines, many more companies adopted codes of conduct, often reciting a company pledge to obey the law. In effect, there was paper and preaching, but little that made use of management techniques for controlling what happened in the organization. One study suggested that codes of conduct in this context did not have any positive impact on a company's likelihood of engaging in wrongdoing.[12] By the late 1980s, there were significant efforts to reach beyond minimal steps in some specific risk areas of compliance. OSHA had issued safety compliance management guides, the major defense contractors had reacted to a wave of scandals and adopted standards for government contractors, and environmental programs typically emphasized audits and monitoring as necessary compliance measures.

In the early 1990s, when the Sentencing Commission adopted its standards for an effective program to prevent and detect violations, it broke from the paper-and-preaching pattern and favored an approach based on management controls and results. The standards went beyond piecemeal approaches and covered misconduct from a broad perspective.

The Sentencing Guidelines are not a cookbook for creating compliance programs. Nor do they attempt to answer the myriad questions that arise in designing compliance management systems for different companies and industries. Rather, they follow a model of "structured flexibility."[13] Primarily, the Guidelines require that for any program to merit credit, it must, above all else, be characterized by due diligence. The Guidelines then proceed to enumerate seven elements that are minimum diligence steps. These elements are designed to be dynamic, however, so no company can ever comfortably examine its own handiwork and put it on the shelf. Instead, companies must continually monitor industry practice and their own histories of problems and adjust their programs accordingly.

The impact of the Sentencing Guidelines has been dramatic in the development of programs for companies and other institutions. (It is worth noting that the Guidelines apply to all types of organizations, including nonprofits, partnerships, unions, universities, and private companies.)

The Guidelines are remarkable in several ways. First, they offer a commitment to companies. The offer of sentencing reduction is a firm one: if a company follows the Guidelines steps, then the sentencing judge is absolutely required to reduce the sentence. Secondly, the Guidelines officially and realistically recognize that no management program, even a highly diligent one, can be expected to prevent all misconduct. One cannot fairly characterize a program as a "failure" merely because one or two of several thousand employees violated one of the many legal restrictions applicable to a business. So the Guidelines definition of an effective program speaks of one designed "to prevent and detect" violations.

Finally, the Guidelines provide a standard that managers can apply. They can grumble that the standard was not specific enough to answer all their questions, but it did provide enough guidance to move them past the stage of endless debates about what to do beyond sterile codes and lectures and to push them toward taking a more management-oriented approach.

The Sentencing Commission may not have anticipated the dynamic genie that took life when the Commission uncorked the bottle of the Guidelines. What started as a standard for sentencing issued by a tiny agency of the judiciary has now taken on a life and evolution of its own. This attention to ethics and compliance is testimony to the Commission's insight in devising a standard that could evolve and grow and could lend itself to use by other agencies, the courts, and compliance practitioners.

Examples Abound

In the United States, the Environmental Protection Agency (EPA) was among the first to adopt the standard for use in its own enforcement determinations. Over time the EPA has refined the standard in ways that may upstage the original version. In healthcare, the Department of Health and Human Services has used the Guidelines' standards to issue standards for healthcare providers. Numerous government enforcement agencies have drawn on the Guidelines' approach in settling cases against companies and requiring those companies to implement compliance programs as part of the settlement.[14] Furthermore, with the Caremark case, the courts have begun to show how the approach will be applied in civil cases. The Caremark court examined approvingly the steps Caremark's management had taken to prevent and respond to misconduct.

The problem of compliance and the nature of large organizations are not issues unique to the United States. The problems—and thus the solutions—are global ones. It is reasonable to expect that voluntary compliance and self-policing programs will be picked up on the global stage as a necessary tool to control organizational conduct.

This trend has, in fact, begun to emerge. In Canada, for example, the Competition Bureau issued a policy statement endorsing compliance programs and explaining how the Bureau would recognize those companies adopting them. The Bureau also gave specific guidance about what it would expect to see in such a program. Not surprisingly, given the managerial nature of the Sentencing Guidelines' standards, the Competition Bureau's expectations are very similar.

In Australia, the Australian Competition and Consumer Commission has taken the lead in developing this white-collar crime prevention tool by aiding the formation of a national association of compliance professionals and by inducing Standards Australia to develop standards for compliance programs.

In the area of environmental compliance, the International Standards Organization's (ISO) 14,000 standards regarding environmental management systems suggest that a global standard will emerge for entities' compliance programs in this area.

What may appear to some to be interesting but isolated trends actually signal an evolution in the definition of organizational culpability. In the past century, a company and its management were judged to be culpable based on what offense was committed by any of the organization's employees, just as if the organization were an individual person. If an employee violated the law, it was the company's fault. Of course, in the past the consequences were usually not so grave. Most managers never faced the prospect of imprisonment, fines were modest, and criminal enforcement was relatively rare. With the change in this framework, however, a change in corporate culpability is also developing. This new standard calls for management to exercise diligence to prevent violations; it recognizes violations will nevertheless occur, but expects management to be diligent in detecting them. If a violation occurs, management is expected to report such events to authorities. And, to complete the picture, management is expected to correct the results of the violations and the circumstances that led to the violation. In shorthand form, the emerging standard is prevent, detect, report, and correct.

What Organizations Are Doing

Against this background, how have managers in companies and other organizations proceeded to build an effective program? The Sentencing Guidelines standards are a logical point of reference, although experience is evolving in this area as ethics practitioners and government agencies share their best practices models.

Due diligence.

The Guidelines require due diligence as the keystone. An effective program is more than a series of formal steps; it involves a flexible understanding of what actually affects the things that employees do on the job. Due diligence is a red-flag warning for practitioners that these standards are not static and that a program can never be considered truly "finished," even in companies with mature programs.

Glenn Coleman, Manager of Ethics Communications and Education at Texas Instruments (TI), explains why TI recently revisited its former code of ethics:

> It is time to focus on the values, not just the rules. We've had a written code since 1961, and five years ago, I would have described it as one of the best around. An international TI team looked at our values within the scope of our company's culture and business objectives and settled on three: integrity, innovation, and commitment. We wrapped these words around some modern graphics, published it in a booklet form, translated it into 12 languages, and passed it out to our 45,000 employees around the world. Our booklet is online and cross-referenced by subject matter, with resources, examples, and information on more than 100 subjects.[15]

The best ethics programs, Coleman believes, are reactive and dynamic.

> This is the most interesting time to be working at TI as we take this giant step into the future, carrying our ethics program to an even higher plateau. But we see ethics and values weaving through everything we do in the company. Everything jives together. We don't feel that the Ethics Office is having to drive ethics anymore; we're being pulled along by the day-to-day operations and decisions of our company and our employees.[16]

Risk assessment.

The Guidelines do not enumerate risk assessment as a specific element, but in practice this is a necessary prerequisite. This step, which Jeffrey

Kaplan, one of the leading writers in the compliance field, has described as a liability inventory,[17] involves management assessing its actual risks and assuring that the program addresses each risk appropriately.

Managers often begin a risk assessment by surveying their industry to consider what ethical issues have faced their competitors and partners, as well as where the company itself has had problems. Companies may also choose to undertake a more in-depth examination at this stage, including employee surveys and focus groups to determine how employees view management and the company; what situations, dilemmas, and questions they face; and what might be the underlying causes of future problems.

Risk assessment can also include an inventory of existing efforts addressed at compliance and ethics. For companies of any significant size, it is rare not to undertake some efforts, although perhaps limited to a few areas such as workplace safety, employment practices, and environmental compliance. A comprehensive inventory also gathers information on available management tools that can be used in the compliance process, such as internal auditing, employee training programs, and company newsletters.

A recent example of this comes from Coopers and Lybrand in reinvigorating their compliance and ethics program in response to internal compliance trouble. According to Harry Britt, extensive risk assessment is essential before rolling out a new ethics initiative.[18] Coopers conducted focus group interviews with approximately 400 employees to identify issues that impacted upon them and reviewed all existing policies before crafting its new policy statement and code-of-conduct book, *The Way We Do Business.*

Standards and procedures.

The Guidelines enumerate seven minimum steps; having standards and procedures is first on the list. Companies have long recognized the need to have a policy more comprehensive than "commit no federal crime." Sophisticated programs endorse objectives such as seeking to act with integrity. Some of the best programs integrate values standards with compliance and ethics initiatives.

Company programs typically use written codes of conduct to set the groundwork. These have evolved to provide both a "values" standard and specific guidance for employees on how to deal with specific conduct issues. A code might tell employees not to discuss prices with competitors, where to get advice on conducting overseas business to avoid missteps, and how to reach the company's compliance/ethics advice line.

Codes are also becoming more user-friendly. Instead of long, turgid text, the best codes use bullet points, clear examples, and question-and-answer formats, as well as color, illustrations, and other publishing techniques designed to capture readers' attention. For example, Bell South's glossy publication, "A Commitment to Our Personal Responsibility," covers 13 subjects, from fair competition to political involvement, and includes policy explanations, questions and answers, excerpts from the law, and a resource directory.

To fulfill the "standards and procedures" element of the Guidelines, companies also examine what procedures need to be developed to give life and ensure adherence to the standards. Actual operating procedures and processes can be instituted to reduce the opportunity for violations to occur—one of the basic principles for any crime control system. One procedure, for example, might require that certain types of activities always pass through a review process to ensure compliance, such as is commonly done in having legal departments review advertising to avoid consumer fraud.

Senior personnel in charge.

The Guidelines require that a senior person or persons take responsibility for the program, so companies commonly designate a compliance or ethics officer. To be effective, the officer must be a well-respected leader and have real clout in the organization. Many companies have the person report to an independent committee of the board, such as the audit committee, to strengthen the position of this officer.

Boards of directors are playing a more important role by specifically authorizing compliance programs and formally electing the compliance officer. Many boards require the officer to report to them on a regular basis regarding the progress in implementing the program. In some instances, compliance officers may be required to specially report certain types of events, such as allegations of misconduct involving a senior manager.

Furthermore, some boards of directors, such as the Michigan Physicians Mutual Liability Company, use board meeting or retreat time to undergo their own customized ethics training, focusing on ethical issues at the board level. Consensus about standards of business ethics is critical at the board level, one director explained, and must be discussed well before a crisis hits. "In short, the buck stops with the board," he said.[19] Thanks to the Caremark opinion, we anticipate that boards will be even more actively involved with ethics and compliance programs in the future.

Companies also recognize that no single person constitutes the entire compliance program. Multidepartmental compliance committees have become an effective supporting structure. With senior managers drawn from diverse departments across the company, the compliance officer has a "kitchen cabinet" to serve as a sounding board and to drive ownership of the program throughout all areas of the business. The committee also helps bring to bear the compliance-related resources available in the participating departments.

Perhaps the most universally recognized ingredient of an effective compliance and ethics program is the commitment and active support of senior management, particularly the chief executive officer. Although the role of top executives is not explicitly discussed in the Sentencing Guidelines, it is clear that the involvement or acquiescence of such managers in violations will negate the sentencing reduction benefits of having a program. Companies with programs that directly impact employee behavior have given this issue much attention. Because substance is always more important than form, if the CEO and the top operating officers actually walk the talk, and support the program, it will have increased credibility with employees.

One aspect of compliance programs that is not in the Guidelines, but is increasingly recognized as important, is the infrastructure that enables a company to ensure that its program actually takes root throughout the company, including remote field locations. For example, in January 1996 the Environmental Protection Agency (EPA) specifically included this element in its evaluation of company environmental due diligence.

The EPA and many companies have recognized that there is a risk that compliance programs will have little influence outside of corporate headquarters. One technique to combat this, captured in the EPA standards, is to have specific managers in the field designated as responsible for their unit's compliance activities. Assigning these "compliance coordinators" or similar positions is an approach that has also been used in workplace safety programs.

Developing the infrastructure for a compliance program may also involve assigning responsibility for coverage for discrete risk areas. After a risk inventory is completed, companies examine the best way to ensure that each area is adequately covered and that employees have a subject matter expert or experts to turn to when they have questions. In some companies, the approach used has been the designation of "responsible officers" for each subject area.[20] Some companies have separate vice presidents for certain high-risk areas, such as environmental compliance. Another method is to create subject matter teams, perhaps consisting of a lawyer and a manager with responsibility in the risk area.

The Guidelines standards refer to the role of agents, which is defined to include independent contractors, a reminder that compliance responsibilities do not end at the formal corporate and employment lines. Thus, companies are extending their programs to reach agents, consultants, partnerships and other joint ventures, and even suppliers. Managers are beginning to use their compliance standards as part of their due diligence in hiring sales distribution networks, researching possible acquisition partners, choosing suppliers, or even deciding to accept a client.

Personnel practices.

One of the early mysteries of the Sentencing Guidelines standards was a step that appeared to be a somewhat obscure requirement—to exercise due diligence not to delegate substantial discretionary authority to anyone managers knew, or should have known, had a propensity to engage in illegal activities. This standard was likely drawn from experience in a few industries in which companies hired employees without regard to their personal records of misconduct. For example, the securities industry maintains public records of complaints against brokers, which are readily accessible to hiring firms. In the defense industry, debarment lists are public and the government expects companies at least to check these lists before retaining someone to engage in sensitive work. In other industries, the approach has been to conduct at least some criminal background searches when hiring employees into high-risk positions, as well as to review internal disciplinary records before promoting individuals into such sensitive positions. As one chief internal auditor succinctly phrased it, "Your big guns should not be loose cannons."[21]

Communicating effectively.

The Guidelines' fourth standard calls for effective communications and lists as examples training and publications that communicate in a practical manner. Training has evolved from pedantic lectures by lawyers to sophisticated uses of high technology involving employee interaction. In the United States commercially produced dramatic video training programs have become a popular training tool. Some larger companies customize their own video training materials especially to cover their own codes of conduct. Even with technology and video, however, personal contact sessions, such as workshops, continue as an essential part of training.

These sophisticated approaches show a recognition that training is more than the mere passive transfer of information to pliant students. The use of dramatic videos and the strength of the messages conveyed in training presentations reflect the philosophy that training must serve both to inform and to motivate. In the compliance area, employees must understand what is required, but they also need to have the motivation to take the subject seriously. In certain areas of the law such as price-fixing and bribery, criminal violations are not committed by lost waifs who have wandered from the trail, unsure of what to do or who to ask. They commit deliberate acts. Companies seeking to deter misconduct in such areas must send a forceful message to capture employees' attention.

Many companies require new hires to participate in an employee orientation and include training on their codes of conduct and values. Some include more detailed training in high-risk subjects at this early stage. These programs are designed to ensure that employees will not start working for the company in high-risk areas until they have first been exposed to the legal and ethical rules of the road.

Sophisticated companies supplement the training programs with periodic reminders about the rules and values of the company. Written, nonlegalistic memos from company counsel, regular features in company newsletters, video programs, and intranet web sites, with real-world examples of recent questions and answers, as well as accounts of actual incidents, are being used with success.

Checking and measuring what is happening.

The Guidelines require reasonable steps to ensure that the program is working, including compliance audits and monitoring, and a system for employees and agents to report concerns without fear of retaliation. Companies recognize the important message here. Managers cannot just send materials blindly out to the field without also checking and measuring what is happening around the company.

Such audits and reviews divide into two general categories: process and substance. On the process side, companies look to determine whether the processes that make up the compliance program are, in fact, functioning as they are designed. Reviews to determine whether the hotline is operating effectively, whether employees have been trained on appropriate risk areas, and whether environmental monitoring devices are properly installed and operating are all part of a process audit.

The second category of review digs deeper to determine whether there are actual violations of the law or of the company's code of conduct. Compliance audits here may examine bidding practices to ferret out signs of price-fixing or may review government contract bids to determine whether acquisition regulations were followed.

Monitoring, as distinguished from auditing, involves real-time observations and measurement. This approach is particularly important where the risk and consequences of a violation are too great to rely on after-the-fact measures. For example, a chemical manufacturing company may monitor its effluents on a continuous basis, and nuclear facilities are kept under constant surveillance. In the retail industry, test shoppers visit a company's retail outlets to ensure compliance with consumer protection requirements. Mutual fund companies regularly monitor their telephone representatives to ensure proper disclosure requirements are followed.

Perhaps one of the most common forms of compliance monitoring is the daily functioning of a company's legal department if lawyers have a preventive law orientation. When company lawyers participate in client meetings and review draft materials on a regular basis, they perform a frontline function in the effort to prevent organizational wrongdoing. Companies that are developing their compliance programs in response to the Sentencing Guidelines frequently do not recognize this activity as part of their compliance programs, possibly because they are so familiar with the function that they fail to recognize it in this different light.

The standard for compliance auditing has been expressed in the EPA due diligence standards, making clear that the audits must be systematic. Companies must assess their compliance risks and determine where to audit and when to monitor, based on a realistic assessment of the compliance risks.

One practical, cost-effective approach to compliance auditing is to utilize any internal audit functions that already exist. While conventional financial audits contribute to the overall control environment of a company, they are not the same as compliance audits. But companies are bridging that gap by expanding the scope of the auditors' work, including compliance within the scope of their duties. Specific compliance training and materials help auditors identify questionable areas in which to focus.

Not specifically expressed in the Guidelines, but necessary for any effective management program, is the measurement of what is being done. Is the training working? Is the program reaching people? How do you measure a violation that did not occur because it was prevented? Ethics officers report that even in the most well-developed programs, the issue of measurement is still a challenge. They are using surveys, focus groups, "helpline" totals, and other techniques to measure the impact of their programs, including feedback obtained through the compliance auditing process.

Reporting and information systems.

Part of the Guidelines' standards was a system to report criminal conduct. The initial response of companies was to institute hotlines, toll-free numbers promoted as a means to report wrongdoing. Soon companies realized that employees would not limit their calls to reporting actual crimes, since not even lawyers can discern whether a particular set of facts constitutes a crime or some other level of misconduct. Companies also saw a value in softening the tone of the message, labeling their report lines as a "helpline" or "guideline," to serve as a source of advice and counsel on ethical and compliance issues. This function is more consistent with a program to prevent and detect violations and is received more receptively by employees.

Some companies believed it was sufficient to have an "open door" policy, without a system for anonymous calling. Not surprisingly, open door systems that require a subordinate to directly confront a boss or a boss's boss are viewed with skepticism, so the present trend is to permit anonymous calls. Some companies staff hotlines with their own personnel, but a significant number have turned to outside professional services, which provide 24-hour-a-day, 365-days-a-year coverage.

Concern about retaliation and the expectation that fear would inhibit callers were motivating forces for the Sentencing Commission in requiring a reporting system that could be used "without fear of retribution." There is, however, survey evidence to suggest that the impact of retaliation is overstated and that the biggest deterrent to whistleblowing is fear that no action will be taken in response to the call.[22] Nevertheless, companies typically have included a statement in policies that adamantly promise no retaliation for whistleblowing, at least if done in good faith. Much rarer are specific procedures and processes designed to actually protect whistleblowers from organizational ostracism.

The ability to receive communications from any employee who suspects misconduct is recognized as a key element in effective programs, but it does not complete the picture regarding information flow in an organization. Bad news—or at least worrisome trends—must rise to senior levels of the company. Thus, companies with the best practices programs also require reports to the board of directors, often through the audit committee or another independent committee of the board. Such reports are designed to inform the board of what is working and what is not, where more attention is needed, and how well the company is pursuing the board's direction to implement an effective program.

Consistent discipline and rewards.

The Guidelines require a disciplinary system consistent and strong enough to deter wrongdoing. Punishment must be imposed for failure to detect wrongdoing, and companies will try to have standards and a procedure to ensure that those standards are consistently applied. The most effective way to undercut an ethics program is to discipline a low-level employee but to ignore the same wrongdoing by a senior executive or a star performer. For that reason, companies may use a disciplinary manual and require the compliance officer or a compliance committee to review disciplinary cases involving misconduct. This will help to avoid double standards.

While the Guidelines' standards address punishment, they do not specifically address incentives, evaluations, and rewards. In contrast, under the EPA standards, a compliance program must also provide incentives that encourage commitment to compliance. Experts in ethics and compliance have also emphasized the importance of positive motivators. In some companies, evaluations of compliance and ethical conduct are integrated into annual personnel review forms, although unfortunately they may be little more than checkoffs. But in other companies, managers have specific compliance-related objectives that are important in their evaluations, more common in easily quantified areas such as safety and environment.

Another useful incentive method can be awards and other forms of recognition for positive performers. One of the easiest of these to implement is the recognition letter from a senior executive such as the compliance officer, presented in a way that brings credit to the employee and the work group, thus reinforcing the positive behavior.

Responding to violations.

The Guidelines do not require perfection; despite the best compliance programs, there will be violations. Companies are expected to respond to violations responsibly, investigating allegations of wrongdoing, disciplining the wrongdoers, stopping the violation, and correcting the wrongs done.

Companies devote substantial attention to investigating misconduct. In serious cases they may hire lawyers, accountants, or investigators. Such investigations can be global in scope, involving interviews of hundreds of employees and reviews of large volumes of documents.

The Guidelines require companies to take steps to prevent the recurrence of violations. For that reason companies must look for the underlying causes of the violations and then take steps to prevent them. This "root-cause analysis" can be incorporated into the processes of a company's interdepartmental compliance committee.

There has also been increasing pressure on companies to voluntarily disclose violations that are uncovered. Some government agencies have formal programs granting amnesty to companies that self-report.[23]

Under the Guidelines, failure to report results in loss of sentencing credit for the company's compliance program. Companies may make voluntary disclosure part of their compliance policy and establish procedures to facilitate decisions on such sensitive questions.

Being at least as good as industry practice.

Under the Guidelines, the failure of a program to meet industry practice weighs against credit for an effective program. Therefore, companies must look outside to be sure they are familiar with the best programs established by their peers. Compliance managers do this by reading the literature and attending symposia about compliance programs. Some industry groups convene compliance practices forums in which companies freely exchange information and experiences regarding their compliance programs.[24]

Keeping the program dynamic.

One of the clear but indirect policies of the Guidelines is that programs must adjust to the dynamics of a company and its industry. The reference to industry practice, the requirement to respond appropriately to findings of violations, and the overarching standard of due diligence send this message.

Managers responsible for compliance and ethics face this challenge shortly after getting their initial program off the ground. They continually have to assess and reassess risks resulting from changes in the company and its industry. They modify training, revise the scope of auditing, and respond to reports of potential trouble areas or questions that arise from the hotline. They recognize that the nature of misconduct is dynamic and that any program designed to keep pace with violations must be similarly flexible and vibrant.

Some compliance managers with well-developed domestic programs now face the challenge of tailoring their values statements, codes of conduct, and compliance infrastructures to a global marketplace. They realize they cannot simply use a compliance program designed for their own country in other countries without carefully understanding each specific country's culture, customs, and legal requirements. "Different" may not necessarily be "wrong," but some standards and values may be inviolate. Crafting and communicating ethics in many countries are daunting tasks.

Documenting what was done.

The Sentencing Guidelines do not address record-keeping, but the EPA's standards require "accurate and complete documentation" of a company's program. In dealing with the legal system, keeping sufficient records to prove the diligence of a company's efforts is an essential element in a company's defense. As a skeptical prosecutor would say, "If it isn't in writing, it didn't happen."[25]

The Emergence of a New Professional: Compliance/Ethics Constituencies

The success of a compliance program depends greatly on the staff who are responsible for its implementation. This is a point that is sometimes misunderstood by managers who believe that ethics and compliance are the responsibility of all employees and therefore that compliance managers are unnecessary. Those with experience in this area recognize, however, that these are two essential but separate ingredients. It is true that buy-in by all employees is a key objective of any program, but there is still a need for specific managers to participate in a more detailed way and take responsibility for the program. Here there is an apt analogy to a company's internal auditing function. Every employee in a company is responsible for financial integrity, but it is still recognized that a separate internal auditing group is needed to give this focus and direction and to serve as a check on the process.[26] So, too, compliance managers serve a similar purpose.

In-house compliance staffs internalize the external integrity standards they are charged with implementing throughout the company. The values and commitment of the ethics and integrity program become part of their personal missions, often with an enthusiasm that cannot be explained merely as the product of their company paycheck. Compliance teams often include professionals such as lawyers, auditors, and engineers who are already required to act under specific professional standards that require more than allegiance to the employer.

These compliance-oriented groups have the potential to act as a check and balance on organizational misconduct if given the clout to do so. These groups and the compliance and ethics officers they support often operate with a value standard not reflected in the company's compensation system.

"Teamwork" and pressure to meet the short-term goals of the organization may be signs of company loyalty for employees, but compliance professionals must take the long view, operating to protect the company's reputation and to avoid misconduct. For that reason, compliance officers and staff may have to step outside of the "team" and raise uncomfortable questions, imposing requirements on their peers that may seem like unnecessary bureaucracy.

As a counter to this internal pressure, it is crucial for compliance professionals to network with other compliance professionals for valuable, cost-effective ideas and experience. But perhaps more important, such contacts help bolster the determination and strength of the compliance professional. Meetings with those in other companies who are experiencing the same pressures and frustrations serve as support groups for these inside warriors. This resource can help reinforce their resolve to persist in the face of determined opposition in their own corporate home.

Perhaps in recognition of this need, several organizations exist for compliance and ethics managers. In 1991, Bentley College's Center for Business Ethics (CBE) hosted a gathering of ethics managers, which led to the formation of the national Ethics Officer Association (EOA) in 1992. By 1998 its membership had grown to over 500 professionals who serve as managers of internal ethics or compliance programs. The EOA sponsors two national conferences a year and, in partnership with the CBE, executive education programs for ethics officers.

Other organizations, such as the Ombuds Association, take a functional approach, representing the interests of those who act as ombuds in companies. Some organizations are designed just to reach those in a specific industry, such as the Healthcare Compliance Association, open to both in-house and outside compliance professionals.

One of the most noteworthy examples of a full-scale association comes from Australia. There, at the initiative of the Australian Consumer and Competition Commission, a nation-wide organization was formed for anyone with an interest in compliance and ethics who shares the mission of promoting the evolution of this area. The Association for Compliance Professionals of Australia publishes a newsletter and holds annual conferences at which attendance rivals similar conferences held in the United States, a nation with almost 20 times Australia's population. Active participants include members from industry, government, and academia.

Prognosis and Recommendations

The shift to increased utilization of voluntary internal ethics and compliance programs is a necessary and beneficial one for industry and society. When organizations support the mission of preventing and detecting misconduct, it is more likely that disasters will be prevented before they occur. Given the constraints on resources available to government for traditional policing techniques, diligent organizational self-policing is an irreplaceable adjunct.

Because the potential benefit is so great, it is an easy prognosis to say that this initiative will continue and its momentum will increase over time. However, this is not a completely safe assumption. This effort can be derailed or at least discredited over the short term.

Those adopting compliance and ethics programs need to act in good faith and recognize that a successful program takes true diligence. The focus of such programs must shift away from the old patterns of paper and preaching to an orientation toward results that constantly challenges whether any given program element actually achieves its purpose. Training, written materials, and other compliance efforts that do not reach employees and do not actually change conduct are not worth the expenditure of resources. This results orientation also requires a realistic assessment of organizational politics and power. Those given compliance management responsibility must be given the authority and protection needed to accomplish this difficult job.

Governments and legal systems need to evolve to support this effort as well. When an organization engages in diligent self-policing, it places itself in an extraordinarily vulnerable position. By relentlessly looking for weaknesses and misdeeds, the compliance office will inevitably gather highly sensitive information. Taking the steps necessary to enforce compliance programs may lead to acrimony and litigation aimed at the organization.

In the United States, the legal system frequently shows a jealous intolerance to alternative means of exerting control over wrongdoing. If compliance officers, ombudsmen, and the results of compliance audits become nothing more than weapons for litigators and government enforcers to use against companies, the legal system will kill this evolution at its early stage. It is necessary, therefore, for companies that pursue such diligent programs to receive full recognition from the government and the courts that they are undertaking an effort that benefits society. Good faith compliance efforts would then be immune from exploitation in litigation. If a company met the test of the Guidelines' steps to prevent, detect, report, and correct misconduct, a due diligence defense would protect it from the buzzsaw of the legal system.

On the plus side, some litigators have begun to realize that benchmark standards of business ethics exist. Companies that act with integrity in all business dealings have an advantage in civil disputes. Companies that do not often find themselves embarrassed when business ethicists appear as expert witnesses and explain why their conduct does not meet contemporary business ethics norms.

Compliance professionals should be able to find assistance in the academic community in answering their questions about the efficacy of compliance efforts. Far more work needs to be done to study what efforts work to affect organizations and how to fine-tune existing programs to improve their impact.

We can confidently predict that society will benefit from this trend . . . but with an important caveat. This benefit is not inevitable and will call for diligence both from those inside engaged in the daily heroic tasks self-policing requires and from those of us who stand to benefit from their work.

Notes

1. United States Sentencing Commission. "Sentencing of Organizations." *Federal Sentencing Guidelines Manual,* Chapter 8. Washington, D. C.: United States Sentencing Commission. http/www.ussc.gov/1994guid/table1994.htm.

2. United States Sentencing Commission. Section A12, Comment (n3(k)).

3. *In Re Caremark International Inc. Derivative Litigation,* 1996 WL 549894. 1996. (Del. Chancery C.A. 13670), 15 Sept.

4. Driscoll, D.-M., and W. M. Hoffman. 1994. "Doing the Right Thing: Business Ethics and Boards of Directors." *Directors' Monthly* 18 (Nov): 1–7.

5. "Independence, Integrity, and the Governance of Institutions." 1998. *Directors' Monthly* 22 (Jan): 14.

6. "Independence, Integrity, and the Governance of Institutions," 15.

7. *Report of the Advisory Group on Personal Investing.* 1994. Washington, D. C.: Investment Company Institute.

8. Moore, N. G. 1998. "Ethics: *The* Way To Do Business." Presented as the Inaugural Sears Lecture in Business Ethics at the Center for Business Ethics, Bentley College, Waltham, Massachusetts, 9 February.

9. Britt, H. 1998. Interview with author. 9 February.

10. Giffin, W. E. 1998. Introductory remarks at the Sears Lecture in Business Ethics at the Center for Business Ethics, Bentley College, Waltham, Massachusetts, 9 February.

11. Kelley, T. 1998. "To Do Right, or Just to Be Right?" *The New York Times* 8 February, Section 3, 12.

12. Mathews, M. C. 1988. *Strategic Intervention in Organizations.* Newbury Park, CA: Sage Publications.

13. Swenson, W., and N. Clark. 1991. "The New Federal Sentencing Guidelines: Three Keys to Understanding the Credit for Compliance Programs." *Corporate Conduct Quarterly* 1 (Winter): 1–3.

14. Jordan, K., and J. Murphy. 1996. "Compliance Programs: What the Government Really Wants." *ACCA Docket* 14 (July/Aug): 10.

15. Coleman, G. 1998. Interview with author. 3 March.

16. Coleman, G. 1998. Interview with author. 3 March.

17. Kaplan, J., J. Murphy, and W. Swenson. 1993. *Compliance Programs and the Corporate Sentencing Guidelines,* Chapter 6. Deerfield, IL: Clark Boardman Callaghan.

18. Coleman, J. 1998. Interview with author. 3 March.

19. Interview by author with unnamed director.

20. Kaplan, J. 1996. "Sundstrand's 'Responsible Executive' Program." *Corporate Conduct Quarterly* 4: 33.

21. Author's discussion with a company's chief internal auditor.

22. Miceli, M. P., and J. P. Near. 1992. "Blowing the Whistle." *The Organizational and Legal Implications for Companies and Employees*, 296. New York: Macmillan.

23. United States Department of Justice, Corporate Leniency Policy, Environmental Protection Agency, Antitrust Division. 1995. *Incentives for Self-Policing: Discovery, Disclosure, Correction, and Prevention of Violations, Federal Register 60*, 66,706.

24. Gill, A. 1995. "Telecommunications Industry Practice Forum." In *Corporate Crime in America: Strengthening the "Good Citizen" Corporation*, 89. Washington, D. C.: United States Sentencing Commission.

25. Kaplan, J. 1998. "Retaining Compliance Records: When, Where, and for How Long?" *Ethikos/Corporate Conduct Quarterly* 11 (Jan/Feb/Mar): 7, 16.

26. Driscoll, D.-M., W. M. Hoffman, and E. S. Petry. 1995. *The Ethical Edge: Tales of Organizations That Have Faced Moral Crises*, 105. New York: MasterMedia Ltd.

Annotated Bibliography

Chambliss, D. F. 1996. *Beyond Caring: Hospitals, Nurses and the Social Organization of Ethics.* Chicago: University of Chicago Press. An anecdotal and illuminating discourse on the effect of organizational realities on professional behavior.

Haron, D. 1998. "Waste and Neglect: Fraud and Abuse in the Health Care Industry." *Health Care Supervisor* 6 (4): 61–67. A comprehensive and up-to-date analysis of the fraud and abuse issue.

Izraeli, D., and M. S. Schwartz. 1998. "What Can We Learn From the U.S. Federal Sentencing Guidelines for Organizational Ethics?" *Journal of Business Ethics* 17 (4): 1045–55. A clear and penetrating description and impact analysis of federal compliance requirements.

Nash, L. L. 1990. *Good Intentions Aside: A Manager's Guide to Resolving Ethical Problems.* Boston: Harvard Business School Press. An insightful overview of organizational ethics from a business corporation perspective stressing the relationship of organizational climate to individual behavior.

Potter, R. L. 1996. "From Clinical Ethics to Organizational Ethics: The Second Stage of the Evolution of Bioethics." *Bioethics Forum* 12 (2): 3–12. Provides perspective on the relationship of corporate ethics to clinical ethics.

Rovner, J. 1998. "Organizational Ethics: It's Your Move." *Health System Leader* 5 (1): 4–12. A terrific update on the status of organizational ethics in hospitals including case examples.

Schyve, P. M. 1996. "Patient Rights and Organization Ethics: The Joint Commission Perspective." *Bioethics Forum* 12 (2): 13–20. Written by a vice president of the Joint Commission, this article provides clarity on the Joint Commission's view of organizational ethics.

Worthley, J. A. 1997. *The Ethics of the Ordinary in Healthcare: Concepts and Cases.* Chicago: Health Administration Press. A unique look at the power of healthcare professionals within the organizational setting and the ethical implications involved.

2

ETHICS AND ORGANIZATIONAL STRUCTURES

OBVIOUSLY ORGANIZATIONAL ethics in healthcare is about ethics—ethical principles, theory, and reasoning. That is where bioethicists come in. But organizational ethics is equally about healthcare organizations—what they consist of and how they work— and that is where management theorists and organization behaviorists come in. The nature of organizations and how ethics can be structurally integrated with organizations is the focal question of this chapter. Answering that question is essential in developing a working understanding of the compliance notion.

CASE STUDY

Case Two: The Code or the Cash?

Some years ago St. Serena's chief executive officer, Samantha Savage, instituted a corporate code of ethics that was consistent with the codes of both the American Hospital Association and the American College of Healthcare Executives. Among the code's provisions were the following:

1. *St. Serena's will neither engage in nor facilitate discriminatory organization practices.*
2. *St. Serena's will openly advise patients or others served of their rights, opportunities, responsibilities, and the risks regarding available healthcare services.*

> *3. St. Serena's will operate through processes that ensure the autonomy and self-determination of patients and others served.*

A copy of the code is given to every new employee during orientation. Each employee is required to sign a form stating that the code has been read and understood. Additionally, a beautifully framed, laminated copy of the code hangs on the wall of every unit. Annually, the trustees of St. Serena's sponsor a high-profile lecture by a noted ethicist.

Shortly after the institution of the code of ethics, St. Serena's acquired a long-term skilled nursing facility in an attempt to situate itself more favorably in the healthcare marketplace. When the nursing home was acquired, it not only adopted the St. Serena's code of ethics but also formulated specific policies to implement the principles of the code and to ensure compliance with governmental and Joint Commission regulations and standards. Among these policies is the following:

> *All applicants for admission to the St. Serena's nursing home will be treated equally and fairly without regard to race, creed, color, national origin, sex, handicap, or source of payment.*

Andrew Able, the administrator of the facility, proudly speaks of the nursing home as one of the finest and most ethical long-term care facilities in the state.

Although the hospital and nursing home are separate entities within the St. Serena's complex, they are governed by the same board of trustees. St. Serena's executive vice president, Lance Larue, oversees the operations of both the hospital and the nursing home. He made the final decision to hire Andrew as the facility's administrator.

Within the past few years St. Serena's has experienced severe financial pressures while adjusting to the managed care environment. Although its long-term position looks promising because of shrewd strategic planning, short-term realities promise to be challenging. Indeed, St. Serena's recently engaged a consulting firm to help bring more discipline to the financial management practices of administrators, directors, and supervisors, all of whom—including Andrew Able—have been receiving regular reminders and training to increase revenues and decrease expenditures.

Enter Mrs. Livingston. A prominent citizen in the community served by St. Serena's, she is currently a patient in the hospital. At 86 years of age she is being treated for heart disease and chronic pulmonary ailments. Her attending physician, in consultation with the family, has determined that she will require nursing home placement upon discharge. The family strongly expressed to the hospital discharge planner a desire to have Mrs. Livingston placed in St. Serena's nursing home. The discharge planner explained that policies require the hospital to refer every nursing home candidate to all similar facilities in the area, with the next available vacancy going to the next person on the waiting list. The discharge planner further explained that because Mrs. Livingston would be a private-pay patient she could—unlike Medicare/Medicaid patients who would lose benefits—refuse placement offers from undesired facilities and remain on the list.

However, when a bed at St. Serena's will become available is unknown. In fact, when the St. Serena's nursing home preadmission committee added Mrs. Livingston's name to the waiting list there were 60 people ahead of her. Shortly thereafter Andrew received a call from Lance requesting that priority for the next bed be given to Mrs. Livingston. Lance reminded Andrew that not only is Mrs. Livingston a high-level donor to St. Serena's, but that the consultants had strongly encouraged the nursing home to increase its percentage of private-pay residents. In percentage of higher revenue-producing private patients, St. Serena's facility is currently well below the norm among area facilities, and as a result the facility is at a competitive disadvantage.

Questions for Discussion:

1. What should Andrew do and why? What is he likely to do? If your answers to these questions are different, explain the variance.
2. What organizational structures are mentioned in the case description? What influence are these likely to have, if any, on Andrew's behavior? Will the code or the boss have more influence?
3. Does this situation involve a compliance issue? Is ethics integrated into the organizational structure of St. Serena's? Structurally, what could be instituted to help everyone conform with policy?
4. What effect is the code of ethics likely to have on Andrew? Will it ensure ethical behavior as intended? Why?
5. What are the likely outcomes if Andrew moves Mrs. Livingston to the top of the list? If he keeps her at her current position on the list?
6. What is the ethical thing for Andrew to do? What organizational structures might be put into place to increase the likelihood of Andrew doing the ethical thing?

COMMENTARY

Andrew Able has some decisions to make. As an ethical individual he wants to make ethical decisions. But, as Jansen and Von Glinow articulate in their reading attached to this chapter, behavior—ethical or

Figure 2.1 The Nature of Organizations

	Corporate (Macro)	Group (Middle)	Individual (Micro)
Formal			
Informal			

otherwise—is a function of both the person and the environment. Andrew's task is complicated by the reality that the situation has unfolded in an organizational setting with a code of ethics, a hierarchy, ethics symbols and words, financial pressures, competition, and consultant expertise. Therefore, the nature of this organizational setting and its effect on Andrew's commitment to behave ethically must be determined.

Such a determination is all the more important for healthcare organizations given the American College of Healthcare Executives ethics policy statement that healthcare executives should "evaluate and continually refine organizational processes for addressing ethical issues,"[1] given the Joint Commission's increasing insistence on organizational ethics standards, and given the Federal Sentencing Commission's requirement of rigorous attention to organizational means of ensuring ethical behavior.

Formal Versus Informal Realities

A simple matrix can be helpful in describing the formal and informal structures of ethics in healthcare organizations (see Figure 2.1).

I call this the Whorton-Quinn Matrix in honor of former colleagues who refined it.[2] The matrix provides a window through which to better see and analyze the nature of healthcare organizations. The official, and fairly obvious, aspect of organizations, typically termed the "formal organization" or structural element, refers to all the visible realities of organizations that usually come to mind—things like organizational charts and written policies. The much less obvious, unofficial realities of organizations—like unwritten policies and "grapevines" are usually termed the "informal organization" or elements of organization "culture." The formal structure concerns what presumably *should* characterize organizational life; the informal culture concerns what *actually* characterizes organizational life. Of course, a close interaction exists between the two, and each affects the other.

An analogy of highway driving illustrates the distinction. Formally, we have official speed limits, radar equipment, and traffic courts.

Culturally, most drivers travel a bit above the official limits, most police officers set their radars at 8 to 10 m.p.h. above the official limit, and most traffic courts reduce speeding violations to "non-moving violations" if an attorney plea bargains. Traffic safety agencies continue to seek effective ways to change the actual driving behavior of Americans both by adjusting formal structures and by direct efforts to adjust the "culture" of driving. So too, to affect behavior in healthcare organizations, we need to reflect on realities and seek effective ways to facilitate ethical behavior. This requires reflection on the nature of organizations, which entails analysis of both the formal and the informal structures. The present chapter focuses on the formal structures, and Chapter three will explore the informal aspect.

These formal and informal aspects of organizations can be more easily explored by recognizing that each consists of a corporate (macro), a group (middle), and an individual (micro) dimension. Each interact with and affect one another. Using this construct we can identify six significant elements in the nature of organizations:

1. Formal corporate structures and processes;
2. Informal corporate culture and processes;
3. Formal group structures and processes;
4. Informal group culture and processes;
5. Formal individual structures and processes; and
6. Informal individual culture and processes.

By isolating each of these elements we can better focus on the ethical dimension of the organization. For each element we can identify specific realities of the ethical situation and then determine what the organization can do to better facilitate ethical behavior (see Figure 2.2).

At the formal corporate level we can look at and for policies, codes, authority structure, department and committee structure, procedures, and systems of control, monitoring, and rewards. At the formal group level we look for work group structure and relationships, group tasks, and local group procedures; at the formal individual level job descriptions, performance evaluations, degree of isolation or interaction, and training requirements are sought. We can probably analyze the St. Serena's situation more easily, and better understand the points in the attached readings, with the help of these categories.

More specifically, we can examine—at the corporate level—whether, for example, a code of ethics exists and whether it is prominent or little known, whether an ethics committee exists and whether it has corporate-wide representation, and whether there are mechanisms in place to monitor compliance with codes and policies. At St. Serena's we find that a solid code exists and is highlighted. Some corporate-wide

Figure 2.2 Elements of the Ethical Dimension at Each Level of the Formal Organizational Structure*

Corporate	Group	Individual

Policies
Codes
Authority Structure
Department and
  Committee Structure
Procedures
Systems of Control,
  Monitoring, and
  Rewards
	Work Group Structure
	Work Group
	  Relationships
	Tasks
	Procedures
		Job Description
		Performance
		  Evaluation
		Degree of Isolation
		  or Interaction
		Training Requirements

*Compare to Figure 3.2 in Chapter three.

ethics training is given in the form of an annual lecture. Although a well-developed hierarchy exists, no mechanism to monitor compliance with policies is apparent. An ethics committee has been established but it does not seem to deal with issues of management (it probably deals well with clinical issues).

At the group level we could look for a departmental or professional codes of ethics, ethics focus groups, and targeted training related to the ethical dimension of each specialized work group. St. Serena's does seem to have group-level ethics policies (at least for the long-term care facility group), but apparently has little training or monitoring mechanisms in place at this level.

At the individual level the job description of the administrator at the St. Serena's nursing home should be evaluated. Does it include any mention of compliance with written policies? Does it stress authority relationships more than compliance? Does the performance evaluation of the administrator include an ethics rating? Is ethics training provided for managers like Andrew and for his boss, Lance?

Before-During-After

A second helpful concept for thinking through organization structural positioning with regard to ethics is the simple "before-during-after" construct. In financial management jargon the concept is usually termed the more arcane "budgeting-accounting-auditing," but the idea is the same for ethics management: (1) What does the organization do

Figure 2.3 Structuring Organizational Ethics

	Before	During	After
Planning			
Monitoring			
Evaluating			

structurally *before* behavior? Does it plan for ethics? (2) What does the organization do structurally *during* behavior? Does it monitor its ethics? (3) What does the organization do structurally *after* behavior? Does it evaluate its ethics? Or, does the organization simply plan for ethics but then fail to perform structural follow-up? Figure 2.3 depicts the concept and provides a lens through which to identify and analyze specific structural mechanisms in an organization. Notice how the matrix suggests that each structural function needs to be addressed continuously even though only one function might be stressed at a particular phase.

At St. Serena's appropriate measures have been taken in the before phase. The code of ethics is a mechanism of structural planning and sets forth what the organization intends its behavior to be. However, neither monitoring nor auditing mechanisms appear to be in place to manage behavior in the direction of the stated plan. Lance Larue can cavalierly direct Andrew toward unplanned behavior probably because no one will notice given the apparent absence of ethics accounting and auditing systems. St. Serena's fine code, to borrow from Brien's analysis in the reading attached to this chapter, is not really part of the organizational infrastructure. If we consider a code of conduct to be a sort of ethics "program plan," would we not reasonably expect, as with any planned program, that an associated program evaluation mechanism with, for example, identified evaluation measures and benchmarks, be in place? We would normally expect some effort at testing the plan and auditing its track record. The before-during-after concept can be a reminder of these kinds of managerial expectations.

Organizational Values

A third relevant concept for probing the ethical nature of organizations is the notion of organizational values. A perusal of any corporate or professional code of ethics in healthcare and of nearly all healthcare ethics literature reveals the very prominent place values take in healthcare ethics discourse. The problem, as I have discussed elsewhere,[3] is that while healthcare ethics is about values in theory, in reality it is about *conflicting* values, and that modifier makes all the difference. Clearly ethics is about upholding the time-honored values of healthcare such as patient's rights and professional integrity. With the managed care environment of recent years, cost-consciousness values have come to the fore. St. Serena's code highlights the values of patient dignity and patient rights; but its operating administration correctly places great importance on economic values as well. Indeed, Andrew Able faces a problem of conflicting values within the organization.

Instead of dealing comprehensively with such conflict, most discussions of values in healthcare seem to seek escape.[4] Patients and providers speak of quality care often with merely lip-service to the values of economic care. Insurers and healthcare managers speak of cost consciousness often with seeming lip-service to quality of care values. Bioethicists have embraced the notion of "values ascendency," which is a convenient way to avoid confrontation of conflicting organizational values. In this construct some values (usually patient-care related) are judged more valuable than other values (usually finance related)—they "ascend" to a level beyond conflict. Recently, the notion of "deep values" has emerged as a way of reminding cost-conscious managers of the traditional values upon which most healthcare facilities—particularly those with religious roots like St. Serena's—were founded. Under this construct conflict can be deflected by reminders of sacred traditions.[5]

For purposes of organizational ethics analysis a more useful notion may be that of values emphasis. What values does the organizational structure emphasize? What values does the organization's behavior emphasize? What values should be emphasized in healthcare organizations? St. Serena's code and policies seem to emphasize quality care and patient rights, and its hierarchy emphasizes economics. What values will Andrew Able emphasize? What values should he emphasize? By structurally emphasizing some values and understating others, organizations risk denial of realistic conflict. They then make what Andrew Brien in the attached reading calls "pious affirmations" instead of practical accommodations.

Recognizing the reality of values conflict requires structural efforts at values balance, values reconciliation, and equal values emphasis. The situation at St. Serena's is a timeless challenge and has been confronted throughout the centuries. Historically, the dilemma has typically been viewed as the individual versus the community, or freedom versus order. Figure 2.4 attempts to combine ancient concepts with modern healthcare concepts.

Figure 2.4 Organizational Values Conflict

Individual	⟷	Community
Quality	⟷	Cost
Patient Rights	⟷	Organization Concerns
Freedom	⟷	Order

The tension between individual freedom and community order has been experienced and debated since the days of ancient Greece and later. The conflict was central to the deliberations of the writers of the American Constitution[6] who, rather than avoiding the real conflict with pious ideals, dealt with it head-on and developed structures of balance and values reconciliation (for example, a free-wheeling House of Representatives and an ordered Senate must agree for anything to happen). In healthcare today the tension is played out in the stress between the economic needs of organizations and the rights of each individual patient to freely chose quality care. Demands for maximum quality at minimum cost present a values conflict that is part of organizational reality today.

At St. Serena's, codes and policies seem to structure the values of individual freedom and quality, while hierarchy seems to structure the values of community order and finance. A confrontational rather than an avoidance approach might help the organization deal better with this reality. Efforts at values balance and reconciliation are needed. Could the code, for example, equally emphasize the financial well-being of the organization and patient rights? Could the hierarchy more equally emphasize patient rights and quality care as well as financial concerns? Are there ways to structure a values balance such that the rights of patients on the nursing home waiting list *and* the financial concerns of St. Serena's are honored and dealt with?

A recent study of organizational justice suggests the importance of structural process in dealing with such conflict in a balanced way.[7] Schminke, Ambrose, and Noel distinguish formalism from utilitarianism in decision making; formalism stresses process and procedure, utilitarianism stresses outcomes. They suggest the possibility of structuring ethical decision making in organizations so that both outcomes (for the individual and the organizational community) and process are recognized and managerially addressed. Would St. Serena's do well to establish a process for dealing with admissions situations such as Mrs. Livingston's? Would it do well to clarify the financial outcomes and the patient rights outcomes involved?

Structural Mechanisms

The importance of solid organizational mechanisms for structuring ethical behavior cannot be overemphasized. Some of the more widely suggested mechanisms follow.

Codes.

As probably the most common ethics mechanism employed in healthcare organizations today, codes—or mission statements—vary tremendously in content, design, and rigor. This mechanism is thoroughly described and critically analyzed in depth by Andrew Brien in his reading following this commentary.

Health ethics committees.

Ethics committees have become the central structural unit for most healthcare organizations' attention to ethics. Although their charters, membership, and procedures have been somewhat diverse, they have been largely limited to clinical issues; they have, as Heitman and Bulger put it, "considered economic issues to be outside their official purview."[8] In 1984, for example, as ethics committees were emerging, bioethicist John Monagle wrote a "blueprint" for health ethics committees. It focused on "treatment decisions."[9] That same year the Hastings Center defined a health ethics committee as "a group established by a hospital or healthcare institution formally charged with advising, consulting, discussing, or otherwise being involved in ethical decisions and policies that arise in clinical care."[10]

More recently, ethicists like Robert Potter have urged the broader development of health ethics committees. He calls for a "paradigm shift" through which committees learn how to integrate clinical and corporate aspects of bioethics. But, he laments, "the typical ethics committee is not prepared for, and may even be resistant to, the task of organizational ethics." He argues for a second generation of institutional ethics committees as "the mechanism" to more completely integrate ethics with the organization.[11] Similarly, Holmes and Meehan[12] as well as Weber[13] see a need for expanded membership and scope for ethics committees. Weber contends that the mechanism of a health ethics committee "must be prepared to say when cost factors trump other considerations and when they do not." Citing Joint Commission developments, Spencer[14] urges the broader use of institutional ethics committees so that organizational issues are addressed together with clinical concerns. Is this what St. Serena's should do? Develop an institutional ethics committee to which Andrew Able may turn?

Ethics officer.

Many corporations, including healthcare organizations, are reorganizing in the face of the compliance and ethics challenge. They are creating new, high-level positions in the hierarchy to oversee their organizational ethics thrust. Some—such as Quorum Health Group—are establishing the position at the vice president level; others—such as Harvard Pilgrim Health Care—are designating it as a directorship. In any case, responsibilities of an ethics officer generally include "managing internal reporting systems, assessing ethics risk areas, developing and distributing ethics policies and publications, investigating alleged violations, and designing training programs."[15] Reflective of this thrust, a professional association of corporate ethics officers has emerged with more than 300 major corporations represented.[16]

Compliance programs.

Owing to the force of the Federal Sentencing Guidelines, a corporate compliance program is the most rapidly evolving structural mechanism. This emphasis has developed from the severe governmental response to the Office of the Inspector General's empirical study that found 14 percent of Medicare payments—amounting to an astounding $23 billion—to be erroneous.[17] The government promulgated major criminal and civil sanctions—commonly known as "fraud and abuse" provisions—that address the following areas:

- Filing false claims;
- Solicitation, receipt, or offering of kickbacks, bribes, or rebates;
- Misrepresentation of institutional qualifications;
- Violation of assignment agreements;
- False representation of Medicare; and
- Assorted other financial records problems.

Compliance programs are typically organizational responses to the incarcerative and financial penalties attached to fraud and abuse violations in these areas.[18] Such programs seek to ensure more responsible and honest behavior by establishing rigorous organizational measures for ethical healthcare management. Seven elements are essential to compliance programs:

1. Written standards and procedures;
2. Designated high-level oversight;
3. Due care in delegation of authority;
4. Effective communication of standards;

Figure 2.5 Organizational Rewards Systems

	Formal	Informal
Positive		
Negative		

5. Monitoring and reporting systems;
6. Disciplinary enforcement; and
7. Appropriate response after detection.

According to Gunn, Goldfarb, and Showalter,[19] development of an effective compliance mechanism requires six steps:

1. Adoption of a board resolution;
2. Designation of a corporate compliance officer and committee;
3. Completion of a risk assessment;
4. Development of an organization-specific program;
5. Delivery of education and training; and
6. Implementation of the program.

The reading attached to Chapter one further elaborates on organizational structuring of the compliance mechanism. St. Serena's does not appear to have moved in this direction,[20] and when it does, as Whitley and Heeley articulate, the limitations of compliance programs may require that it be complemented by a broader ethics program.[21]

Reward systems.

Conscious and systematic attention to structural reward systems in the organization is becoming widespread, largely because federal compliance pressure has raised this mechanism to a new level of awareness. The Jansen and Von Glinow reading attached to this chapter provides sophisticated insight on the subject.

Reward systems can be negative or positive, formal or informal. Figure 2.5 provides a matrix lens for identifying and analyzing a health-care organization's specific rewards portfolio. Formal rewards are part of organization structure and include negative mechanisms like disciplinary procedures and positive mechanisms like bonus programs. More subtle informal mechanisms include negative incentives like denial of promotion and positive incentives like inclusion in social gatherings. The key measure for ethical analysis is identification of what behaviors are rewarded. At St. Serena's, for example, is compliance with written

Figure 2.6 Ethics Survey as Suggested by Quorum Health Group

1. Do you believe that members of senior management are committed to ethical practices?
2. Do you understand the organization's code of conduct?
3. Do you know the procedure for reporting unethical practices?
4. Do you feel comfortable reporting ethical issues or dilemmas?
5. Are you given the education and tools necessary to perform your job in an ethical manner?

policies rewarded in performance assessment, or is obedience to hierarchy rewarded through formal promotion systems that stress the "team player" notion and informal processes that embrace obedient subordinates into the inner circle of decision makers? Will Andrew Able be given a salary raise for upholding the written policy or for obeying Lance Larue? Will he be invited to the CEO's golf club for following hierarchical direction or for complying with official policies? Analysis of reward systems is a key to the development of organizational ethics.

Surveys.

A simple but rarely used structural mechanism is an ethics survey instrument. As part of a reasonable monitoring effort, a healthcare organization could design and implement a survey of its employees on the ethics environment as they perceive it. Something as concise as the survey in Figure 2.6, suggested by—though curiously not used in—the Quorum Health Group, illustrates the concept.[22]

Of course many variations of the survey in Figure 2.6 are possible. Professional design and administration of such surveys are essential to usefulness. Would such a survey at St. Serena's be useful? What might it reveal? Notice how a survey could be a tool for practical use at all stages—before, during, and after—of ethics management.

Administrative case rounds.

Some commentators have suggested administrative case rounds as a viable mechanism for developing the ethical organization.[23] Just as the case has become a central instrument in the teaching of clinical medicine, so too, argues Reiser, can it help in the ethics dimension:

> Cases illuminating the relationships and actions of organizations can be used to test how effectively the values in institutional statements of purpose are applied in practice, to formulate and critique policies and goals, to analyze

troublesome problems, and to create institutional memory to guide future policies.[24]

He advises that rounds should include different organizational constituencies and maintains that they should be a routine feature of institutional life. A case round of admissions situations at St. Serena's might be helpful to Andrew as well as to Lance.

Numerous other mechanisms, such as establishment of hotlines for reporting or seeking counsel, provision of periodic training, and funding of ethics research within the organization are available to structurally develop the ethics dimension of a healthcare organization. Taken together, these structural mechanisms constitute what Weaver, Trevino, and Cochran call a "formal ethics program." They see this as an organizational control system aimed at standardizing employee behavior within the domains of ethics and legal compliance.[25]

Process of structure development.

Developing a structure for supporting the ethical dimension of healthcare organizations requires time and care. The AHA's Julie Rovner, for example, emphasizes the nurturing of consensus and commitment before any organizational ethics program is launched.[26] Establishing fair and open forums for this purpose and carefully designing mechanisms that make sense for the particular organization are key steps to a successful process. For example, Harvard Pilgrim Health Care—one of the first healthcare organizations to embark on a comprehensive organizational ethics effort—chose not to develop a code of ethics initially. Unlike most healthcare organizations that typically begin with a code Harvard Pilgrim began its effort by forming an ethics advisory group consisting of a cross-section of the organization as well as outsiders. This group analyzes cases brought to it and publishes the results of its deliberation. The work of the group is viewed as a learning tool that will enable development of a meaningful structure.

Similarly, United HealthCare has developed a committee structure to study cases and develop policy recommendations. On the other hand, under the pressure of a court order, Tenet Healthcare—owner of a 130-hospital network—quickly developed a comprehensive ethics training program and a systemwide "ethics action line" staffed by trained personnel. Under the direction of a corporate integrity program management committee of its board of directors, Tenet requires every employee to receive ethics training within three months of hire and once annually thereafter. Tenet also developed a detailed "standards of conduct" brochure. The ethics action line receives 500 calls per month, some reporting suspected wrongdoing but most seeking advice. This ethics structure is independent of the system's organizational compliance program.

Does St. Serena's need to design a process to further build its ethics structure? Should it provide regular ethics training and establish an "action line" instead of simply a "hotline" that Andrew could consult? Would that really help? Some kind of formal structure is essential in addressing organizational ethics; however, weaving in the informal culture of the organization is equally important. The following readings demonstrate such integration in their presentation of structural approaches to organizational ethics. The ensuing chapter then provides more focus on the informal reality of ethics within an organization.

Notes

1. American College of Healthcare Executives. 1997. "Ethical Policy Statement."
2. Joseph Whorton of the University of Georgia and Robert Quinn of the University of Michigan.
3. Worthley, J. 1997. *The Ethics of the Ordinary in Healthcare*, 111–46. Chicago: Health Administration Press.
4. Stark has argued that the same problem exists among business ethics analysts. See Stark, A. 1993. "What's the Matter with Business Ethics?" *Harvard Business Review* 71 (3): 38–48.
5. See, for example, Veatch, R. 1995. "Abandoning Informed Consent." *Hastings Center Report* 25 (2): 5–12.
6. See the *Federalist Papers* for the classic dialogue between public order proponents like Hamilton and individual freedom advocates like Madison.
7. Schminke, M., M. Ambrose, and T. Noel. 1997. "The Effect of Ethical Frameworks on Perceptions of Organizational Justice." *Academy of Management Journal* 40 (5): 1190–207.
8. Heitman, E., and R. Bulger. 1998. "The Healthcare Ethics Committee in the Structural Transformation of Health Care." *HEC Forum* 10 (2): 153.
9. Monagle, J. 1984. "Blueprints for Hospital Ethics Committees." *California Hospital Association Insight* 8 (20): 1–4.
10. Levine, C. 1984. "Questions and (Some Very Tentative) Answers About Hospital Ethics Committees." *Hastings Center Report* 14 (3): 9.
11. Potter, R. 1996. "From Clinical to Organizational Ethics." *Bioethics Forum* 12 (2): 3–9
12. Holmes, P., and M. Meehan. "Ethical Awareness and Healthcare Professionals." *Journal of Pastoral Care* 52 (1): 33–40.
13. Weber, L. 1997. "Taking on Organizational Ethics." *Health Progress* 78 (3): 20.
14. Spencer, E. 1997. "A New Role for Institutional Ethics Committees." *Journal of Clinical Ethics* 8 (4): 372–376.
15. Petry, E. 1998. "Appointing an Ethics Officer." *Healthcare Executive* 13 (6): 35.
16. Weaver, G., L. Trevino, and P. Cochran. 1999. "Corporate Ethics Programs as Control Systems." *Academy of Management Journal* 42 (1): 41.

17. Forgione, D. 1998. "Corporate Compliance Plans in Health Care Organizations." *Journal of Health Care Finance* 24 (4): 87.

18. For description of a model plan, see Matusicky, C. 1998. "Building an Effective Corporate Compliance Program." *Healthcare Financial Management* (Apr): 77–80.

19. Gunn, J., E. Goldfarb, and J. Showalter. 1998. "Creating a Corporate Compliance Program." *Health Progress* 79 (3): 62–63.

20. St. Serena's and other healthcare organizations could benefit from Withrow, S. 1999. *Managing Healthcare Compliance.* Chicago: Health Administration Press in designing a comprehensive corporate compliance program.

21. Whitley, L., and G. Heeley. 1998. "Beyond Compliance." *Healthcare Executive* (May/June): 62.

22. Batts, C. 1998. "Making Ethics an Organization Priority." *Healthcare Forum Journal* 41 (1): 42.

23. Reiser, S. 1991. "Administrative Case Rounds." *Journal of the American Medical Association* 226 (15): 2127–28.

24. Reiser, S. 1994. "The Ethical Life of Health Care Organizations." *Hastings Center Report* 24 (6): 34.

25. Weaver, Trevino, and Cochran, *op.cit.*, 42.

26. Rovner, J. 1998. "Organizational Ethics: It's Your Move." *Health System Leader* 5 (1): 5.

READINGS

The following pieces are interestingly disparate yet similar in their unusually realistic perspective on organizations. The first article was written by business experts in America more than a decade ago; the second, by a philosophy professor in New Zealand just recently. Jansen and Von Glinow's contribution is among the earliest but still best analyses of the relationship of the organizational setting—specifically reward and sanction systems—to the behavior of corporate members. The authors illuminate the influence not only of the formal structural realities discussed in this chapter, but also the informal realities probed in the next chapter. Their discussion of organizational rewards and sanctions can well be used to clarify the situation at St. Serena's and to design an effective ethics compliance program.

Andrew Brien is an unlikely winner in the management ethics literature. Despite a focus on codes, despite his philosophical calling, and despite this New Zealander's distance from the American corporate experience, his article is one of the most comprehensive and clear views of the nature of organizations from an ethics perspective. After observing that, notwithstanding the popularity of codes, little evidence indicates that codes actually improve ethical standards, Brien convincingly argues that "no matter how well-formulated a code may be, compliance will not result naturally. . . . Effective compliance requires a compliance mechanism, that is, a structural approach that takes into account the capacities and features of the code's constituency." His analysis might help St. Serena's focus on development of institutional mechanisms to make its code more than a superficial part of the organization structure. Brien's kind of analysis is also evident in recent federal judicial sentencing decisions.

Ethical Ambivalence and Organizational Reward Systems

Erik Jansen and Mary Ann Von Glinow*

Issues of corporate morality and business ethics are of concern to both management and business schools (Garrett 1985; Snoeyenbos, Almeder, and Humber 1983; Walters 1978). These issues include social responsibility (Heilbronner 1972), conflict of interest (Snoeyenbos et al. 1983), payoffs (Pastin and Hooker 1980), product safety (Vandevier 1978), liability (Berenson 1972), and whistle-blowing (Nader, Petkas, and Blackwell 1972). On the popular front, CBS's *Sixty Minutes* offers continuing glimpses of corporate and managerial misbehavior. Despite all the attention, such inquiries rarely explicitly examine the pressures that organizational reward systems exert on individuals to behave "unethically." It is far more common and dramatic to focus on individual culpability, a practice organizations may support out of sheer self-interest. However, greater knowledge of the organizational context of the behavior may change attributions of individual culpability, for example, Vandevier's (1978) disclosures about B. F. Goodrich's handling of the aircraft brake scandal. To some extent, villains begin to resemble scapegoats as one sees how a system's reward structure shapes and maintains actions that are judged to be unethical.

Behaviors judged to be unethical, like other classes of behavior, are a function of the person and the environment (Lewin 1951; Magnusson and Endler 1977). It is acknowledged that individuals are intentional,

*Reprinted with permission of Academy of Management, P. O. Box 3020, Briarcliff Manor, NY 10510. Academy of Management Review 1985. 10 (4). Reproduced by permission of the publisher via Copyright Clearance Center, Inc. The authors were on the faculty of the Business School of the University of Southern California.

active agents, but a complementary situational approach is pursued here. Attention is focused not on the individual per se, but on the rewards and sanctions that help define the individual's situation. This reward system perspective views rewards and sanctions not only as direct determinants of the individual's definition of the situation, but as determinants of group norms, which also define the individual's situation. This paper focuses on organizational and institutional norms and counternorms as they are shaped and maintained by reward systems.

Ambivalence, Ethics, and Reward Systems
Sociological ambivalence.

Merton and Barber (1963) and Merton (1963, 1976) argue that ambivalence—the experience of being pulled in psychologically opposite directions—requires a sociological analysis to complement the dominant psychological approach. Merton argues, as do the present authors, that ambivalence often is "built into the structure of social statuses and roles" (1963, 93). Sociological ambivalence may be defined as incompatible normative expectations of attitudes, beliefs, and behaviors assigned to a role or set of roles in a social system (Merton 1976). Sociological ambivalence thus is an attribute of a social system and is inherent in social positions.

According to Merton and Barber, "Major norms and the minor counternorms alternatively govern role behavior to produce ambivalence" (1963, 103). Norms are common beliefs about appropriate and required behavior for group members as group members (Katz and Kahn 1978). Counternorms thus are viewed as inappropriate, and yet they also are viewed as necessary. Merton and Barber argue:

> Behavior oriented wholly to the dominant norms would defeat the functional objectives of the role. Instead, role-behavior is alternatively oriented to dominant norms and to subsidiary counternorms in the role. The alternation of subroles evolves as a social device for helping men in designated statuses to cope with the contingencies they face in trying to fulfill their functions (1963, 104).

Thus, given the different contingencies faced in any given role set, the oscillation between roles and subroles, between norms and counternorms, is functional.

The lay observation that an organization would come to a grinding halt if everyone narrowly followed the rules expresses the need for inconsistency and maneuvering room provided by counternorms. As Mills notes:

> Just as sociological ambivalence allows individuals to create autonomy for themselves by means of legitimated inconsistent behavior, so at the social

system level the presence of contrasting norms and values assures a ferment of differences which both encourages innovation and inhibits system efficiency in goal attainment (1983, 281–82).

Counternorms are viewed here as generally inappropriate and socially undesirable. Although they may be tolerated as counternorms, important stakeholders may find them intolerable as norms. Thus, if the reward system inadvertently supports these counternorms, a special type of sociological ambivalence, which the authors call ethical ambivalence, is likely to result.

Ethical ambivalence.

Ethical ambivalence is based on the somewhat neglected construct of sociological ambivalence. Ethical ambivalence is a form of sociological ambivalence in which (a) the behaviors, attitudes, and norms that are shaped and maintained by the organizational reward system conflict with (b) the behaviors, attitudes, and norms congruent with the ethical values and judgments of organizational stakeholders. Stakeholders are classes of individuals who have a vested interest in the outcomes of actions and the solutions of problems. They include customers, government, and stockholders (Mason and Mitroff 1981).

Merton (1976) gives, as an example of sociological ambivalence, the physician who alternatively behaves with affective neutrality and emotional involvement toward patients. Such ambivalence is not ethically problematic because both classes of behavior contribute to the goals and well-being of patients. When, as in many mental institutions, active, emotional involvement is not rewarded or is disapproved, then the well-being of patients may suffer as patients are neglected (Scheff 1981). Ethical ambivalence is revealed by stakeholder claims that they have been harmed. Stakeholder (i.e., patient) advocates thus may seek redress of past wrongs. Legal actions have resulted in court rulings mandating the care of institutionalized mental patients.

Ethical ambivalence is conceptually close to role conflict, even as norms are conceptually close to roles. Katz and Kahn (1978) note that roles differentiate positions and norms integrate positions. Role conflict deals with differentiated positions; ethical ambivalence deals with norms that are intended to integrate positions and counternorms that allow individuals to retain some personal autonomy (Mills 1983). Furthermore, role conflict refers to proximate interactions of individuals with others in their role set. Conceptually, one may imagine situations of ethical ambivalence even when everyone in an individual's role set is sending consistent messages on role behavior. Even in the absence of face-to-face role conflict, ethical ambivalence can result if distal stakeholders (e.g., customers, citizens, stockholders) claim that they have been harmed.

Ethical theory and ethical judgments.

> [Ethical theory] does not ask such questions as 'What decision would society (or the American Medical Association, or the church, or any other group) approve?' Ethics seeks the principles that will tell us the right thing to do, or what things are worth doing, no matter what these groups in fact approve or disapprove and no matter what people will be damaged by the decision. (Jones et al. 1977, 5–6)

Thus judgments about the rightness or value of norms and counternorms require ethical theory, which is within the domain of philosophical inquiry.

Here, by contrast, there is more concern with patterns of organizational approval and disapproval, with patterns of norms and counternorms, than with ethical judgments per se. Although ethical theory guides judgments about the morality of counternorms and norms, ethical ambivalence serves to structure one's thinking about organizational research. Thus, one condition of ethical ambivalence requires that a class of individuals (stakeholders) assert that they have been harmed through morally culpable actions.

Organizational reward systems.

The reward system perspective observes that organizational actors "seek information concerning what activities are rewarded, and then seek to do (or at least pretend to do) those things often to the virtual exclusion of activities not rewarded" (Kerr 1975, 769).

The reward system comprises the related set of processes through which behaviors are directed and motivated to achieve individual and collaborative performances; the set of processes comprise goal setting, assessing performance, distributing rewards, and communicating feedback. Kerr (1975) argues that reward systems frequently shape and maintain behaviors that they are trying to discourage while punishing or ignoring desired behaviors. If contingencies alter the dialectical balance of norms and counternorms, ethical ambivalence is likely to result.

The reward system is viewed as the structural source of ethical ambivalence. It is important to explore the linkages between the organizational reward system and the extent to which employees behave "unethically." The concept of ethical ambivalence directs attention to characteristics of ethically enabling and disabling reward systems and the norms and counternorms that such systems shape and maintain.

A fascinating example of ethical ambivalence induced by an alteration in the reward system can be seen in current business sponsorship of what traditionally has been basic scientific research (e.g., genetic engineering; Dickson 1984). The norms of academic scientists are norms of open communication that support knowledge as a public commodity. However, business research tends to be surrounded by norms of secrecy that support knowledge as private property. Secrecy has long been a counternorm of science; it protects scientists from later involvements in priority disputes (Merton 1957). However, advocates now argue that academic departments and the public, who support the universities, are being hurt by secrecy. Lawyers advise scientists going to scientific meetings to "have their proposed remarks notarized, giving details of when and where they came up with their ideas and where they were going to discuss them" (Dickson 1984, 77). Scientists, "having delivered research papers at an open meeting, have subsequently refused to divulge details of the techniques" (Dickson 1984, 77). Thus, an associate professor of physics asserts: "It is absolutely unethical for people who are employed academically to put themselves in the position where they cannot speak about a major thrust or development of their research freely to their cohorts" (Dickson 1984, 77).

In short, ethical ambivalence is being experienced by individuals as the reward system alters the balance between norms and counternorms.

Norms and Counternorms

In the absence of conceptual and empirical research on the norms and counternorms leading to ethical ambivalence, two strategies are offered here to address this issue. The first strategy looks at the literature on professional and scientific norms to determine if these norms are relevant to a wider range of organizational behaviors. The second is a consideration of "strategic behaviors" (Lawler and Rhode 1976) that maximize appraisals and rewards at the expense of effective performance (Kerr and Slocum 1981).

Table 1 gives a list of norms and counternorms that are shaped and maintained by the reward system. The first three pairs are discussed to give the reader a sense of how norm-counternorm shifts can create ethical ambivalence. They are chosen because they are relatively global in nature and are from the professionalism literature; the last eight pairs stem from reward systems research (Jansen 1983; Sethia and Von Glinow 1985.) Given the exploratory stage of inquiry into ethical ambivalence, it is unlikely that this represents a comprehensive listing of norm-counternorm pairs; they are meant to be illustrative of common

Table 1 Norms and Counternorms

Norms	Counternorms
1. Openness, honesty, candor; "open covenants openly arrived at"	1. Secrecy and lying; stonewalling; "playing your cards close to the chest"
2. Emotional neutrality, disinterestedness, objectivity	2. Emotional involvement, investment, intuition
3. Organized skepticism within the rules	3. Organized dogmatism within the rules
4. Follow the rules	4. Break the rules to get job done
5. Be cost-effective	5. "Spend it or burn it"
6. Develop and mentor subordinates	6. "Watch out for number one"
7. Take responsibility	7. Avoid responsibility, "pass the buck"
8. Maintain corporate loyalty	8. "Bad-mouth" the company
9. "All for one and one for all"	9. Achieve your goals at the expense of others
10. Maintain an appearance of consensus, support the team	10. Maintain high visibility; "grandstanding"
11. Take timely action	11. "Never do today what you can put off to tomorrow"

norms and counternorms that arise in discussing dysfunctions of reward systems (Kerr 1975; Lawler and Rhode 1976).

Counternorms are difficult to express in socially desirable terms. Although the counternorm of secrecy may be an inevitable and even a necessary part of organizational life, openness typically is viewed as more socially desirable. Theories of cognitive dissonance and of defense mechanisms suggest that even unethical actions can be rephrased and rationalized into more socially desirable statements. Note also that although ethical ambivalence typically results from the dialectical interplay between norms and counternorms, tension also may develop between some of the dominant norms, for example, Number 1: Openness, honesty, and candor versus Number 8: Maintain corporate loyalty (see Table 1).

Openness and honesty versus secrecy and lying.

One set of seemingly common organizational norms comprises openness, honesty, and full disclosure or, in Woodrow Wilson's terms, "open covenants, openly arrived at." Full disclosure acts, sunshine laws, and the Freedom of Information Act are indicators of the normative expectations surrounding honesty and openness.

The counternorms of secrecy, lying, and deceit clearly are more socially undesirable as well as ethically problematic (Bok 1978, 1983).

Stonewalling indicates the counternorms of withholding and hiding relevant information. However, such counternorms may be necessary and functional. Bennis (1980) suggests that the nation seems to be suffering from "full disclosure" mania, which requires more inventive forms of secrecy. Secrecy may be made more socially desirable when presented in terms of confidentiality of sources. However, when a pattern of secrecy and lying begins to appear to be the normal appropriate action to take, then ethical ambivalence may occur if (a) the reward system supports secrecy and lying and (b) the withholding of information is harmful to the welfare of a group of stakeholders.

Organizational reward systems may punish honesty and reward dishonesty. The case of B. F. Goodrich in the aircraft brake scandal is one example: falsifying data required to win certification was rewarded by the company (Vandevier 1978). The attempts by Metropolitan Edison's Vice President of Generation to manage the press during the Three Mile Island crisis provides a second example (Gray and Rosen 1982). In both cases the counternorm of secrecy and stonewalling toward important stakeholders (the government, press, and community) placed organizational actors in positions of ethical ambivalence. Academic examples of dishonesty include deceiving research subjects, plagiarizing, and fudging data to achieve expected results, all of which may be rewarded and become acceptable to subgroups.

Emotional neutrality and objective rationality versus emotional involvement and intuition.

The norm of emotional neutrality has been described as an instrumental condition for the achievement of scientific rationality and professional decision making (Barber 1952; Kerr, Von Glinow, and Schriesheim 1977; Merton 1963; Mitroff 1974). Hays and Abernathy indicate the importance of this norm in justifying management decisions when they assert:

> During the past two decades American managers have increasingly relied on principles which prize analytical detachment and methodological elegance over insight, based on experience, into the subtleties and complexities of strategic decisions (1980, 70).

Merton (1963, 80) noted that few scientists or professionals are exempt from "affective involvement with his ideas and his discoveries." Mitroff (1974) found that Apollo moon scientists often tightly held to their own pet theories in the face of objective and contradictory data. Indeed, emotional investment in one's theories appears to be an a priori condition for involvement with granting agencies and clients. Mitroff (1974), Polanyi (1958), and others argue that the whole of scientific decision making is infused with personal, emotional, and subjective forces. There thus is a dialectic between the dominant norm of impersonal disinterestedness and the counternorm of personal involvement in decision making. It seems even more likely that managers also must disinterestedly analyze and invest themselves in their decision making.

Organized skepticism within the rules versus organized dogmatism within the rules.

The last norm borrowed from the scientific and professionalism literature is described by Storer, who observes:

> The scientist is obliged . . . to make public his criticisms of the work of others when he believes it to be in error . . . no scientist's contribution to knowledge can be accepted without careful scrutiny, and . . . the scientist must doubt his own findings as well as those of others (1966, 79).

The counternorm is:

> The scientist must believe in his own findings with utter conviction while doubting those of others with all his worth (Mitroff and Kilmann 1978, 103).

The norm of organizational skepticism within the rules is found in the professions and, to a lesser extent, in the field of management. For example, in human resource management, selection, promotions, and performance appraisal all are accomplished within the framework of Title VII, which may be regarded as a way of opposing organized dogmatism. The Equal Employment Opportunity Commission may scrutinize personnel decisions with respect to discrimination and to job relatedness. Employment procedures are required to go through elaborate validation tests to establish conformity with legal standards of equality. The idea that one can assess job performance is acceptable and reinforced as long as it is done within a framework of rules and procedures. Organized skepticism allows doubt of particular findings. Similarly, rules for the conduct of appraisals and grievances provide an acceptable framework for questioning organizational decisions and sanctions.

The counternorm of organized dogmatism is revealed when organizational members report that they are rewarded for such behaviors as going along with the majority, never bucking a rule to get the job done, and never questioning rules or policies (Kerr 1975). Groupthink (Janis 1972) exemplifies the counternorm of organized dogmatism overwhelming the norm of organized skepticism.

A more obvious, alternative way of violating the norm of organized skepticism within the rules is to carry the skepticism outside the rules (see Table 1, Number 4). Some employees report that they are rewarded for breaking the rules in order to get the job done. If getting a desperately needed employee on board requires violating the rules and procedures that operationalize Title VII, sanctions for such actions may be suspended.

The last eight norms in Table 1 also tend to be socially desirable and are almost certainly the preferred norms of management. Cost effectiveness and staying within the operating budget are full of social desirability. The phrase "spend it or burn it" captures the well-known result of a reward system that bases future allocations on past spending habits. Similarly, management typically espouses values of developing subordinates but may fail to reward the time and energy such development requires. Cooperation ("all for one and one for all") may be expected by major stakeholders but "achieving one's own goal at the expense of others" may be rewarded. Ethical ambivalence may result when the espoused values behind dominant norms conflict with reward system practices.

Managing Ethical Ambivalence

Table 1 offers some of the norms and counternorms that reward systems may affect. Following Merton and others, it can be assumed that organizational norms and counternorms arise in every organizational setting. This is problematic when the counternorms are supported by the reward system and they violate the ethical expectations of important stakeholders. The resulting ethical ambivalence can interfere with the well-being of employees and other stakeholders. What academic responses can serve those who face ethically ambivalent situations and those who have the authority to redesign dysfunctional reward systems?

Managers usually are not well trained or educated to develop facility in surfacing and debating ethical dilemmas. Ethical issues may take a subordinate role to more pressing "bottom line" issues. There have been few incentives to discuss ethics and ethically enabling reward systems. Nonetheless, to the extent that managers aspire to professionalism (Kerr, Von Glinow, and Schriesheim 1977), they must develop facility in dealing with ethical dilemmas. As a construct, ethical ambivalence may support such inquiry.

Given the absence of conceptual and empirical research into ethical ambivalence, unanswered questions abound, including the following:

1. How pervasive are corporate reward systems that reinforce behavior that stakeholders consider unethical and thus produce ethical ambivalence for members?

2. Are there common attributes of dysfunctional reward systems or of the processes that lead to such reward systems?

3. Under what conditions (e.g., resource scarcity, high differentiation, and low integration) are instances of ethical ambivalence likely to occur?

Given the need for education and research, what advice can be suggested for those facing ethically ambivalent situations? The easiest advice to suggest often is agonizingly difficult to enact: resign. Leaving the field is one of the classic solutions to cognitive dissonance, and it may have symbolic value that contributes to forces for normative change.

Managers and employees who intend to work to reform the system must seek to redesign the reward system and affect the dialectical norm-counternorm balance. The difficulty of this varies with one's position. Some individuals are designers and decision makers who have power and influence to change the system. Others are in positions of system maintenance, collecting assessment data and distributing rewards according to rules. Others are in the assessed and rewarded position.

Managers and employees facing ethically ambivalent situations need to determine whether support is available from decision makers who have the authority to redesign the system or whether reports of ethical ambivalence are likely to be ignored or even challenged with intimidation rituals (O'Day 1974). Furthermore, transforming organizational norms may be much more difficult and threatening than seeking to reestablish norms that were once dominant. Although more research and discussion is certainly needed, the following directions are offered to managers and researchers. The focus is on generating information and action strategies that are useful to those who are in positions to redesign the reward system or are in positions to influence those who are in such positions.

1. Diagnose the reward system.   Diagnosing the reward system directly assesses the perceptions of employees and managers. A diagnosis may take the form of asking about the consequences—reward, punishment, no consequences, uncertain consequences—of different actions—breaking the rules to accomplish a task or giving management inaccurate but optimistic-sounding information. A similar strategy inquires directly into the norms that exist and those that should exist (Kilmann 1984). Diagnosis is useful in showing what the case is in a relatively objective format. Survey feedback, process interventions, and redesign of the reward system may result from this diagnosis.

2. Analyze the rules and procedures of the organization.   Interviews with those who administer and maintain the system and an analysis of written documents also may reveal important information about the system. This is compatible with an organizational learning perspective (Argyris and Schon 1978). For example, performance appraisal based on ranking may contribute to a competitive climate in which information sharing is not perceived by incumbents as rewarding. When used with the diagnosis, management can determine the extent to which the formal procedures and rules of the organization are supported or opposed by the actual pattern of rewards and punishments. Norms are one component of culture, and commonly told stories reveal aspects of the culture; thus, examining stories of how people "beat the system" may help in locating ethically ambivalent situations.

3. Training and education. Training groups can raise members' consciousness of norms, counternorms, and ambivalence. Training strategies that seek to surface assumptions and identify problems (Mason and Mitroff 1981) seem especially likely to surface counternorms and identify dysfunctional rewards. In addition to developing facility in identifying ethically ambivalent norms and the dialectical character of such norms, training might develop process skills helpful in surfacing such ambivalence. The information that emerges in discussions and exercises facilitated by trainers could function as a feedback loop for those managers who have authority to redesign the reward system or otherwise affect norms and counternorms.

4. Develop investigative structures. When counternorms develop to the point that they violate rules and procedures of the organization, the organization may have to rely on investigations and sanctions. For example, a city government that received public and internal complaints about abuses of breaks and lunch time by building maintenance crews hired private investigators to follow workers in the division. Based on the evidence and internal interviews, a number of employees were discharged or demoted (Hall 1984). Police departments have internal affairs divisions that investigate unethical or illegal behavior. Organizations may find that investigative structures can locate the aspect of a reward system that fails to signal the importance of dominant norms and allows counternorm-driven behavior to be rewarded. (This is not to say that organizations need secret police to eliminate the dialectical interplay between norms and counternorms and, in the process, harm the climate of trust. Trust also may be harmed by failing to sanction actions that major stakeholders are likely to judge as unethical.)

5. Government regulations and laws. Reward system dysfunctions may be traced to the way an industry does business so that legal regulation is necessary to eliminate rewards for misbehavior. In such cases, internal redesign is insufficient to alter the conditions leading to ethical ambivalence. Changes in interorganizational relationships are required. The $12 million in payments made by Lockheed to Japan did not violate American laws. Lockheed's President Kotchian testified:

> From a purely ethical and moral standpoint I would have declined such a request. However, in that case, I would most certainly have sacrificed commercial success (Snoeyenbos, Almeder, and Humber 1983, 141).

Lockheed officials felt that they had played by the "rules of the game"; it was up to Congress to alter the rules and hence the rewards contingent on "unethical" behaviors.

Ethical ambivalence refers to the conflicts that result from the malintegration of the reward system with the dominant norms and the desired culture of the organization. Although not denying that individuals are active, intentional agents, the reward system perspective is sympathetic to Milgram's observation that "we are all fragile creatures entwined in a cobweb of social constraints" (1974, 71). Ethical ambivalence focuses on the external control of behavior and provides a perspective complementary to the more common emphasis on individual moral judgments and actions. It is believed that ethical ambivalence is a pivotal construct for descriptive research in the functioning and design of ethically enabling and disabling reward systems. It also has potential value for educating managers in practical ethical inquiry and the design of reward systems that are less likely to lead employees into temptation.

A Final Ethical Note

It is commonplace in philosophy to distinguish between the domain of facts ("is" statements) and the domain of values and ethics ("ought" statements). The "normative fallacy" involves attempting to derive value statements from factual relationships. Although the present authors have attempted to remain within the descriptive domain of organizational research, they also believe that their research has implications for design. Design is a value-laden activity (Cummings 1981).

Systems theorists have challenged the assumption of these two separate domains and the assertions of the normative fallacy. As Laszlo notes, "The real reason why the fact-value gap is obsolete is that human beings . . . are themselves goal directed systems" (1972, 259). Goals presuppose values. Thus, Maslow (quoted in Laszlo) argues that "inclusive generalization, namely that increase in the factiness of facts, of their fact quality, leads simultaneously to increases in the ought quality of these facts. Factiness generates oughtiness, we might say" (1972, 260). The present authors believe that understanding how reward systems function has implications for how reward systems ought to function. Understanding how individuals yield to or resist organizational temptations has implications for understanding human nature and developing ethical theory for analyzing management and professional decisions.

References

Argyris, C., and D. A. Schon. 1978. *Organizational Learning: A Theory of Action Perspective*. Reading, MA: Addison-Wesley.

Barber, B. 1952. *Science and the Social Order*. New York: Collier.

Bennis, W. 1980. "The Cult of Candor." *The Atlantic Monthly* (Sept): 89–91.

Berenson, C. 1972. "The Product Liability Revolution." *Business Horizons* 15 (5): 71–80.

Bok, S. 1979. *Lying: Moral Choice in Public and Private Life*. New York: Vintage Books.

Bok, S. 1983. *Secrets: On the Ethics of Commitment and Revelation*. New York: Vintage Books.

Cummings, T. G. 1981. "Designing Effective Work Groups." In *Handbook of Organizational Design*, edited by P. C. Nystrom and W. H. Starbuck, 250–72. New York: Oxford University Press.

Dickson, D. 1984. *The New Politics of Science*. New York: Pantheon Books.

Garrett, T. 1985. *Business Ethics*. Englewood Cliffs, NJ: Prentice-Hall.

Gray, M., and I. Rosen. 1982. *The Warning*. New York: Norton.

Hall, D. 1984. "Torrance Tails Workers—And Cleans House." *Torrance Daily Breeze* (July 25): B1, B7.

Hays, R. H., and W. J. Abernathy. 1980. "Managing Our Way to Economic Decline." *Harvard Business Review* 58 (4): 67–77.

Heilbronner, R. L. 1972. *In the Name of Profit*. New York: Doubleday.

Janis, I. L. 1972. *Victims of Groupthink*. Boston: Houghton-Mifflin.

Jansen, E. 1983. "Turning Around Plant 10 (A)" [A Research Case on the Lockheed California Company's L-1011 TriStar program]. Unpublished paper available from the author.

Jones, W. T., F. Sontag, M. O. Beckner, and R. J. Fogelin (eds.). 1977. *Approaches to Ethics*. New York: McGraw-Hill.

Katz, D., and R. L. Kahn. 1978. *The Social Psychology of Organizations*. New York: John Wiley & Sons.

Kerr, S. 1975. "On the Folly of Rewarding A While Hoping for B." *Academy of Management Journal* 18: 769–83.

Kerr, S., and J. W. Slocum. 1981. "Controlling the Performance of People in Organizations." In *Handbook of Organizational Design*, edited by P. C. Nystrom and W. H. Starbuck, 115–34. New York: Oxford University Press.

Kerr, S., M. A. Von Glinow, and C. Schriesheim. 1977. "Issues in the Study of Professionals in Organizations: The Case of Scientists and Engineers." *Organizational Behavior and Human Performance* 18: 329–45.

Kilmann, R. H. 1984. "Five Steps to Culture Change: Vultures vs. Beavers." *New Management* 2 (1): 20–21.

Laszlo, E. 1972. *Introduction to Systems Philosophy.* New York: Harper & Row.

Lawler, E. E., and J. G. Rhode. 1978. *Information and Control in Organizations.* Glenview, IL: Scott, Foresman.

Lewin, K. 1951. *Field Theory in Social Science.* New York: Harper.

Magnusson, D., and N. S. Endler (eds.). 1977. *Personality at the Crossroads: Current Issues in Intentional Psychology.* Hillsdale, NJ: Erlbaum.

Mason, R. O., and I. I. Mitroff. 1981. *Challenging Strategic Planning Assumptions: Theory, Cases, and Techniques.* New York: John Wiley & Sons.

Merton, R. K. 1957. "Priorities in Scientific Discovery." *American Sociological Review* 22: 635–59.

Merton, R. K. 1963. "The Ambivalence of Scientists." *Bulletin of the Johns Hopkins Hospital* 112 (2): 77–97.

Merton, R. K. 1976. *Sociological Ambivalence and Other Essays.* New York: Free Press.

Merton, R., and E. Barber. 1963. "Sociological Ambivalence." In *Sociological Theory, Values, and Sociocultural Change,* edited by E. A Tiryalcian, 91–120. New York: Free Press of Glencoe.

Milgram, S. 1974. "The Frozen World of the Familiar Stranger." *Psychology Today* 17 (6): 70–80.

Mills, E. W. 1983. "Sociological Ambivalence and Social Order: The Constructive Uses of Normative Dissonance." *Sociology and Social Research* 67: 279–87.

Mitroff, I. 1974. "Norms and Counternorms in a Select Group of the Apollo Moon Scientists: A Case Study of the Ambivalence of Scientists." *American Sociological Review* 39: 579–95.

Mitroff, I., and R. H. Kilmann. 1976. *Methodological Approaches to Social Science.* San Francisco: Jossey-Bass.

Nader, R., P. Petkas, and K. Blackwell. 1972. *Whistleblowing.* New York: Grossman.

O'Day, R. 1974. "Intimidation Rituals: Reactions to Reform." *Journal of Applied Behavioral Science* 10: 373–88.

Pastin, M., and M. Hooker. 1980. "Ethics and the Foreign Corrupt Practices Act." *Business Horizons* 23 (8): 43–47, 1.

Polanyi, M. 1958. *Personal Knowledge: Towards a Past-Critical Philosophy.* New York: Harper & Row.

Scheff, T. 1981. "Control over Policy by Attendants in a Mental Hospital." *Journal of Health and Human Behavior* 2: 93–105.

Sethia, N., and M. A. Von Glinow. 1985. "Arriving at Four Cultures by Managing the Reward System." In *Gaining Control of the Corporate Culture,* edited by R. H. Kilmann and Associates, 400–20. San Francisco: Jossey-Bass.

Snoeyenbos, M., R. Almeder, and J. Humber. 1983. *Business Ethics.* Buffalo, NY: Prometheus Books.

Storer, N. W. 1966. *The Social System of Science.* New York: Holt, Rinehart and Winston.

Vandevier, K. 1978. "The Aircraft Brake Scandal: A Cautionary Tale in Which the Moral is Unpleasant." In *Interpersonal Behavior: Communication and Understanding Relationships,* edited by A. G. Athos and J. J. Babarro, 529–40. Englewood Cliffs, NJ: Prentice-Hall.

Walters, J. A. 1978. "Catch 20.5: Corporate Morality as an Organizational Phenomenon." *Organizational Dynamics* 6 (1): 3–19.

Regulating Virtue: Formulating, Engendering and Enforcing Corporate Ethics Codes[1]

Andrew Brien*

Amongst the most popular instruments used when attempting to inject ethics into organizational life is the code of ethics (or code of practice—I use the expressions synonymously).[2] In fact, such codes are often the first formal structure to be established when the attempt is made to raise the ethical profile of an organization.[3] The popularity of codes stems from the fact that they are very adaptable; they are used in all types of regulatory environments, from external regulatory regimes to self-regulatory and enforced self-regulatory regimes. As well, all sorts of organizations—government departments and agencies, universities, along with many professions,[4] have codes of ethics—and many businesses do, too. For example, one global study of business organizations found that 76 percent of respondents had codes,[5] while over 90 percent of Fortune's 500 firms and almost half of U.S. companies have codes, or mission statements, or practice statements.[6]

The rapid growth in the number of ethical codes is a phenomenon characteristic of the past two decades. It is, largely, a result of widely publicized ethical failures that have affected many people and have caused disquiet within the government and the professional, business, and civic community about the behavior of powerful sectors of the societies concerned. Writing in 1989, L. J. Brooks reported that 60 percent of codes were less than ten years old.[7] Six years earlier Cressey and Moore reported that 43 percent of their sample of codes in the United States "were either drafted or revised in 1976, the year following the first nationwide publicity about corporate bribery," and almost two-thirds were written or revised between 1975 and 1977.[8] Codes of ethics are also popular amongst academic theorists, many of whom consider them to have an important role to play in instiutuionalizing ethics.[9]

Despite the popularity of codes, there is no evidence that they actually improve ethical standards.[10] Violations are frequent, and compliance is a major practical problem.[11] The reasons why compliance is a problem are well-known and fall into two categories: internal factors and external factors. Internal factors are those features of the code itself that predispose the code's constituents to violate it. The most common internal problem of codes is that they are poorly formulated.[12] They may contain

*Reprinted with permission from Business and Professional Ethics Journal 1996. 15 (1): 21–52. Andrew Brien is executive director of the Centre for Professional and Applied Ethics at Charles Sturt University in Australia.

inconsistencies, ambiguities, confusions, or provisions that invite non-compliance and the development of cynical attitudes towards the code because, for example, the code may be directed only at employees while management may be exempted, or the code may be self-serving and ignore the interests of other stakeholders, as many codes seem to do.[13] Thus, codes may lack an *internal* authority, and organizational actors will be encouraged by this to develop a disposition to ignore them or to evade their provisions.

Codes may also possess inadequate *external* authority. This can be of two sorts. First, the ethical culture of the organization may be weak. This sort of weakness is manifested in two areas.

1. The leaders of the organization may not fully support the code or affirm the importance of ethics in organizational life. Yet, enthusiastic support for codes, as well as ethics in general, by the leaders of an organization is crucial to a code's success and, more generally, to the project of injecting ethics into organizational life.[14] Without such support a code is unlikely to be observed. The problem, however, is that since high-level executives have been frequently implicated in (or are the perpetrators of) much of the ethical misbehavior that many of the codes have been formulated to correct,[15] their support is unlikely to be forthcoming.

2. The code may not have been internalized by its constituency. Often, this means that the members of the organization may not believe that the code embodies values that are important to their activities as members of the organization. Actors may not respect a code, for example, because they have not been encouraged to see that the values embodied in the code are important in the everyday functioning of the organization. Consequently, they will not be disposed to follow it, or in ethically ambiguous situations, they may defect from it. Internalization is important for the success of a code since people are more likely to behave in compliance with a norm if they hold the norm themselves. Therefore, such internalization is essential to maintaining high levels of voluntary compliance.

Second, the code may not be adequately institutionalized. For example, the code may not be part of the organizational infrastructure, the mechanisms that promote the code may not exist or they may not be used effectively, or there may be no systematic attempt to use the code, even if the infrastructure exists. So, codes may fail because the structure and culture of the organization is not conducive to ethical action. Actors may be presented with mixed and confusing messages—ethical ideals and an ambivalent or confusing organizational infrastructure for codes (for example, ethics committees, interpretation and adjudication mechanisms that are poorly coordinated, empowered, or which are not serious or clear about their respective roles) are often reinforced by pious affirmations from management and other organizational leaders—while they work within an organizational climate that is, overall, antagonistic to ethics. The lack of institutions such as an ethics committee, an adjudication and interpretation committee, and an appropriate organizational climate are well-known problems that undermine the success of ethical codes. This is widely recognized in the literature where it is often noted that such institutions are essential to the success of a code and its successful implementation,[16] and it has been the absence of these bodies (or inactivity on their part), that has been a primary cause of their failure.[17] Surprisingly, while the drafters of codes seem to be aware of the importance of promoting compliance judging by the fact that many codes include compliance procedures,[18] few codes have compliance institutions, such as ombudsmen, ethics or watchdog committees,[19] or well-developed, systematic, and routine compliance programs.[20]

The upshot is that while there is clear evidence that the organizational climate and institutionalization of codes often have a more profound effect in promoting ethical action than behavior modification and enforcement, which is usually at the heart of the project of implementing ethical codes,[21] appropriate measures are seldom taken. In practical terms, this means that there must be effective and authoritative institutions within the organization that interpret the code, clarify it, apply it to quandaries, resolve ambiguities and contradictions, communicate it, conduct ethical audits, and enforce the code by adjudicating on alleged violations and responding to those found to have violated it.

The internalization and institutionalization problems by codes include difficulties with grounding a code's external authority in the behavior patterns of organizational actors. These problems are, to be sure, implementation problems. How can the promulgator of a code encourage it to be internalized so that it becomes part of the culture of the organization? How can she make it part of the fabric of the organization, a "cultural artifact," by establishing it as part of the stable institutions of the organization? How can she enforce it most effectively?

While there are many suggestions for implementing and enforcing codes,[22] surprisingly, there does not seem to be any discussion of the theory that grounds the formulation of codes or their implementation, nor does there seem to be any discussion of the criteria to be used to distinguish a good code from a bad one. There is, to be sure, an air of "ad hocery" in this entire area. It is, specifically, this lack of a theoretical discussion that I want (at least to start) to make good in this paper.

I shall begin by developing an account of the nature of ethical codes. Using this, I shall then discuss the desiderata that determine the nature of a well-formed code. These desiderata are necessary conditions for the development of a code's internal authority. In the third section, I shall discuss the nature of the implementation mechanism—a code's external authority.

II

A code of ethics is, ideally, a statement of the organizational norms against which the actual or proposed actions of an actor, as a member of an organization, are evaluated. Codes embody these norms in a variety of different forms as rules, principles, tenets, credos, and ideals. They express, in effect, the criteria for good and bad, right and wrong action, within an organizational setting.

Codes can be used in two ways, reactively and proactively. Reactively, an ethical code may be used as a basis upon which to *regulate* the behavior of organizational actors because it provides the criteria for the evaluation of (performed) action. In that way, an ethical code may constitute the basis for discipline and deterrence. Proactively, an ethical code may be used as a standard to resolve ethical quandaries or, more simply, it may serve as a standard to which action must conform. In these ways, it guides the proposed behavior of organizational actors and educates and nurtures their ethical awareness.

Given this analysis of the nature of codes, prima facie, there seem to be both similarities to, and differences from, the institution of law that society has. To be sure, codes do differ from the laws of a society in that they are not typically punitive in orientation nor do they expressly stipulate the result of non-compliance.[23] Nevertheless, they do have a number of fundamental similarities to law. Like law, an ethical code operates on a one-way projection of power, from those who create and enforce the code, to those whom it regulates, guides, and educates. And like the law, a code relies for its success upon the voluntary cooperation of the code's constituency and acceptance by it of the code.

Such cooperation and acceptance will occur and be nurtured only if the code is seen to possess some inherent moral authority and legitimacy. In order that this aura of authority and legitimacy may develop, a code, like the law, must be framed so as to foster voluntary cooperation with the code by its constituent. It will do this by taking account of the constituency's capacity to obey, by being and being seen to be "reasonable," by taking into account the views of the constituency during the formulation and periodic reformulation processes, and by being adopted through discussion and consent. This occurs in civil society with law, for example, when interested parties are invited to make submissions on a proposed law to a select committee of parliament and through the conduct of regular, free, and fair general elections. Therefore, a code, like law, relies upon a projection of influence by its intended constituents upon the drafters of the code when it is formulated, as well as a sensitivity on the part of the legislators to the needs, desires, aspirations, and capacities of the governed.

This points directly to the similarities between codes and law: codes operate in an environment similar to that of law, and they serve a similar function. First, they are the private laws of a private state; their efficacy is grounded ultimately upon the consent and support of the governed. On this analysis, a code's makers have a role in the formulation of the code that is analogous to that of the law's makers.[24]

Second, codes have a similar function to the law in society: they embody criteria that are used within the institutional context to guide and evaluate conduct, proactively and persuasively, and sometimes, reactively and coercively. They have the capacity to provide the basis for discipline and a foundation upon which one member of the organization may be empowered to behave in a certain sort of way towards another, when in the ordinary course of events such behavior would not be permitted. In this way, like the law, codes may enjoin certain actions and prohibit others. In their general outlook, however, codes embody the values and ideals of the organization in the same way that the law as a body of practice and knowledge embodies the values and ideals of society.

Now, these similarities to law are important. Just as there can be well—or poorly—drafted laws, there can be well—or poorly—drafted codes of ethics, and, it seems, given the extensive similarities, that codes, like laws, may be well-drafted or poorly drafted for the same sorts of reasons. The question then is "What are the criteria to be used to distinguish well-drafted laws from poorly drafted ones?" One influential account of such criteria has been given by Lon Fuller. According to Fuller, these criteria "are like the natural laws of carpentry, or at least those laws respected by a carpenter who wants the house he builds to remain standing and serve the purpose of those who live in it."[25] Just as the natural laws of carpentry—the rules that a carpenter must obey in order to attain his purpose—are determined by the purpose he has, the natural laws or criteria governing the nature of well-drafted law—the rules that a lawmaker must obey in order to attain her purpose—are determined by the purpose she has in making laws.

This leads to the next question: Do the criteria that a law must meet in order to be considered well-drafted or well-formed also apply to codes of ethics? Clearly they must. The activity of lawmaking is, according to Fuller, "the enterprise of subjecting human conduct to the governance of rules."[26] The activity of code making is similar, since the aim is to regulate human conduct by using criteria for right and wrong conduct.

Moreover, the purpose of law, according to Fuller, is to provide a "firm base-line for human interaction" in order to secure the good life.[27] In order that they fulfill this purpose (that is, are effective), laws must be such that they are capable of being obeyed and of guiding action, and laws that do this are considered well-drafted. Codes share the same purpose. They are designed, as we saw, to provide a base-line against which behavior can be evaluated and regulated and, as such, to promote the flourishing of the organization. This, in turn, promotes the well-being of the stakeholders. In order for this purpose to be fulfilled, like the law and individual laws, codes must be capable of being obeyed and guiding action, and, like laws, codes that do this are well-drafted. Since the activity and the purpose of the law and codes are identical and the contexts of their operation analogous, it is reasonable to conclude that the properties that the law must have in order to be capable of attaining its purpose must also be possessed by ethical codes.

What properties does a well-drafted law (or, as I have been arguing, a code of ethics) possess? Fuller's answer to this question consists of eight necessary criteria[28]:

1. There must be rules or laws that ground evaluation of action rather than ad hoc evaluation.
2. Laws must be publicized.
3. Laws cannot be made retroactively.
4. Laws must be understandable.
5. Laws should not be contradictory.
6. Laws must be within the power of the citizens to obey them.
7. Laws must maintain a degree of stability through time.
8. Laws as announced must be in agreement with their actual administration.

Fuller claims that a total failure in any one of these eight desiderata does not simply result in a "bad legal system." He claims that it "results in something that is not properly called a legal system at all, except perhaps in the Pickwickian sense in which a void contract can still be said to be some kind of contract."[29] Fuller's point is that what makes a putative legal system a genuine legal system is the capacity of the putative system to fulfil the purpose that legal systems have in societies. The proximate purpose of the legal system is to "subject human conduct to the governance of rules" in order to procure the ultimate purpose of promoting human well-being and flourishing. A total failure in any one of these desiderata will result in there not being general rules that can be used to regulate human conduct; consequently, the proximate and ultimate purposes will be prevented from being realized. In virtue of this, the system will fail to be a *legal* system. Similarly, a putative code of ethics would fail to be a "code of ethics," since it would fail to embody (in a useful manner), the norms of the organization that are used to guide, regulate, and evaluate action in order to promote, ultimately, the nourishing and well-being of the organization's stakeholders. It would be unable to fulfill its purpose and would, for this reason, fail to be a code of ethics.

Fuller's justification for each of the desideratum is based upon the capacities that human agents possess: that actors are rational, that there must be a point to action, that actors require certainty as to outcome and guarantees that the laws will not be used against them capriciously or whimsically. Fuller[30] says:

> Certainly there can be no rational ground for asserting that a man can have a moral obligation to obey a legal rule that does not exist, or is kept secret from him, or that came into existence only after he acted, or was unintelligible or was contradicted by another rule of the same system, or commanded the impossible, or changed every minute. It may not be impossible for a man to obey a rule that is disregarded by those charged with its administration, but at some point obedience becomes futile—as futile, in fact, as casting a vote that will never be counted.

Such reasons apply also to codes of ethics, since the nature of human agency within organizations is substantially similar, and the role of a code of ethics is analogous to that of the law, in civil society.

Are there only eight desiderata? It would seem not. Actors must be able to trust the code, have confidence in it, and see that it is not an instrument of repression, but one of protection which promotes the good of the organization and its stakeholders. Fuller's eight desiderata fail to do this completely, since by themselves they fail to promote adequately the well-being of the code's stakeholders and the subjective sense of security that is essential if a code is to be capable of being effectively implemented and followed. They fail to provide grounds upon which to base trust in the code.

Such trust is based ultimately on agreement between the organization's governors and governed, and the capacity of the governed to be certain that the agreement is being honored. In other words, a culture of trust must be cultivated.[31] Fuller's eight desiderata do not, however, provide an adequate means whereby the code's constituents can see that the agreement legitimating the code is being honored. To be sure, the moral and rational basis of a code is the same as it is for law. Like the law, a code rests upon a contract between the code-makers and the code's constituents. The contract embodies the interlocking responsibilities of the governors of the (corporate) state and its citizens. These responsibilities arise from the same source, an offer which must be made by the organization's governors if the code is to be effective: "These are the rules we ask you to follow. If you will obey them, you have our promise that they are the rules we will apply to your conduct."[32] Once accepted, the code attains legitimacy and the contract at the basis of the code's legitimacy embodies a bond of reciprocity; a person, in virtue of being a member of the organization with this code, has an obligation to obey the code, and the organization's governors have an obligation to abide by the rules they have made.

To be effective, however, contracts must be nurtured by appropriate institutions and practices (something that Fuller seems merely to assume). That is, unless the constituents can see that it is being honored, the code, like the law, will be ineffective. It will not be trusted, and it will not attain the purpose set for it. Now, to be effective, a code must have a form that promotes trust, that does not discourage voluntary compliance but rather promotes it, and which provides a means whereby the constituents can see and be assured that the contract that is the foundation of the code is being honored. For these reasons codes must offer their constituents clear guarantees as to their application and use. These guarantees provide clear grounds upon which to trust the code and trust that it will not be used against them without justification. Ultimately, such guarantees provide a basis upon which to evaluate whether the contract is being honored and a criterion for continued compliance and acceptance. To Fuller's eight desiderata must be added:

9. Due process;
10. Procedural justice; and
11. Substantive morality and justice.[33]

In other words, the code must contain explicit provisions stating that:

- The implementation and enforcement will be carried out in a particular, known and settled way, rather than secretly or haphazardly.
- The code will be applied to all members of the organization, from the chief executive officer down.
- The code and its use rest upon legitimate authority, typically the consent of the governed.
- People will be treated in accordance with their culpability, in the case of wrongdoing, or praiseworthiness in the case of exemplary service.

This is not all, however. Two further conditions concern the nature that the provisions themselves should have. The provisions must be general. Provisions, however, can be general in two quite different senses, both of which are important here[34]:

12. Provisions must be general in the sense that they must refer to types or classes of actions.
13. Provisions must be general in the sense that laws must not be directed at one individual but at classes of individuals.

Why should the provisions of a code be general in any of these senses? Provisions directed at individuals, rather than individuals occupying a certain role, will smack of victimization. And even if initially such a provision is benign, it will provide a precedent upon which an organization may base future victimization of individuals. It is best to avoid mention of individuals altogether and talk instead of "role duties" and ideals.

Moreover, provisions should be directed at classes of actions since it is impossible to construct a workable code that will specify in advance all the vagaries and nuances of human action. Provisions must refer to general rules or principles in order to remain a code of ethics, rather than a code of directions, as one might find in an instruction manual.

Codes should be general so that the organization's governors will not have to expend enormous energy formulating precise ordinances, and monitoring and enforcing compliance with individual ordinances. It is more sensible to have general rules or principles aimed at all, bolstered by organizational ideals where possible, and to leave the observance, interpretation, and implementation to the common sense of individuals, stepping in only when justified—in much the same way that the law does.

In addition to these extra desiderata, codes must be seen to address real issues and not be merely another mechanism for social control. A code which did that would destroy the trust between the organization's governors and citizens. This would not only erode support for the code, but would also weaken the morale of the organization. Therefore,

14. There must be a point to having the code and any particular precept in it.

Moreover, the precepts of the code must not be outside the capacity of the organization to implement. Just as a law that is never enforced because the state lacks the capacity to do so or because it is too complex quickly becomes a sham, so too a code or any provision in it. So, like a law,

15. A code and its provisions must be practical and usable from the point of view of the code maker.

Finally, there is a general requirement that any guide to behavior must actually improve matters. If the ultimate purpose of a code is to promote the well-being of the organization and in that way its stakeholders, a code that fails to do so lacks a moral justification. So,

16. A code or an individual provision must not leave an organization worse off than it would be through it not having the code or the individual ordinance.

These desiderata work together to constitute an ideal against which any code (or element of a code) can be evaluated as "well-drafted." They determine whether a code will have an effective and credible internal authority—one of the areas that must be strong if a code is to succeed. Given that an organization has developed a well-drafted code, how does it then go about implementing it, so as to promote compliance—that is to say, how does it develop an effective and credible external authority?

III

No matter how well-formulated a code may be, compliance will not result naturally or from haphazard efforts which implement the code in an uncoordinated manner. Effective compliance requires a compliance mechanism, that is, a structured approach that takes into account the capacities and features of the code's constituency. It is well known that an effective compliance mechanism would, of course, contain various elements—or institutions—that implement, interpret, and enforce the code. It would operate within a sympathetic organizational culture. It would enjoy unequivocal support from the management and leadership of the organization. As well, the code would be developed and promoted in such a way as to encourage "ownership" of it by the organizational community.[35] The question remains, however, "What structure would the compliance mechanism have?" To answer this we must look at the nature and foundation of compliance.

As a matter of stipulation, I shall define "compliance" as,

An actor A is acting in compliance with a standard X if and only if that actor knowingly, consciously, and deliberately selects and performs an action precisely because it conforms (reflects, honors, instantiates) with standard X which is known to A.

A compliance mechanism, on this analysis, would be a group of settled institutions that work together to motivate the selection and performance of the appropriate act-option. How can actors be motivated to select the appropriate option? Acts of compliance rest primarily upon two, often mixed, motives. An actor may be motivated to comply because she believes some standard is right and ought to be obeyed, or she may be motivated to comply out of fear of the consequences for failing to do so. Since the motivational sources of compliance are, by and large, limited to these sorts of motivation, a successful compliance mechanism will consist in measures that create in actors one or another, or some mixture of both. How can these two types of motivation be developed?

These motives rest upon certain beliefs: belief in the rightness of values or belief that certain unwanted consequences will follow certain actions.[36] In the former case, the aim of the compliance mechanism is to encourage the actor to internalize the code—that is, to have the actor develop a strong belief that the code of ethics embodies values that are (in an organizational context) good and right and which ought to be obeyed. Such values are engendered in each actor, become part of her belief system, and become part of the organizational culture.

Compliance produced through the fear of the consequences also rests upon beliefs—the actor believing that non-compliance will be discovered and that certain unwanted consequences will follow. This is a deterrence theory: actors are deterred from wrongdoing by the likelihood of discovery and fear of the consequences. There is no change in the actor's beliefs about the merits of the code, whether it is right or wrong, good or bad. The code exists, and actors must comply—or face the consequences. Thus, actors are coerced into complying. The coercive approach attempts to enforce the code through credible sanctions and inducing actors to believe that discovery will be highly likely.

Creating compliance-inducing motivation on this analysis rests upon beliefs generated by two different sorts of mechanism: *engendering* mechanisms based upon persuasion, discussion, affirmation, and demonstration, and *enforcement* mechanisms based upon surveillance, coercion, threats, and sanctions, leading to deterrence. What is the relationship between these two approaches? Is one preferable to the other?

Enforcement is a very blunt instrument. It seems, however, to be the approach favored by some of the most influential writers and business leaders. For example, they speak of "vigorous," "savage," or "routine" enforcement, "(credible) sanctions," and codes imitating the deterrence (and even retributive) nature of the criminal law.[37]

Such an approach is mistaken. Empirical evidence, from the study of the regulation of business, suggests that persuasion and trust (reinforced by firm action only if persuasion and trust fail) are more effective and less costly regulatory approaches than enforcement through the use of surveillance and sanctions alone.[38] There are good reasons to infer that within any organization such findings would be replicated, since agents are similar in all organizations, and similar sorts of relationships and causes of unethical behavior are at work. For example, most agents prefer to be trusted, given responsibilities, left to act autonomously, rather than work under intense supervision and surveillance. They prefer to be assessed by known, reasonable, and transparent procedures. Further, in business corporations as well as other organizations, the regulator and the regulated are individual people within whose responsibility wrongdoing and rightdoing resides. Corporate wrongdoers often face a trade-off between corporate goals, customs, mores, and ethics (which are often perceived not to be paramount corporate goals), while organizational wrongdoers face a similar trade-off between organizational goals, customs, mores, and ethics.

As well, the effectiveness of any enforcement program relies upon adequate levels of detection of code violators. Few organizations, however, possess the capacity to marshal resources so as to ensure the high levels of surveillance and detection required in order to make an enforcement program credible. It is simply too costly, and in many different ways: for example, in the use of time, financial, and material resources; in the maintenance of an extensive and formal adjudication system and other institutions that ensure due process in what is effectively a private justice system[39]; distractions from the purpose of the organization; and employee goodwill and trust, since the organization may become like a mini police-state. The very act of enforcement may lead to a cure far worse than the disease.

In general, the enforcement approach assumes that the members of an organization cannot be trusted. It fails also to respect individuals, their autonomy and integrity, and their capacity to assume personal responsibility for actions they perform. Respecting these things has been identified as a major factor in an organization having a strong ethical culture. The enforcement approach, relying upon the blunt use of power, fails to affirm, promote, and encourage the engendering[41] of the very values at the heart of a strong ethical culture—the feature of an organization that is essential if a code of ethics is to be successful. Used alone, enforcement fails to develop the motivational base for reliable compliance and is, ultimately, self-defeating.

Moreover, the enforcement approach is focused upon decontextualized individuals. It addresses only the violation and the possibility of repetition, while ignoring the causes of non-compliance[42] such as a poor ethical culture, an unsupportive organizational culture, and alienation from the organizational community and its values. However, an ethics program that makes pious pronouncements about the importance of ethics but does nothing to remove the causes of unethical behavior is simply not credible and therefore unlikely to serve a regulatory role. Further, since it is concerned with results only, there is the possibility that it will license victimization, the use of "scapegoats," and impose solutions that are inappropriate and perceived to be so.

Since such an approach maintains alienation from the ethical culture of the organization (because it uses power to deter and is unconcerned with what an actor believes is valuable), it fails to promote organizational "citizenship," inclusion and ownership of the values that drive the organization. In a nutshell, such an approach fails to foster organizational virtue. This has unwanted consequences: people who are alienated from their community, who feel that they have no investment in it, and who have not developed and cultivated organizational virtue, are more likely to offend when the opportunity presents itself. (This, it might be worth pointing out, is as true of society in general as it is of organizations, where the analogue for organizational virtue is civic virtue, and the analogue for code-compliance is lawfulness or law abidingness.)

Finally, if the enforcement strategy is to succeed, then the penalties for violations must be set at a level that is credible; that is to say, at a level that deters the majority of potential miscreants. In the majority of cases, if not all, this level is likely to be higher than the level that seems appropriate given the intrinsic wrongness of the violation. Thus, an effective enforcement strategy would violate one of the principles of retributive justice, namely that a person should be punished only in proportion to the gravity of her wrongdoing. Such a principle is important for the citizens of any community, since it plays an important role in grounding their confidence in the system. In addition, the level may be so high that it paralyzes decision making within the organization: actors become fearful of acting lest they breach the code. This engenders a "better do nothing than risk everything" policy.

These problems are all paradoxes of deterrent-orientated enforcement programs. Should they arise, they lead to cynicism and disenchantment amongst the members of the organization about the compliance mechanism. That such paradoxes would arise is highly likely, given the nature of the system and because the sanction levels must be high if the system is to be credible and deter would-be wrongdoers.

The alternative to enforcing a code of ethics is engendering it. Is this approach any better? It is attractive for a number of reasons. Such an approach tends to produce ethically reliable actors. Most agents prefer, other things being equal, to do what they believe to be right and good— that is, act, as it seems to them, ethically. Now, getting actors to believe in something, or believe that it is right, is what engendering involves. If the code of ethics has been engendered, it will be perceived to be an ethical reference point, and actors will believe that it embodies relevant ethical values. They will be disposed, other things being equal, to ensure that their acts comply with it. Since the code means something to the actors because it has been engendered, the rate of compliance will be higher.

There are many ways to foster such beliefs. They may be promoted through demonstration, such as by the upper-echelon managers and leaders of the organization behaving ethically. They may be affirmed through ethics education programs within the organization which explain the code and the values in it, or by creating institutions that encourage ethical action—for example, employee involvement in the formulation and administration of the code, as well as ethics "hotlines" or advisers who will clarify, interpret, or apply the code and resolve a quandary, or provide ethics counselling. All of these measures serve to educate the code's constituents, persuade them of its merits, and generally foster belief in the code and, in that way, promote ethical motivation.

Moreover, engendering ethics involves fostering values and traits of character—such as autonomy and integrity—that are at the heart of a strong ethical culture and organizational virtue. This is likely to be a more effective regulatory approach than enforcement since it is more likely to result in higher rates of compliance. The reason is that people prefer to act in ways that accord with their values, and people are more likely to do what they want to do (which in this case is to act ethically) than what they have been coerced to do. There are, then, sound motivational reasons to select engendering programs over enforcement programs.

Apart from the motivational advantages that engendering offers, such an approach avoids many of the costs associated with enforcement. Unlike the enforcement strategy, it does not require as much intrusive surveillance or monitoring of actors, with the consequent loss of employee goodwill and trust. Engendering mechanisms address causes (since to fail to do so would undermine the credibility of the mechanism). Consequently, an engendering approach addresses matters of concern or potential concern, specific problems, and so on. It is for this reason that it provides a more honest way for actors to interact with each other, since reasons are given, the motivation underlying decisions and directives is clear, and problems are dealt with. This encourages confidence in the system and the organization, fosters citizenship (a reduction of alienation), and ultimately it fosters compliance with organizational norms. It fosters organizational virtue.

Furthermore, in the special case of miscreants, the engendering process reincorporates them into the life of the organization, offering them a chance of "redemption" and forgiveness (i.e., an actor's wrong-doing is not held against her). They have the opportunity of once again exercising full membership in the organization. This process strengthens and repairs the relationships between actors and tailors the response to violation of the code to the causes of the wrongdoing and the needs and situation of the perpetrator. This has the effect of reducing alienation from the life of the organization on the part of all organizational citizens. They can develop a sense of involvement and ownership in the process of ethical action. This can be heightened if they are incorporated into the process of developing and administering the code. And this, in turn, fosters compliance since actors are reluctant to destroy those things in which they have a personal investment or which they value.

Finally, engendering ethics is a more ethically sound approach than enforcement. Unlike enforcement strategies, which treat actors as self-interested players and a means to an end, engendering ethics assumes that actors are rational (since it attempts to persuade them), that they are autonomous and deserving of respect for no other reason than they are rational human beings. Such moral defenses of engendering should not be discounted. Actors evaluate in moral terms what they do to others and how they are treated themselves. A program that seems ethically suspect will not obtain and maintain the support of a group of people. The capacity of such a program to promote compliance will be diminished.

Such an approach does not abandon entirely some level of en-forcement through the use of coercive programs. In any community there will be willfull wrongdoers displaying all levels of culpability, from trivial offenders against organizational norms to egregious actors who play the system but who never believe in it, so-called "organizational sociopaths." Enforcement should focus only on those actors who cannot be reformed through engendering programs alone. The type of response to an actor's particular wrongdoing should be determined by her level of culpability and capacity for reform. For some code violators, it may mean a period of supervised work and education about the values of the organization; for others, a warning or demotion; for yet others some combination.

This approach keeps coercive programs in the background, as an avenue of last resort to be used only against wanton and negligent actors. The organization does not develop the thorough, far-reaching, and intrusive programs to detect wrongdoers that enforcement programs assume. This approach uses targeted audits aimed at known weak spots and reported problem areas, rather than constant, general surveillance. The organization encourages reporting and disclosure, that is, proactive behavior on the part of corporate citizens. However, having become aware of wrongdoing, the coercive programs become an option, if warranted—that is, if education and reform fail. This sends a clear message to organizational citizens, that they are trusted but that their actions are subject to assessment, as in civil society.

Such a system operates on a similar basis as ordinary, nonorganizational life—something with which actors are comfortable and familiar. Such familiarity encourages support. In this way, the autonomy of the individual is promoted and respected, while the organization demonstrates clearly that it possesses the capacity and the willingness to deal with egregious miscreants. Actors know, however, that only willfull wrongdoing will attract institutional sanctions and that inexperience, ignorance and mistakes will not be held against them.

Such a system further promotes the engendering of the code and compliance with it since it reinforces the grounds upon which such engendering occurs. For example, it appears to be a reasonable and fair system. As such, it fosters feelings of security and trust, rather than feelings of vulnerability.

From this, it is clear that the aim of any compliance mechanism should not initially merely be to deter. Deterrence rests on nothing more than a threat and is power at its crudest and most unimaginative. It obtains its credibility from the capacity of the powerful agent to induce the vulnerable agent to believe that she is willing and able to use her power. Such flaunting of power breeds resentment, mistrust, and fear. A more imaginative use of power is to use the threat of deterrence and coercion as a last resort in a program of ethical education. The (albeit veiled) threat of power focuses the attention on wrongdoers; having done that, education can begin. The problem, of course, is finding a balance between enforcement programs and engendering programs. This will be determined largely by the local conditions, such as the nature of the organization, the state of its ethical and organizational culture, and the behavior of its citizens.

On the model sketched here, engendering the values of the organization is the first option and enforcement is a last resort. In all events, the compliance mechanism should be internal to the organization. There is good reason for this. It is cheaper, tailored to the needs and circumstances of the organization, and, because it comes from within the organization, the members feel that they own it, and it seems to work; studies have shown that keeping discipline within the organization may in fact promote compliance.

What emerges is a compliance mechanism which consists in an ordering of compliance programs, based upon the level of coercion involved. Engendering programs and enforcement programs are organized so as to form a unified, progressive compliance mechanism. It begins with engendering programs such as education, affirmation, persuasion, information, counselling, and so on which involve no coercion. It then moves to programs designed less to engender and more to deter and educate from a position of power, each with increasing levels of coercion, moving finally to pure deterrence. The levels should not be seen as exclusive, and practices from one level may be mixed with those from another. The following diagram expresses this code of ethics compliance mechanism.[45]

The amount of effort invested in engendering ethics decreases as one ascends the triangle, while the amount of coercion increases. At the top of the pyramid only the most blatant, obvious, and egregious actors are dealt with, that is to say, those who are unable to be convinced of the relevance of organizational norms. Often they will be reoffenders for whom the best engendering efforts were unable to nurture allegiance. They become, in effect, a self-selecting group that does not require the expenditure of vast amounts of resources to deter. As a result, the organization has to expend fewer resources in dealing with them and is exposed to fewer of the risks and costs associated with surveillance and punitive enforcement measures. There is, for the organization, an economy of effort.

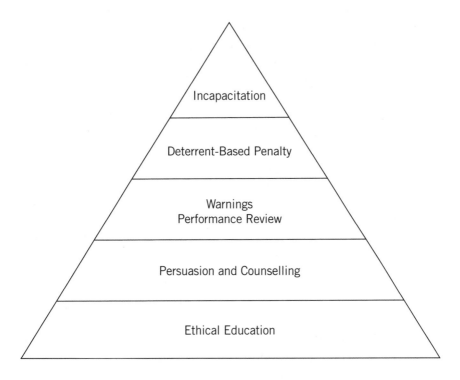

Resources can be reallocated and the organization can use proactive programs, such as targeted ethical audits (which can often be quite effective since internal auditors often know "where the bodies are buried") to identify problem areas, to provide opportunity for confession, and to encourage actors to seek help, guidance, and the clarification of ethics policies. As a result, actors will not be caught in a web of perpetuating unethical behavior, but will have clear exits, and fewer cases will go so far as to require the most drastic coercive responses—the sorts of responses that may easily use enormous resources compared to the return and which often end up being resolved in the civil courts. Throughout this process the coercive level of the response must be limited by the culpability of the actor and the seriousness of the offense, rather than by the harshness required to attain some desired level of deterrence. In this way, the enforcement paradoxes will be avoided, but the lessons that can be learned from deterrence programs will be communicated to the citizens of the organization without the costs.

This strategy seeks to educate all, redeem those who can be redeemed, while providing a mechanism to incapacitate the most dangerous offenders. It rests upon the assumptions that agents are rational actors who are capable of choosing and weighing reasons, that most of them care about ethical concerns, and that they desire to "do the right thing." Such a mechanism promotes and fosters the engendering of ethics in the organization since it nurtures the ethically confused or ignorant as well as the virtuous; it reforms the ethically wayward, it deters the ethically uncommitted and venal actor. Ultimately, it may be used to incapacitate the ethical rogue. It does all these things while minimizing enforcement costs and redirecting resources into the most important part of any organization: its people.

This structure sends the message to the members of the organization that they are valued and trusted by the organization as individuals, and not as the mere recipients of coercive treatment. This is reinforced by the fact that at all stages, agents are respected as autonomous, rational, and responsible for their own decisions. In this way, this *structure* promotes participation in the life of the organization and a reduction of alienation from it and organizational goals. It enfranchises (and re-enfranchises) them as members of the organizational community, as well; it promotes confidence and trust in the overall compliance system, further promoting the engendering of ethical attitudes. This is particularly important. Trust encourages ethical action and ethical action further encourages trust, in a self-reinforcing circle.[46] This structure provides the foundation for that trust, and in that way, grounds the trust necessary for actors to internalize the code and live by it. Finally, embodied in the *structure* of this mechanism (as opposed to being merely stated in the code) are three guarantees that actors in vulnerable positions value highly and which underpin the credibility of any ethics program. First, this system embodies a due process. There is a definite, known, public, and agreed-upon process that must be worked through, and a progression through a system of steadily escalating responses towards actors who violate the code. They know that organizational power cannot be wielded capriciously, that they do not live at the whim of their superiors, and that the possibility of victimization—one of the criticisms of codes—is minimized. This further engenders trust in the organization, the ethics program, and fosters ethical action.

Second, there is procedural justice. In other words, the due process and the substantive elements of the code are applied to all institutional actors alike. Why? Without procedural justice there would be no guarantee that the compliance mechanism would be applied to all similar cases. This would tend to encourage cynicism about the mechanism and the motives of its proponents, thus weakening support for it. If it is not to be self-defeating, the compliance process must assume and utilize procedural justice.

Third, there is substantive justice or fairness. It would be unfair to hold a person accountable who violates the code accidentally or through ignorance or because of pressure from her superiors, if she has unavailable to her appropriate mechanisms that allow her to ignore with impunity such pressure. In the compliance mechanism developed here, an actor's individual circumstances are taken into account, the causes of a violation are determined, and an appropriate response is developed. Again, so that it is not self-defeating the compliance process must assume and do substantive justice or fairness.

Moreover, opportunities are given whereby actors can seek assistance and guidance, as well as be given it before violations occur. This accords with received opinion of what counts as fair and just. Such received opinion is important. Fairness and justice (along with reasonableness) are principles that actors prize highly in all sorts of circumstances. No system can long maintain the support of citizens and be as successful as it has the capacity to be, unless it makes some effort to abide by at least the principles of fairness and justice. Organizations as mini-communities are no different in this respect from general society.[47] Such principles serve as criteria that actors use to evaluate the organization, and in grounding any commitment to the organization and appropriation or internalization of organizational values. For this reason, if a compliance mechanism is to be successful, it and its constituent elements must operate on the basis of substantive justice and fairness.

IV

This paper has been concerned with examining the theory that underlies ethical codes and which grounds the development of a code's internal and external authority—the features which determine whether a code will be successful or not. I have attempted to set out the desiderata that an ethical code must satisfy in order to be well-formed, and so be capable of fulfilling the purpose that was intended for it. I have also attempted to set out the structure of the compliance mechanism that well-formed codes must use in order to be effective. This structure, along with the desiderata, is determined by the purpose that codes of ethics have in organizational life: to guide human conduct, raise the ethical profile of an organization, and in that way promote the well-being of stakeholders.

It is surprising that more research has not been done on the theory underlying ethical codes. Over the past few years the citizens of the Western democracies have shown an increased intolerance of those who, holding various sorts of positions of power, abuse the trust placed in them. Such intolerance has been directed not only at legislators, but also at the paradigm professions, such as law and medicine, business people, public servants, and even university lecturers and school teachers. "Accountability" has become the "buzz-word" of the 1990s. Apart from various pieces of legislation, ethical codes are often an integral part of the attempt to ensure accountability and exert some measure of control by the community over people who live largely without constraint. Such codes, however, need to be well-formulated and implemented adequately. The theory expounded here provides a basis for assessing codes and their implementation mechanisms. It remains to be seen, however, whether this approach to reining-in the power of influential sectional interests will be successful.

Notes

1. This is a much longer version of a paper originally presented at the Ethics in Business and the Professions Conference, Massey University, Palmerston North, New Zealand in June, 1993. My thanks to conference participants for their very helpful comments and to Jim Battye and Peter Schouls for reading the penultimate version.

2. But not all writers do. See L'Etang, 1992, 737; Davis, 1991, 17.

3. Although codes are used in many different sorts of organizations—for-profit organizations, charities, public and private and governmental—the focus of this paper will be corporate codes of ethics. While my paper has this focus, it does seem to me that, although codes vary between organizations, their underlying structure is the same if for no other reason than all codes have the same sort of function in organizational life. Thus, many of the theoretical points that I make may well apply across the board though I shall not argue for these conclusions in this paper.

4. Abbott, 1983, 857.

5. Brooks, 1989, 120.

6. Center For Business Ethics, 1992, 863–67; Hoffman, 1990, 630; Murphy, 1988, 908. Again, I consider these terms to be largely synonymous. In terms of my argument, nothing hangs upon the distinction, if any, between codes of ethics and mission statements, credos, and so on. I am in fact using the term "code of ethics" generically to refer to all statements of values and norms of good and bad practice. My interests here are the principles that underpin their formulation, engendering, and enforcement.

7. Brooks, 1989, 120.

8. Cressey and Moore, 1983, 55.

9. For example, Purcell, 1978; Mathews, 1988, 79; Snoeyenbos and Jewell, 1983, 129; Ferrell and Gardiner, 1991; Weber, 1983, 534; Hoffman, 1990; Maitland, 1990, 513–14.

10. See Cressey and Moore, 1983; Mathews, 1988; Barber, 1983, 139, 142–63; Tomasic and Bottomley, 1993, 94–96; Abbott, 1983, 859; Cullen, 1978, 161; Newton, 1982, 35; Davis, 1991a, 160, note 9; Beder, 1993, 36, 40.

11. Brooks, 1989, 123; Snoeyenbos and Jewell, 1983, 103. I say "practical problem" here. Codes may face, as well, a number of moral problems. It has been noted that codes are often authoritarian and paternalistic (Cressey and Moore, 1983, 63) or they can form a foundation upon which the unethical treatment of employees and other stakeholders may be based. For example, they can be used to empower unjustifiably organizational officers to violate the privacy and personal dominion of employees; they can act as mechanisms for grounding capricious and arbitrary control of organization members (*Ibid.*, 71), for placing blame where it does not belong, or for creating scapegoats or conducing witchhunts or purges (Toffler, 1991, 338); they may be used to deflect responsibility from poor organizational practices (for example, working conditions that are stressful and promote stress-related illnesses); or they may be used primarily to advance organizational interests, rather than ethical concerns generally (Cressey and Moore, 1983, 58; Mathews, 1988, chs. 4–5, 83 *et seq.*). I do not consider these problems here.

12. Starr, 1983, 104.

13. Arthur, 1987, 68; Cressey and Moore, 1983, 58; Mathews, 1988, chs. 4–5, 83 *et seq.*; Starr, 1983, 104.

14. Mathews, 1988, 46–47, 60, 78; Murphy, 1988, 910, 914; Snoeyenbos and Jewell, 1983, 101–102; Bowie, 1990, 507; Arthur, 1987, 63; Weeks and Nantel, 1992, 758; Hoffman, 1990, 632; Dean, 1992, 286; Kotter and Heskett, 1992, 60–61; Brooks, 1989, 123; Cressey and Moore, 1983, 66; Fleming, 1984, 219; Fasching, 1981.

15. Cressey and Moore, 1983, 63.

16. Bowie, 1990, 506; Hoffman, 1990, 630; Mathews, 1988, 78; Ferrell and Gardiner, 1991, 129–30; Snoeyenbos and Jewell, 1983, 104–106.

17. Barber, 1983, 145, 151–52; Tomasic and Bottomley, 1993, 94–96.

18. Mathews, 1988, 55, says 80 percent of her sample of Fortune 500 companies and Cressey and Moore, 1983, 64, reported that 75 percent of their sample contained

information on compliance procedures. See also Hoffman, 1990, 630; Mathews, 1988, 58–59.

19. Hoffman, 1990, 630, claims that just 18 percent of his sample of Fortune 500 companies had ethics committees and eight percent had ombudspeople; and three companies out of the 279 that responded to his questionnaire had judiciary boards.

20. Cressey and Moore, 1983, 71.

21. *Ibid.*, 74.

22. Amongst the most detailed, Bowie, 1990; Hoffman, 1990; Murphy, 1988; Snoeyenbos and Jewell, 1983; Fleming, 1984; Purcell, 1984.

23. Cressey and Moore, 1983, 69.

24. *Ibid.*, 67–68.

25. Fuller, 1969, 96.

26. *Ibid.*, 106, 122.

27. *Ibid.*, 205.

28. *Ibid.*, 39, 46–91. It must be pointed out that Fuller claims that he is not dealing with the substantive aims of legal rules. He is not suggesting that these criteria form the basis by which to judge that a particular law is well-drafted or that these criteria can be used to determine whether any particular law will attain the purpose the lawmaker had in mind when formulating it. Rather, Fuller claims that he is concerned with the ways in which a system of rules for governing human conduct must be constructed and administered if it is to be efficacious and at the same time remain what it purports to be [a system of laws]" (97). In contrast, I am arguing that most of these criteria (including the additional ones I suggest) not only function as a basis upon which to distinguish well-drafted codes of ethics from poorly drafted codes, but that most of them can be used to identify well-drafted provisions from poorly drafted ones. For example, if the law as a body of rules is unknown, it will fail to regulate conduct; similarly, if a particular law is unintelligible then it will be unlikely to regulate conduct in the direction desired, and certainly no agent could be held culpable for failing to obey it. A person cannot be held culpable for failing to obey a rule that is secret, or which, for other reasons, could not be known, or which does not exist.

29. *Ibid.*, 39.

30. *Ibid.*

31. On this, see Brien, 1997.

32. Fuller, 1969, 216–17.

33. It may be argued that Fuller assumes some of these criteria within the eight he sets down. For example, he talks about "procedural due process" [sic] (81) and fairness (211), though he does seem to exclude considerations of a law's substantive justice (47). If this is the case, then Fuller would seem to be confusing logically distinct criteria under the one heading. It may be true that in order for there to be congruence between a law and its administration there need to be devices within the system that promote congruence. But the principle that there be congruence between a law and its administration is distinct from how we should go about ensuring it. It would be a defect in a system if it did not explicitly commit itself, not only by affirmation (an explicit rule), but by device (such as a court), to

ensuring that the laws that existed were enforced and implemented in an orderly and fair way, if only because the explicit absence of such a commitment would weaken support for the system, that is, its potential for efficacy. Consequently, these elements must be separated into distinct desiderata.

34. Is this assumed in criterion 1? After all, what I have described as the requirement that there be rules to guide action, Fuller himself calls the criterion of "the generality of law." Moreover, he seems to include in criterion 1 the requirement that laws be general (46–49) and not apply to individuals (214–15). Fuller seems to have confused two distinct issues. In his discussion of criterion 1 (39, 46–49) quite clearly Fuller is thinking about general rules or principles; that is, there must be guides to action of some sort, and rules to ground the evaluation of behavior rather than ad hoc decision making. While Fuller does talk about general rules, he does not, however, seem to be as focused upon the generality of a law with respect to actions or people, as upon the fact that rules or principles are required to regulate action. The generality of law is a logically distinct question from questions about the form that laws should take: Should laws be directed at individuals or groups of individuals? Should they be directed at types of acts? How are the guides to action to be formulated, as categorical roles or as general or universal rules or as prescriptions? Or can they be even more general and be formulated as principles or even tenets? Since there is a logical distinction here, I separate the points.

35. Mathews, 1988, 46–47, 60, 78; Murphy, 1988, 910, 914; Snoeyenbos and Jewell, 1983, 101–102; Bowie, 1990, 507; Arthur, 1987, 68; Weeks and Nantel, 1992, 758; Hoffman, 1990, 632; Dean, 1992, 286; Kotter and Heskett, 1992, 60–61; Brooks, 1989, 123; Cressey and Moore, 1983, 66; Fleming, 1984, 219; Fasching, 1981.

36. Of course, there may be other beliefs that support these, such as beliefs about the sincerity of the program or about the capacity of the organization to detect violations of the code. There may be beliefs that count against these, such as that the organization is more concerned with profit than ethics. I am assuming, for the sake of argument, that such countervailing pressures are insignificant.

37. See, for example, the people quoted in Cressey and Moore, 1983, 65–70; Tomasic and Bottomley, 1993, 95. See also, Mathews, 1988, 78; Bowie, 1990, 507.

38. Fisse and Braithwaite, 1993, 85. See also Braithwaite, 1993; Braithwaite and Makkai, 1993; Cressey and Moore, 1983, 66; Ayres and Braithwaite, 1992, 49.

39. Cressey and Moore, 1983, 70–71.

40. Pastin, 1986, 221–25; Peters and Waterman, 1982, 3, 55–88, cited in Newton, 1986, 253; Kotter and Heskett, 1992, 60–67.

41. Ayres and Braithwaite, 1992, 49.

42. Cressey and Moore, 1983, 68.

43. The obvious criticism is that such engendering of values seems not that far removed from brainwashing. I shan't pursue that question here, as it is not the focus of this paper. However, I would argue that there are important moral differences. Brainwashing aims to change a person's values, beliefs, and attitudes without that person exercising her critical and analytic faculties to freely select and adopt the values. Engendering involves persuading the agent through rational argument, discussion, and demonstration that invites discussion, testing, and so

on. Engendering, unlike brainwashing, involves an act of free will on the part of the agent, whereas brainwashing does not.

44. Henry, 1983, 146, cited in Fisse and Braithwaite, 1993, 170. For example, in a study of private sector disciplinary proceedings, Stuart Henry discovered that some employees felt that they received fairer treatment from the company than the state. Employees viewed employer-based discipline as more individualized, more contextualized to, and understanding of, the accepted way of doing things within the organization. Such a system is perceived as fairer and more likely to determine the cause of the wrongdoing. Since the process is fairer and perceived to be so, the decision is more likely to be accepted, leading to reform of the miscreant and education of others; and since such a process is more likely to identify the cause, proactive measures can be adopted to prevent a repetition.

45. This model and the diagram have been derived from Ayres and Braithwaite, 1992a, 45. See also Ayres and Braithwaite, 1992b, 35ff and Fisse and Braithwaite, 1993, 142ff.

46. See Braithwaite, 1993; Brien, 1997.

47. Cotter and Heskett, 1992, 52; Pastin, 1986, 222.

Bibliography

Abbott, A. 1983. "Professional Ethics." *American Journal of Sociology* 88 (5): 855–85.

Arthur, E. E. 1987. "The Ethics of Corporate Governance." *Journal of Business Ethics* 6 (1): 59–70.

Ayres, I., and J. Braithwaite. 1992. "Designing Responsive Regulatory Institutions." *The Responsive Community* 2 (Summer): 41–47.

———. 1992. *Responsive Regulation: Transcending the Deregulation Debate*. New York: Oxford University Press.

Barber, B. 1983. *The Logic and Limits of Trust*. New Brunswick, NJ: Rutgers University Press.

Beder, S. 1993. "Engineers, Ethics and Etiquette." *New Scientist* 25: 36–41.

Bowie, N. E. 1990. "Business Codes of Ethics: Window Dressing or Legitimate Alternative to Government Regulation?" In *Business Ethics: Readings and Cases in Corporate Morality*, edited by M. Hoffman and J. M. Moore, 505–509. New York: McGraw-Hill.

Braithwaite, J. 1993. "Power and the Architecture of Trust." Photocopy ms., Division of Philosophy and Law, Australian National University.

Braithwaite, J., and T. Makkai. 1993. "Trust and Compliance." *Policing and Society* 4:1–12.

Brien, A. 1997. "Professional Ethics and the Culture of Trust." *Journal of Business Ethics* 16: 21–33.

Brooks, L. J. 1989. "Corporate Codes of Ethics." *Journal of Business Ethics* 8 (Nos. 2 and 3): 117–29.

Centre For Business Ethics. 1992. "Instilling Ethical Values in Large Corporations." *Journal of Business Ethics* 11 (11): 863–67.

Cressey, D. R., and C. A. Moore. 1983. "Managerial Values and Corporate Codes of Ethics." *California Management Review* 25 (4): 53–77.

Cullen, J. B. 1978. *The Structure of Professionalism: A Qualitative Examination.* New York: Petrocelli Books.

Davis, M. 1991. "Do Cops Really Need a Code of Ethics?" *Criminal Justice Ethics* 10 (Summer/Fall): 14–28.

———. 1991. "Thinking Like an Engineer: The Place of a Code of Ethics in the Practice of a Profession." *Philosophy and Public Affairs* 20 (2): 150–67.

Dean, P. J. 1992. "Making Codes of Ethics Real." *Journal of Business Ethics* 11 (4): 285–90.

Fasching, D. J. 1981. "A Case for Corporate Management Ethics." *California Management Review* 23 (4): 62–76.

Ferrell, O. C., and G. Gardiner. 1991. *In Pursuit of Ethics: Tough Choices in the World of Work.* Creve Coeur, MO: Smith Collins.

Fisse, B., and J. Braithwaite. 1993. *Corporations, Crime and Accountability.* Cambridge: Cambridge University Press.

Fleming, J. E. 1984. "Managing the Corporate Ethical Climate." In *Corporate Governance and Institutionalizing Ethics,* edited by W. M. Hoffman, J. M. Moore, and D. A. Fedo, 217–26. Lexington, KY: D. C. Heath.

Fuller, L. 1969. *The Morality of Law,* Rev. ed. New Haven, CT: Yale University Press.

Henry, S. 1983. *Private Justice: Towards Integrated Theorising in the Sociology of Law.* London: Routledge and Kegan Paul.

Hoffman, W. M. 1990. "Developing the Ethical Corporation." In *Business Ethics: Readings and Cases in Corporate Morality,* 2nd ed., edited by W. M. Hoffman and J. M. Moore, 628–34. New York: McGraw-Hill.

Kotter, J. P., and J. L. Heskett. 1992. *Corporate Culture and Performance.* New York: Free Press.

L'Etang, J. 1992. "A Kantian Approach to Codes of Ethics." *Journal of Business Ethics* 11 (10): 737–44.

Maitland, I. 1990. "The Limits of Business Self-Regulation." In *Business Ethics: Readings and Cases in Corporate Morality,* edited by W. M. Hoffman and J. M. Moore, 509–18. New York: McGraw-Hill.

Mathews, M. C. 1988. *Strategic Intervention in Organizations: Resolving Ethical Dilemmas,* vol. 169. Newbury Park, CA: Sage.

Murphy, P. E. 1988. "Implementing Business Ethics." *Journal of Business Ethics* 7 (12): 907–15.

Newton, L. 1986. "The Internal Morality of the Corporation." *Journal of Business Ethics* 5 (3): 249–58.

———. 1982. "The Origin of Professionalism: Sociological Conclusions and Ethical Implications." *Business and Professional Ethics Journal* 1 (4): 33–43.

Pastin, M. 1986. *The Hard Problems of Management.* San Francisco: Jossey-Bass.

Peters, T. J., and R. H. Waterman. 1982. *In Search of Excellence.* New York: Harper & Row.

Purcell, T. V. 1984. "Ethics Committees on Boards of Directors?: The Norton Experience." In *Corporate Governance and Institutionalizing Ethics,* edited by W. M. Hoffman, J. M. Moore, and D. A. Fedo, 193–204. Lexington, KY: D. C. Heath.

———. 1978. "Institutionalising Ethics on Corporate Boards." *Review of Social Economy* (Dec): 41–53.

Snoeyenbos, M., and D. Jewell. 1983. "Morals, Management and Codes." In *Business Ethics: Corporate Values and Society,* edited by M. Snoeyenbos, R. Almeder, and J. Humber, 97–108. New York: Prometheus.

Starr, W. 1983. "Codes of Ethic—Towards a Rule Utilitarian Justification." *Journal of Business Ethics* 2 (2): 99–106.

Toffler, B. L. 1991. *Managers Talk Ethics.* New York: John Wiley & Sons.

Tomasic, R., and S. Bottomley. 1993. *Directing the Top 500: Corporate Governance and Accountability in Australian Companies.* Sydney: Allen and Unwin.

Weber, J. 1983. "Institutionalizing Ethics into the Corporation." In *Ethical Theory and Business,* 2nd ed., edited by T. L. Beauchamp and N. E. Bowie, 533–41. Englewood Cliffs, NJ: Prentice-Hall.

Weeks, W. A., and J. Nantel. 1992. "Corporate Codes of Ethics and Sales Force Behavior: A Case Study." *Journal of Business Ethics* 11 (10): 753–60.

Annotated Bibliography

Guinn, J., E. Goldfarb, and J. Showalter. 1998. "Creating a Corporate Compliance Program." *Health Progress* 79 (3) 60–63. A clear and concise presentation on structuring a compliance effort.

Haron, D. 1998. "Waste and Neglect: Fraud and Abuse in the Health Care Industry." *Health Care Supervisor* 16 (4): 61–67. A concise and clear presentation of the fraud problem and of managerial responses.

Rovner, J. 1998. "Organizational Ethics: It's Your Move." *Health System Leader* 5 (1): 4–12. A practical report on recent experience with organizational ethics programs in healthcare organizations.

Spencer, E. 1997. "A New Role for Institutional Ethics Committees: Organizational Ethics." *Journal of Clinical Ethics* 8 (4): 372–76. Provides an approach to development of organizational ethics structure that begins with the existing ethics committee structure.

Tuohey, J. 1998. "Covenant Model of Corporate Compliance." *Health Progress* 79 (4): 70–75. Offers a sound framework for developing ethics structures.

3

ETHICS AND ORGANIZATIONAL CULTURE

WHAT IS the informal nature of healthcare organizations and how can ethics be integrated with it? Following our previous reflection on the formal structural aspects of organizations, this chapter focuses on that informal culture question. What is the ethical situation in the informal arena, and what can a healthcare organization do there to facilitate ethical behavior?

As noted by Trevino, Butterfield, and McCabe in their reading attached to this chapter, the structural and cultural are intertwined. We discuss them in separate chapters for conceptual clarity purposes only. Figure 3.1 recalls the "nature of organizations" matrix.

Each of the six aspects of organizational life interacts with and affects the other five aspects. Corporate, group, and individual realities interact with one another; formal realities interact with informal realities. Indeed, some view this interaction as the very essence of organization ethics, defining the field as "the study of ethical issues related to how an organization influences its members and how members influence each other and the organization."[1]

Figure 3.1 Cultural Aspects of Organizations

	Corporate	Group	Individual
Informal	X	X	X
Formal			

But the informal cultural reality is much more subtle than the formal structural reality. Although unofficial and undocumented, the informal culture of an organization is a very real aspect of organizational life and behavior. A key part of organization analysis is discernment of the consistency, or lack thereof, between what is formally stated and established and what is actually done and informally effectuated. The following case anchors our reflection on this aspect of an organization.

CASE STUDY

Case Three: Do What We Do

Aware of the Federal Sentencing Guidelines—and fearful of severe financial consequences for failing to comply with compliance standards—St. Serena's recently promulgated a strong business code of conduct and a corporate compliance program. Among the provisions in the code is the following:

> *Section I.5.c.(ii): Any personal or other non-work related use of any corporate data communications system or computer system, including Internet access for non-business purposes, is prohibited.*

The corporate compliance program established a network of compliance coordinators representing every unit of the St. Serena's complex. They have been specially trained to ensure that the compliance program is effective. The compliance program has also provided for a telephone hotline to receive anonymous reports of any suspected code violation. In addition, the code of business conduct contains the following provision:

> *Section II: Every employee has the obligation to report promptly any suspected violation of the corporate code of conduct to their supervisor or divisional compliance coordinator.*

Clare has worked in the medical records unit of St. Serena's for two years. She had originally heard of the job through a friend whose husband, Charley, is the unit supervisor. Clare has been an average employee and is attending night school to obtain a college degree in healthcare administration to improve her career opportunities. She regularly uses her office computer—on breaks only—to do school assignments and occasionally uses the Internet connection for research. Because her school program seems somewhat job-related, Charley told her this practice is okay so long as she does her schoolwork only on breaks. (A card game addict, Charley occasionally plays hearts on his office computer during lunch.)

Mike, a friend of Charley's, is the compliance coordinator for the admissions unit. Last week on their way to lunch together they walked past Clare's cubicle and noticed her computer screen with a game of solitaire displayed. Mike asked Charley, "What's that all about?" to which Charley replied, "I'll take care of it later." That afternoon, Charley told Clare she could no longer use her computer for personal purposes. Mike did not report what he had seen to his supervisor. He did ask Charley the next day what he had done about the matter.

Yesterday Mike stopped by Frank's office in financial affairs. Mike and Frank have both worked at St. Serena's for 12 years, and have become great friends. Both are highly respected and productive managers. That morning Frank had received a phone call from his wife. They had been planning a long-awaited vacation, and she had called to say that she had heard from a friend that reduced air fares had been announced for reservations made that day. Frank's wife was unable to get through to the airline by phone apparently because of public response to the special offer. Because their home computer is broken, she asked Frank to make electronic reservations on the Internet before the deal sold out. "It will save us $1000," she stressed.

On entering Frank's office, Mike finds his friend on the computer with the airline home page on the screen. Frank excitedly tells Mike about the deal and asks if he wants a reservation too.

Questions for Discussion:

1. What should Mike do? Why?
2. What formal structural aspects of St. Serena's are relevant to this situation?
3. What informal cultural elements are operative?
4. Is there consistency between the formal and informal realities of St. Serena's?
5. Based on this case, is St. Serena's a compliant organization? Is it an ethical organization?
6. Do situations like this warrant ethical analysis?

COMMENTARY

As a compliance coordinator Mike is officially bound to report suspected violations of the corporate code to his supervisor. As a close friend of Frank he may unofficially feel bound to protect his brother worker. There is organizational meaning to the old saw about a rock and a hard place. Has the organization created this predicament? Has the Federal Sentencing Commission created it? Odds are that Mike will stand by his friend, perhaps tell him not to use the Internet again, but probably not report the code violation. However, a pattern of code neglect has been a major factor in harsh judicial sentences. Determining what St. Serena's can do organizationally to confront rather than deny situations like that described becomes essential, especially because such action will thus qualify St. Serena's for the leniency provided for in the Federal Guidelines. Some conceptual crutches can help the reflection.

Micro Versus Macro

We first need to address the notion that situations like this seem blatantly trivial and are not matters for serious ethical deliberation. Clearly the situation involving Mike is a micro matter as previously distinguished from macro matters. Let us assume that Frank does not routinely use the Internet at work for personal matters, that his violation is exceptional because of the specifics of his wife's request, the deadline for the airline deal, and the broken home computer. Mike is very likely—especially with his perception affected by the emotional factor of friendship—to view the matter as trivial and as an exception to the code. After all, isn't Frank's action eminently reasonable?

But what about the clear violation of the code that stipulates that *any* personal use of the office computer for non-business purposes is prohibited? Is that a micro or a macro matter? And what about the code's stipulation that Mike and everyone else is to report *any* suspected violation? Would Mike's failure to report Frank be a micro or a macro ethics matter? Furthermore, how did Mike seem to view the situation of personal use of the office computer by Clare? Does his speaking to Charley twice about it suggest that he deemed that situation as not so trivial a matter? Was his lack of a friendship with Clare a factor in that perspective?

In thinking this notion through, three considerations are in order. One, in the compliance context, any violation of a code stipulation is likely to be judged as a macro matter subject to harsh penalty. Two, the "slippery slope of sin" saw contends that precisely this kind of "seemingly trivial" exception to standards leads eventually to headliner exceptions. Experience strongly suggests that, after a while, Mike will find difficulty in seeing the harm in overlooking his friends' violation of, say, fraud provisions in the code. Three, organizational analysis of the situation would suggest that the structural mechanism of the code is defeated by the cultural norm of loyalty to friends, and that unless those cultural norms are recognized and addressed, compliance in any sense will be undermined. This approach highlights the interaction of the structural and cultural aspects of organizations. In this situation, as in many organizational situations, a macro matter of violating a formally structured code of conduct may easily be viewed as a micro matter through the lens of informal cultural norms. Undoubtedly in recognition of this the Compliance Guidelines from the Office of the Inspector General state that, "fundamentally," compliance efforts are designed to establish a *culture* that promotes prevention, detection, and resolution of instances of conduct that do not conform to federal, state, and private payor healthcare program requirements, "as well as to [an organization's] ethical and business policies."[2]

Informal Culture

A structural approach to Mike's situation would focus on the code itself and on monitoring mechanisms. Is the provision in the code prohibiting "any" personal use unrealistic and unreasonably rigid? Does such wording unnecessarily invite difficult situations by not providing for a measure of approved exceptions or approvals? Can the answer be found in providing a more flexible code? Or, do inadequate monitoring mechanisms invite short-circuiting behaviors such as Mike's accommodation to his friend? This structural approach—common in compliance-focused organizations—might lead to a recommendation, for example, that St. Serena's employ more sophisticated computer software that would monitor and report Frank's use of the Internet.

At a deeper analytical level, the structural approach might recall the "3 Ds" concept from Chapter one, and ask whether St. Serena's rushed to ethical dogma when it might better have spent some time and analysis in ethical development. How did St. Serena's develop the code? Did it emerge hastily from the office of legal counsel or was there broad organizational participation—by groups and individuals—in an extended process? Was there an effort to obtain organizational "ownership" of the code or was it simply promulgated as a fait accompli?

A cultural approach to the situation, on the other hand, would focus on informal realities such as power, norms, patterns, social groups, stress, feelings, and attitudes. Figure 3.2 depicts the differences in approach. As a manager and compliance coordinator Mike has specific authority, but obviously he also has the power to question Charley or not to question him, to report his friend or not report him, to reprimand or not. How does the reality of *power* in the organization affect ethics and compliance efforts? The code declares specific organizational values

Figure 3.2 Elements of the Ethical Dimension at Each Level of the Informal Organizational Culture*

Corporate	*Group*	*Individual*
Patterns	Social Groups	Feelings
Power	Habits	Attitudes
Grapevines	Norms	Role Models

*Compare to Figure 2.2 in Chapter two.

of St. Serena's. But what are the operating *norms* of the organization? Is, for example, the norm of loyalty to friends prevalent? How does this affect the compliance effort? Is there a *pattern* of personal use of computers at St. Serena's or are Clare, Charley, and Frank exceptions to the pattern? Do existing patterns need to be specially addressed?

Mike and Frank are clearly part of a *social group* that probably includes Charley and others. Clare is undoubtedly not part of that group. Does the reality of social groups in organizations affect behavior in organizations? Is this a factor in Mike's behavior regarding Clare and Frank? And what about the reality of *feelings*? Mike's feelings when he saw Clare's computer were certainly different from his feelings at seeing Frank's. In the former case there may have been some intense outrage; in the latter case the feeling was probably more like mild concern. Did feelings affect Mike's perception and behavior? Should ethics and compliance programs confront these kinds of informal realities? Do informal realities like these significantly affect the way organizational members perceive job situations? Do informal cultural realities tend to skew our ethical analysis? Does this explain Mike's behavior as well as Charley's and Frank's and Clare's?

The importance of confronting and dealing with the informal cultural realities of healthcare organizations is suggested by a recent Ethics Officer Association–sponsored study that has become "one of the most widely referenced pieces of business ethics research."[3] This major survey of American workers found that a 60 percent majority feel a "substantial amount" of pressure on the job to act unethically. Healthcare workers reported among the highest levels of pressure of any industry, and the pressure came predominantly from informal realities. Most of the organizations represented in the survey had structural mechanisms—like codes of conduct—that exerted positive pressure for ethical behavior, but the survey suggests that the cultural realities exerted stronger negative pressure.

The most frequently cited misbehaviors were cutting corners on quality control, covering up incidents, lying about sick days, deceiving clients, falsifying reports, withholding information, and misusing corporate property. (As far as we know Charley, Clare, and Frank had not participated in the survey!) Note that all of these behaviors are in the informal cultural realm and run counter to formal official policies and procedures. In other words, this landmark survey strongly suggests that rampant inconsistency exists between the formal ethical dimension and the informal ethical dimension of healthcare organizations.[4]

Helpfully, the survey asked workers to identify factors that contribute to the pressure felt to behave unethically. Among the most cited factors were poor leadership, poor internal communications, lack of management support, emphasis on financial goals like cost-cutting requirements, and increasing competition.

These findings are supported in the healthcare field specifically by a more recent survey of 207 healthcare executives from across the United States. The study found that pressure from a superior and the desire to gain a competitive advantage were the top factors to cause a reduction in ethical standards: "The desire to win or advance would appear stronger than the desire to maintain a normative standard of ethical performance."[5] The findings are also consistent with an earlier survey of healthcare human resource professionals that found favoritism in promotion, differences in discipline based on friendship, and inconsistent use of discipline as among the ten most serious ethical situations in healthcare organizations.[6]

This "attitudinal" informal organizational reality has apparently been resistant to common formal structural efforts—such as codes— at generating ethical attitudes. Indeed, the seemingly harsh Federal Sentencing Guidelines and the rigorous formal structural compliance mechanisms they require undoubtedly stem from the prevalence of this attitudinal reality and are fundamentally aimed at changing such attitudes. The Guidelines heavily stress, for example, that "patterns of indifference" are being just as significant as intentional misdeeds when fraud and abuse violations exist.

In the St. Serena's case, Charley's use of his computer to play hearts is probably well known and is a significant factor in his department's attitude toward use of office equipment for personal purposes, the code of conduct notwithstanding. Mike's sense of "competitive advantage" for his friend Frank also most likely influences his attitude toward reporting him, the code provision notwithstanding.

The good news from the Ethics Officer Association survey is that most workers are optimistic that organizational ethics can happen: "This survey shows that today a majority of workers believe that business and ethics can mix and that ethical dilemmas can be reduced."[7] The association identified specific steps that could relieve pressure in the workplace for unethical behavior. Consistent with their responses about poor communication and inadequate leadership being key sources for unethical pressure, the workers identified open dialogue and serious commitment by top management as the best solutions to the problem. The executive director of the Ethics Officer Association observes: "It is encouraging that the solutions were low cost and easily attainable within most organizations."[8] We should also observe that such measures are addressed to the more subtle informal dimension of organizational life.

This informal dimension—unlike the formal dimension—is characterized by subtlety. As Bowen McCoy has put it: "The stories people tell, rather than printed materials, transmit the organization's conceptions of what is proper behavior."[9] At St. Serena's, is the tenor of the stories about Charley's games and Frank's saving of $1,000 in airfare more significant than written provisions of the code? Chambliss points to subtle practices in hospitals like "the slow code" and "snowing" and the way they are discussed among healthcare personnel as being at least as significant to ethical analysis as formal rules about euthanasia.[10] Similarly, Frank Navran of the Ethics Resource Center maintains that even when values and policies are in print but not adhered to by leaders of the organization, employees receive "very mixed messages."[11]

As suggested above, understanding the notion of informal organization culture requires an analysis of *attitude*. What is the attitude of Charley and other employees of St. Serena's toward the code of conduct, and specifically toward the provision of personal use of computers? What is Mike's attitude toward the reporting provision? In stressing the importance of attitude, business ethicist Lynn Paine says: "Though integrity strategies may vary in design and scope, all strive to define companies' guiding values, aspirations, and patterns of thought and conduct." Paine describes this cultural dimension as "the governing ethos of an organization."[12] In a similar vein, hospital board chairman Raymond Andrews emphasizes the role of the attitude of an organization's board of trustees toward organizational ethics. He writes: "Believe it or not, trustees contribute heavily to the pressures felt far down the line. . . . Many trustees see their role as protecting their institution's finances, first and foremost. . . . They send subtle messages that may mislead workers as to priorities or practices expected of them."[13] What is the attitude of the board of St. Serena's toward the code of conduct and its provisions?

Potter refers to this informal culture when he argues that the field of organization ethics "will have to enter into the dynamics of corporate culture and experience first-hand how to meaningfully interpret organizational behavior."[14] Toward this he urges development of "systems thinking" in ethics analysis to enable a "learning organization" to emerge: "The attitude of a learning organization will enlist everyone in understanding the subtle dynamics of corporate decision making and seek out opportunities to introduce moral reflection at the right moment of that process."

Recall the systems thinking concept of before-during-after introduced in Chapter one. Has St. Serena's provided for feedback on its code of conduct provision *during* its implementation? Has the organization learned about the difficulties faced with the rigid prohibition of personal use of office equipment? Might it evaluate the code after this experience and consider modifications?

Self-Interest Versus Covenant

John Tuohey, ethicist at Mercy Health System in Oklahoma, has recently articulated an approach to corporate compliance requirements that stems from an appreciation of the power of the informal culture over behavior in healthcare organizations.[15] Drawing from an analysis of business ethics, he distinguishes between a "self-interest" model and a "covenantal" model of organizational ethics: "The purpose or goal of business in the self-interest model is primarily, if not exclusively, to maximize returns. The main mode of operation is the contract." The covenant model, in contrast, conducts business not just through contracts but through covenants meaning "business decisions are made with an awareness of their impact on corporate relationships." Under this notion[16] the attitude of the healthcare organization is that its first responsibility is to its relationships—its people relationships (patients and staff); its business relationships (insurers and vendors); and its community relationships (government, local populace). "When a corporation faces a problem, one option is to address it according to the norms of efficiency and expediency. The covenant model addresses the problem from the perspective of fidelity to relationships."

This perspective resonates with the study of Jurkiewicz and Thompson that found dominance of a self-interest model—seeking "competitive advantage" above all—to be a key source of unethical behavior in healthcare organizations,[17] and with Stanley Reiser's contention that "organizations declare what really counts by their treatment of staff, students, and community, the institutional goals they set, and how they handle controversy and conflict. What they do tells what they value."[18]

Which model dominates the informal culture of St. Serena's? Does its code's reliance on legality and reporting suggest a contractual emphasis at the corporate level? Do Mike and Charley's adaptation to Clare and Frank suggest a covenantal construct at the group and individual levels? Is this inconsistency at the heart of the problem? Is it reasonable to suggest that a covenantal emphasis could include fidelity to the code, to governmental regulations, and to personal friendships? St. Serena's might, for example, have the contractual code revised through an open process that invites feedback from its people, thus respecting their key relationship with the corporation.

Moral Approbation

Finally, the concept of "moral approbation" can be helpful in reflecting on St. Serena's from a cultural perspective. Jones and Ryan have developed "moral approbation" to mean "the desire of moral agents to be seen as moral by themselves or others,"[19] and contend that such a desire plays a critical, informal role in ethical decision making and behavior. They argue that organization members have a "referent group" whose approval is important. The referent group might consist of colleagues and coworkers or friends who work elsewhere in the organization. Professional groups often serve as these referents. In police work, for example, the notorious "blue wall of silence" is an expression of the moral approbation against reporting a colleague. Similarly, doctors often form their own referent group, and part of the purpose of such solidarity is mutual protection.

What are the referent groups at St. Serena's? What referent groups are desirable? Perhaps Charley's initial referent is his work group. The desire for approval from his work group might have pressured him to allow Clare's use of the office computer. Perhaps Charley also has a higher level referent group that includes managerial colleagues such as Mike. Mike's question upon seeing Clare's use of the computer seemingly influenced Charley's behavior. Similarly, Mike's initial referent group may have been a friendship group that included Frank. His desire for that group's approval may influence his decision of whether to report Frank. A higher level referent group does not seem to be present. Had the code been developed and revised by the corporate body, and had participation of all levels of St. Serena's been emphasized, the corporate body may have constituted a higher level referent group. Indeed, a necessary question when analyzing organizational culture is what referent groups exist and what they value.

Notes

1. Tuohey, J. 1998. "Covenant Model of Corporate Compliance." *Health Progress* 79 (4): 74.

2. United States Department of Health and Human Services, Office of the Inspector General. 1998. *Compliance Program Guidance for Hospitals* February, 63 Federal Register 8987.

3. Petry, E., A. Mujica, and D. Vickery. 1998. "Sources and Consequences of Workplace Pressure: Increasing the Risk of Unethical and Illegal Business Practices." *Business and Society Review* 99 (1): 25.

4. *Ibid.*, 26.

5. Jurkiewicz, C., and C. Thompson. 1999. "An Empirical Inquiry into the Ethical Standards of Healthcare Administrators." *Public Integrity* 1 (1): 50.

6. Brodeur, D. 1998. "Health Care Institutional Ethics: Broader than Clinical Ethics." In *Health Care Ethics,* edited by J. Monagle and D. Thomasima, 498. Gaithersburg, MD: Aspen Publishers.

7. Petry et al., *op. cit.*, 29.

8. *Ibid.*, 30.

9. McCoy, B. 1997. "The Parable of the Sadhu." *Harvard Business Review* (May/June): 59.

10. Chambliss, D. *Beyond Caring*, 150–79. Chicago: University of Chicago Press.

11. Navran, F. quoted in Rovner, J. 1998. "Organizational Ethics: It's Your Move." *Health System Leader* 5 (1): 6.

12. Sharp Paine, L. 1994. "Managing for Organizational Integrity." *Harvard Business Review* (March/April): 107. This article appears as the reading in Chapter nine.

13. Andrews, R. 1998. "When Good People Do Bad Things." *Trustee* 51 (2): 27.

14. Potter, L. 1996. "From Clinical Ethics to Organizational Ethics." *Bioethics Forum* 12 (2): 7.

15. Tuohy, J. 1998. "Covenant Model of Corporate Compliance." *Health Progress* 79 (4): 70–75.

16. For elaboration of the concept see Nash, L. 1990. *Good Intentions Aside.* Boston: Harvard Business School Press.

17. Jurkiewicz, C., and C. Thompson, *op. cit.*

18. Reiser, S. 1994. "The Ethical Life of Health Care Organizations." *Hastings Center Report* 24 (6): 28.

19. Jones, T., and L. Ryan. 1998. "The Effect of Moral Forces on Individual Morality." *Business Ethics Quarterly* 8 (3): 433.

READING

The following is a conceptually rich article that rewards the concentration it requires. Trevino, Butterfield, and McCabe nicely summarize previous research as they distinguish between organizational climate and culture. The former attempts to describe the formal context, while the latter is what I have categorized as the informal—emphasizing underlying values, beliefs, assumptions, and patterns that have developed over time. The findings of their study (methodological details of which are omitted in this reprint) suggest that culture "more explicitly guides and shapes behavior." Their study does stress the strong relationship between informal and formal realities in terms of ethical outcomes, but also suggests that a healthcare organization's emphasis on formal rules and procedures over development of values and attitudes is likely to be counterproductive. A focus on the good of employees, customers, and the public rather than on self-interest is the key. This comprehensive and sophisticated article has important implications for the current compliance craze. In particular, the study finds that reliance on compliance mechanisms alone is likely to produce non-compliant behavior with the resultant heavy penalties, and that managerial failure to develop an ethical context of behavioral values would likely be viewed by the courts as unacceptable "benign neglect." Healthcare managers need to understand the climate and culture concepts and address them in any compliance program.

The Ethical Context in Organizations: Influences on Employee Attitudes and Behaviors

Linda Klebe Trevino, Kenneth D.
Butterfield, and Donald L. McCabe[*]

Recent research has focused on understanding the factors that influence ethical conduct in organizations. Most ethical decision-making models propose that ethical conduct is influenced by a combination of individual characteristics such as values and cognitive moral development, and contextual factors such as reward systems, rules, and codes (e.g., Ferrell, Gresham, and Fraedrich 1989; Jones 1991; Trevino 1986). Although individual characteristics are clearly important, the role of contextual factors seems important from a practical perspective because managers have more control over the work environment than they do over individuals' values or moral development. Further, given the significant resources being invested in organizational ethics initiatives, research is needed

Reprinted with permission from Business Ethics Quarterly *1998. 8 (3): 447–76. Linda Klebe Trevino is professor of organizational behavior at the Pennsylvania State University. Kenneth D. Butterfield is assistant professor of management and decision science at Washington State University. Donald L. McCabe is professor of organization management at Rutgers University.*

to investigate the relationship between "ethical context" and employee attitudes and behaviors.

In the descriptive business ethics literature, ethical context has been represented primarily by two multidimensional constructs, ethical climate (e.g., Victor and Cullen 1987, 1988) and ethical culture (Trevino 1990). These constructs were developed more or less independently and were based on somewhat different assumptions and literatures. Although both constructs have been theoretically associated with individual ethical conduct, empirical support for these relationships is lacking. A number of other issues concerning ethical climate and culture also remain unresolved: Are measures of ethical climate and ethical culture tapping the same or different aspects of the ethical context? Do ethical culture and ethical climate predict the same or different outcomes (e.g., attitudes, behaviors)?

These questions are related to discussions in the broader organizational studies literature about the relationship between organizational climate and organizational culture and the relationship between these context variables and attitudes and behavior (Kopelman, Brief, and Guzzo 1990). Denison (1996) recently proposed a somewhat controversial thesis—that the purported differences between the climate and culture literatures are differences of theoretical roots, perspective, and preferred methodology rather than differences of substance. Both literatures concern the organizational context—"the internal social psychological environment of organizations and the relationship of that environment to individual meaning and organizational adaptation" (Denison 1996, 625). Denison argued that the tendency to focus on the contrasts between these literatures may serve the self-interest of researchers in each camp, but a more integrative approach may be needed if we are to understand the phenomenon that is organizational context. We agree. In this study, we explore the similarities and overlaps as well as the differences between these constructs. Most of all, we hope to gain a better understanding of the relationship between the ethical organizational context and employee attitudes and behaviors.

Ethical Climate

Ethical climate theory and research can be considered a subset of the organizational climate literature. Schneider (1975) argued that there are many types of work climates, one of which Victor and Cullen (1988) labeled "ethical climate." In his recent review of the culture/climate literature, Denison (1996, 624) defined climate as "rooted in the organization's value system." Climate represents the organization's social environment "in terms of a fixed (and broadly applicable) set of dimensions . . . that are consciously perceived by organizational members."

Victor and Cullen (1988, 101) defined ethical climate as "the prevailing perceptions of typical organizational practices and procedures that have ethics content" or "those aspects of work climate that determine what constitutes ethical behavior at work." They proposed nine ethical climate types based upon three major classes of philosophy (principle, benevolence, and egoism), and three loci of analysis (individual, local, and cosmopolitan).

Each of their nine ethical climate types is accompanied by a particular normative expectation (Cullen and Victor, 1993). In the egoistic-individual climate self-interest is the normative expectation. In the egoistic-local climate, company interest guides ethical decisions. In the egoistic-cosmopolitan climate, efficiency is the normative criterion. In the benevolent-individual, local, and cosmopolitan climates, the welfare of individuals, groups inside the organization, and those external to the organization, respectively, guide decisions. In the principled-individual climate, personal morals guide decisions. In the principled-local climate, organizational rules and regulations are the normative criterion. Finally, in the principled-cosmopolitan climate, external laws and codes guide ethical decisions.

To empirically test for the existence of these nine ethical climate types, Victor and Cullen developed the ethical climate questionnaire (ECQ). Across a series of survey studies, they validated the existence of some, but not all, of the proposed climate types (Cullen and Bronson 1993; Victor and Cullen 1987, 1988). In a key test of their typology (Victor and Cullen 1988), the nine dimensions reduced to five that they labeled caring, law and code, rules, instrumental, and independence. Three of these dimensions were consistent with the proposed typology. Law and code was comprised of items representing the original principle-cosmopolitan dimension. Rules was comprised of items representing the original principle-local dimension. Independence was comprised of items representing the original principle-individual dimension (but it had a relatively low reliability of .60). The instrumental dimension was comprised of egoism items from all three levels. Finally, the caring dimension was comprised of a variety of items from all three levels and the benevolence and egoism categories. Thus, the empirical evidence suggested that a reduced number of ethical climate di-mensions could be used to describe some aspects of an organization's ethical context. Further, Victor and Cullen (1987, 1988) found that different ethical climates exist within and between organizations, and that most organizations appear to have a dominant ethical climate type.

In a study of subclimates within an organization, Weber (1995) hypothesized that employees' responses to an adapted ECQ would differ by type of department because of differences in departmental tasks and stakeholder accountability. A study in a financial institution found support for the idea that employees in different departments, from the technical core to boundary spanners, perceived different loci of analysis and different ethical decision-making criteria, leading to differences in perceptions of ethical climate by department.

Having determined that the measure of ethical climate captures some aspects of organizations' ethical context and can differentiate between organizations and departments, researchers have also explored the relationship between ethical climate and attitudinal and behavioral outcomes. General work climates have been found to influence a number of organizational outcomes such as performance and satisfaction (e.g., Pritchard and Karasick 1973). Accordingly, Victor and Cullen (1987, 1988) suggested that ethical climates should influence attitudes and behaviors by providing information about the organization and guidance regarding appropriate conduct.

With regard to organizational commitment, Cullen and Victor (1993) argued that, to the extent that people prefer certain types of normative climates, employees should be more committed to organizations with these climate types. Thus, organizational commitment should be higher in organizations with principle- or benevolence-based climates than in organizations with egoism-based climates. Employees may feel more attached to and may identify more with the values of organizations that increase felt responsibility for others and encourage concern for employees and the community (Mowday, Steers, and Porter 1979; Cullen and Victor 1993). In an empirical study, Cullen and Victor (1993) found that perceptions of a benevolent climate were positively related to commitment and perceptions of an egoistic climate were negatively related to commitment. These relationships are also investigated in this study.

A somewhat more difficult question concerns the relationship between ethical climate and behavior. Victor and Cullen (1988) suggested that "the most important questions focus on identifying the characteristics of ethical climates that affect future ethical behavior" (Victor and Cullen 1987, 68). However, they did not specify those characteristics. Conceptual work by Wimbush and Shepard (1994) suggested that different climate types might be related to different behaviors (e.g., egoism should be associated with unethical behavior, whereas principled climates should be associated with ethical behavior).

Victor and Cullen (1988, 101) also stated that ethical climate "encompassed the range of perceptions that answer, for a member of an organization, the Socratic question: 'What should I do?' " (Victor and Cullen 1988, 101). However, they did not specify exactly how that question would be answered. An examination of the ethical climate dimensions suggests little behavioral guidance for some climates, broad behavioral guidance for others, and specific behavioral guidance for only a few climate dimensions. For example, the independence climate suggests that people should follow what they think is right as individuals. Therefore, in response to the question, "what should I do," the independence climate suggests something like the following—"decide for yourself." Thus, it is not clear that individual behavior could be predicted in a strong independence climate except to say that people will do as they see fit.

The instrumental climate combines a focus on personal and company interests. Therefore, it may be unclear to individuals in this type of climate whether they should act in their own self-interest or in the company's interest, particularly if these interests conflict as they frequently do.

The other three dimensions may be more helpful in answering the "what should I do?" question. The rules climate says to follow the rules. Assuming that the organization has clear rules guiding behavior in a particular situation (such as rules about conflicts of interest in an ethics code), the guidance would be to follow those rules. The law-and-code climate suggests compliance with the law and/or professional standards. This is helpful where the law or professional standards apply. However, in the many situations not governed by law or professional standards, individuals would presumably be left with little guidance. Finally, the caring climate says that one should look out for other people including customers and the public.

The above analysis leaves questions about the relationship between ethical climate and ethical conduct. Few of the specified ethical climates provide specific behavioral guidance. It may be that only certain climates (e.g., rules, law-and-code, caring climates) predict ethical conduct. Further, most organizations have a climate profile that combines a number of climates, and climates may differ across departments, further complicating behavioral prediction.

With regard to empirical support for the ethical climate/conduct relationship, Gaertner (1991) found that although ethical climate did not directly influence behavior, a number of ethical climate dimensions did influence ethical decision making indirectly by affecting the decision-making criteria individuals used. However, empirical support for a direct relationship between ethical climate and behavior is still lacking.

Ethical Culture

The organizational culture literature views the organization as "both the medium and the outcome of social interaction" (Denison 1996, 635). It also emphasizes broad patterns of underlying values, beliefs, and assumptions, the uniqueness of individual social settings, evolution of patterns over time, and qualitative research methods. Kopelman, Brief, and Guzzo (1990, 283) point out that the many approaches to the study of culture can be divided into two categories: the phenomenal, "focusing on observable behaviors and artifacts"; and the ideational, focusing on underlying shared meanings, symbols, and values. The ethical culture construct as explicated by Trevino (1986, 1990) emphasizes the phenomenal level of culture—the more conscious, overt, and observable manifestations of culture such as structures, systems, and organizational practices, rather than the deeper structure of values and assumptions.

Trevino (1986) initially conceptualized the organization's ethical culture as a situational moderator of the relationship between the individual's cognitive moral development stage and ethical/unethical conduct. In that model, culture was comprised of the organization's normative structure (norms about what is and is not appropriate behavior), referent others' behavior, expectations about obedience to legitimate authority, and the extent to which the organization encourages individuals to take responsibility for the consequences of their actions.

In a subsequent conceptualization, Trevino (1990) further developed the ethical culture construct and proposed direct influences of ethical culture on individual conduct. She defined ethical culture as a subset of organizational culture, representing a multidimensional interplay among various "formal" and "informal" systems of behavioral control that are capable of promoting either ethical or unethical behavior. "Formal" cultural systems include such factors as policies (e.g., codes of ethics), leadership, authority structures, reward systems, and training programs. "Informal" systems include such factors as peer behavior and ethical norms. To the extent that these formal and informal cultural systems support ethical conduct, individual behavior is expected to be more ethical. For example, ethical conduct should be higher in organizations where leaders and norms encourage and support ethical conduct, and where ethical conduct is rewarded and unethical conduct is punished, than in organizations without such characteristics.

Underlying the proposed ethical culture/behavior relationship is the assumption that culture can exert a powerful influence on individual behavior. An important characteristic shared by most conceptualizations of organizational culture is the expected relationship between culture and conduct (for a review, see Jelinek, Smircich, and Hirsh 1983). Culture helps to establish what is considered legitimate or unacceptable in an organization. Whether defined as an informal organizational control system (Martin and Siehl 1983; Deal and Kennedy 1982), or an instrument of domination, organizational culture is thought to provide direction for day-to-day behavior.

Cohen (1993) relied upon the sociological concept of anomie (Merton 1938) to explain the relationship between ethical culture (or moral climate, as she labeled it) and behavior in organizations. Anomie is defined as "a condition of formlessness and social disequilibrium where 'the rules once governing conduct have lost their savor and force.'" (Merton 1964, 226). Anomie results from a social system that focuses on goal attainment without a corresponding focus on the means that are used to achieve those goals. It produces detachment from the social system and loss of motivation for moral behavior. Cohen (1993) analyzed a number of Trevino's (1990) ethical culture dimensions and their potential relationship to the development of anomie and to unethical conduct in organizations. For example, leaders can encourage anomie and unethical conduct by ignoring rules and regulations in order to achieve financial objectives, or senior managers can provide reliable leadership that is consistent with stated organizational values. Cohen argued that "in order to develop and maintain work climates which facilitate ethical conduct, it is necessary to reduce any discord between goals and means expressed in various aspects of the culture" (Cohen 1993, 355).

To date, little empirical work has been conducted to support the existence of an ethical organizational culture or its proposed relationship with ethical or unethical conduct. For example, research on culture components such as reward systems (Hegarty and Sims 1978; Trevino and Youngblood 1990) and codes of ethics (e.g., McCabe and Trevino 1993) suggests that these aspects of organizational culture can influence ethical conduct in organizations. Additional research is necessary in order to develop a measure of the proposed multidimensional ethical culture construct and to investigate its influence on ethical conduct.

Although Trevino (1990) did not propose a relationship between ethical culture and employee attitudes, we will also explore this relationship. The theoretical relationship between ethical culture and employee attitudes is based upon the notion that most people will feel more attached and committed to an organization if they perceive that the organization supports and encourages ethical conduct and discourages unethical conduct. Previous research provides some support for such a relationship. For example, Trevino and Ball (1992) found employees' justice evaluations and emotional responses to be most positive when ethical rule violators were punished and punished harshly, suggesting that employees not only approved of ethical rules but wanted them to be enforced. In addition, popular press surveys have suggested that employees prefer working for ethical organizations (Kleiman 1989; Sandroff 1990).

Ethical Climate and Ethical Culture: The Same or Different?

Both ethical climate and ethical culture refer to aspects of an organization's context that are thought to influence attitudes and/or ethical behavior. But the few statements regarding the connection between ethical climate and ethical culture in the literature suggest confusion rather than clarity. For instance, according to Victor and Cullen, "the ethical climate questionnaire, then, is simply an instrument to tap, through the perceptions of organizational participants, the ethical dimensions of organizational culture" (1988, 103).

It may be helpful to consider the metaphors evoked by the notions of "ethical climate" and "ethical culture." The term "climate" suggests meteorological climate and qualifiers such as temperature, humidity, precipitation, wind, and other atmospheric conditions that can affect individuals (e.g., feelings), although it is unclear exactly what the effects will be. In contrast, the notion of "culture" evokes notions of rules, codes, rewards, leadership, rituals, and stories—sense making devices that more explicitly guide and shape behavior (cf. Smircich 1983). In this metaphorical sense, ethical climate may characterize organizations in terms of broad normative characteristics and qualities that tell people what kind of organization this is—essentially what the organization values. If so, ethical climate is likely to be associated with attitudes, but may influence decision making and behavior only indirectly as Gaertner found. Ethical culture, on the other hand, characterizes the organization in terms of formal and informal control systems (e.g., rules, reward systems, and norms) that are aimed more specifically at influencing behavior. Therefore, we may find a stronger relationship between dimensions of ethical culture and ethical conduct. Ethical climate and ethical culture, although somewhat different, are also likely to be related to each other. For example, a culture that supports ethical conduct through codes of conduct is likely to be related to a climate that values rules and laws. However, in order to answer questions about the relationship between these constructs, and their relationship with attitudes and behaviors, both must be included in the same study as has been done here. . . .

Discussion

In this study, Victor and Cullen's (1987, 1988) and Trevino's (1990) conceptualizations of ethical climate and ethical culture were used to characterize the ethical context of organizations and both were discussed in terms of potential influences on employees' attitudes and behaviors. This study is the first investigation to include measures of both constructs in a single study, to factor analyze them together, to investigate the relationships between them, and to examine their relative influences on unethical conduct and organizational commitment.

Ethical context—The relationship between ethical climate and culture.

The initial principal components factor analysis (all of the ethical climate and ethical culture items) revealed ten ethical context factors. Each of these ten factors consisted of items that were derived from either the ethical climate or the ethical culture measures. None of the resulting factors combined items from both the climate and culture measures. Thus, this factor analysis provided some empirical evidence of differentiation between the ethical climate and ethical culture constructs.

This study also provided further support for the existence of a number of ethical climate dimensions. The factor analysis results were generally consistent with previous research findings suggesting that future research can continue to use these measures. However, two of the climate dimensions do not meet conventional reliability standards (.70) and should be improved.

The study also provided the first reliable scales for the measurement of ethical culture that can be used in future research. A number of the proposed dimensions became part of a single factor we labeled overall ethical environment. This factor encompasses ethical leadership, norms, and reward systems that support ethical conduct, and (in code organizations) a code of conduct that is consistent with organizational norms. These aspects of ethical culture varied together in the responses and did not turn out to be "separate" culture dimensions as originally proposed. Future investigations that include both culture and climate (as this one did), should use the scales derived from the combined factor analysis . . . because the combined analysis removed items that did not discriminate between the two constructs.

The correlational analysis suggested that the factors derived from the ethical climate and ethical culture constructs, although somewhat different, are strongly related. Correlations were particularly high between ethical environment (the main culture-based factor) and employee-focused climate, community-focused climate, law-and-professional-code climate, and self-interest climate (negative correlation).

These results suggest that dimensions of ethical climate and ethical culture are tapping somewhat different aspects of the ethical context of the business organizations represented in this study. Clearly, the ethical culture-derived dimensions are capturing an aspect of the organization's ethical context excluded from the ethical climate construct (e.g., leadership and reward systems). And, as we will see below, this aspect of ethical culture seems important for ethical conduct, especially in code organizations. But, the strong relationships between ethical climate– and ethical culture–based factors suggest a large degree of overlap and important relationships between these constructs as well. We should not be surprised at a finding suggesting that an organization whose leaders represent high ethical standards and who reward ethical conduct is also an organization that focuses on its employees and community and on obeying the law. The finding that ethical climate and ethical culture are strongly related is aligned with recent work in the broader organizational climate/culture literature suggesting the close relationship between them (Denison 1996; Pettigrew 1990). A number of researchers are currently using the terms together when talking about creating a particular type of organizational context—for example, one that supports change or success (e.g., Schneider, Brief, and Guzzo 1996; Schneider, Gunnarson, and Niles-Jolly 1990).

Relationship Between Ethical Context and Attitudes/Behaviors

Ethical context and ethical conduct.

We proposed that ethical culture would be more strongly associated with ethical conduct than would ethical climate. The empirical results were mixed. Code organizations, where ethical culture–based factors were most strongly associated with observed unethical behavior, provided support for this proposition. However, in non-code organizations, ethical climate factors emerged as better predictors.

In code organizations, when culture dimensions were entered first, climate dimensions did not add significantly to the variance explained by overall ethical environment and obedience to authority. When climate dimensions were entered first, a single climate dimension (self-interest) was significant and positively associated with unethical conduct.

However, when culture was added, the same two ethical culture dimensions as before (overall ethical environment and obedience to authority) added significantly to the variance explained.

In non-code organizations, the results were quite different. When the culture dimensions were entered in the regression equation first, they explained the same amount of variance (29 percent) as they did in the code sample, suggesting that ethical culture influences ethical conduct similarly in the two types of organizations. However, two climate dimensions (law and professional code and self-interest) explained an additional eight percent of the variance. When ethical climate dimensions were entered first, a full 36 percent of the variance was explained, with only self-interest being significant. Culture was non-significant. Therefore, in non-code organizations, the key variable was self-interest. To the extent that respondents perceived a focus on self-interested behavior in the organization, they also reported observing more unethical conduct. This finding for self-interest is consistent with Wimbush and Shepard's (1994) prediction that egoistic climates would be associated with unethical conduct. However, a note of caution in interpreting this finding is in order because it may represent a tautology. To the extent that unethical conduct (e.g., lying, cheating, stealing) is defined, to a large degree, as self-interested, it is not surprising to find that respondents who perceive self-interest in their organization will also say that they observe more unethical conduct. With that caution in mind, we believe that organizations might find it useful to know that they can survey their employed about self-interest climate and simultaneously learn quite a bit about unethical conduct.

The finding for law and professional codes suggests that a company's more general emphasis on obeying the law and adhering to professional conduct standards is associated with less observed unethical behavior. As suggested earlier, this climate dimension is one of the most behavior-focused in that laws and professional standards are quite specific about behaviors that are acceptable and unacceptable. Future research may want to consider whether an emphasis on laws and professional codes can substitute for a company code, particularly in certain types of organizations such as professional organizations (e.g., accounting, law) or organizations in highly legalized or regulated industries (e.g., banking).

It is also important to consider the climate and culture dimensions that did not enter significantly into the regression equations. Four of the seven ethical climate dimensions (employee focus, community focus, personal ethics, efficiency) had no significant association with observed unethical conduct. One of the three ethical culture dimensions (code implementation) did not contribute significantly. This may suggest that a number of aspects of the ethical context are unrelated to conduct, although they may be related to attitudes.

In sum, we found that two ethical culture–based (overall ethical environment and obedience to authority) dimensions were the best overall predictors of unethical conduct, and they operated similarly in code and non-code organizations. A climate focused on self-interest was also associated with unethical conduct in both code and non-code settings, but was the most important contextual variable in non-code settings. In non-code settings, a focus on adhering to laws and professional standards was also associated with unethical conduct.

These analyses suggested that the context influenced behavior some-what differently in code and non-code settings. In code settings, un-ethical conduct was primarily a function of a behavior-based cultural dimension (overall ethical environment). Observed unethical conduct was lower in a context that encouraged ethical conduct and discouraged unethical conduct through leadership, reward systems, and a meaningful code of conduct. In non-code settings, unethical conduct was primarily a function of an ethical climate dimension (self-interested climate) that was associated with observed unethical behavior. Support for ethical conduct came from a focus on law and professional codes. These findings suggest that researchers and managers may need to think somewhat differently about contextual influences on ethical conduct in code and non-code organizations.

When considering ethical conduct in organizations in general (with-out the code/non-code distinction), selected dimensions from both the ethical climate and culture constructs are clearly relevant. Therefore, future studies of the relationship between ethical context and unethical conduct should, at a minimum, incorporate the select combination of variables from the original ethical climate and ethical culture constructs that were found to be predictive in this research—overall ethical en-vironment, obedience to authority, self-interest, and law and profes-sional code.

Ethical context and organizational commitment.

In this study, we found that measures of ethical climate and ethical culture were almost interchangeable in their ability to predict employee attitudes in both code and non-code organizations, providing organiza-tions with multiple options for influencing organizational commitment. Interestingly, the ethical culture dimensions (overall ethical environ-ment and obedience to authority) associated with ethical conduct were also associated with commitment, making them the most consistently influential study variables. Overall ethical environment was the most consistent culture dimension to be associated with organizational commitment. However, two new climate dimensions emerged as significant in relation to organizational commitment. Employee-focused and community-focused climates were the most consistent climate dimensions to be associated with commitment. These employees were more likely to identify and feel a sense of shared values with organizations that supported and rewarded ethical conduct and that emphasized the good of employees, customers, and the public. The finding for employee and community-focused climate was also similar to Victor and Cullen's finding that benevolence-based climates were positively related to commitment. In non-code organizations, self-interest also had a significant (negative) effect on commitment, again similar to Victor and Cullen's (1993) finding regarding egoistic climates. Therefore, a climate focused on self-interest not only appears to promote unethical conduct, it also has a negative influence on organizational commitment.

Implications for Theory

The findings support the general theory driving this research—that the ethical context of the organization is associated with employee attitudes and behaviors. However, questions remain about how best to conceptualize the ethical context of organizations and its relationship with attitudes and behaviors. Since this study was designed, Cohen proposed another way of conceptualizing the ethical context of firms. She defined "moral climate" as "prevailing employee perceptions of organizational signals regarding norms for making decisions with a moral component" (Cohen, in press). Climate provides a psychological environment of shared perceptions in which certain expected behaviors are more likely to occur. In Cohen's model, cultural processes (e.g., political and technical processes) serve as stimuli that signal managerial expectations for certain types of behavior. Shared interpretations of these cues create a climate that makes certain behaviors more likely. Thus, in the model, cultural processes influence climate which influences ethical behavior. Ethical behaviors are also influenced by other mediating variables such as individual differences and conditions outside the firm. Cohen's model provides a way of integrating culture and climate into a single model that offers a broader framework for thinking about ethical context and how climate and culture components may be related. Additional research will be needed to explore the relationships among contextual dimensions, attitudes, and behaviors. We believe that theory in this area may also be advanced by conducting inductive qualitative research. Employees could be asked to discuss what drives their ethics-related attitudes and behaviors, and specifically to focus on the firm's context. These findings could then be combined with previous theorizing and empirical findings to develop a more complete understanding of ethical context.

Implications for Management

The study findings certainly suggest implications for management. In order to decrease unethical conduct, an organization should have leaders who encourage and model ethical behavior, reward systems that reward ethical conduct and discipline unethical conduct, an ethics code that is consistent with norms, a focus away from strict obedience to authority and away from self-interest at the expense of other considerations, and a focus on adherence to the law and professional standards when they apply. Some of the management prescriptions are quite clear (e.g., discipline unethical conduct) while others raise concerns about common management practices. For example, many organizations base their reward systems almost exclusively on self-interest (e.g., commission-only systems). Does this type of reward system produce an ethical climate high on self-interest and a corresponding high level of unethical conduct? Recent theorizing (Kurland 1996) and media reports about the unethical practices of financial advisers and others suggest that such a relationship can develop. If so, can these reward system pressures be countered by a culture characterized by a strong ethical environment (leadership, codes, norms, etc.)? Or, must the reward system be fundamentally changed? Additional research will be needed to answer these questions.

These findings also suggest a number of routes managers can take to obtain the commitment of employees through the ethical context. They can focus on developing a culture that supports ethical conduct and discourages unethical conduct through leadership, reward systems, codes, and norms. They can focus on developing climates that emphasize the good of employees, customers, and the public rather than self-interest. Or, even better, they can do all of these things. As with prescriptions for decreasing unethical conduct, many questions remain about the best ways to develop these ethical contexts. Hopefully, future research can answer these questions. . . .

Normative Implications of the Study

This study was driven by an empirical approach to the study of business ethics—questions about the association between contextual factors and employee attitudes and behaviors. However, the normative and empirical are certainly intertwined in this work in ways that suggest a symbiotic relationship between the normative and the empirical. Normative ethical theories can provide relevant and useful input into the theorizing that guides descriptive empirical work. Further, empirical findings can provide input that normative theorists can use (Weaver and Trevino 1994).

This study relied on several normative inputs. First, we began with the assumption that it would be normatively better to have an organization in which commitment is high and unethical conduct is low. Second, the ethical climate typology proposed by Victor and Cullen (1988) was based, in part, on normative ethical theory. In this empirical study, several of the ethical climate dimensions (self-interest, employee-focused climate, community-focused climate, and law-and-professional-code climate) were associated with attitudes and behaviors. From a normative perspective, these findings focus our attention on the importance of benevolence and egoism-based normative theories. Egoism (operationalized as self-interest in this study) was negatively associated with organizational commitment and positively associated with unethical conduct, while benevolence (to employees and the community) was positively associated with commitment. Given our assumption that ethical conduct and organizational commitment are normatively good organizational outcomes, the empirical findings have clear implications for how organizations can achieve such preferred outcomes. The findings suggest that organizations should find ways to demonstrate to employees that they care about them and the larger community. Further, organizations should not support an exclusive focus on individual self-interest or strict obedience to authority in the firm. If they do, they are indirectly supporting and encouraging unethical conduct and individuals' commitment only to themselves, not their coworkers or the organization. These findings are consistent with recent prescriptions about the need for trust, cooperation, and teamwork in business.

When the culture-based findings are considered from a normative perspective, additional issues emerge. As stated earlier, our notion of ethical culture assumes that organizations can influence individual ethical behavior—a deterministic perspective that may be distasteful to philosophers who believe that "ethically significant action is autonomous" (Weaver and Trevino 1994, 118). Yet, the empirical results support the claim that cultural factors influence conduct. Therefore, the important normative question may be whether organizations should be managing the ethics of their members, or should employees be left to follow their own principles.

We believe that organizations should be proactively managing the organization's ethical context. If contextual factors do influence conduct, management's lack of attention to these factors can be characterized as benign neglect. In such instances, cultural factors from the broader business environment are likely to take over in the absence of firm-level influences (Trevino 1990). Self-interest is central to the highly competitive global business environment, and individual business persons work within and are influenced by that environment. As we discussed above, an exclusive focus on self-interest is associated with more unethical conduct and lower organizational commitment. In order to balance the influences of this broad self-interested business environment, individual firms must create a sub-context in which moral values other than egoism are encouraged and rewarded. The culture findings from this study provide managers with guidance about the management tools they can use to achieve more ethical conduct in the firm as well as more commitment to the organization. Reward systems that support ethical conduct and discipline unethical conduct and top management role modeling appear to be the most important aspects of an overall ethical environment. This suggests that reward systems should be scrutinized carefully to be sure that "good guys (gals) are rewarded" and "bad guys (gals) are punished." It also suggests that top managers need to become aware of the important role they play as moral leaders in their organizations.

Conclusion

Our analysis suggests that the ethical climate and ethical culture constructs are tapping somewhat different but strongly related aspects of the ethical context. Several climate- and culture-based dimensions were strongly associated with observed unethical conduct and organizational commitment. Employees observed less unethical behavior and were clearly more committed to organizations that supported ethical conduct and that emphasized the good of employees, customers, and the public. The findings suggest that ethical climate and ethical culture are not alternative ways of conceptualizing the ethical context. Rather, both are important because some dimensions are more strongly associated with behavior and others are more strongly associated with commitment. Further, a number of interesting differences were found across code and non-code organizations. Based upon the findings presented here, researchers should think carefully about their research questions and the organizations studied in determining which dimensions of the ethical context to include in future investigations. Future research in this area should also ask whether the combination of dimensions emerging from this study captures all relevant dimensions of ethical context, or whether there are others (Cohen, in press).

The normative implications of the study suggest that normative theories and normative assumptions can provide useful inputs to the design of empirical work. Further, the results of this empirical study suggest that organizations should take responsibility for creating a context in which ethical conduct is supported and encouraged and unethical conduct is discouraged. Employees will not only be more ethical, but they will be more committed to the organization.

Bibliography

Akaah, I. P. 1992. "Social Inclusion as a Marketing Ethics Correlate." *Journal of Business Ethics* 11 (8): 599–608.

Cohen, D. 1993. "Creating and Maintaining Ethical Work Climates: Anomie in the Workplace and Implications for Managing Change." *Business Ethics Quarterly* 3 (4): 343–58.

———. "Moral Climate in Business Firms: A Conceptual Framework for Analysis and Change." *Journal of Business Ethics* (in press).

Cullen, J. B., and J. W. Bronson. 1993. "The Ethical Climate Questionnaire: An Assessment of the Development and Validity." Presented at the Annual Academy of Management Meeting, Atlanta, GA.

Cullen, J. B., and B. Victor. 1993. "The Effects of Ethical Climates on Organizational Commitment: A Multilevel Analysis." Unpublished manuscript.

Darlington, R. B. 1968. "Multiple Regression in Psychological Research." *Psychological Bulletin* 79: 161–82.

Deal, T. E., and A. A. Kennedy. 1982. *Corporate Cultures.* Reading, MA: Addison-Wesley.

Denison, D. 1996. "What Is the Difference Between Organizational Culture and Organizational Climate? A Native's Point of View on a Decade of Paradigm Wars." *Academy of Management Review* 21 (3): 619–54.

Ferrell, O. C., L. G. Gresham, and J. Fraedrich. 1989. "A Synthesis of Ethical Decision Models for Marketing." *Journal of Macromarketing* 9 (2): 55–64.

Folger, R., and M. A. Konovsky. 1989. "Effects of Procedural and Distributive Justice on Reactions to Pay Raise Decisions." *Academy of Management Journal* 32: 115–30.

Gaertner, K. 1991. "The Effect of Ethical Climate on Managers' Decisions." In *Morality, Rationality and Efficiency: New Perspectives on Socio-economics.* Armonk, NY: M. E. Sharpe.

Hegarty, W. J., and H. P. Sims, Jr. 1978. "Some Determinants of Unethical Decision Behavior: An Experiment." *Journal of Applied Psychology* 63: 451–57.

Jelinek, M., L. Smircich, and P. Hirsh. 1983. "Introduction: A Code of Many Colors." *Administrative Science Quarterly* 28: 331–38.

Jones, T. M. 1991. "Ethical Decision Making by Individuals in Organizations: An Issue-Contingent Model." *Academy of Management Review* 16: 366–95.

Kleiman, C. 1989. "Heading the List of Worker Wishes Isn't More Money!" *The Morning Call* 2 October: B-10.

Kopelman, R. E., A. P. Brief, and R. A. Guzzo. 1990. "The Role of Climate and Culture in Productivity." In *Organizational Climate and Culture*, edited by B. Schneider, 282–318. San Francisco: Jossey-Bass.

Kurland, N. 1996. "Trust, Accountability, and Sales Agents' Dueling Loyalties." *Business Ethics Quarterly* 6 (3): 289–310.

Martin, J., and C. Siehl. 1983. "Organizational Culture and Counterculture: An Uneasy Symbiosis." *Organizational Dynamics* (Autumn): 52–64.

McCabe, D. L., and L. K. Trevino. 1993. "Academic Dishonesty: Honor Codes and Other Contextual Influences." *Journal of Higher Education* 64 (5): 522–38.

Merton, R. K. 1938. "Social Structure and Anomie." *American Sociological Review* 3: 672–82.

———. 1964. "Anomie, Anemia, and Social Interaction." In *Anomie and Deviant Behavior*, edited by M. Clinard, 213–42. New York: Free Press.

Mowday, R. T., R. M. Steers, and L. Porter. 1979. "The Measure of Organizational Commitment." *Journal of Vocational Behavior* 14: 224–47.

O'Reilly, C., and J. Chatman. 1986. "Organizational Commitment and Psychological Attachment: The Effects of Compliance, Identification, and Internalization on Prosocial Behavior." *Journal of Applied Psychology* 71: 492–99.

Paulhus, D. 1989. "Measurement and Control of Response Bias." In *Measures of Social Psychological Attitudes*, edited by J. P. Robinson, P. R. Shaver, and L. Wrightsman. New York: Academic Press.

Pettigrew, A. 1990. "Organizational Climate and Culture: Two Constructs in Search of a Role." In *Organizational Climate and Culture*, edited by B. Schneider, 413–33. San Francisco: Jossey-Bass.

Pritchard, R. D., and B. W. Karasick. 1973. "The Effects of Organizational Climate on Managerial Job Performance and Job Satisfaction." *Organizational Behavior and Human Performance* 9: 126–46.

Randall, D. M., and M. F. Fernandes. 1991. "The Social Desirability Bias in Ethics Research." *Journal of Business Ethics* 10: 805–17.

Sandroff, R. 1990. "How Ethical Is American Business?" *Working Woman Magazine* (Sept): 113–16.

Schneider, B. 1975. "Organizational Climate: An Essay." *Personnel Psychology* 28: 447–79.

———. 1983. "Work Climates: An Interactionist Perspective." In *Environmental Psychology: Directions and Perspectives*, edited by N. W. Feimer and E. S. Geller, 106–28. New York: Praeger.

Schneider, B., A. P. Brief, and R. A. Guzzo. 1996. "Creating a Climate and Culture for Sustainable Organizational Change." *Organizational Dynamics* 24 (4): 7–19.

Schneider, B., S. K. Gunnarson, and K. Niles-Jolly. 1994. "Creating the Climate and Culture of Success." *Organizational Dynamics* 23 (1): 17–29.

Schneider, B., and A. E. Reichers. 1983. "On the Etiology of Climates." *Personnel Psychology* 36: 19–39.

Smircich, L. 1983. "Concepts of Culture and Organizational Analysis." *Administrative Science Quarterly* 28: 339–58.

Trevino, L. K. 1986. "Ethical Decision Making in Organizations: A Person-Situation Interactionist Model." *Academy of Management Review* 11: 601–17.

————. 1990. "A Cultural Perspective on Changing and Developing Organizational Ethics." *Research in Organizational Change and Development* 4: 195–230.

Trevino, L. K., and G. A. Ball. 1992. "The Social Implications of Punishing Unethical Behavior: Observers' Cognitive and Affective Reactions." *Journal of Management* 18: 751–68.

Trevino, L. K., and S. A. Youngblood. 1990. "Bad Apples in Bad Barrels: A Causal Analysis of Ethical Decision-Making Behavior." *Journal of Applied Psychology* 75: 378–85.

Victor, B., and J. B. Cullen. 1987. "A Theory and Measure of Ethical Climate in Organizations." In *Research in Corporate Social Performance and Policy*, edited by W. C. Frederick, 51–71. Greenwich, CT: JAI Press.

————. 1988. "The Organizational Bases of Ethical Work Climates." *Administrative Science Quarterly*. 33: 101–25.

Weber, J. 1995. "Influences upon Organizational Ethical Subclimates: A Multi-departmental Analysis of a Single Firm." *Organization Science* 6 (5): 509–23.

Wimbush, J. C., and J. M. Shepard. 1994. "Toward an Understanding of Ethical Climate: Its Relationship to Ethical Behavior and Supervisory Influence." *Journal of Business Ethics* 13: 637–47.

Weaver, G., and L. Trevino. 1994. "Normative and Empirical Business Ethics." *Business Ethics Quarterly* 4 (3): 129–44.

Annotated Bibliography

Hicks, H., and C. Gullett. 1975. *Organizations: Theory and Behavior.* New York: McGraw-Hill. Chapter six probes the informal aspect of organizations and is wonderfully clear and insightful on the basic concepts needed to understand this dimension.

Nash, L. 1990. *Good Intentions Aside.* Boston: Harvard Business School Press. A clear and practical presentation of the informal culture of organizational covenant.

Ritti, R., and G. Funkhouser. 1997. *The Ropes to Skip and the Ropes to Know: Studies in Organizational Behavior.* Columbus, OH: Grid. Probably the most realistic, fun-filled, and enlightening exposé of the informal nature of organizations in print.

Tenbrunsel, A. 1998. "Misrepresentation and Expectations of Misrepresentation in an Ethical Dilemma: The Role of Incentives and Temptation." *Academy of Management Journal* 41 (3): 330–39. A good example of organizational ethics analysis using informal, cultural constructs.

Trevino, L., and B. Victor. 1992. "Peer Reporting of Unethical Behavior." *Academy of Management Journal* 35 (1): 38–64. A particularly important analysis given compliance programs' emphasis on peer reporting.

Victor, B., and J. Cullen. 1988. "The Organizational Bases of Ethical Work Climates." *Administrative Sciences Quarterly* 33 (1): 101–25. Still among the best insights to the informal nature of organizations.

Weick, K. 1979. *The Social Psychology of Organizing.* New York: Random House. The classic and still illuminating study of organizational culture.

4

CONFLICTS OF INTEREST AND ORGANIZATIONAL ETHICS

A MONG THE more widely recognized issues of organizational ethics in healthcare has been the conflict of interest concern. What does "conflict of interest" entail, how do ethics deliberations apply to it, and what can organizations do to facilitate ethical handling of situations that are subject to conflict of interest problems? These are the questions we probe through the following case and reading.

CASE STUDY

Case Four: Mr. Roger's Neighborhood

Roger is manager of the purchasing department at St. Serena's. As a 15-year veteran employee he has experienced numerous changes at the facility and over the years has developed many helpful relationships both with administrators at St. Serena's and with vendors and suppliers. He is an avid basketball fan. In his managerial position he is responsible for millions of dollars in annual purchases at St. Serena's. His decision making is often complicated by realities on two sides: On the one hand, healthcare providers pressure him to have items readily available, and sometimes to have certain manufacturer-specific items. His decisions not only affect the financial well-being of vendors and suppliers, but also the quality and timeliness of healthcare provided at St. Serena's.

Recognizing the importance and sensitivity of not only Roger's decisions but also those of other professionals and executives in the corporation, St. Serena's code of conduct includes a whole section dealing with conflicts of interest. Among its provisions are the following:

Section I.2: Employees must avoid situations in which their personal interests, or the interests of immediate family members or close relatives, would conflict, or reasonably appear to conflict, with the interests of the corporation. An example of conflict of interest is an opportunity for personal gain apart from the normal compensation provided through employment.

Section I.2.a: All employees have a continuing obligation to fully and accurately disclose any and all interests and activities that are in conflict with or may potentially conflict with or that may create the appearance of a conflict with their obligations and responsibilities to the St. Serena's corporation.

Section I.4.c: No employee may accept or solicit gifts of money under any circumstances, nor may they solicit non-monetary gifts, gratuities, or any other personal benefit or favor of any kind from St. Serena's suppliers or clients. Employees may accept unsolicited non-monetary gifts from a business firm or individual doing or seeking business with St. Serena's only if the gift has a value of $100 or less. . . . Any entertainment offered or accepted should be a reasonable extension of a business relationship.

Over the years Roger has developed a relationship with Phil Fellows, who represents a major pharmaceutical company. Many times over the years Phil has helped Roger by providing materials that were temporarily in short supply; and over the years Roger's purchasing decisions have resulted in Phil being St. Serena's major supplier of pharmaceutical products. Through this interaction Phil and Roger have developed a working business relationship. They have also become friends.

This year Roger's alma mater, Sam Houston Institute of Technology, produced an extraordinary basketball team. When they made it to the Final Four and the NCAA site for the games was the Michael Jordan Arena near St. Serena's, Roger desperately hoped to get tickets to the game. None were to be found. The $90 tickets were being scalped for $750, and even these were impossible to come by. Knowing of Roger's basketball addiction and zeal for his alma mater, Phil called the night before the game offering Roger a ticket that had become available in the company. Roger was thrilled!

Phil and Roger had terrific seats and watched Sam Houston Tech upset the favorite in its semi-final game. Also at the game was Pat Pauper, the local representative of a small pharmaceutical firm that for years had been trying to garner more of St. Serena's business. When Pat saw Roger at the game and recognized Phil with him, he again realized his competitive disadvantage. Pat's small firm could little afford to host customers at such an expensive event. He wondered whether he should speak to someone about the situation, but feared that any complaints would get back to Roger and thus make increasing his business with St. Serena's even more difficult.

Questions for Discussion:

1. Was it ethical for Roger to accept the ticket to the game? If yes, why? If no, what should he have done?
2. What, if anything, is likely to happen if Pat reports what he saw to the CEO of St. Serena's?
3. What formal organizational mechanisms are in place for situations like that described? Are they adequate? What additional organizational mechanisms might help?
4. What informal realities are at play in the situation?
5. Is Roger's situation a macro or a micro matter? (To phrase the question another way, what's the big deal here?)

COMMENTARY

Roger was surely excited at the chance of going to the game. Who wouldn't be? He also knew that although the ticket was worth $750 on the street, its face value of $90 was within the $100 limit specified in the code of conduct. Further, he did not solicit the ticket, at least not directly. Still, we might wonder whether emotion or reason carried the day when he was offered the seat. To him was it a personal matter or an institutional matter?

Did Roger commit a code violation given the actual value of the ticket? Did St. Serena's fail in its ethics structure by not defining the basis of "value"? Was this game a "reasonable extension" of a business relationship? Once again, let us get help from basic concepts as we reflect on the issue.

Nature of Conflict of Interest

Just what is meant by a conflict of interest anyway? St. Serena's code seems to define it as a situation in which personal benefits encounter tension with corporate interests. Has Roger's option for his personal interest in basketball undermined the corporate interests of St. Serena's? Would the institution be getting a better deal were Roger not so beholden to Phil? Legalists have defined conflict of interest as "any influence, loyalty, or other concern" capable of compromising a professional's ability to meet professional obligations: "Conflict of interest is a matter of professional judgment, a problem of arranging things so that competent judgment can function as it ordinarily does."[1] Is Roger's professional judgment in purchasing decisions compromised by the influence of basketball tickets from a supplier? He would adamantly deny any influence on business decisions, as would most of us. Is that a clear or a clouded perception?

Business analysts attempt to clarify the notion by distinguishing "conflicting interests" from "conflicts of interest," the former being situations of competing considerations that are presumed to be legitimate; the latter being situations of role competition deemed inappropriate: "Because of the potential for abuse, performing both roles simultaneously is considered inappropriate, even if the individual has good intentions, never exploits the conflict, and does not harm anyone."[2] Is Roger's situation a matter of conflicting interests (alma mater basketball and St. Serena's business) or conflict of interest (the best purchasing decisions for the institution versus friendship with Phil and admission to the Final Four?)

George Khushf, in a brilliant article challenging existing paradigms, argues that the traditional understanding of conflict of interest stressed fiduciary interests of individual healthcare providers but that today's healthcare arrangements make the notion of conflict of interest a different reality: "Medicine is no longer practiced by individuals," he contends, "it is practiced by institutions."[3] He thus maintains that conflict of interest now is a matter of healthcare professionals' roles and obligations interacting within an institutional setting. "To address conflicts of interest properly one must consider administrative and organizational ethics together with the ethics of the medical profession."[4] Furthermore, in this dialogue on conflict of interest, "institutions must emerge as the central focus of reflection."[5]

In the St. Serena's situation Khushf would certainly view the institution, not Roger, as the heart of the matter. Roger's friendship with Phil cannot be separated from the institutional setting through which it developed. What is St. Serena's doing, or what could it do, about endemic situations like that involving Roger, Phil, and Pat at the basketball game? That, according to Khushf, would be the primary question.

In any case, we can identify five hallmarks of the conflict of interest concept (see Figure 4.1). One, a conflict of interest always involves competing obligations of some sort. Roger's obligation to St. Serena's is obvious: The only reason he knows Phil and is in the position to

Figure 4.1 Hallmarks of Conflict of Interest

Competing Obligations

Appearance

Myopia

Fairness

Power

receive wonderful tickets is his official position in the organization. Less obvious, but no less existentially forceful, may be his sense of obligation to himself and to his friendship with Phil. After all, seeing his alma mater play in the Final Four is probably a once in a lifetime opportunity. Should he surrender that opportunity over an ambiguous provision in a corporate code of conduct? Further, he and Phil really have become friends. Should their relationship be compromised because of institutional interests?

Two, particularly in public service enterprises like healthcare, the mere appearance of impropriety constitutes a major facet of the conflict of interest notion. Even when absolutely no crossover occurs between business decisions and the receipt of coveted basketball tickets (or patient care in clinical situations), to most reasonable people the appearance of such a conflict exists. The well-being of St. Serena's patients is ultimately on the line even in purchasing decisions, therefore, can any chance be taken? The "appearance standard" says no. If you were a Sam Houston Tech alumnus, and heard about Roger getting tickets to the game from a company with which he does million-dollar business, would you be suspicious?

Three, conflict of interest seems to engender a cloudiness or myopia —if not outright blindness—in the conflicted person. More often than not, the one in the middle simply does not see things as those outside do. Does Roger appreciate the perspective of Pat? Would an ethics committee tend to view the situation in the same or similar manner as Roger? Do emotional involvements tend to cloud rational perception? Indeed, conflicts of interest have been so problematic because good and decent people have not been able to see an untowardness in their action when others have seen it clearly.

Four, a subtle but powerful element of the conflict of interest concept is the value of fairness. Decisions made and actions taken within a conflict of interest situation can be fundamentally unfair to some legitimate stakeholder. Advantages accrue to someone because a conflict of interest situation reduces the equal opportunity that would otherwise be available to others. This is precisely what bothers Pat Pauper in the St. Serena's situation.

Five, conflict of interest situations almost always entail some confusion around the fact of official authority and the reality of unofficial power. For example, Roger has the official organizational *authority* to make purchasing decisions, but he also has a lot of unofficial *power* over how those official decisions are made. Unless officially and specifically prohibited, he has the power to include informal social interactions in the process of doing his official job. Roger does have the power to ask for advice when situations arise although perhaps he is not officially required by authority to ask. Do you think he called St. Serena's legal counsel the night before the game? Did he call an ethics officer? Should he have called someone?

Formal Organization

These facets of conflict of interest can be addressed by both formal and informal organizational action. What structural organizational mechanisms are engaged in Roger's situation? What formal mechanisms might be helpful? St. Serena's seems to have a detailed written code of conduct that addresses the conflict of interest reality extensively. Does it also have a formal ethics committee? Does that committee deal only with clinical matters, or does it also probe business issues? Is there a formal procedure for contacting committee members—or an "ethics officer" for consultations when things like $90 basketball tickets enter the picture? Or would that be viewed culturally as too small (micro) a matter to warrant an ethics consultation? Is a telephone hotline available to Roger after he receives Phil's offer? In this vein we might also wonder whether St. Serena's code requires any formal permission in situations like the one Roger faced, and what the operational procedure is when last-minute situations like a ticket offer arise. Finally, there could be a structural requirement and mechanism for formally reporting acceptance of gifts that seem to fall within the guidelines.

Note that at the core of formal mechanisms is the notion of open dialogue before, during, and after conflict of interest situations arise. Vinicky, Edwards, and Orlowski emphasize this in the reading that follows this commentary. The importance of open dialogue stems from the elements of appearance, cloudiness, and power discussed above. The more dialogue that is opened the more likely conflict of interest situations will be ethically handled. At St. Serena's dialogue evidently took place *before* in the process of developing the code of conduct. Some ethics training in the conflict of interest area might also have been

Figure 4.2   Conflict of Interest Organizational Lens

	Corporate	Group	Individual
Formal			
Informal			

provided. But are there mechanisms for dialogue—such as hotlines and consultations—*during* such situations? And are there any mechanisms—such as reporting procedures and review processes—for dealing with conflict of interest situations *after* the fact? Are there, for example, audit mechanisms that monitor and review Roger's purchasing decisions precisely to discourage any favoritism? These are important formal organizational ethics questions.

Mark Rodwin, in his influential tome, *Medicine, Money and Morals*, takes a formal approach to the conflict of interest issue. He argues for direct regulation, contending that legal prohibitions on certain behaviors—such as pharmaceutical gift giving and accepting—is the way to go. He also calls for organizational monitoring and review mechanisms such as "conflict-of-interest review boards."[6]

The problem with sole reliance on the formal organizational approach, of course, is that it can lead to a legalism mentality in which anything not expressly prohibited is okay. Indeed, might it have been a formal and legalistic approach that led Roger to discern that, since the $90 face value of the ticket was within the $100 code limitation, acceptance was ethical? What might Pat say to this argument? Perhaps clear situations can be formally regulated, but subtleties can be hard to legislate.

Informal Organization

What informal organizational realities are at play in Roger's situation? What could St. Serena's do at the informal cultural level to better deal with the conflicts of interest issue? Let us adapt the organizational realities matrix to the conflict of interest issue. Figure 4.2 provides a lens for this analysis.

At the formal corporate level we have identified the code of conduct; at the formal group level we have suggested audit possibilities for the purchasing department; and at the formal individual level we have wondered about prohibiting purchasing agents from accepting any gifts. What about the informal level?

At the informal corporate level we might look at organizational norms and patterns of behavior. For example, are senior managers at St. Serena's enthusiastic golfers who regularly accept invitations to play at the clubs of business associates? Is this considered a "reasonable extension of a business relationship" (code Section I.4.c)? Do these senior managers report these rounds of golf in the spirit of code Section I.2.a? Would you guess that what they do here might affect Roger's perspective on the basketball tickets? Might the senior executives' example be important in determining how the formal code is to be interpreted?

At the informal group level we should note the apparent existence of the social group consisting of Roger, Phil, and probably others. Should St. Serena's recognize the reality of social groups like this and formally address their behavior? Finally, at the informal individual level, although Roger is the formally described purchasing manager, informally he has feelings. In this case those feelings include an emotional attachment to his alma mater, a love of basketball, and a friendship with Phil. Do those feelings count? Should their existence be recognized in any strategy by St. Serena's to deal with conflicts of interest? And what about Pat's real feelings including his apparent fear of reporting Roger? While analysts may tend to underplay the effect of informal realities, good business people never do. They recognize and deal with the reality of corporate norms, social groups, and individual feelings in doing business. They know that personal relationships, as opposed to merely official business relationships, go a long way in determining who gets what business. Is that not precisely why "wining and dining" is found extensively in corporate budgets? We organizational ethicists would do well to learn from the realistic perspective of practicing business people as we try to concoct effective means of advancing organizational ethics. For example, an organizational ethicist might analyze Roger's situation and recommend that any conflict of interest could be formally resolved by Roger paying Phil the $90 value of the ticket; but any shrewd business person is likely to respond that Roger's informal feeling of indebtedness to Phil will not diminish.

Self-Interest Versus Covenant

Finally, the concept of self interest versus covenant can be helpful in our analysis of conflicts of interest. St. Serena's apparent reliance on the "contract" it calls its code of conduct may have guided Roger's "contractual" approach to dealing with the tickets situation. Legally, Roger can surely argue that accepting the $90 ticket is not a conflict of interest given the $100 limit established in the code. This approach, coincidentally, serves his self-interest—he gets to go to the game of a lifetime. But this approach also seems to affect his relationship with Phil: It may increase their friendship bond and it certainly increases Roger's indebtedness to Phil. Roger's relationship with Pat seems to be negatively affected. Some might also contend that Roger's relationship with St. Serena's patients and with the community is affected. Had Roger taken a covenantal approach to the situation instead of the legalistic, contractual approach, his behavior might well have been different.

Notes

1. Davis, M. 1988. "Conflict of Interest: The Lawyer's Analysis." In *Ethical Theory and Business*, edited by T. Beauchamp and N. Bowie, 482–85. Englewood Cliffs, NJ: Prentice-Hall.
2. Margolis, J. 1979. "Conflicts of Interest and Conflicting Interests." In *Ethical Theory and Business*, edited by T. Beauchamp and N. Bowie, 361–72. Englewood Cliffs, NJ: Prentice-Hall.
3. Khushf, G. 1998. "A Radical Rupture in the Paradigm of Modern Medicine: Conflicts of Interest, Fiduciary Obligations, and the Scientific Ideal." *Journal of Medicine and Philosophy* 23 (1): 112.
4. *Ibid.*, 114.
5. *Ibid.*, 120.
6. Rodwin, M. 1993. *Medicine, Money and Morals.* Oxford, UK: Oxford University Press.

READING

The following article from a noted bioethics journal presents and analyzes several cases of conflict of interest in healthcare. The discussions illustrate the method that bioethicists can bring to bear on organizational ethics issues. Note that although no evident comprehensive framework is used, the authors implicitly employ the concepts of formal and informal organizational realities. Their solutions seem to emphasize formal mechanisms such as written guidelines and institutional procedures, but their analyses inevitably confront informal realities such as the power (as opposed to formal authority) of the Health Maintenance Organization (HMO) physicians in the second case; furthermore, consistent in their approach is an emphasis on dialogue, openness, and communication—all factors in organizational culture. How would they analyze Roger's situation? What kinds of questions would they likely ask?

The authors correctly observe that "an ever-changing healthcare system in which hospitals and physicians contract for services, and in which group insurers contract with hospitals and groups of physicians" means that organizational ethics issues such as conflicts of interest will become more and more significant. Organization ethics analysis such as demonstrated in these discussions will become part and parcel of healthcare organizational reality.

Conflicts of Interest, Conflicting Interests, and Interesting Conflicts

Janicemarie K. Vinicky, Sue Shevlin
Edwards, and James P. Orlowski*

The role of clinical bioethics consultation is inevitably changing as the delivery of healthcare from various providers and systems of providers evolves, and it is our opinion that "conflicts of interest" will become part and parcel of the day-to-day business of the ethics consultant and ethics committee. Even the new edition of the *Encyclopedia of Bioethics* has an index entry on conflict of interest that had not appeared in the prior edition (1978).[1] This entry, written by E. Haavi Morreim, quite adequately addresses conflicts of interest concerning one's obligation to a particular person or group, and also addresses issues of third-party payers, institutional providers, private industry, physicians' investments, and the legal system. This section also thoughtfully addresses notions of conflicts of interest in the research setting as they relate to institutions, physicians, and other health professionals. And although much more has been written on such conflicts in the arenas of business ethics and professional ethics, we are of the opinion that those of us who do ethics consultation ought to become familiar with some of the types of conflicts of interest that already face us, and with those likely to arise in an ever-changing healthcare system in which hospitals and physicians contract for services and in which group insurers contract with hospitals and groups of physicians. We will consider a variety of situations that involve these sorts of conflicts as a means to begin the dialogue in a series of

Reprinted with permission from The Journal of Clinical Ethics 1995. 6 (4): 358–66; 1996. 7 (1): 69–76; and 1996. 7 (2): 184–86. Copyright 1995–1996 by The Journal of Clinical Ethics. Janicemarie K. Vinicky is director of the department of bioethics at the Washington D. C. Hospital Center. Sue Shevlin Edwards is coordinator of the department of bioethics at the Washington D. C. Hospital Center. James P. Orlowski is medical director of pediatric intensive care at University Community Hospital and professor of pediatrics and medical ethics at the University of South Florida, Tampa.

articles in this and the next two issues of *The Journal of Clinical Ethics.* We were asked to consult on these cases both within and outside of our respective institutions, and we have had long and analytic discussions regarding them.

Part 1

In the present article we will discuss two cases. The first case involves an author who was a member of an international Commission on Classification who submitted a manuscript to the international society for the study of this disorder for publication in its journal at the invitation of its editor. The author's manuscript was rejected, and she was accused of unethical behavior. The Commission, like every organization, had goals, missions, and norms—stated and tacit—that created conflicts of interest within the organization.[2] When a member of an organization unknowingly steps into an organizationally created, but hidden area of conflicting interests, can she credibly be reprimanded and charged with unethical behavior? Is it ethical for a body to reprimand a member who fails to meet its unstated expectations?

The second case involves the conflicts surrounding the treatment of an elderly patient in an HMO clinic, the rotating attending physicians at the clinic, the "real" attending physician, and the HMO, which had narrowly defined the roles and responsibilities of the various players.

Background on Conflicts of Interest

Before launching into specifics, we will provide some general background on conflict of interest for the professions. Conflicts of interest have been defined in many settings and for many professions. It is clear that a conflict of interest is, to some extent, in the eyes of the beholder. In the legal profession, for instance, distinctions are made between having a conflict of interest (potential, latent, or actual) and acting in a conflict of interest situation. The American Bar Association's Code of Professional Responsibility is probably the most lengthy and specific professional code on this issue:

> 'Interest' [in the ABA Code] is just shorthand for any influence, loyalty, or other concern capable of compromising a lawyer's ability to act for the benefit of his client (within the bounds of his role as a lawyer). . . . Conflict of interest is a matter of professional judgment, a problem of arranging things so that competent judgment can function as it ordinarily does. The 'conflict' of conflict of interest is a collision between competent judgment and something that might make that judgment unable to function as a lawyer's

role requires. . . . The Code understands a conflict of interest to require only (a) one relatively formal role (with occupants), the role of being someone's lawyer, and (b) at least one interest tending to interfere with acting properly in that role.[3]

In the world of business ethics, Joseph Margolis distinguishes between conflicting interests and conflicts of interest in the following way:

The former occur in any situation where competing considerations are presumed to be legitimate. Conflicts of interest, on the other hand, are characterized by an individual occupying dual roles which should not be performed simultaneously. Because of the potential for abuse, performing both roles simultaneously is considered inappropriate, even if the individual has good intentions, never exploits the conflict, and does not harm anyone.[4]

In the context of research ethics, Roger J. Porter informs us that the oldest definition of a conflict of interest is also the best:

'No one can serve two masters, for either he will hate the one and love the other, or he will be devoted to one and despise the other. You cannot serve God and mammon' (Matthew 6:24). A person with a conflict of interest has two masters to serve, and these two masters do not always have coincident needs. . . . It is also an oversimplification to say that scientific motivations are always in conflict when two masters are served. When the two masters appear to have coincident interests, then the conflict may best be described as a potential conflict of interest. Theoretically, at least, the two masters must have divergent interests in the same endeavor for conflict to be present. Unfortunately, the boundaries of what is a potential conflict of interest and what is a genuine conflict of interest are fuzzy and in the eye of the beholder. Investigators who wish to downplay a conflict of interest in their research often refer to the serving of two masters as a 'potential' problem, whereas others—perhaps more objectively—may simply call it a 'conflict of interest.'[5]

Thus, there is again a "fuzziness" of description and perception. Some have written more generally on conflicts of interest in the medical setting. One hospital task force, convened to consider the issue of inappropriate gifts, used a definition set forth by the British Medical Association, a simple statement asking only, "Would you be willing to have these arrangements [this situation] generally known?"[6] At the Cleveland Clinic, a task force was formed to determine appropriate and ethically justifiable policy on the notion of conflicts of interest in the healthcare setting. That task force described a conflict of interest as "a discrepancy between the personal interests and the professional responsibilities of a person in a position of trust."[7]

In his book *Medicine, Money and Morals*, Marc A. Rodwin suggests that although much lip service has been given to the notion of conflicts of interest for physicians, there is a paucity of analysis of such issues:

As yet, no efforts have been made to identify systematically the existing range of physicians' conflicts of interest, to analyze their similarities and differences, or to suggest which of these are of particular concern to society. The literature generally assumes that these issues should be left to the individual physician and resolved through informal means or through professional self regulation. . . . Moreover, no studies have compared the problems of physicians with the experience of other professionals or with policies and problems in other countries. The lack of a generally accepted analytic framework for approaching physicians' conflict of interest hampers the development of effective social policy.[8]

For individual physicians, guidelines on conflicts of interest have been proposed by the American Medical Association's Council on Ethical and Judicial Affairs, which states:

Under no circumstances may physicians place their own financial interests above the welfare of their patients. The primary objective of the medical profession is to render service to humanity; reward or financial gain is a subordinate consideration. For a physician unnecessarily to hospitalize a patient, prescribe a drug, or conduct diagnostic tests for the physician's financial interest is unethical. If a conflict develops between the physician's financial interest and the physician's responsibilities to the patient, the conflict must be resolved to the patient's benefit.[9] (II)

We will consider these definitions of conflict of interest in the following two cases and in two cases in two subsequent articles, as described above.

Case One

Dr. A was the chair of a specialty department at a tertiary care hospital, and had been invited to sit on an international Commission on Classification for a particular disorder. The editor of the journal of the official society for this disorder had invited Dr. A to submit a manuscript (MS) that described "Dr. A's classification" of the disorder. The MS was rejected according to Dr. A, not because of "technical arguments," but because the individuals who had been selected to peer review the article for the journal stated that it was inappropriate (even unethical) for a member of the Commission on Classification to "publish her opinion on matters that will be discussed by the Commission" in the future. Dr. A had approached the chairman of the bioethics committee at her hospital for an ethical opinion; the chairman referred Dr. A to the first author of this article because the chairman believed an outside ethical opinion was most appropriate. Dr. A spoke with the authors and provided us with various documents and resources that we used to form our reactions and analysis.

Dr. A said that she was interested in having "her classification" published in another journal, as it had been rejected by her journal of choice, but she was concerned that publication of the MS elsewhere could be considered unethical, especially because she was a member of the Commission on Classification.

We spoke with Dr. A and used her documentation in our analysis, addressing the following concerns: When and why was Dr. A appointed to the Commission? What role were members of the Commission expected to play? Were Dr. A's opinions and previous publications relevant to her membership on the Commission and in its activities, and how were they relevant? How was "ethical behavior" defined in light of the allegations against Dr. A, which revolved around what the peer reviewers alleged to be a conflict of interest?

Comments on professional ethics, values, and biases in research.

As professionals, the authors of this article have frequently had the opportunity to review articles for peer-reviewed professional journals. In this role, we believe it is appropriate for us to comment on the content of the MS to be reviewed (whether or not we agree with the author's or authors' position) and on the appropriateness of the article for the journal. We believe that a sound article that is likely to provoke discussion should be published; in some sense, professionals are in the business of challenging the status quo (in science, applied philosophy, or clinical bioethics) for the good of society.

Most ethical codes recognize the responsibility of professionals to enhance the public good. As Bayles stated in *Professional Ethics,*

> Responsibility for the public good has three main facets. First are activities of social leadership, such as service with charitable organizations, government commissions, and so on. . . . A second facet of responsibility for public good is the improvement of professional knowledge, tools and skills. . . . A third facet of this responsibility is to preserve and enhance the role of the profession itself.[10]

Generally speaking, the physician's professional responsibilities for the public good occur as they perform and publish their research or as they care for their patients. In either instance, the primary responsibilities of researchers and clinicians are candor and independence. As Bayles noted "Few people would dispute that researchers must be candid and independent in their judgments. The purpose of research is to discover the truth. A lack of candor or independence thwarts this purpose."[11]

Further, what is the role of values in science? A major socially relevant value in science is the desire to do accurate work. However, one cannot deny that every individual comes to his or her scientific endeavor with his or her own set of values and personal biases. As the Committee on the Conduct of Science of the National Academy of Science noted in *On Being a Scientist,* although scientists have developed criteria by which more promising scientific hypotheses may be distinguished from those which are less promising, "those values relate to the epistemological, or knowledge based, criteria applied to hypotheses. But, values of a different kind can also come into play in science. Historians, sociologists, and other students of science have shown that social and personal values unrelated to epistemological criteria—including philosophical, religious, cultural, political, and economic values—can shape scientific judgment in fundamental ways."[12]

Although such values tend to influence science and scientific progress, peer review by one's colleagues in the field tends to minimize such influences. Publication in a peer-reviewed journal remains the standard means of disseminating scientific information. The Committee on the Conduct of Science continued, "This process of public, systematic skepticism is critical in science. It minimizes the influence of subjectivity by requiring that research results be accepted by other scientists. It also is a powerful inducement for researchers to be critical of their own conclusions, because they know that their objective must be to convince their ablest colleagues, including those with contrasting views."[13]

Observations on the peer-review process.

Regarding Dr. A's case, it seemed apparent that she had acted in accordance with the basic "rules" of scientific investigation and publication when she submitted her definitive MS on the classification of this disorder to be published in the premiere peer-reviewed journal—at the invitation of the editor of the journal. It was, however, less apparent that the peer reviewers gave the MS a fair peer review.

When we read the reviews of Dr. A's MS, we saw a great deal of emotion, and little, if any, comment on its scientific content. One reviewer spent an entire paragraph explaining what the current chair of the Commission might "feel" if this MS were to be published. The reviewer spent one sentence attesting to the need for a revision of the current classification, another sentence suggesting that "everyone would be best served if these ideas could be incorporated in a revision of the Classification" rather than be published in the organization's peer-reviewed journal, and another expressing the concern that the Commission "will have the wisdom to do this." This reviewer did comment, in less than one sentence, on the scientific/technical content of the article: "There is equally little doubt that the ideas and suggestions of the physician in this respect are most valuable and should receive all possible attention." The reviewer went on to state that he or she would strongly disfavor publication of the proposed classification. In sum, there was little peer review and a great deal about the feelings of the current chair of the Commission regarding the MS.

The second reviewer revealed an even greater amount of concern and emotion regarding the potential publication of Dr. A's classification in the journal at that particular time. The concern expressed by this reviewer was entirely one of what he/she perceived to be "a maverick performance" with an "ethical allegation" regarding what the reviewer described as a conflict of interest on the part of Dr. A. This reviewer perceived "the present opus as a flagrant attempt to preempt the work of the Commission by one of its members." The reviewer went on to state that he or she "would not presume to abridge the authors' First Amendment rights but while persons are members of a duly appointed Commission they have the responsibility of refraining from clearly conflicting interests vis-à-vis those of the Commission particularly when using the vehicle wherein to publish."

The then editor-in-chief of the society's journal decided, "after considerable thought and discussion," to reject Dr. A's MS for publication, and apologized that "what [I] had naively anticipated to be a simple matter turned out to be far more complicated and to have more political and other complications than [I] had foreseen."

Based only on this data, it appeared to us that this MS received a review and subsequent rejection for publication based on an acknowledged political agenda, rather than on scientific peer review of its content. From an ethical perspective, we wondered whether the peer reviewers reviewed this MS using the same criteria they would use for other submissions to the journal. We wondered if the reviewers had an interest that conflicted with a fair review of the MS. If there was a "conflict of interest" in Dr. A's role on behalf of the Commission on Classification and in her role as an author who subjected her classification to peer review by the society's journal, there was also a conflict of interest for the peer reviewers: fair review of Dr. A's MS versus their interest in protecting the role of the Commission and the feelings of its chairman.

Specific case-related issues and ethical analyses.

Dr. A had already published an article in another journal that briefly described her perspective on her proposed classification. Following (and perhaps unrelated to) that publication, she was appointed to the Commission on Classification. As described above, Dr. A submitted her

MS for peer review and publication, and it was rejected by the editor with apologies regarding the complex and "political" nature of its rejection.

If Dr. A had a conflict of interest in having developed a scientifically based and well-researched classification, the conflict was well known by the commissioners prior to her appointment to the Commission. Thus, the allegation of a conflict of interest on the part of Dr. A could not be supported, as her interests and actions were previously disclosed, were known, and were accepted by at least the then-current president of the Commission who had appointed Dr. A. Someone (the president of the society at least) must have thought that Dr. A's position on classification would be a benefit rather than a liability to the Commission. Even the editor of the journal did not perceive the publication of Dr. A's classification in the journal to be a conflict of interest. Also, some of her colleagues must have respected her position on classification, or there would have been little justification (other than perhaps the "old-boy" network, or the buddy system) for her appointment to the Commission. It was also plausible (although it would have been scientifically small-minded) that this physician was placed on the Commission to dissuade her from further independent publication or discussion regarding her proposed classification. The latter would have been unethical on the part of the Commission, as its stated mandate included a review of the classification in light of scientific advances.

The appointment of Dr. A to the Commission and the subsequent rejection of her MS could also be viewed (as one of the reviewers of the article stated) as an infringement of Dr. A's First Amendment rights, as an attempt to try to silence her about her personal professional opinion on classification while she sat as a member of the Commission. This type of behavior could not have been representative of the behavior of the Commission on Classification or of the peer-review process of the society's journal. We would expect that both the workings of the Commission and the peer-review process of the journal should easily pass the British Medical Association's litmus test: scrutiny by the public.

However, to be fair, we considered it to be possible, as one of the reviewers did, that Dr. A's publication and scientific defense of her own classification could conflict with her requisite collegial role as a member of the Commission. In this scenario, Dr. A could have intended to set forth her own criteria as definitive, and to sit as a closed-minded, non-collaborative Commission member incapable of open-minded, critical science. If this had been the case, Dr. A's loyalty to her own scientific research would have been in serious conflict with her duty to sit as a member of a commission whose goal was to set forth a scientifically supportable, current, revised classification that was consistent with some degree of scientific opinion. It would also have been necessary to see Dr. A's two "masters" (loyalty to herself and her publication and her work as a member of the Commission) as having diverse goals rather than coinciding goals.

It was our perception, based upon our review of the previously discussed documents and facts, that the work of the Commission (to reclassify a disorder via a consensus based on current knowledge) and the personal professional work of Dr. A (her classification) were not, at face value, in conflict. Both were trying to achieve the same goal, but with differing views of the process by which the classification ought to occur. One could argue that, as the Commission continued to exist with the mandate of reclassification, the most appropriate forum for submission and presentation of proposed new classifications was directly and only to the Commission. We believed that this view failed to support the standard approach to scientific review by the broadest representation of one's peers, namely publication in a well-respected, peer-reviewed journal. One could also have been concerned that the masses might have become confused if multiple and diverse classifications were to be proposed by peer professionals, and that such confusion could have negatively affected communication and research throughout the world, justifying the control that was exerted by the Commission on Classification. This view, in our opinion, would not be consistent with the workings of many commissions, which require broad representation and diversity of views and which frequently present reports of their work that include the views of those who are in dissent. An example of this is *Are Scientific Misconduct and Conflicts of Interest Hazardous to Our Health?*—the 19th Report by the Committee on Government Operations together with dissenting and additional views.[14]

Conclusions Regarding Case One

Both the Commission and Dr. A had some weighty decisions about how to proceed. The following are what we perceived to be the ethically supportable options:

1. Dr. A could resubmit her article to the society's journal, requesting a fair review by experts who did not sit on the Commission on Classification and who would not be influenced by its members.

2. Dr. A could resign from the Commission, resubmit her article to the society's journal, requesting a fair review by non-Commission members. By doing so, even the

"appearance" of a conflict of interest would be removed (although the journal could again reject her article).

3. Dr. A could choose to submit her MS to another well-respected peer-reviewed journal, and disclose her intent to the Commission on Classification. Since this type of action could be politically volatile, and could "appear" to be in conflict with her role as a Commission member, it may or may not have proven to be acceptable to the Commissioners. If the Commissioners were to perceive Dr. A's behavior as being in conflict with her duty to the Commission (and it is possible that they could, depending on their notion of conflict), they would likely inform her of their position and its justification and offer her these options:

    A. Retract her classification while sitting as a Commission member;

    B. Add a disclaimer to her classification (that is, "this does not in any way represent the views of the Commission"); or

    C. Ask that she resign from the Commission. Such an action would, in our opinion, require a majority vote of the members of the Commission and perhaps a hearing at some higher level (the board of the society?). Such an action, we would assume, would be based upon "rules of professional conduct," either for members of the society or for members of the Commission.

4. Another option is that Dr. A could choose to remain a member of the Commission on Classification and decide not to publish her classification, but rather submit her classification to the Commission for its scrutiny, scientific review, and incorporation into its work as a commission on classification. This would mean that Dr. A would relinquish her intellectual property rights to the classification and allow it to become the intellectual property of the Commission. In this way, all appearances of a conflict of interest would definitely be put to rest.

In our opinion, many assumptions were made about Dr. A's participation as a Commission member. She did not receive any information either in the materials provided to her by the Commission or in any memo stating that there were restrictions placed upon her as a professional researcher while she sat as a member of the Commission. There was no evidence that she had been explicitly informed of some Commission "policy" that required that all Commission members were to refrain from publishing an article in any journal on either terminology or classification. It sounded to us, however, as though there may have been some unspoken "understanding" among the Commission members that such publications ought not occur; we were unclear about the bases for such an assumption.

It is our opinion that since Dr. A was not asked, nor did she promise, not to publish specifically on the issue of classification while sitting as a member of the Commission, there was no logically supportable reason for her to refrain from doing so. We suggested that she submit the article on classification to another well-respected, peer-reviewed journal and that she inform the Commission of her intent to do so. We also recommended that she add a disclaimer to her article stating that these opinions were hers and did not represent the views of the Commission.

As Dr. A had made no promises not to publish on the classification (at least as far as we knew), it was certainly ethically preferable that she maximize the good that could come out of this rather difficult situation. Therefore, if she could achieve both the publication of her classification scheme in some other well-respected, peer-reviewed journal, thus making her ideas accessible to a broad spectrum of professionals for review, as well as continue to sit as a collegial Commission member who was willing to consider and critique other classifications, then she, her co-authors, the Commission, and society at large were likely to benefit.

Case Two

A bioethics consultation was requested regarding a patient who belonged to a local HMO. The patient, Mrs. N, was a 77-year-old married African American woman. At the time of this admission, the patient's diagnoses included acute renal failure and a past medical history of diabetes mellitus (30+ years), multiple cerebrovascular accidents resulting in quadriplegia and blindness, and Stage IV ovarian cancer. Mrs. N was extremely obese and was aphasic, although she could clearly render "yes" and "no" answers according to her family, her nurses, and her physicians. Upon admission she was placed on dialysis, although she consistently told her primary HMO physician that she wanted dialysis stopped and that she wanted to be allowed to die. Although she was judged to be competent by a psychiatric evaluation, the patient's family was opposed to her stopping dialysis and consistently demanded that it be performed.

Like all patients belonging to this HMO, Mrs. N had a new hospital attending physician each week. This gave the family multiple individuals from whom to demand continued dialysis. As one might expect, bioethics consultation attempts with the multiple providers were a miserable failure. One physician clearly informed the family members that Mrs. N was not "really" his patient, but was rather another physician's responsibility. "You see," he said, "we all have our own clinic patients with whom we have developed a relationship. When we're on hospital service, we cover everyone's hospital patients—even if we don't know what their wishes are. We barely have time to talk with the primary attending of each of these patients once a week. Sometimes we're lucky if it happens at all." Meanwhile, the nurses at Mrs. N's bedside were feeling morally stressed by the daily overriding of her current and previously expressed wishes. One nurse decided to call Mrs. N's "real" attending physician, Dr. B, to determine what Dr. B's perceptions of Mrs. N's wishes were. The nurse felt that he needed to express to Dr. B his concerns regarding this competent patient whose wishes were being overridden because no physician who wasn't the patient's "real" attending was willing to withdraw dialysis and allow Mrs. N to die.

Finally, Dr. B asked for a bioethics consultation to see what could be done. When the bioethics consultant spoke with her by phone, Dr. B said that she felt a serious conflict between her obligations to her patients in clinic and to her patients who really needed her in the hospital. She was a working mother who could not spend evenings and early mornings caring for her hospitalized patients. In addition, she had been led to believe that this system was supposed to work. Dr. B went to her medical director at the HMO to express her concerns, and was informed that this was really a colleague-to-colleague communication problem. In other words, it was up to Dr. B to communicate the long- and short-range goals for each of her patients to the hospital attending physician of the week. Dr. B informed her medical director that even when she did have those conversations, her colleagues were unwilling to call family meetings, especially if there was a life-sustaining therapy to be withheld or withdrawn or if "bad news" was to be given.

Dr. B felt a serious conflict of interest in two areas. First, she felt that her clinic requirements in terms of numbers of patients seen allowed little, if any, time to communicate with her colleagues about her hospitalized patients. She also felt what she called a conflict of interest regarding the care of her hospitalized patients. She felt that although she was assured that her patients in the hospital were well cared for by her colleagues, she had the ultimate responsibility for their care. Families of her hospitalized patients would frequently call her in the clinic to get information on their loved one, since the "doc of the week" hadn't spoken with them.

In this case, Dr. B agreed to meet with Mrs. N, Mrs. N's family members, and members of the bioethics consult team on her own time after clinic. This meeting was, at best, difficult to arrange. However, once it had been arranged, Mrs. N was encouraged to express her wishes in front of both her family and the bioethics consult team as well as in front of her primary caregivers. Mrs. N had expressed her desire for no heroic measures years ago in the "real" attending physician's office, and this note was also brought to everyone's attention. After this discussion, the dialysis was stopped and Mrs. N was allowed to die. This was accomplished, however, after a 33-day hospital stay and at least four different hospital bedside attending physicians. Only Dr. B was willing to place herself in a potentially adversarial relationship with Mrs. N's family, perhaps because she was the only physician who had attempted to establish and maintain any sort of significant physician-patient relationship.

Conclusions Regarding Case Two

Whether one chooses to categorize this case as a conflict of interest or as a conflict of obligation, it is apparent that the changing nature of the healthcare system and of provider/patient relationships is causing the duties and obligations of physicians to their patients to come into question. Did Dr. B really have a conflict of interest? Weren't her interests coincident with those of Mrs. N? They were not, however, consistent with the duties required of her at her place of employment.

Conflicts of interest affect providers pervasively, powerfully, and personally. Where once the fiduciary duty consisted mainly in refraining from vulgar exploitation, the obligation to place the patient's best interest before one's own can no longer be an unlimited obligation. Providers must exercise great care to avoid conflicts where possible, and to uphold a strong fiduciary presumption to favor patient's interests over their own. However, they cannot be expected routinely to commit professional self-sacrifice in an often futile unilateral attempt to battle economic forces beyond their control. Therefore, one of the most important and difficult moral challenges of medicine's new economics is to consider not just what providers owe their patients, but also the limits of those obligations.[15] It appears that the further physicians move from their place at the bedside and the more they enter into confusing employer/employee relationships, the more these questions arise. As to whether they are actual conflicts of interest or more appropriately categorized as conflicts of obligation, they are not usually in any single patient's best interest, as this case so vividly illustrates.

Final Remarks

As can be seen from the preceding discussions, cases and issues involving allegations of a "conflict of interest" are not black and white; at the very least, they are varying shades of gray. Whether the situation at hand involves a conflict of interest, the appearance of conflict of interest, or a conflict of obligation; or involves acting in a situation where the potential for conflict of interest exists, is sometimes in the eyes of the beholder. However, some very real conflict situations do exist, and these situations require accurate identification and careful analysis. Issues concerning conflicts of interest are just beginning to be recognized in the clinical ethics arena. It is our opinion that as organizational ethics issues become "part and parcel" of ethics consultation, knowledge of how to appropriately identify and address such conflicts will become even more essential. These issues will be discussed in the next two articles in this series.

Notes

1. Reich, W. T. (ed.). 1994. *Encyclopedia of Bioethics*, vol. 5, 2nd ed., 2876. New York: Simon and Schuster Macmillan.
2. For example, the case of the AMA and managed care described in Miles, S. H., and R. Koepp. 1995. "Comments on the AMA Report, Ethical Issues in Managed Care." *The Journal of Clinical Ethics* 6 (4).
3. Davis, M. 1988. "Conflict of Interest: The Lawyer's Analysis," In *Ethical Theory and Business*, 3rd ed., edited by T. L. Beauchamp and N. E. Bowie, 482–85. Englewood Cliffs, NJ: Prentice-Hall.
4. Margolis, J. 1979. "Conflict of Interest and Conflicting Interests." In *Ethical Theory and Business*, 1st ed., edited by T. L. Beauchamp and N. E. Bowie, 361–72. Englewood Cliffs, NJ: Prentice-Hall.
5. Porter, R. J. 1992. "Conflicts of Interest in Research: The Fundamentals." In *Biomedical Research: Collaboration and Conflict of Interest*, edited by R. E. Porter and T. E. Malone, 125–26. Baltimore, MD: Johns Hopkins University Press.
6. Royal College of Physicians. 1986. "The Relationship Between Physicians and the Pharmaceutical Industry." *Journal of the Royal College of Physicians of London* 20 (4): 235–42.
7. Orlowski, J. P. 1994. "The HEC and Conflicts of Interest in the Health Care Environment." *HEC Forum* 6 (1): 3–11.
8. Rodwin, M. A. 1993. *Medicine, Money and Morals*, 254–55. Oxford, UK: Oxford University Press.
9. AMA Council on Ethical and Judicial Affairs. 1994. *Code of Medical Ethics: Current Opinions with Annotations*, 99. Chicago: American Medical Association.
10. Bayles, M. D. 1981. *Professional Ethics*, 109–11. Belmont, CA: Wadsworth Publishing.
11. *Ibid.*, 111–12.
12. National Academy of Science, Committee on the Conduct of Science. 1989. *On Being a Scientist*, 6–7. Washington, D. C.: National Academy Press.
13. *Ibid.*, 10.
14. Orlowski, "The HEC and Conflicts of Interest," 3.
15. Morreim, E. H., " Conflict of Interest." In *Encyclopedia of Bioethics*, vol. 1, 2nd ed., edited by W. T. Reich, 459–64. New York: Simon and Schuster Macmillan.

Part 2

As we wrote in Part 1 of this article in the Winter 1995 issue of *JCE*, the role of clinical bioethics consultation is inevitably changing as the delivery of healthcare from various providers evolves. It is our opinion that "conflicts of interest" will become part and parcel of the day-to-day business of the ethics consultant and ethics committee. In Part 1 we presented the background on conflicts of interest, and considered some already established guidelines by the British Medical Association, the Cleveland Clinic, Marc A. Rodwin, and the American Medical Association's Council on Ethical and Judicial Affairs. In this, the second of three articles in this series, we will continue to examine some of the types of conflicts of interest that already face us.

The Case

An individual who is the recipient of a donated organ has, as part of her job responsibility, the role of requesting organ donation in a large, urban hospital emergency room. A member of the local organ procurement board expressed some concern about her ability to retain her objectivity when making requests, as the individual was herself an organ recipient. Was this a conflict of interest? Should the obligation to request organs be removed from her list of job responsibilities? The individual did not believe that a conflict of interest existed, and believed that her experience was an asset. No complaints had been received regarding the individual's conduct, nor was there any indication that there would be. The Department of Bioethics was asked to assess the issue.

History of the Problem

Cadaveric donation. The current policy regarding the donation of transplantable organs and tissues has been directed toward increasing the number of organs available. Most states have passed some form of "required request" legislation that mandates that families be given information about donating organs and tissues upon the death of a loved one. These required request laws were the result of the limitations of the Uniform Anatomical Gift Act (UAGA), which simply allowed individuals to donate their organs to increase organ and tissue donations to meet the growing demand for organs.[1] For a variety of reasons, current practice in American society is to seek familial consent before taking an individual's organ for the purposes of transplantation. The reasoning behind this stems from the need to obtain consent for organ donation. Absent direct consent from the donor (before death) in the form of an organ donor card or some other directive, the role of providing such consent falls to the decedent's family. It was thought that by approaching families at the time of a loved one's death and asking them to consider the option of donation, more transplantable organs and tissues could be obtained. Despite the fact that most families are willing to donate a loved one's organs, in the stress and grief that they often experience at the time of the decedent's death, the option of donation is often forgotten or not even considered.[2]

Family members are included in the organ procurement process for many reasons, including both the protection of the donor's autonomy and the protection of the family itself. By allowing the family to provide informed consent for organ donation on behalf of the donor, the autonomy of the donor may be protected while he or she is still alive, as well as after death. But allowing the family to provide consent may also be helpful as a mechanism for helping family members deal with their own issues. As Chad D. Naylor points out in his article, "The Role of the Family in Cadaveric Organ Procurement,"

> Social values necessitate familial involvement in order to protect the family members themselves. When organ donation opportunities arise, the family will be in great emotional distress. This is especially true because most people leaving bodies suitable for organ donation died unexpectedly. . . . Giving family members a consenting role will alleviate their grief and provide a means of protecting their sensibilities and emotions.[3]

As it turns out, much of the difficulty encountered in obtaining organs for transplantation results not from families' unwillingness to donate, but rather from the failure of medical professionals to identify suitable donors and obtain consent from the family.[4] In fact, a variety of studies, including a Gallup survey undertaken for Partnership for Organ Donation in 1991, have reported that the general public has a positive attitude toward donation.[5] Further, families who have agreed to donate the organs of a loved one after death have often said that the decision to donate has helped them deal with their grief over their loss. Psychologically, it seems clear that the process of donation can assist grieving families in dealing with the tragic and often sudden loss of their loved one by allowing them to feel that something good has come out of what may otherwise be a senseless and tragic death: namely, the fact that another person or persons will be able to continue to live because of their choice to donate.

Concerns Regarding Asking the Family to Donate

Despite the fact that providing the family of a deceased individual with information and the opportunity to donate can be a positive experience, there are some concerns that must be considered. For instance, in most cases, potential organ donors are young, otherwise healthy persons who have been the victim of some kind of violent death, such as a motor vehicle accident or a gunshot wound. Death is often unexpected and occurs quickly, leaving the grieving family little if any time to assimilate what has happened. Furthermore, in light of the time constraints involved (organs must often be procured rapidly in order to ensure their viability), a decision regarding donation must often be made quickly, with little time to deliberate. Often, the request for donation comes at the end of what has been a traumatic series of events for the family, beginning with a call informing them that their loved one has been hurt and ending with the grave news that he or she has died or will die soon. Family members may not even have had the opportunity to deal with their shock and grief before someone comes along to ask them about the option of donation. Given the difficulty of the situation, the family may find it difficult to understand and accept the death that has occurred. It is hard to imagine that any consent given at this time could truly be "informed." As William DeLong, in his article "Required Request: Who is Asking?" comments:

> The initial request [is] critical to a successful donation, principally as a matter of timing and support. The number one difficulty families have with the donation process is that they are approached too soon, before they have accepted the death of the family member.[6]

DeLong also notes that, given the nature of organ procurement, grief is one of the primary emotional elements that need to be addressed. Yet, in many places, those who are charged with the responsibility of discussing organ donation with grieving families (often physicians and nurses) may not be adequately prepared and trained to deal with such situations. DeLong proposes that the creation of teams, consisting of social workers and chaplains, as well as physicians and nurses, might be more effective in terms of addressing families' questions and concerns regarding donation.

Different healthcare institutions and organ procurement agencies (OPAs) have devised a variety of ways to meet the requirement to offer information about the option of organ donation to family members. Regardless of who is given responsibility for addressing this issue, however, it is imperative that they receive comprehensive and appropriate education and training. It is essential that they have effective communication skills and experience in dealing with grief-stricken and emotionally vulnerable families.

Potential Conflicts of Interest

As a result of the less-than-optimal circumstances surrounding the death of a potential organ donor, it is possible that undue pressure may be exerted on family members by members of the organ procurement team. Clinical conflicts, social and economic conflicts, and conflicts regarding requests for donation are all potential areas of concern. Such conflicts arise because of competing values. In the case of cadaveric organ donation, it has been difficult to ethically obtain usable organs in a way that respects cadaver donors, their families, and social values. This has proven, over time, to be a consistent stumbling block in providing the needed organs for transplantation.

There is an inherent conflict between society's need for transplantable organs and the rights of the patient/donor (and/or family members). This conflict first becomes apparent at the time that a patient is identified as a potential organ donor. The question arises: When should the medical staff cease trying to "save" the patient and begin trying to maintain the patient/donor's organs so that they will be suitable for transplantations? As the clinical management of the patient/donor differs depending upon the goal to be achieved, there is clearly a potential for tension in relation to physical care and professional responsibility.[7]

The UAGA attempted to remove some of this conflict by separating the medical team who cares for the patient and who actually certifies death from the team who is involved in the transplantation process. Section 7(b) states, "The time of death shall be determined by a physician who tends the donor at his death, or, if none, the physician who certifies the death. The physician shall not participate in the procedures for removing or transplanting a part."[8] However, it is possible for both teams, as well as for a representative from the local OPA, to be part of a larger institutionalized organ procurement and utilization program. In such cases, special attention must be paid to maintaining the separation of the goals and actions of the two teams.

On the larger social scale, organ donation and transplantation may come into conflict with other forms of medical therapy that compete for scarce resources. The funds for organ procurement and transplantation must come from somewhere, with the two most likely sources being private insurance and Medicare/Medicaid. While it is difficult to show that the resources that are expended on one type of medical treatment directly decrease the resources that are available for other treatments, it is not unreasonable to assume that increased spending in one area will affect the overall resources that are available. Recognition of this potential conflict does not necessarily mean that society should not spend its resources or organ procurement and transplantation; rather, it is yet another example of the conflict that is inherent in the process.

Probably the area of greatest concern is the potential that undue pressure will be placed on potential donors or, more likely, on the families of potential donors. This is an area of particular concern, especially because of the high value that our society places on the preservation of life and on organ transplantation as a means to achieve this goal. Generally speaking, those individuals who are involved in the organ procurement process truly believe in it, and believe that organ transplantation has the potential to provide a real good for those with end-stage organ disease. Unfortunately, a problem may arise when a family becomes an impediment to procuring the needed organs. In these situations, the goal of saving lives comes into direct conflict with the goal of protecting the interests of the family members, and extreme caution must be exerted in order to ensure that the former does not override the latter.

In his article "Organ Procurement: Coercion or Informed Consent?" Daniel Helwig addresses the concern expressed by Pat Houlihan, an organ procurement officer at a hospital in Halifax, Nova Scotia, regarding the coercion of family members. Ms. Houlihan suggested,

> Members of transplant services can pressure bereaved persons by telling them about patients who are dying because donor organs are not available. . . . To let someone who is treating a possible graft recipient talk to the wavering family of a potential donor is allowing a 'grandstander' into the intensive care unit. . . .[9]

Ms. Houlihan's remarks were made in response to certain comments made by Dr. Calvin Stiller, chief of the multi-organ transplant service at a hospital in London, Ontario. Dr. Stiller argued that telling the family what will be done with the organs is part of fully informed consent, emphasizing the need to give "total information" to the family.[10] Ms. Houlihan responded, however, that while informing and educating people about transplantation and the need for donation is a good thing, those individuals who have a stake in the donation may try to unduly influence family members' decisions regarding donation, and that this is not appropriate. What is important in discussing the option of donation with family members, she argued, is the way in which the information is presented and the ability of the person asking to establish a rapport with grieving people. These individuals should believe in transplantation but should function as advocates for the family, not the recipient.[11]

The arguments presented in Helwig's article, even though they addressed circumstances that occurred in Canada, are especially pertinent to the issue of potential conflicts of interest that surround requests for organ donation. Families are often influenced by what those around them say, especially in situations where they are particularly vulnerable—as one would expect them to be when a loved one is dying or has died. In this time of emotional upheaval, family members will often rely upon the advice and counsel of healthcare professionals. Sydney Lange, in "Psychological, Legal, Ethical, and Cultural Aspects of Organ Donation and Transplantation," reports,

> The potential donor family may ask the intensive care (ICU) nurse for guidance about their decision on organ donation. . . . ICU nurses often are asked to share their feelings about organ donation with the family. Potential donor families who were initially unsure about organ donation eventually viewed it favorably after dealing with ICU nurses whose attitudes toward donation were positive and favorable.[12]

While this is by no means conclusive, it does point out the need for healthcare professionals to exercise caution when they discuss donation with family members.

It is important that the family's consent for organ donation be valid, that is, informed and voluntary. This means that the family must not be subjected to psychological pressure to donate or to the efforts of over-aggressive organ procurement personnel. Informed consent is an absolute requirement for the donation of an individual's organs and/or tissues for transplantation. Any attempt to force or coerce the donor, or the donor's family, renders the consent invalid and is unacceptable from a medical, ethical, and legal perspective. Families of potential donors are entitled to be treated with respect and consideration, regardless of whether they give consent or not.

It is important, however, to be cognizant of the distinction between "coercion" and proper informed consent. Webster's defines "coerce" as "1. to restrain by force; 2. to compel; 3. to enforce."[13] "To coerce" connotes compelling another to act against his or her will. Clearly, any attempt to lead family members to donate against their will is unacceptable. The use of force or pressure should never be involved. Placing pressure on family members defeats the spirit and intent of the gift of the donation of an organ to help another in need.

Let us contrast coercion with the notion of advocacy or support for the donation of an organ. Advocacy implies pleading a cause or seeking support for an ostensibly worthwhile goal. This would seem to be more in keeping with the sort of process that is acceptable with regard to organ donation. Clearly, those who are placed in the position of discussing the option of donation have some emotional stake in obtaining the consent of family members. After all, they are people who are closely involved in the process and who are committed to the belief that transplantation is an important and worthwhile endeavor. One would assume that if they did not believe in transplantation—if they did not care one way or another—they wouldn't be involved in the process.

To some extent, then, it can be argued that virtually any individual who is involved in the process of requesting consent for organ donation has some degree of interest in obtaining that consent. By the same token, this commitment need not be mutually exclusive with respect to the needs and the rights of the families of potential donors. A cause for concern may arise when it is felt that the interest of the "requestor" might conflict with the rights and concerns of the family, or that it may, in some way, cause the requestor to act in a way that places undue pressure on the family to give consent, consent that they might otherwise not have given. People who are likely to act in that way clearly ought not be allowed to be in a position where they might attempt to coerce the family.

The question becomes "How do we determine which individuals present such a risk?" When the "required request" legislation was developed, an attempt was made to address this concern. It was pointed out that treating physicians should be expressly prohibited from making requests in order to avoid any suggestion of conflict of interest. It was also suggested at that time by Arthur Caplan that a variety of persons, including doctors, nurses, clergy, social workers, or organ procurement specialists, could be allowed to make requests. What was important was not so much their professional background, as the fact they had been adequately trained in how to appropriately request consent for donations.[14] It was assumed that, with proper education and training, those who were placed in the position of requesting consent for donation would be able to handle the situation appropriately; that is, they would be able to present the necessary information to the family, to answer any questions the family might have, and to competently (and without placing undue pressure) make the request for donation in an emotion-laden situation.

It would seem to be true that no matter what the requestor's profession, it would be likely that he or she would have some interest in the organ donation process. Certainly it is reasonable to expect that clinicians would be committed to the organ procurement and transplantation process, by virtue of their commitment to medicine, if nothing else. And, as Caplan pointed out,

> If health care professionals are actually put in an untenable moral bind due to a genuine 'conflict between encouraging hope (through caregiving) and causing

the family to lose hope (through the donation request),' then no form of organ request is ethically acceptable. . . .[15]

It would stand to reason that even members of other professions who become involved in the process would be equally committed to the desirability of obtaining organs; otherwise, one would assume, they would not continue to be involved. And what about those individuals who are employed by OPAs? Certainly it could be argued that they have a stake in obtaining consent for organ donations. After all, the continuing operation of the agency for which they work depends on a constant supply of organs being obtained for transplantation. Such persons are routinely given the responsibility of requesting consent for organ donation.

Is it reasonable, then, to suggest that those who have the responsibility of making this request will not attempt in any way to influence the decision of the family? It seems clear that such complete objectivity or neutrality is both impossible as well as undesirable. As noted above, those involved in the organ procurement process, by their very natures, have an interest in obtaining consent for donation. Furthermore, it would seem that we should encourage such commitment and interest in the process of procuring organs for donation. A positive attitude toward donation—sharing the feeling with the family that donation is a good thing to do—should be regarded as a desirable aspect of the request process. If donation is not a positive act, if it is not something to be encouraged, then why are we asking families to consent to it at all? If families do not believe that those requesting the donation think it is important and worthwhile, why should they give their consent? If we believe that transplantation is a good thing, a sentiment that seems to be accepted in our society, shouldn't we try to encourage the family to share this belief? The attitude that the person requesting is completely neutral about donation, that it doesn't really matter whether or not consent is given for the donation, may lead the family to believe that the donation is not important. As Caplan reported, "if you simply ask relatives about organ donation by citing the law the consent rate is zero."[16]

Addressing the Conflicts

It would therefore appear to be unreasonable—as well as undesirable—to insist that no one who has any sort of interest or "stake" in the obtaining of organs for donation be allowed to discuss the option of consenting to donation with family members. Instead, it would seem more sensible to recognize and acknowledge those situations in which the potential for coercion of family members exists, and to take appropriate measures to counteract them. There are a variety of ways in which this could be accomplished.

First of all, an attempt needs to be made to identify those situations in which the potential for undue pressure to donate may be placed on the family. Such situations would include conditions in which, for whatever reason, the family is particularly vulnerable and open to suggestion. Examples of such situations might be the case of a death that was particularly traumatic, a particularly troubled or dysfunctional family, a situation in which the family member from whom consent is being sought was estranged from or had a particularly strained relationship with the deceased, or circumstances involving special social, cultural, or psychological concerns. Situations in which the person who is requesting consent has a special interest or bias toward donation should also be identified. Examples of persons who may have such a bias are employees of OPAs, persons who have a relationship with someone who is in need of or has received an organ transplant, or persons who themselves are in need of or have received an organ transplant. It is important to remember that the identification of such potentially coercive situations does not necessarily imply that consent for donation should not be sought; rather, it suggests that the process should proceed under extreme caution.

In an instance where a potentially coercive situation has been identified, the actual risks of coercion need to be assessed. Despite the fact that the potential for coercion exists, it does not mean that coercion will necessarily occur. Depending on the circumstances, it may be possible to address the concerns in a way that ameliorates the fear of undue pressure. For instance, if the concern revolves around a family member who had a poor relationship with the potential donor, it might be possible to ascertain from other family members or friends what the decedent's wishes were regarding donation. If the decision of the estranged family member who has decision-making authority is in agreement with those wishes, then the consent for the donation would seem to be appropriate. By the same token, if the cause for concern involves a potential bias for donation on the part of the requestor, it may be possible to address these concerns. If, for example, the requestor is a person who is in need of or has received an organ transplant, there may be some fear that he or she would try to inappropriately influence the decision of a wavering family member. If this fear is based on the past performance of the requestor (if he or she has done this in the past or has indicated a likelihood of doing so), then the concern may be legitimate, and perhaps this person should no longer be involved in the donation process. However, if this person has been adequately trained, if his or her past performance has indicated no inappropriate attempts to influence family members, and he or she has demonstrated the ability to appropriately handle delicate situations regarding consent for donation, then there is no reason to prohibit that person from continuing to be involved in the process of requesting consent. As long as the person refrains from using his or her own situation to influence the family's decision, there need be no cause for concern.

The question may rise as to what the responsibilities of a requestor with a potential bias toward donation might be in the instance that he or she were asked directly about his or her own experience. For example, suppose that an individual who is a transplant recipient is asked by the family of a potential donor, "Do you personally know any one who has received an organ donation?" It may be suggested that if such an individual answers this question truthfully, he or she will unfairly influence the decision of the family. After all, how could a family look such a person—a person who owes his or her very life to another family's willingness to donate an organ for transplantation—in the eye and refuse to give consent to donate their loved one's organs?

Clearly the responsibilities of such a requestor in this sort of situation will depend upon the actual circumstances of the case. If the family has not expressed a desire to donate their loved one's organs, their questions may simply be a matter of seeking further information regarding how their loved one's organs are to be used and whether their "gift" will truly benefit another. In such an instance, the truthful reply of the requestor may be helpful, as he or she can comment directly on the positive (and negative) aspects of transplantation. Furthermore, it must remembered that coercion implies that one is trying to force or compel another to act in a way contrary to his or her will. If the family has not indicated that they are opposed to donation, but rather are simply seeking more information in order to make their decision, the requestor's own experiences could be viewed as influential, perhaps, but not as coercive. And, as noted earlier, encouraging families to donate because one believes it is a good thing is not necessarily undesirable or inappropriate. What would be inappropriate is to try to "talk the family out of" their choice not to donate. For a requestor to use his or her personal experiences to make the family change their minds about their choice not to donate would, in fact, be coercive and therefore unethical.

There may be instances in which, during the course of the discussion with the family regarding the option to donate, the requestor becomes aware that the family is being unduly influenced. This may occur regardless of who the requestor is or his or her particular background. Clearly, in such a case, the requestor has an obligation to take whatever action is necessary to address this situation and may even, in extreme circumstances, need to remove him or herself from the case. Such a situation will be the exception rather than the rule; however, organ procurement personnel must have guidelines in place for such occurrences and be prepared to address them should they arise.

Of course, it may be argued that we cannot simply "take it on faith" that someone with a potential bias or conflict of interest will not take advantage of the situation in order to unfairly obtain consent for donation from a vulnerable family member. For this reason, in circumstances where the potential for coercion exists (and it exists in virtually any donation request), it may be appropriate to monitor the consent process. This monitoring could be accomplished by having another person present during randomly selected discussions with the family, or by having the family complete an anonymous evaluator form in which they reported their experience regarding the discussion. In fact, it would be beneficial to have such a monitoring process as a routine activity to ensure, in general, that the process for obtaining consent is being carried out appropriately.

Conclusion

In light of the fact that we are all human and therefore imperfect, it must be accepted that the process of obtaining consent from family members for organ donation will be problematic. While every effort should be made to ensure that the autonomy of the donor and the donor's family members are respected regardless of whether they decide to donate or not, it must be acknowledged that the possibility of conflicts within the process do exist. Instead of discounting the validity of the process, perhaps we should work toward addressing the areas of our concern. For example, if we are worried that a particular individual may possess a certain bias regarding donation that may cause him or her to unduly pressure family members, instead of simply prohibiting that person (who may be a particular asset professionally and an integral part of the organ procurement team) from participating in the process, perhaps we should explore options by which the potential for coercion can be removed, or at least lessened.

We must keep in mind the fact that organ donation and transplantation provides a once-impossible opportunity for those suffering from end-stage organ disease to continue living when they otherwise would have died. This, in itself, is a goal worth pursuing. And while the goal cannot justify overriding the autonomy of potential donors and their families or forcing them to consent to donation against their will, it does compel us to be as creative and as committed as possible to finding ways to achieve ethically, medically, and legally appropriate ways to increase the supply of transplantable organs.

As a final thought, it worth noting that, as Caplan and Welvang tell us:

> There have been few problems associated with families who have been approached under the new [required request] laws. There is some evidence that, whether they decide to donate or not, they do not feel pressured or coerced by being asked.[17]

It is important, if we hope to maintain a constant supply of organs, to continue to encourage the goodwill and the positive attitude of the public toward organ donation. The general public seems to believe that organ donation is a positive thing, and this sentiment seems to be generally supported by those who have donated the organs of loved ones. Furthermore, it has been reported that those families who do express regret tend to express regret for not having taken the opportunity to donate organs.[18]

The option to donate organs and tissue provides many people with an opportunity to participate in doing good for those in need of organ transplantation. While we should do everything in our power to ensure that individuals are not unfairly taken advantage of in our efforts to reduce the shortage of available organs for transplantation, we also owe persons the opportunity to choose to donate their organs or their loved one's organs (providing the potential donor did not express a desire not to donate his or her organs). We must maintain the commitment to ensure an ethically, medically, and legally acceptable process for soliciting the donation of organs and tissues that respects the autonomy of donors and their families, as well as society's commitment to save lives through the process of organ procurement and transplantation.

Notes

1. National Conference of Commissioners on Uniform State Laws. 1968. *Uniform Anatomical Gift Act*, 182–93. (approved by the American Bar Association at its Annual Meeting in Philadelphia, PA, 7 August).
2. Lange, S. S. 1992. "Psychological, Legal, Ethical, and Cultural Aspects of Organ Donation and Transplantation." *Critical Care Nursing Clinics in North America* 4 (1): 25–42.
3. Naylor, C. D. 1989. "The Role of the Family in Cadaveric Organ Procurement." *Indiana Law Journal* 65 (1): 167–89.
4. Lange, "Psychological, Legal, Ethical, and Cultural Aspects."
5. *Ibid.*

6. DeLong, W. D. 1989. "Required Request: Who Is Asking?" *Nursing Management* 20 (5): 112R, 112V, 112X.

7. Martyn, S., R. Wright, and L. Clark. 1988. "Reconsidering Required Request." *Hastings Center Report* (Apr/May): 27–28.

8. National Conference of Commissioners on Uniform State Laws. *Uniform Anatomical Gift Act.*

9. Helwig, D. 1988. "Organ Procurement: Coercion or Informed Consent?" *Canadian Medical Association Journal* 139 (1): 59–61.

10. *Ibid.*, 61.

11. *Ibid.*

12. Lange, "Psychological, Legal, Ethical, and Cultural Aspects," 26.

13. Guralnik, D. B. (ed.). 1993. *Webster's New World Dictionary of the American Language*, 120. New York: Warner Books.

14. Caplan, A. L., and P. Welvang. 1989. "Are Required Request Laws Working? Altruism and the Procurement of Organs and Tissues." *Clinical Transplantation* 3 (3): 170–76.

15. Caplan, A. L. 1988. "Professional Arrogance and Public Misunderstanding." *Hastings Center Report* (Apr/May): 34–37.

16. Caplan, "Professional Arrogance," 35.

17. Caplan and Welvang, "Are Required Request Laws Working?" 176.

18. Caplan and Welvang, "Are Required Request Laws Working?" 171.

Part 3

This is the third and final part of a series of articles by the authors on conflicts of interest as they relate to medical practice and clinical ethics. This article deals with enticements and inducements by vendors to influence prescribing patterns. The particular case chosen involves the token gifts and free food given resident physicians by pharmaceutical firms' sales representatives as well as the more blatant expense-paid medical seminars offered practicing physicians. The take-home message is that gift-giving entails a subliminal expectation of reciprocity.

Accepting Gifts and Changing Prescribing Practices: The Case

While riding on the elevator, a member of a hospital ethics committee overheard a conversation between a resident physician and a pharmaceutical company representative. The pharmaceutical representative informed the resident that unless he increased his prescribing of that company's drug, the residents would no longer be offered free lunches, token pens, calendars, and other gifts. The resident openly acknowledged his "duty," almost, to get his fellow residents to increase their prescriptions of the company's drugs.[1] With that conversation in mind, the ethics committee member approached the hospital pharmacy only to discover that the pharmacy had yet another concern: lavish gifts were being bestowed on attending staff physicians and their spouses in return for changing the drugs they prescribed.

This issue was brought before the hospital ethics committee, and it decided that more data was needed. A task force was appointed to review hospital policy. The existing hospital policy stated, in part:

> No employee shall accept any money, gift, favor, entertainment, or accom-modation for himself or herself or any relative or friend from anyone having current or prospective commercial activities with [the hospital] if this would tend in any degree to prevent the employee from acting solely in the best interests of [the hospital].[2]

Since the policy seemed to favor the hospital's best interest rather than the patients' best interests, the task force recommended that both the task force and the Pharmacy and Therapeutics Committee study this issue further. Orlowski and Wateska examined whether physicians changed the drugs that they prescribed when pharmaceutical firms offered all–expense paid trips to popular sun belt vacation sites to attend symposia sponsored by pharmaceutical companies.[3] The authors monitored the drugs that physicians prescribed for a minimum of 20 months prior to the symposia and a minimum of 17 months after the symposia. They found that physicians had, in fact, been influenced by the practices of the pharmaceutical company, despite the fact that all 10 physicians interviewed denied that they had been influenced. The authors concluded that there were serious questions

> about conflicts of interest and the ethics of physician–pharmaceutical firm relationships. A conflict of interest [according to these authors] is a discrepancy between the personal interests and the professional responsibilities of a person in a position of trust [the physician]. Patients have a right to expect that a service or a product is recommended because it is needed and because it is the best, most efficacious, safest, and most cost-effective, based on sound professional judgment unbiased by extraneous factors or inducements.[3]

The ethics committee concluded that its policy regarding conflicts of interest was in the institution's and not the in the patients' best interests and that the policy did, in fact, need significant revision.

Comments

Pharmaceutical firms are well aware of the effects and results of visits from pharmaceutical firms' sales representatives (or "detail men") and the gifts they bear. Each visit costs a pharmaceutical firm between $75 and $100, and pharmaceutical firms obviously would not continue this practice if it did not pay off in the long run.

The small, token gifts establish a relationship between the giver and the recipient. The sociocultural expectation is that the recipient will reciprocate with some favor in return. The reciprocity sought by the pharmaceutical firms is that physicians will prescribe their products.

Even such mundane gifts as pens, calendars, or textbooks engender a subconscious, if not conscious, desire to reciprocate. Most physicians would consider giving the "detail man" a token gift in return as unthinkable or absurd. What they may not realize is that they unconsciously feel compelled to reciprocate in some other way, and do so by prescribing that representative's products, or at least by being reminded subconsciously about them. Clinical decisions often involve choosing a medication, and accepting gifts from drug companies creates an obligation to a drug company that may conflict with a patient's best interests and threaten the relationship between the physician and patient. Free meals carry even greater sociocultural entanglements, because sharing a meal, with its conviviality and camaraderie, often engenders a feeling of a special relationship between the partakers, report Chren et al.[4]

Gifts from pharmaceutical representatives cost money, and the cost is ultimately passed on to patients without their knowledge. Patients already complain about the high cost of drugs. That physicians accept these gifts may erode the public's confidence that physicians act in the best interests of patients.

Equally important is the effect that such practices as free meals for residents have on patients. In a sensitive piece called, "The Pizza Parade," Robert Noble, MD, reminds us that pharmaceutical representatives often parade carts, boxes, or luggage carriers laden with pizzas, sandwiches, or Chinese food past patients who don't even know where their next meal is coming from (or if there will be a next meal). At large university medical centers, as many as a dozen detail men may be seen trekking through the outpatient clinics laden down with food for the resident physicians and medical students, while the patients can only look on and salivate.[5]

Since the article by Chren et al. and the study by Orlowski and Wateska[6] were published, a number of major changes in the way pharmaceutical firms are allowed to interact with physicians have been made. Both the American Medical Association (AMA) and the Pharmaceutical Manufacturers Association (PMA), in response to hearings conducted by the U.S. Senate Labor and Human Resources Committee chaired by Senator Edward Kennedy (D-Mass.), adopted guidelines that prohibit subsidies to pay physicians for the costs of travel, lodging, or other expenses to attend medical education meetings; cash payments of any kind; "honoraria" for physicians to attend medical educational conferences at which they are not speakers; and any gifts to physicians that are of substantial value and do not primarily entail a benefit to patients. Under the latter guidelines, textbooks, modest meals, and other gifts are appropriate or acceptable if they serve a genuine educational function. Any gifts tied to how physicians prescribe products are also forbidden.[7] The AMA Council on Ethical and Judicial Affairs recommended that physicians should not accept free samples of drugs and other gifts for personal or family use (a common practice), because these gifts do not improve the care that patients receive. The General Assembly of the AMA has returned this latter issue to the Council on Ethical and Judicial Affairs for further study.

Final Remarks

As can be seen from the discussions in the three parts of this series, cases and issues involving allegations of a "conflict of interest" are not black and white; at the very least, they are varying shades of gray. Whether the situation at hand involves a conflict of interest, the appearance of conflict of interest, a conflict of obligation, or acting in a situation where the potential for conflict of interest exists is sometimes in the eyes of the beholder. However, some very real conflict situations do exist, and these situations require accurate identification and careful analysis. Issues concerning conflicts of interest are just beginning to be recognized in the clinical ethics arena. And it is our opinion that as organizational ethics issues become "part and parcel" of ethics consultation, knowledge of how to appropriately identify and address such conflicts will become even more essential.

Notes

1. Orlowski, J. P. 1994. "The HEC and Conflicts of Interest in the Health Care Environment." *HEC Forum* 6 (1): 3–11.
2. Orlowski, J. P., and L. Wateska. 1992. "The Effects of Pharmaceutical Firm Enticements on Physician Prescribing Patterns: There's No Such Thing as a Free Lunch." *Chest* 102 (1): 270–73.
3. *Ibid.*
4. Chren, M. M., C. S. Landefeld, and T. H. Murray. 1989. "Doctors, Drug Companies, and Gifts." *Journal of the American Medical Association* 262: 3448–51.
5. Noble, R. C. 1990. "The Pizza Parade." *Annals of Internal Medicine* 112: 237.
6. Orlowski and Wateska, "The Effects of Pharmaceutical Firm Enticements."

7. AMA Council on Ethical and Judicial Affairs, American Medical Association. 1991. "Gifts to Physicians from Industry." *Journal of the American Medical Association* 265: 501.

8. Page, L. 1994. "AMA Opposes Free Drug Samples for Family Use." *AMA News* 24 (31 Jan): 9.

Annotated Bibliography

Hall, S. 1998. "Conflicts of Interest: Disclosure and Resolution." *Cost & Quality* 4 (1): 21–25. Although focused solely on physicians, this article provides an insightful analytical method.

Khushf, G. "A Radical Rupture in the Paradigm of Modern Medicine: Conflicts of Interest, Fiduciary Obligations, and the Scientific Ideal." 1998. *Journal of Medicine and Philosophy* 23 (1): 98–122. The most current and challenging analysis of conflicts of interest in the modern healthcare setting.

Orlowski, J. P. "The HEC and Conflicts of Interest in the Healthcare Environment." *HEC Forum* 6 (1): 3–11. A sound probe of organizational approaches to conflict of interest issues.

Rodwin, M. 1993. *Medicine, Money and Morals.* Oxford, UK: Oxford University Press. An insightful though somewhat limited foray into the economic dimension of conflict of interest in today's healthcare.

Spece, R., D. Shimm, and A. Buchanan (eds.). 1996. *Conflicts of Interest in Clinical Practice and Research.* Oxford, UK: Oxford University Press. An outstanding and balanced collection of analyses on a full range of conflict of interest issues.

ETHICS OF INFORMATION PRIVACY AND CONFIDENTIALITY

S TANDARD IM 2 of the Joint Commission's *Accreditation Manual* stipulates that: "Confidentiality, accuracy and integrity of data and information are maintained."[1] The standard goes on to specify that compliance requires healthcare organizations to determine "appropriate levels of security and confidentiality." The American College of Healthcare Executives has promulgated an ethical policy statement on health information confidentiality.[2] Federal and state governments have enacted extensive privacy statutes.[3] The ethical dimension of these information management issues and how healthcare organizations deal with that dimension is the focal issue of this chapter.

CASE STUDY

Case Five: Whose Record Is It Anyway?

Joseph Coughlan entered the St. Serena's emergency room on Friday afternoon bloodied from a fall. At 84 years of age, his legs had been getting progressively weaker and he occasionally became disoriented and confused when in stressful and strange settings. Upon examining him the resident physician ordered x-rays and an EKG. A month previously Mr. Coughlan had been hospitalized after an abnormal heart rhythm was detected during a routine cataract procedure. Extensive tests over the ensuing seven days revealed the condition was apparently an asymptomatic congenital anomaly. The extensive stay and tests, however, had produced considerable confusion in Joseph during his hospitalization.

Hospital records—apparently not yet updated—did not reveal that recent experience. When the new EKG again indicated a heart abnormality, Mr. Coughlan was admitted. The hospital call to his son, Donald, did not get through because the phone number in the hospital record was incorrect. Four hours later, when Dr. Elsie, Mr. Coughlan's primary care physician, saw him, she had her office call the family from the correct number in her records. By this time Mr. Coughlan was again showing signs of disorientation. When Donald arrived and spoke with Dr. Elsie they agreed that he should be released and sent home.

During the previous seven-day hospitalization, son Donald had been irritated at the lack of information provided when he questioned the extent of the testing being performed on his father. He was particularly irate when, on examining his father's chart, he noted that "patient exhibits hallucinations" was recorded. In fact, his father was completely clear when in the presence of his son, and Donald felt that the confusion at other times was his way of coping with the hospital ordeal. Mr. Coughlan had always been good at "tuning out" things he did not want to hear. Donald was most aggravated when he overheard an orderly telling an aide, "Don't worry about things Mr. Coughlan says. He's senile!"

Two months later a bill arrived from St. Serena's for the eligible charges not covered by Medicare for both the week-long hospitalization and for the emergency room episode. Donald had specifically informed the hospital during the original admission of his father's secondary coverage through a labor union. The hospital had indicated that the union would be billed directly.

St. Serena's code of conduct, in Section I.5.b. states:

> *All reports and records, whether computerized or on paper, are accurate and proper. Employees must never create false or misleading records, nor suppress, alter, or destroy operating data. . . . Employees are required to advise clients of any clerical or other errors made as they become known, and to ensure prompt correction of such errors.*

Questions for Discussion:

1. Is there an ethical dimension to the situation involving Mr. Coughlan? Is there a compliance issue?
2. What privacy and confidentiality questions might arise from this case?
3. Distinguish the formal and informal organizational elements evident in the situation.

4. What Joint Commission standards or other issues of organizational ethics might be relevant to Mr. Coughlan's case?

5. What organizational action could St. Serena's take in response to situations like this?

6. Does there appear to be a pattern of indifference toward information management at St. Serena's? If there is, how might it affect governmental compliance initiatives?

COMMENTARY

Clearly St. Serena's had some difficulty managing the personal information that had been collected on Joseph Coughlan. But did the organization violate any ethical obligation? Were any principles of confidentiality and privacy compromised? Are there any compliance concerns involved?

The principle of confidentiality in healthcare goes back to the Hippocratic oath: "The things I may see or hear in the course of the treatment or even outside of treatment . . . I will keep to myself." But, as Thompson observes, "confidentiality looks quite different in the modern hospital than one would expect from the traditional statements of the principle. The qualifications to patient confidentiality are not merely exceptional, they are routine."[4] He goes on to note the extensive access to personal information available today both formally and "through the corridors," and argues that it is disingenuous to collect personal patient information, purportedly under the confidentiality principle, and then dispense the information "under an institutional system that offers much less protection." Thompson concludes that healthcare organizations need to establish and enforce more explicit standards for institutional confidentiality that balance the various interests involved. Would this include, for example, at least informing Mr. Coughlan and his family that personal and sensitive information might be recorded and accessed? Might it include training directed at preventing aides from accessing and interpreting patient charts?

The issue of patient information is complex and, often subtle, so let us turn again to clarifying concepts.

Security, Confidentiality, and Privacy

First, we need to be clear about the terms used in our reflection. The Joint Commission and federal guidelines speak of security, confidentiality, and privacy often in the same sentence. What do these terms mean? What is the difference among them? What is their relationship?

Figure 5.1 Conceptual Distinctions

Although sometimes used interchangeably, confidentiality and privacy are not synonymous. Confidentiality normally refers to the notion of secrecy, whereas privacy refers to the broader notion of safeguarding, the former being only one aspect of the latter (see Figure 5.1). These are policy, social, and ethical issues. What information should be kept secret or restricted only to certain "need to know" standards? Should some personal information specifically not be restricted? What kinds of safeguards or managerial measures should be applied to personal information about patients and staff? The answers are debatable.

Information security, on the other hand, is a technical and administrative matter (see Figure 5.1). What measures are available to implement the decisions made on the confidentiality and privacy questions? Are they in place? Are they working? The privacy/confidentiality issue concerns what *should* be done to control information, but the security matter deals more with what *can* be done to protect personal information. There is general agreement about the security problem and its solution, but the privacy/confidentiality issue involves considerably less certainty and consensus. In Mr. Coughlan's case, for example, whether the "hallucinations" information should be recorded and accessible to aides is an information privacy and confidentiality issue; the determination of how to effectively implement whatever restrictions are decided is a security issue.

Information privacy, in connoting "safeguarding," means not only designating certain information as secret or restricted—that is, safeguarding access—but also

1. Determining what personal information can or cannot be collected in the first place;
2. Ensuring that the information collected is accurate, complete, and up-to-date;
3. Deciding whether and when certain personal information should be purged; and
4. Limiting the purposes for which the information collected can be used.

Whatever determinations are made on these matters, note that security then becomes essential in actually making those decisions happen. When the Joint Commission speaks of the "integrity of information," these are the elements implied.

The ethical dimension of these issues for healthcare organizations develops from consensus that personal information should not be collected unless it is demonstrably relevant to the provision of healthcare services; that healthcare organizations have a responsibility to ensure that any information collected is accurate and complete; that any personal information collected should be used only for the purpose for which it was given; and that certain personal information should be purged after a reasonable period of time. These information "norms" have developed because the following problems have been recognized in the healthcare system:

- Healthcare organizations require vulnerable patients to reveal personal information as a condition of service.
- Healthcare organizations use personal information for purposes other than that for which it was given, that is, the delivery of healthcare.
- Healthcare organizations maintain and use inaccurate information with resultant harm to patients.
- Healthcare organizations permit sensitive information to be accessed by unauthorized people having no demonstrable need to know.

In the case of Mr. Coughlan, we could ask a number of questions related to these concepts. Was the information about his confusion collected and recorded but then used for other purposes by the aides? Was that ethical? Did such use cause a breakdown in the hospital's covenant with Mr. Coughlan to treat him with respect? The personal medical record that St. Serena's had maintained on Mr. Coughlan seems to have been incomplete or at least not up-to-date in that it did not reveal his previous diagnosis to the physician—who had a need to know. Because that failure resulted in inconvenience if not harm to Mr. Coughlan, are there ethical implications to St. Serena's record-keeping system? Is the problem an organizational ethics issue of privacy? Or is it rather an organizational ethics issue of security? Perhaps the information was not available to the emergency room because security mechanisms prevented access.

Is the matter of an inaccurate phone number in his record a matter of organizational ethics? Does it ethically matter that this error contributed to an inappropriate admission as well as a failure to connect with the family? Did St. Serena's fail in not providing a structure for Mr. Coughlan and his family to review his record for purposes of verifying accuracy? Regarding billing, does it ethically matter that the patient and family were inconvenienced because the personal record of Mr. Coughlan had, apparently, not been updated as specifically requested? Finally, do the incidents involving Mr. Coughlan suggest a pattern of information management problems? Does this then have serious compliance implications given the federal government's "fraud and abuse" priority?

Evaluating the ethical dimension of these matters becomes serious when the organizational effect on Mr. Coughlan is realized, and all the more serious when legal developments are tossed into the reflection. That is, although considerable ambiguity remains, courts are beginning to recognize personal information as the private property of the person. Currently any violations of privacy and confidentiality regulations are judged under the law of torts, meaning that violations are a civil matter involving financial penalties. Were the law of property applied, however, those same violations would become criminal matters involving possible jail sentences. In Sweden this has already happened: that country now recognizes "data trespassing" as a felony. This crime includes improper organizational collection and use of personal information, maintenance of inaccurate and incomplete records, and allowing unauthorized access to personal data.

If we consider Mr. Coughlan's personal information as his private property, would St. Serena's corporate ethical obligation to safeguard his personal files—including their accuracy, completeness, and accessibility—become a matter of more serious concern? Furthermore, in today's competitive and litigious healthcare environment, does the seriousness of this issue intensify? Dowd and Dowd think so: "Patients who feel that their privacy has been violated will probably not return to that institution for care and may, in fact, feel compelled to sue for what they see as a breach of care."[5] Furthermore, as Guglielmo clarifies, sloppy information practices are now targeted by government regulators and such practices are subject not only to large financial penalties but even to criminal prosecutions.[6]

The reality of computerization further enriches these concepts. Confidentiality, for example, becomes at once both more simple and more complicated. Access to personal information in a computerized database now becomes a gigantic possibility given remote entry capability. On the other hand, computerization can make limiting access easier through software security mechanisms like passwords and automatic logs. Privacy becomes more complicated in that, for example, once inaccurate information gets on the system, correction at all retrieval points can be extra challenging. Restricting access and use of personal information—given creative minds, hackers, and the like—now requires rigorous, structural mechanisms of technology and administration.

So, what is the ethical obligation of St. Serena's, and all healthcare organizations, with regard to these confidentiality, privacy, and security realities? Is it reasonable to hold that when an organization collects personal information that organization also "collects" a responsibility to manage that information carefully—maybe not perfectly, but with care? Fortunately, information management is a straightforward concept, but it does require understanding and attention.

Information Management

Mismanagement of sensitive personal information can be financially devastating, legally disastrous, and politically debilitating; it is also ethically intolerable. Information management is analogous to driving a car: Once we take control we are legally and financially responsible for what we do with the automobile. If we misuse it by, for instance, speeding, we pay a fine. If we hurt someone by driving while intoxicated, we go to jail. When we get behind the wheel we have an ethical responsibility to know what we are doing. So, too, with information: Once we take control of a patient's or employee's information we are responsible for what happens to it.

In an age that is defining personal information as the private property of the subject, healthcare organizations have an obligation to take care of that property when they "borrow" it to provide health services. Care, or due diligence, implies management. What, then, is involved in basic information management?

In another work[7] I suggested that there are five generic characteristics of information: relevance, conciseness, accuracy, timeliness, and completeness. In the context of this book we might add a sixth: accessibility. Information management is simply organizational attention to those attributes; they are the keys to ethical management of the privacy, confidentiality, and security issues. Figure 5.2 depicts them.

Relevance.

Relevance, in the operational sense, means that healthcare organizations get the information needed to accomplish their goals and objectives. In the ethical sense it means that organizations collect the personal information they need, and *only* that which they need. If there is no demonstrable relationship of, for example, the collection of details of a patient's sex life to the provision of a healthcare service, is it ethical to request such information from a vulnerable patient? Such information may be interesting to note—and there may be some future research

Figure 5.2   Keys to Ethical Information Management

Relevance
Conciseness
Accuracy
Timeliness
Completenes
Accessibility

significance—but it might not be ethical to collect it. On the other hand, is it ethical to provide a healthcare service when lacking information needed to provide that service safely and effectively? Information relevance is essential to the ethics of information management; failure to manage the relevance issue—such as collecting personal information that is not needed—violates the privacy principle. Failure to collect the personal information needed violates the competence principle. For this reason careful organizational clarification of information needs is a first step in information management.

Conciseness.

The property of conciseness, closely related to relevance, implies a discipline to organizational information systems to prevent misuse of computers to store as much information as possible whether or not operational need has been demonstrated.

In Mr. Coughlan's case, we might wonder whether an effort was made to gather information on the recent EKG before the order and interpretation of the new one was determined. A question of relevance in collecting and recording the information about Mr. Coughlan's "hallucinations" also exists, although that might be more a matter of accuracy.

Accuracy.

A critical step in information management is procedural effort at accuracy. Does a healthcare organization have an ethical obligation—given the consequences of acting in error—to ensure the accuracy of the personal information it collects? Does it have an ethical responsibility to provide for reasonable mechanisms to verify accuracy? In Mr. Coughlan's case was the term "hallucinating" accurate? Was "senile" accurate? Were these pieces of information subject to any verification check? Should they have been? Mr. Coughlan's phone number seems to have been inaccurately recorded. Does St. Serena's have in place any structural mechanism to check the accuracy of such important personal information? Does the organization have a responsibility to have such a structure, especially given its stated policy quoted previously? Are patients like Mr. Coughlan and his family routinely invited to review and confirm the accuracy of their records? Is there an ethical as well as an operational rationale for such a procedure?

Timeliness.

A fourth key to ethical information management is structured attention to timeliness. St. Serena's may have properly collected and verified the accuracy of Mr. Coughlan's previous EKG report; but was there a problem in getting that needed and accurate piece of information into Mr. Coughlan's record? Did it get there a week after the emergency room episode? Was it simply not timely? More to the point, we could well wonder whether St. Serena's has a policy—beyond that required by Joint Commission standards—on time limits for information record-ing and a procedure to ensure that records have been updated. Does personal information typically pile up on a data-entry clerk's desk? Does the clerk—through training sessions—have any sensitivity to the importance of recording the information accurately and in a timely manner?

Completeness.

A fifth step involves managing completeness. Joseph's record was appar-ently lacking complete billing information. Was that a result of untimely recording of the information given by son Donald, or was provision for secondary insurance information not procedurally attended to?

Accessibility.

Finally, a big part of the privacy, confidentiality, and security manage-ment challenge is organizational attention to accessibility. Is relevant, accurate, and complete information available to the healthcare providers and administrators who need it to provide safe and effective health-care? Is the information accessible to anyone else, or is it restricted structurally? In Mr. Coughlan's case, perhaps the information on his previous EKG was, in fact, accurately and timely recorded but the record was not accessible to the emergency room. And perhaps his chart with the "hallucination" notation was accessible to aides who should not have had such easy access. The organizational ethics question concerns whether St. Serena's has working access procedures and systems in place to provide availability to need-to-know staff, to prevent availability to others, and to protect against inaccurate changes and deletions by those with legitimate access. The retrieval stage in St. Serena's information systems would be the object of scrutiny (see Figure 5.3).

Figure 5.3   Stages of Information Management

Information Needs Specification → *Relevance Check*

↓

Information Collection → *Accuracy Verification*
→ *Completeness Review*

↓

Information Recording → *Timeliness Policy*

↓

Information Storing → *Access Protections*

↓

Information Retrieval → *Access Procedures*

Heads-up information management is essential to ethical treatment of the information privacy and confidentiality issues in healthcare. A return to the concepts of formal and informal organization can further empower organizational action in this regard.

Formal and Informal Organization

The previous discussion—in emphasizing steps, procedures, and policies of information management—highlights the formal structural aspect of this issue. At the corporate level, for example, we might examine whether St. Serena's has pertinent written policies beyond the item from the code of conduct quoted in the Coughlan case. Do these policies include privacy initiatives of information collection, use, and completeness, as well as the confidentiality issue of access? Are there corporate procedures for implementing information management policies? Is there a department of information management to oversee the information resource? If not, who performs this task? What privacy and security software is employed?

At the group level—such as the emergency room and the billing office—we could look at implementation procedures of information management. Are information verification checks routine, for example? How is privacy and security software used? Are passwords, for example, taped to terminals such that anyone nearby could circumvent the access restriction? Is access monitored? At the individual level we might ask about training. Is staff regularly trained in information management? Does it include training to sensitize personnel to privacy and security issues?

These and other structural measures are important in ethically managing sensitive, personal information. But informal reality of organizational life probably poses the greatest risk for the ethics of privacy and security. For example, was it through the corporate informational grapevine that the aides at St. Serena's heard about Mr. Coughlan's "senility"? Is this grapevine fueled through conversations in the hospital cafeteria, in the elevators, and in the staff restrooms? Do the informal norms of the emergency room group emphasize speed of treatment rather than information review, as indicated in Mr. Coughlan's case? Do individual staff in the emergency room and on the ward feel stressed and thus less able to attend to things like accuracy, timeliness, and completeness? Ongoing training to sensitize staff to the ethical importance of information management is a recommended response to this informal reality, as is reinforcement—through newsletters, case rounds, and the like—and monitoring of actual handling of personal information.

Before-During-After

Finally, the before-during-after concept can be helpful in illuminating the organizational ethics of information privacy and confidentiality. An organization like St. Serena's needs to *plan* for information management and privacy protection through formal structural measures like written policies, established procedures, and training, and through informal measures like newsletters and visual displays. St. Serena's needs to *monitor* what is actually happening through things like case rounds that include information handling observations, software audit systems that report access activities, and "grapevine audits" that observe informal conversations. And it needs to evaluate what is happening through things like privacy task force reviews.

Notes

1. Joint Commission on the Accreditation of Healthcare Organizations. 1996. *Accreditation Manual for Hospitals*, 172. Oakbrook Terrace, IL: JCAHO.
2. American College of Healthcare Executives. 1997. "Ethical Policy Statement: Health Information Confidentiality."
3. Beginning with the Federal Privacy Act of 1974 numerous privacy laws and regulations have been promulgated.
4. Thompson, D. 1992. "Hospital Ethics." *Cambridge Quarterly of Healthcare Ethics* 1 (3): 204.
5. Dowd, S., and L. Dowd. 1996. "Maintaining Confidentiality: Health Care's Ongoing Dilemma." *Health Care Supervisor* 15 (1): 25.

6. Guglielmo, W. 1998. "The Feds Take Aim at Fraud and Abuse." *Medical Economics* 75 (15): 166–78.
7. Worthley, J., and P. DiSalvio. 1995. *Managing Computers in Healthcare,* 29–55. Chicago: Health Administration Press.

READING

The following piece is particularly helpful in two ways: one, it is written by social workers who have a high sensitivity to subtleties of the information privacy and confidentiality issue, and two, the writers exhibit a not-so-common business sense, thus giving a realistic tone to their analysis. The Davidsons consider the ethics of information privacy and confidentiality within the managed care environment, which, they note, includes compliance realities. Recognizing that the economic determinants of healthcare have changed, they illuminate a need for new insight on the information ethics challenge. Observe how they contend that a covenantal—as opposed to a self-interest—approach to the information management issue correlates with sound marketing strategy, thus making "good ethics" a matter of "good business." What might their comments be on the case of Joseph Coughlan?

Confidentiality and Managed Care: Ethical and Legal Concerns

Jeanette R. Davidson and Tim Davidson*

Abstract

As managed care companies take over the allocation of funds, the monitoring of treatment, and the measurement of outcomes, social workers encounter an ethical and legal dilemma with the demise of confidentiality in the professional-client relationship. Given that the profession has long heralded the protection of client confidentiality, it is timely that social workers re-examine traditional ethical and legal responsibilities to clients

*Reprinted with permission from Health & Social Work 1996. 21 (3): 208–15. Copyright 1996 National Association of Social Workers. Jeanette R. Davidson is associate professor of social work at Columbia University. Tim Davidson is director of Putnam County, NY Mental Health Services.

and challenge managed care personnel to protect clients' right to confidentiality. This article highlights problems concerning confidentiality that often arise for social workers working with managed care systems. It focuses also on ethical and legal standards related to confidentiality and social work responsibilities regarding informed consent.

Before managed care, social work services in the field of mental health tended to be needs driven. Increasingly, these services are resource driven, and there is a profit motive for the managers whether the resource is the public or the private dollar. As managed care companies take over the allocation of funds, the monitoring of treatment, and the measurement of outcomes, social workers encounter an ethical and legal dilemma with the demise of confidentiality in the professional-client relationship. The dilemma appears to be rooted first in the essential difference in primary purpose between social workers and managed care companies, and second in the heavy reliance of managed care companies on burgeoning information systems.

Specifically, many social workers providing services within managed care systems are concerned about the quantity of information sought about the client; the sensitive nature of that information (which if exposed leaves the client entirely vulnerable); the way in which the client is, for all intents and purposes, forced to permit the disclosure of the information to ensure third-party payments (unless able to pay directly for services); the potential use of the information to deny rather than provide needed services to the client; and the all-too-often suspect security of the information systems involved. Social workers are also uncomfortable when they consider the potential negative effect that the loss of confidentiality may have on the client-worker relationship as well as the possible liability issues that may ensue.

Given that the profession has long heralded the protection of client confidentiality, it is timely that social workers re-examine traditional guidelines within this new context of managed care. If safeguarding confidences is still valued, then social workers, individually and in consortium, need to negotiate with managed care policymakers and government regulators to develop new mechanisms to protect client information.

Clash of Essential Purposes

Difference in mission.

Social workers need to be aware of the fundamental differences in mission between managed care personnel and themselves as providers and the effect of those differences on the treatment of client data. Because managed care companies primarily serve the funding bodies, they have an essential disparity of purpose from social workers. They are concerned with capitated risk for groups of people, and therefore any individual's particular need is evaluated in the context of all the other covered lives. Thus, managed care companies have gatekeepers in place who examine intimate details about a person from a distance and who may use that information to deny rather than provide needed services. In contrast, social workers' general aim is to work with all who request and need services. With managed care, then, the mission is restrictive and generalized, whereas with social workers service delivery is inclusive and individualized.

Difference in Reasons for Documentation

When care is managed, client data become determinative. Recordings undertaken for managed care companies are first and foremost meant to establish the saving of health care dollars for employers and insurance companies. A document containing highly confidential material, in the hands of a managed care administrator, will be used whatever way is most profitable from a business perspective. This contrasts with the traditional use of social work records, which has been to chronicle, in the context of trust, individuals' treatment and progress for the purpose of assisting recovery.

Difference in Use of Outcome Measures

An impetus for adopting a managed care format in behavioral health care is to promote the measurement of treatment outcomes. This purpose, seemingly laudable at first, belies another agenda. Marketers of managed care companies stress that health professionals will be better prepared to deliver the optimum treatment for each disorder once reams of outcome data are analyzed. Although managed care research is often flawed because of inappropriate questions (Shapiro 1995), simplistic and reductionistically defined variables, and economic controls over the process, it may in fact produce some interesting and helpful conclusions.

In practice, however, outcome measures for managed care have ultimately been used to determine which populations are healthy and which populations predictably could drain the profits of the managed care company. Chronic, heavy users of health care services are not usually recruited by managed care unless there is a guaranteed safety net provided by state or local governments. The legitimate clinical principle of "least-restrictive alternatives" has been transliterated by managed care to mean "severely restricted alternatives." "Stop-loss" and "hold harmless" are fundamental operating procedures written into managed care contracts. Stop-loss clauses require the government to step in when providing care for those who are needy proves too costly, and hold-harmless clauses require providers to shoulder the burden of further treatment and liability when managed care companies discontinue payments because it does not appear that a positive treatment outcome is cheap and imminent.

Social workers have traditionally advocated for people who need services, and so it seems perverse to contribute client data to a system that takes that information and uses it to figure out who should not receive treatment. For clients who have been approved for some managed care payments, the social worker's report of positive treatment outcomes frequently inclines the case reviewer to stop payment for further services because the clients' needs are then determined to be not great enough. Outcome measures are used, then, both to disenfranchise those most in need and to limit funding for others. Social workers support efficacy studies, but not at clients' expense.

Problems with Managed Care's Reliance on Information Systems

Irrespective of the form of managed care, whether a health maintenance organization, an employee assistance program, a preferred provider network with horizontal or vertical layers, or a management service designed to manage these and other kinds of managed care, client information is now shared in a much less discriminate manner than traditionally occurred in fee-for-service delivery systems. Before managed care, even in agencies with several layers of bureaucracy, strict guidelines governed the release of information to the various levels of administration and accounting.

With the use of managed care information systems that include telephone reviews, voice mail, faxes, cellular telephones, and highly unregulated computerized databases, there are few guarantees, if any, that sensitive information is stored securely. Rather, it appears that information, once passed from the social worker to a managed care service and logged into the medical database of a third-party insurance payer, may be as accessible as credit card information or mortgage payment records to people who know how to proceed with the electronic inquiry. As noted by the Legal Action Center (LAC) (1995), "The potential for wrongful disclosure of confidential information has expanded right along with the expansion of the capability of computers to move information from location to location" (104).

Unprotected Databases

Press reports from a number of sources delineate various problems within the managed care industry with respect to information systems. In an article in the *New York Times*, concerns about unprotected databases were cited and clearly indicated a clinical predicament involving trust for both clinicians and clients (Henneberger 1994). A scathing article in the *Wall Street Journal* noted how "open" all medical information is as "it lies unprotected in a patchwork of databases where it is so easy to see" and how people who file for managed care visits to psychotherapists "build up especially detailed records" (Schultz 1994, A5) that are easy to access. One defense lawyer, representing insurance companies and employers on work-related cases, blatantly admitted that he examined confidential therapy notes within managed care files to see if he could get clients to "look like Charlie Manson" (Schultz 1994, A5). Not surprisingly, the public's generally held belief that sensitive records are protected by doctor-patient confidentiality is considered by lawyers to be more myth than reality. Medical benefits experts report that once therapy files are in the possession of employers and insurance companies, "so are the temptations to tap it, for a variety of reasons that have nothing to do with keeping employees healthy" (Schultz 1994, A1).

Violation of Federal Law

Federal law is in place to protect certain client rights, but managed care companies often do not adhere either to disclosure or to redisclosure regulations. Even in the area of alcohol and drug abuse treatment, for which by law confidentiality requirements are very strict (Confidentiality Law 1992), private insurance carriers and managed care entities "routinely share information through vast computerized networks" (LAC 1995, 19). For example, one insurer "placed information about claims for reimbursement for drug abuse treatment on recorded telephone messages easily retrievable by anyone who has access to the patient's social security number" (LAC 1995, 19). Such a cavalier approach to sensitive information is reflected again by managed care personnel who "frequently redisclose to third parties (e.g., insurance companies, other health care providers, or governmental agencies) information that identifies the client as having received alcohol or drug services" (LAC 1995, 86), even though such a practice is prohibited by statute and tradition.

Violation of Research Protocol

It is important to recognize that research conducted within managed care systems, based on client information submitted by providers, ostensibly may be very helpful with regard to "practice guidelines," and "efficacious, effective and efficient" treatments (Landers 1994, 3). However, reflecting managed care companies' general tendency to conduct business in an unregulated fashion, the collection of such data may well be out of compliance with accepted guidelines for scholarship and research as outlined in the NASW *Code of Ethics* (NASW 1994) and federal guidelines about alcohol and drug abuse client records (*Regulations for Confidentiality of Alcohol and Drug Abuse Patient Records* 1987). In drug and alcohol treatment, for example, when programs permit access to patient-identifying information without the client's specific consent for purposes of research, there must be compliance with a protocol that is independently reviewed and approved by a group of three or more individuals; with regulations about securing data, including electronically stored data; with procedures for locking and blocking protected information; and with rules about access to the data only by authorized and qualified researchers (*Regulations for Confidentiality of Alcohol and Drug Abuse Patient Records* 1987, sect. 2.52). In the evolving managed care industry, it is evident that such protection of research data is frequently breached.

Absence of Known Boundaries for Information Transfer

Before managed care and the widespread use of information systems, social workers could more reasonably assume that those who were privy to client information were identifiable, occupied a role specific to the provision of client care, were relatively motivated by the best interests of the client, and were able to safeguard the information disclosed by the client. Similarly, the location of hard copies of client records, which were gathered and stored by the clinician or agency, was "more knowable and securable" (LAC 1995, 103) than is presently the case with managed care systems. Now, with a revolving system of unidentified case reviewers, social workers may not know who knows what or who will have access in the future to client disclosures they divulge for the purposes of being included in a managed care network.

Pressures on Social Workers and Clients to Comply

Clients in managed care environments find themselves compelled to sign consent forms to release information from the social worker to the gatekeeper of managed care services in the hope that doing so will ensure that third-party payments are paid to the provider. Social workers find themselves prevailing on clients to sign these release forms, which in effect relinquish the client's right to privacy, for management purposes, without there being a valid clinical reason to do so.

Confidentiality as a Core Value and Ethical Standard

Confidentiality has traditionally been regarded as a core value of the social work profession (Lindenthal et al. 1988; Loewenberg and Dolgoff 1992; McGowan 1995). The importance of confidentiality has been emphasized by its inclusion as an ethical standard in the NASW *Code of Ethics*, adopted in 1979 and revised in 1990 and 1994, to "serve as a guide to the everyday conduct of members of the social work profession" (NASW 1994, v).

The NASW *Code of Ethics* (NASW 1994) exhorts practitioners to "respect the privacy of clients and hold in confidence all information obtained in the course of professional service" (6) and guides social workers to "share with others confidences revealed by clients, without their consent, only for compelling professional reasons" (6). Furthermore, social workers are directed to "inform clients fully about the limits of confidentiality in a given situation, the purposes for which information is obtained, and how it may be used" (6) and "to obtain informed consent of clients before taping, recording, or permitting third-party observation of their activities" (6).

A resource guide on managed care recently published by NASW specifies that "it is imperative that all clinicians continue to protect the confidential nature of the patient-therapist relationship" (Jackson 1995, 8.5). The guide urges managed care managers and agency staff to develop clear protocols for communicating about clinical issues, and it states that these protocols should be comfortable to clinicians and in accord with state laws and statutes.

Legal Responsibilities to the Social Work Client

It is clear that the social worker's ethical responsibilities and legal duties converge. McGowan (1995) observed that confidentiality is protected legally by a number of case decisions and by statutes granting licensed or certified social workers privileged information status in many states. Schwarz (1989) stressed the legal rights of clients, pointing out that because the law was created for the protection of the client, technically the privilege belongs to the client, not the professional. He explained, "If a client authorizes the disclosure of a privileged communication for purposes of obtaining insurance, such a client is not deemed to have waived the privilege for other purposes" (224), and "the client has the right to limit to whom and for how long the privileged communication will be disclosed" (224).

Social workers have serious legal obligations to maintain confidentiality. Of the six primary legal duties listed by Cournoyer (1991), two refer directly to the obligation to uphold confidential relationships. Besharov and Besharov (1987), examining categories of lawsuits filed against social workers, found that two of the prominent causes for action included breach of confidentiality and violation of clients' civil rights. Kutchins (1991) emphasized that the social worker has a strict fiduciary responsibility to keep information confidential, to tell the client the truth, and to be loyal to the client. He added that the ethical principles outlined in the NASW *Code of Ethics* "are not just desirable conduct to which social workers aspire" but that "if they ignore these ethical mandates, the law governing fiduciary relationships can make them pay dearly" (107), even if the professional's defense is that he or she acted in accordance with accepted practice. The dilemma facing social workers who practice within a managed care environment is that they have a fiduciary responsibility to clients (which by definition is one that is power laden, protective, based on trust, and without any conflict of allegiance) (Kutchins 1991) and at the same time are asked to give primary loyalty to the managed care network.

Informed Consent to Release Information

Informed consent is much more than the simple matter of signing a piece of paper (Reamer 1987; Torczyner 1991). Torczyner and Reamer highlighted as essential standards for valid consent that the person making the decision be competent; that the decision be voluntary and not a result of coercion or captivity or undue influence; and that the client know all the necessary facts, choices, and risks.

With managed care, the technicalities of consent to release information forms, dutifully signed by the client, have been taken to a new level of complicity. A proper legal format for consent to release information about clients in drug or alcohol treatment as defined by the U.S. Department of Health and Human Services includes among other items the name of the individual or organization that will receive the disclosure, how much and what kind of information is to be disclosed, and a statement that the patient may revoke the consent at any time (*Regulations for Confidentiality of Alcohol and Drug Abuse Patient Records* 1987, sect. 2.31). With managed care systems the reality is often that the name of the individual or organization receiving the disclosure may change without notice, the information to be disclosed may consist of a verbatim account of the client's most sensitive information given to persuade a gatekeeper to continue to authorize services, and the statement about the client's being able to revoke consent at any time is an illusory proposition given the virtual irretrievability of electronic transmissions of data that are stored in various locations.

Under the auspices of managed care, both the spirit and the letter of social work guidelines relating to confidentiality and informed consent are broken regularly. What the social worker may want to give the managed care company—a molehill of sufficient detail about the client—too often develops into a mountain of intimate detail on computer files, the access to which is outside of the worker's control. And although some social workers may believe they are protected legally by formal consent agreements, it should be clear that technical permission to disclose information does not solve the ethical problem of clients losing their right to confidentiality, nor does it excuse the social worker from fiduciary responsibilities to the client.

Rather, when social workers prevail on clients to give consent to release information to obtain third-party payments, the ethical problems around the issue of confidentiality are compounded, either by the social workers' active role in soliciting the consent or by their passive role in not advising the client fully of the uncertainty of keeping the information private. Kutchins (1991) put it succinctly: "Informed consent is a time bomb ticking away for social workers and other mental health professionals" (111).

Questions for the Profession

A number of ethical questions emerge with the demise of confidentiality in the context of managed care. Some of these questions concern ethical decision making by the social worker regarding participation in managed care systems, legal issues, social work purpose, fiscal matters, and professional status.

Deciding to participate.

Social workers may find these questions of importance as they decide whether, or how, to participate with managed care systems:

- With managed care, is more good extended to more people, and is the sacrifice of confidentiality necessary for this to occur?
- Do the ends justify the means (that is, cooperation with managed care)?
- If a utilitarian philosophy rules the day, how might the most vulnerable members of society be protected (see Rawls 1971)?
- Is confidentiality fundamentally good, and to what degree should it be extended or limited in a health enterprise?
- Does managed care perpetuate a class distinction whereby poor and middle-class clients are expected to give up the right to a confidential relationship with social workers while

wealthy people who can pay independently are not required to do so?

- How much should the client bear the responsibility for his or her own decision about trading the right to confidentiality for services, and how much responsibility should the social worker bear?

Legal issues.

Questions social workers may have related to legal issues include the following:

- Is a social worker's cooperation with a managed care company inherently in conflict with his or her fiduciary responsibilities related to confidentiality, truth telling, and loyalty to clients?
- Are social workers colluding with managed care personnel to violate clients' civil rights?
- Because it may not be possible to have a clear understanding or accurate knowledge of the accessibility and distribution potential of information released to a managed care entity, are the customary consent to release information forms valid?
- To what degree is the social worker liable should an unforeseen outcome occur about which the client was given no warning?
- Is it always in clients' best interests for social workers to attempt to explain the limits of confidentiality in a managed care environment (what about the very fragile client?), and if not, how will the social worker justify ignoring the duty to tell clients the truth?

Social work purpose.

Social workers may need to ponder some of the following questions about professional purpose when working with managed care companies:

- Does the social worker's primary duty shift from the client to the managed care company?
- In a bureaucracy where individual rights have been supplanted by principles of group management, are social workers moving subtly into a role in which they will function as agents of social control?
- Is the relationship with managed care a slippery slope, wherein the social worker initially discloses benign information but may be called on later to reveal information that could be used to discriminate against vulnerable

individuals (for instance, to identify clients in gay relationships who may be considered high risk for insurance purposes)?

- What are the ethical obligations of social workers to clients as a collective group who appear to have little freedom to challenge this loss of rights to confidentiality or otherwise influence their situation as an organized group?

- Does this situation with managed care constitute a social justice struggle (forecast by Reid and Billups 1986) against disentitlement and the emphasis on "the minimal rights and statuses of individuals" (14)?

Fiscal matters.

A number of questions arise related to social workers' fiscal concerns:

- Because of the need to be paid for services by third-party payers, are social workers and social services agencies forced to sacrifice clients' rights in order to be recompensed?

- How far does the social worker's duty to aid go when there is an "inconvenience" to the self (for example, "punishment" by exclusion from managed care provider lists if designated "uncooperative") (Shapiro 1995)?

Professional status.

Social workers have been diligent in developing standards of practice and a professional image, both of which are now threatened by dictates of managed care organizations. Practitioners concerned about professional status may ask,

- Does the advent of managed care accelerate declassification (Meyer 1983) of the profession, with social workers being compelled to adhere to the managed care companies' directives that breach confidentiality?

- Is it right for managed care companies to have external authority over traditional social work standards of ethics, hierarchical ethical guidelines developed within the profession (Loewenberg and Dolgoff 1992; Reamer 1987; Rhodes 1991), and even the social worker's internal ethical judgments?

- What are the costs of turning back the clock on social worker's fight for privileged communication with their clients?

- By agreeing to an administrative plan that undermines confidentiality, have social workers and social services agencies allowed professional honor to give way to expedience?

Recommendations for Change

Managed care appears to be here to stay, and soon almost all social work services, whether public or private, will be influenced by managed care systems. It is hoped that because managed care is a new and developing industry, the profession can influence its various forms and levels of administration. Given that managed care originated from cost-containment efforts of insurance companies and employers, there now needs to be a strong countermovement from social workers intent on serving clients fairly and not simply managing organizations efficiently.

To regain some of the ground that has been lost with regard to confidential care, the following changes are proposed:

- A depersonalized coding system should eventually replace all permanent entries into the computer databases maintained by managed care companies, with the main objective being to camouflage client-identifying information. If managed care companies' genuine purpose in monitoring clients' progress is to improve treatment and to track effective interventions, then these depersonalized records can be used to achieve this end.

- In keeping with NASW guidelines (Jackson 1995), the computer software used in the transfer of client data should be restricted to certain personnel and should block sensitive information that could lead to patient identification. At the same time, tight confidentiality protocols should be maintained by all employees.

- All contracts with managed care companies should state explicitly the expectation of confidentiality in writing (Corcoran and Vandiver 1996).

- Providers should refuse managed care contracts that include nondisclosure clauses (which restrict clinicians' discussion with clients about limitations imposed by the managed care organization). Social workers and their professional organizations should give unequivocal support to members of the profession taking such a stance.

- Outpatient case notes or hospital files should not be copied in part or whole into the databases of managed care or insurance companies.

- Clients should have the opportunity to review records that have been given by the social worker to the managed care company. This review should be made easily and routinely, if desired.

- Any personal information that is put on the files of managed care companies should be destroyed after service is concluded, and managed care companies should comply with federal regulations requiring the elimination of all patient-identifying information on completion of an audit or evaluation.

- If one managed care company is purchased by another company, clients should be notified of the change and guaranteed access to their records.

- If a government body, agency, or person wishes to gain access to information in the database of a managed care company, clients should be notified before the access is made and given veto power over dissemination of the records. In the event this does not occur, managed care companies should be liable for any personal injury that may ensue, based on violations of disclosure or redisclosure laws.

- Gatekeepers and case reviewers for managed care companies should be identifiable and held to the same standards of keeping information confidential as the professionals providing services.

- Managed care companies should be required to have periodic reviews of their record handling and storage of client data by an independent, external examiner with the authority to establish penalties if confidentiality has not been safeguarded.

- Individual social workers, groups of social workers, and organizations such as NASW must recognize their obligation to refuse to comply with managed care directives that contravene clients' rights and should work collectively in this regard.

Implementation of these recommendations would serve to address some of the ethical and legal questions that have been raised. If these recommendations are put into effect, social workers could better work with managed care systems without abrogating their legal and ethical responsibilities to protect confidentiality.

Conclusion

Managed care, with its many facets, has developed with the political, economic, and moral changes in American culture. Health and mental health care costs are high, emphasis is shifting from the care of one to the management of many, and the economic climate is such that managed care personnel are positioned to limit services to clients and to limit the power of social work professionals to provide these services. It would be naive to assume that landmark achievements relating to ethical and legal protection of clients would remain unchallenged when economic determinants are so different.

Within this context, it is important for social workers to resist the temptation to "go along to get along" in an effort to survive alongside an industry that is apparently adjusting to a downsizing economy. Clients' rights and the social work ethical and legal commitment to confidentiality are worth fighting for, particularly given that the managed care approach to confidentiality is determined by business interests in controlling resources, not the scarcity of resources. Huge windfall profits, coupled with the understanding that private client information is essential to the cost-containment efforts of managed care, debunk claims to the contrary.

Like any other industry, however, managed care will seek to protect its consumer base to whatever degree is feasible, including safeguarding confidential information, if doing so retains high currency in the culture of providers and consumers. Social workers can defend the value of confidentiality rationally on the basis of good business practices in a free enterprise system. Specifically, they can highlight to managers the business merits of pleasing the customer by honoring confidentiality and treating client data with respect and of removing the risks of legal action. Thus, social workers' ethical and altruistic endeavors to salvage confidentiality and protect clients can be framed as compatible with businesses' self-interested motives to avoid punitive damages in court and to keep customers satisfied. Alternatively, social workers can develop and support provider-run networks committed to managing data responsibly, maintaining high professional standards, and using sound management principles.

At the same time, social workers must engage in social action to lobby for changes in managed care organizations' approach to confidentiality and for legislative restrictions on dissemination of private client data. Social work leaders, theorists, and researchers need to publicly address the problems around confidentiality that practitioners face on a daily basis. Sadly, members of the profession have been largely silent about these critical challenges to confidentiality or have tended to gloss over problems with euphemistic language or naive optimism.

Because of technological changes and new management initiatives, clients no longer have the right to confidential relationships with their social workers. Confidentiality used to be set within an environment of restrained disclosure but now is lost in a culture of information processing. Social workers need to be clear that client information passed on to managed care companies is data with a purpose beyond the health care needs of a particular individual. Social workers need to reexamine their ethical and legal responsibilities to clients and to challenge managed care personnel to protect the client's right to confidentiality.

References

Besharov, D. J., and S. H. Besharov. 1987. "Teaching About Liability." *Social Work* 32: 517–22.

Confidentiality Law, 42 U.S.C. sect. 290dd-2 (1992).

Corcoran, K., and V. Vandiver. 1996. *Maneuvering the Maze of Managed Care: Skills for Mental Health Practitioners.* New York: Free Press.

Cournoyer, B. 1991. *The Social Work Skills Workbook.* Belmont, CA: Wadsworth.

Henneberger, M. 1994. "Managed Care Changing Practice of Psychotherapy." *New York Times* 9 Oct: A1, A50

Jackson, V. H. (ed.). 1995. *Managed Care Resource Guide for Social Workers in Agency Settings.* Washington, D. C.: NASW Press.

Kutchins, H. 1991. "The Fiduciary Relationship: The Legal Basis for Social Workers' Responsibilities to Clients." *Social Work* 36: 106–13.

Landers, S. 1994. "Managed Care's Challenge: 'Show Me!'" *NASW News* (Sept): 3.

Legal Action Center. 1995. *Confidentiality: A Guide to the Federal Law and Regulations*, 3rd ed. New York: LAC.

Lindenthal, J. J., T. J. Jordan, J. D. Lentz, and C. S. Thomas. 1988. "Social Workers' Management of Confidentiality." *Social Work* 33: 157–58.

Loewenberg, F. M., and R. Dolgoff. 1992. *Ethical Decisions for Social Work Practice,* 4th ed. Itasca, IL: F. E. Peacock.

McGowan, B.G. 1995. "Values and Ethics." In *The Foundations of Social Work Practice,* edited by C. H. Meyer and M. A. Mattaini, 28–41. Washington, D. C.: NASW Press.

Meyer, C. H. 1983. "Declassification: Assault on Social Workers and Social Services (Editorial)." *Social Work* 28: 419.

National Association of Social Workers. 1994. *NASW Code of Ethics.* Washington, D. C.: NASW.

Rawls, J. 1971. *A Theory of Justice.* Cambridge, MA: Harvard University Press.

Reamer, F. 1987. "Informed Consent in Social Work." *Social Work* 32: 425–29.

Regulations for Confidentiality of Alcohol and Drug Abuse Patient Records, 42 C.F.R. Part 2, Sect. 2.31,2.52 (1987).

Reid, P. N., and J. O. Billups. 1986. "Distributional Ethics and Social Work Education." *Journal of Social Work Education* 22 (1): 6–17

Rhodes, M. L. 1991. *Ethical Dilemmas in Social Work Practice.* Milwaukee, WI: Family Service America.

Schultz, E. E. 1994. "Open Secrets: Medical Data Gathered by Firms Can Prove Less than Confidential." *Wall Street Journal* 13 May: A1, A5.

Schwarz, G. 1989. "Confidentiality Revisited." *Social Work* 34: 223–26.

Shapiro, J. S. 1995. "The Downside of Managed Mental Health Care." *Clinical Social Work Journal* 23: 441–51.

Torczyner, J. 1991. "Discretion, Judgment, and Informed Consent: Ethical and Practice Issues in Social Action." *Social Work* 36: 122–28.

Annotated Bibliography

Dowd, S., and L. Dowd. 1996. "Maintaining Confidentiality: Health Care's Ongoing Dilemma." *Health Care Supervisor* 15 (1): 24–31. An excellent discussion of the confidentiality issue in the ethical as well as legal context.

Grumbine, D. 1994. "Revisiting Confidentiality." *Radiology Management* 16 (1): 35–38. A practical probe of implementation challenges of the confidentiality principle.

Joseph, D. 1991. "Confidentiality Versus the Duty to Protect." *Journal of the American Medical Association* 266: 425. A brief but illuminating comment on the practical conflict sometimes involved in limiting access to and use of personal information.

Gilbert, F., and K. Frawley. 1993. "Do Computerized Patient Records Risk Invading Patient Privacy More than Paper Records?" *Hospital and Health Networks* (5 Nov): 8. A good piece for gaining sensitivity to the effect of computers on information privacy.

Worthley, J., and P. DiSalvio. 1995. *Managing Computers in Healthcare*. Chicago: Health Administration Press. Chapter two provides a concise picture of the nature of information management, and Chapters seven and eight illuminate the security and privacy issues.

6

SEXUAL HARASSMENT AND ETHICS

COMMITMENT TO an ethical work environment for employees has become part and parcel of corporate codes of conduct in healthcare. The American College of Healthcare Executives has adopted a policy statement highlighting "freedom from all harassment" as essential to an ethical working environment.[1] Stiff penalties—both financial and reputational—for noncompliance with environmental regulations and sexual harassment laws have prompted the attention. Nevertheless, perhaps because of the subtle and complex aspects of many harassment situations, the issue continues to be a major ethical challenge in healthcare. As Decker puts it: "Healthcare institutions do not seem to realize the financial impact of the problem and are not acting proactively to combat sexual harassment. It is a huge cost."[2] This chapter probes the problem and highlights organizational approaches to address sexual harassment.

CASE STUDY

Case Six: Don't Ask Don't Tell

St. Serena's has prided itself on developing a state-of-the-art radiology and laboratory capacity. Under the leadership of Dirk Williams, Vice President of Ancillary Services, the departments of radiology and laboratory have blossomed and become major sources of revenue for the

St. Serena's complex. Furthermore, during the last Joint Commission accreditation audit these departments received the highest ratings.

Mary Moore, a friend of Dirk's, occasionally pops in to see him in his office. Mary was one of the first women at St. Serena's to be promoted to a vice president position. She had always been considered a team player and in the old days had often been described as one of the boys. One day, while walking through the laboratory office area to visit her friend, Mary noticed the eye-catching cover of a copy of *Playboy* magazine on the desk of the lab director.

This day, as she walked into Dirk's office, his secretary Thelma was leaving with her clothes disheveled. Mary gave Dirk a knowing smile but said nothing about it. As they chatted she noticed what looked like lipstick on Dirk's collar.

A week later Richard, a recently hired lab technician, was in the staff lavatory. While there he overheard a conversation between two supervisors describing in lewd detail the physical attributes of one of their colleagues. "If she plays her cards right," one of them said, "she'll go places here." Because it was part of his recent orientation, Richard thought of Section I.9.a of the St. Serena's code of conduct:

> *Corporate policy strictly prohibits any form of sexual harassment in the workplace. Sexual harassment may include, but is not limited to stating or threatening, either explicitly or implicitly, that an individual's submission to or rejection of sexual advances will in any way influence any decision regarding that individual's terms or conditions of employment.*

Richard also recalled the strong presentation delivered by members of the corporate compliance committee. His divisional compliance officer in particular emphasized Section I.9.b of the code of conduct:

> *Sexual harassment may include, but is not limited to, the existence of a sexually abusive or hostile working environment. This is characterized by unwelcome sexual advances, verbal or physical conduct of a sexual nature, gender harassment (even if the conduct is not sexual in nature), or display of sexually suggestive objects or pictures.*

The committee had also stressed Section II of the code, which states that every employee of St. Serena's *"has the obligation to report promptly any suspected violation of the corporate code of conduct to their supervisor or divisional compliance coordinator."*

That evening Richard's family went out for dinner to celebrate his daughter's birthday. At the restaurant he recognized Lance Larue, St. Serena's executive vice president, at a distant table having what appeared to be a romantic encounter with Bettie Paige, one of the compliance committee members who had addressed his orientation session. Richard had heard through the grapevine that she was a top candidate to head a new home care venture being established at St. Serena's.

Questions for Discussion:

1. What is Richard likely to do? Why? What should he do?
2. If there is a disparity between what Richard is likely to do and what he ethically should do, what contributes to the disparity? If there is no disparity, what facilitates the match?
3. What formal organizational structures for dealing with the sexual harassment issue are apparent at St. Serena's? What further structures might be considered?
4. What informal realities at St. Serena's relate to the sexual harassment issue? What might St. Serena's do to strengthen its informal cultural approach to sexual harassment?
5. Evaluate Mary's behavior. Does the organizational setting affect her judgment?
6. Is Bettie Paige likely to get the new leadership position? Why? Is there any ethical dimension to the matter?

COMMENTARY

Richard seems to be in the middle of a "disconnect." On the one hand formal structures at St. Serena's—especially its code of conduct and its orientation training—nudge him in certain directions with respect to sexual harassment; on the other hand, the culture in the organization seems to direct him in another direction. What to do?!

According to the code, reinforced by the orientation training he received, Richard has apparently witnessed two incidents that, at the very least, could appear to be violations of sexual harassment standards. First, he overheard supervisors use what could well be considered as verbally harassing language about a female employee; further, these supervisors seemed to be suggesting that at St. Serena's a connection exists between "sexual advances" and "conditions of employment," to use the words of the code.

On the other hand, Richard heard these statements behind the closed doors of the men's room; they were not uttered in the presence of the female colleague. Should Richard consider this situation to be within the suspected violation category of Section II of the code, and therefore embrace the obligation to report these supervisors? As a new employee, what might Richard be feeling about that prospect?

Second, Richard has inadvertently witnessed an episode that reasonable people might interpret as inconsistent with the code's admonition about sexual advances being related to conditions of employment. Lance undoubtedly has a significant say in who will be appointed to head the home care venture; therefore, could a romantic liaison with a candidate for the job be ethically inappropriate? Does Richard have an obligation under the code to report this "reasonably suspicious" episode? Or is it any of his business? Afterall, this incident did not occur at work and was witnessed by Richard by sheer chance. We need to decide what Richard's obligation is. To advance the organizational ethics at St. Serena's, we also need to figure out what Richard is likely to do and what St. Serena's could do to maximize the likelihood that Richard will choose to act at least close to how he ethically should act. To help us answer these questions we again turn to fundamental concepts.

Humdrum Versus Headline Events

Remember the distinction between humdrummers and headliners discussed in Chapter one? Surely one could argue that the two incidents confronting Richard are humdrum matters and nothing to worry about. After all, the first episode was in the room where "boys will be boys," where idle chatter occurs, where there is "no harm, no foul" committed. If the discussion occurred in the presence of the female colleague, that would be different. But isn't the incident trivial? Or, is it rather a "seemingly trivial" matter that in subtle ways speaks headlines about a culture of sexual harassment at St. Serena's?

What about poor Lance? He seems to be trying to be discrete about the apparent affair. Might not a reasonable person argue for respect of his privacy, contending that the encounter is after-hours, outside the workplace, and none of Richard's business? Lance and Bettie ogling each other at work might be a headliner meriting report as a suspected violation of the code but a dinner meeting outside of work is more of a gray area. Or is this argument just a clouded perception permitting us—and Richard—to relegate an incident to the triviality trough when in stark (though subtle and complex) reality the incident is a glaring example of a sexual harassment culture at St. Serena's? Is this precisely what Peirce, Smolinski, and Rosen in the attached reading have in mind when they write, "When managers convince themselves that the incident is trivial, they are practicing a form of self-deception . . ."?[3]

Formal Versus Informal Realities

Clearly St. Serena's has taken some strong formal steps—in the form of a written code of conduct and orientation training—to comply with work environment standards and ethical principles. We could inquire about grievance procedures, enforcement mechanisms, and reward systems and we could analyze the code and the orientation program. For example, is the code poorly written? Is the code too broad and vague, inviting justifications for skirting around it? Was this a one-time orientation training, or is such instruction held with regularity? Do training sessions include reflection on, for example, "bathroom talk"?

However, the informal realities at St. Serena's are probably the cause of Richard's agitation. The cultural signals seem to tell employees not to worry too much about the formal policies and training. The code mandates one attitude about sexual harassment, but the supervisors in the lavatory demonstrate another attitude. The training stresses up-front confrontation, but senior manager Mary seems to stress avoidance and senior vice president Lance seems to stress discretion. Socialization à la St. Serena's is underway and a disconnect exists. As Virginia Gibson observes: "What's missing is the heart of the issue—how to achieve behavior changes that ultimately will influence the attitudes and beliefs of the individuals that will lead to increased acceptance and tolerance in the workplace."[4] To get Richard's blood pressure down, St. Serena's will have to attend to its informal cultural reality, not just to the formal reality. Peirce, Smolinski, and Rosen have some ideas in this regard (see reading at end of chapter).

Dignity Versus Denigration

Fundamental to the notion of a harassment-free environment is the value of human dignity. This value holds that every person—no matter what gender, race, title, or hierarchical position—is a dignified human being, and that anything that denigrates rather than dignifies is ethically unacceptable. Today it is also legally unacceptable to denigrate in the workplace: Compliance fundamentally requires organizational respect for human dignity in all its manifestations.

Most codes of conduct, like St. Serena's code, now recognize as denigrating to women and therefore unacceptable the presence in the workplace of pictures that highlight female sexuality. Should Mary have done something when she noticed a visibly suggestive cover of a magazine in the workplace? According to Section II of the code, should she have reported the observation to her compliance coordinator? Has Mary been "culturized" at St. Serena's not to be bothered by such things and not to notice such denigration? Was the conversation Richard overheard in the men's room basically denigrating to all women (and men, too, for that matter) at St. Serena's?

The formal reality at St. Serena's seems to prize and defend the dignity of all employees; the informal cultural reality, in contrast, seems to denigrate at least a certain class of employees. That is the situation Richard entered when he joined the organization. That is the situation in which he must decide what he should do and what he will do.

Power Versus Authority

Underlying most forms of sexual harassment is the reality of power—as opposed to authority—wielded by harassers. A laboratory director has no authority to display offensive pictures, but he does have the power to do so. Dirk has no romantic authority over his secretary, but he may well have romantic power. The supervisors have no authority to speak lewdly about a colleague, but they certainly have the power to do so, especially in the men's room.

Formal structural mechanisms such as codes of conduct address potential abuses of authority. At St. Serena's the abuse of authority for sexual harassment purposes is prohibited formally. Cultural mechanisms are required to control abuses of power, however.[5] Is this relevant to Richard's reflection on what to do? Could he reason that he has witnessed no abuse of authority, which formal mechanisms condemn, but that he has, instead, witnessed possible abuses of power, which is not so clearly prohibited at St. Serena's? This distinction is a key concept in developing organizational ethics.

Moral Approbation

Richard, and anyone else at Serena's who witnesses suspected violations of sexual harassment standards, faces the challenge of moral approbation. Should he, and can he, express disapproval with the behaviors he has witnessed? As we know from Chapter three, the structure at St. Serena's enables him to do this through a hotline. He can report his suspicions anonymously or openly. But does the culture of St. Serena's enable him to report? Richard has—through the code—authority to exercise moral approbation. But does the culture constrain his power to exercise moral approbation? He could have said something disapproving to the supervisors in the bathroom, for example. But does the organizational culture constrain such rebuke? He could have approached Lance in the restaurant, but do cultural norms discourage that?

Figure 6.1 Lens for Addressing Sexual Harassment

	Power	Authority
Formal		
Informal		

Similarly, Mary had both the authority and the power to say something to the lab director about the magazine she saw. And she had the power to say something to Dirk about the lipstick on his collar. She also had the authority to report both incidents to a compliance coordinator or anonymously through the hotline. But Mary did not. Was that because the informal reality at St. Serena's directs her the other way?

As I suggested in Chapter three, moral approbation is a key ingredient of organizational ethics. How does an organization encourage rather than discourage the exercise of moral approbation for inappropriate behaviors? In the reading, Peirce, Smolinski, and Rosen suggest the promulgation of creatively demonstrative policies, the establishment of clear reporting procedures, and the exhibition of clear managerial support. Jones and Ryan[6] emphasize the identification and nurturing of ethically supportive "referent groups." Figure 6.1 suggests that both power and authority realities need to be addressed in both the formal and informal dimensions.

Individual Versus Organizational Ethics

In Chapter one we reflected on the distinction between individual ethics and organizational ethics. At St. Serena's organizational ethics is supported by formal and informal realities; the individual ethics of people like Richard, Mary, Dirk, Lance, and the lab supervisors have been developed from childhood. Richard is a good and decent person— with a high level of personal ethics—who is facing situations within an organizational setting. Recall Chambliss's caveat: "To pretend that someone is good or bad apart from settings that allow or prevent their acting is . . . pragmatically foolish."[7] Will this ethical person take an action that is discouraged by the organization's culture? Or, does the organization need to take action so that its informal realities support good and decent people?

Suppose that the lab supervisors are also good people who have been culturized at St. Serena's to talk in ways they would never speak when in their home bathroom, and that Mary may very well confront her spouse at home but not colleagues at the office where such action is counter-cultural. In effect, Richard and Mary and others may know clearly what they *should* do but, for organizational reasons, may distinguish that action from what they believe they can do.

Notes

1. American College of Healthcare Executives. 1995. *Ethical Policy Statement: Creating An Ethical Environment for Employees.*
2. Decker, P. 1997. "Sexual Harassment in Health Care: A Major Productivity Problem." *Health Care Supervisor* 16 (1): 3.
3. Peirce, E., C. Smolinski, and B. Rosen. 1998. "Why Sexual Harassment Complaints Fall On Deaf Ears." *Academy of Management Executive* 12 (3): 47.
4. Gibson, V. 1993. "Beyond Legal Compliance: What's Next?" *HR Focus* 70 (7): 17.
5. See Worthley, J. 1997. *The Ethics of the Ordinary in Healthcare*, 61–110. Chicago: Health Administration Press.
6. Jones, T., and L. Ryan. 1998. "The Effect of Moral Forces on Individual Morality." *Business Ethics Quarterly* 8 (3): 442ff.
7. Chambliss, D. 1996. *Beyond Caring*, 117. Chicago: University of Chicago Press.

READING

The following piece, although not specifically addressed to healthcare organizations, is arguably the most comprehensive analysis of underlying causes of sexual harassment in healthcare organizations, including St. Serena's. The reading is also the most useful in discerning proactive managerial measures to deal with the situation. The authors stress the business and legal dimensions of the issue, but implicit in their analysis is the ethical dimension based in respect for human dignity. Particularly pertinent to healthcare organizations such as St. Serena's is the emphasis on the relationship of formal structures to cultural realities in identifying reasons for the continuing prevalence of sexual harassment problems despite strong compliance incentives. Peirce, Smolinski, and Rosen find that the roots of organizational difficulties in dealing with the issue are in basic areas such as faulty written policies, reporting procedures, and managerial attitudes. Not surprisingly, the practical measures the authors suggest for improving the organizational ethics of sexual harassment flow from their analysis of these aspects of organizational life. What analysis and recommendations would a consultant report from the authors to St. Serena's contain?

Why Sexual Harassment Complaints Fall on Deaf Ears

Ellen Peirce, Carol A. Smolinski, and Benson Rosen[*]

Executive Overview

Several high-profile sexual harassment cases have been reported in the news media recently. It appears that many organizations are slow to respond to internal complaints of sexual harassment, forcing victims to go outside the organization to seek redress through the court system. These failures to respond to complaints—what we have come to identify as the "deaf ear" syndrome—are surprising in light of the well-publicized costs to human resources, organizational reputation, and the bottom line. This paper investigates some of the factors and dynamics that contribute to organizational inaction. Based on interviews with EEOC attorneys who specialize in sexual harassment litigation, a review of relevant literature, and recent media examples, we identify three themes that are associated with deaf ear syndrome: (1) inadequate organizational policies and procedures, (2) managerial rationalizations, and (3) inertial tendencies. Fortunately, a few responsive organizations provide examples of best practices.

Recent headlines have once again focused on the issue of sexual harassment: "Top Enlisted Man in the Army Stands Accused of Sexual Assault"[1]; "EEOC Sues Mitsubishi Unit for Harassment"[2]; "Abuse of Power: The Astonishing Tale of Sexual Harassment at Astra USA"[3]; "Wall Street Fails to Stem Rising Claims of Sex Harassment and Discrimination"[4]; and "Army Investigates Allegations of Sexual Misconduct and Rape in Training Command."[5] While sexual harassment is not new, the mounting evidence of organizational inaction in the face of repeated sexual harassment complaints is. To date, most of the literature on sexual harassment has focused on how it is defined, and what corporations can do to prevent it. We are aware of no articles which explore the factors contributing to managerial and organizational inaction once sexual harassment is reported. This article examines why reports of sexual harassment fall on deaf ears despite more than a decade of increased awareness, punitive legislation, and extensive media attention,

---

* Reprinted with permission of the Academy of Management, P. O. Box 3020, Briarcliff Manor, NY 10510-8020. Academy of Management Executive 1998. 12: 3. Reproduced by permission of the publisher via Copyright Clearance Center, Inc. Ellen Peirce is professor of law and ethics at the University of North Carolina at Chapel Hill. Carol A. Smolinski is research assistant at the University of North Carolina at Chapel Hill. Benson Rosen is Hanes Professor of Management at the University of North Carolina at Chapel Hill.

and identifies how corporations are likely to fall prey to the "deaf ear" syndrome.

At both Mitsubishi Motors Manufacturing Company of America (Mitsubishi) and Astra USA, Inc. (Astra), Equal Employment Opportunity Commission (EEOC) records and media coverage reveal a long history of harassment complaints. Yet these complaints went unanswered. In the Mitsubishi case, after a lengthy investigation, the EEOC filed a class action suit on behalf of as many as 500 female employees and former employees alleging persistent and unheeded incidents of sexual harassment over a number of years. The EEOC expressed particular dismay over widespread evidence suggesting that Mitsubishi's upper management was aware of the harassment, yet failed to act. In the case of Astra, a 17-year history of sexual harassment complaints against CEO Lars Bildman also went unaddressed.

The High Costs of Organizational Inaction

That Mitsubishi, Astra, the U.S. Army and many other organizations are slow or fail to respond to sexual harassment complaints is particularly puzzling in light of the well-publicized damage that occurs once harassment cases become public. Del Laboratories paid a total of more than $1 million to settle sexual harassment complaints filed by employees with the EEOC in 1995.[6] Chevron recently agreed to pay $2.2 million to four women who alleged that they were the victims of corporate retaliation for filing sexual harassment complaints.[7] In the largest such settlement to date, Mitsubishi agreed to pay $34 million to several hundred women who had alleged unheeded claims of sexual harassment over a period of years at the company's auto assembly plant in Normal, Illinois.

Corporations are faring no better in litigation. The law firm of Baker and McKenzie is currently appealing a $3.5 million judgment to a secretary harassed by a senior partner over a number of months.[8] In 1996, sexual harassment victims received a total of $27.8 million.[9] These awards do not take into consideration the financial toll on the firm in terms of attorney's fees and personnel costs. The negative financial impact on the organization is further supported by a recent study of federal sexual harassment cases. Researchers found that where an individual had been the victim of severe harassment with witnesses and documents to support the allegation, had notified management of the harassment, and management had taken no remedial action upon notification, the individual was virtually guaranteed to win the case against the organization.[10]

Monetary awards to victims represent only a fraction of the total organizational costs for failing to deal rapidly and effectively with sexual harassment complaints. A 1988 survey of 160 Fortune 500 companies reported that a company with 23,750 employees would lose on average $6.7 million per year in decreased productivity, increased rates of absenteeism, and higher turnover attributable to sexual harassment.[11] Such figures represent $282.53 per employee, costs which would be significantly higher in today's dollars. Furthermore, serious harassment charges often lead to the departure of key executives, including both the victims and the harassers. Both Mitsubishi and Astra were compelled to discharge high-level executives following the disclosure of harassment charges. Increasingly, as incidents of sexual harassment are publicized in the media, reputational damage will impact the bottom line. Individuals are refusing to patronize, invest in, or work for organizations that have a poor reputation for enforcing sexual equality. For example, the Reverend Jesse Jackson led a nationwide boycott against Mitsubishi and is currently forming a watchdog organization that will rank U.S. companies on their commitment to managing diversity.

More subtle and troubling costs of sexual harassment include the psychological and physiological harm to victims and their coworkers. Researchers have shown that victims often experience depression, frustration, nervousness, and decreased self-esteem, as well as fatigue, nausea, and hypertension.[12] These symptoms in turn lead to decreased productivity, increased absenteeism, and worker resentment.

With such clear evidence of the costs associated with sexual harassment in the workplace, it seems surprising that corporations would ignore allegations of harassment, yet our research and EEOC records support the fact that they do. Accordingly, understanding why organizations fail to respond in-house to employee allegations of sexual harassment charges is a critical priority.

Exploring the Nature of the Deaf Ear Syndrome
In order to understand the nature of the deaf ear syndrome, we gathered data from several sources. First, we interviewed five veteran EEOC attorneys who are key litigators of sexual harassment cases. Collectively they have 50 years of experience, and have litigated several hundred EEOC sexual harassment cases. Based on their experience of investigating and litigating these cases, we asked them to identify key themes of cases in which companies turned a deaf ear toward sexual harassment complaints. We then asked the attorneys to identify and discuss recently decided cases illustrating organizational inaction. The five EEOC litigators collectively identified nine cases in which organizations had consistently ignored allegations of sexual harassment until, ultimately, victims filed formal charges with the EEOC.[13]

The organizations involved in these cases were Sears and Roebuck, New York Carpet World, Total Systems, Lamplight, Jim Dalley and Associates, Holk Development, Noon's R.V., Featherlite Mfg., and Cafe Vienna. To complete our research, we reviewed management literature relevant to sexual harassment and organizational inaction and culled recent news media examples of organizations that had repeatedly ignored sexual harassment complaints. Drawing from the interviews, literature, and media examples, we extracted common themes regarding deaf ear organizations. It should be noted that our research focused on firms that were troubled by sexual harassment and did not involve a control group of firms that were not so troubled. Although we later discuss what some exemplary firms have done to avoid such problems, our ability to reliably distinguish deaf ear organizations from others awaits well-controlled empirical research. Nevertheless, we believe what we have learned serves as a clear and valuable warning.

We were able to identify three themes associated with organizational inaction: (1) inadequate organizational policies and procedures for managing sexual harassment complaints; (2) managerial reactions and rationalizations for failing to act in the face of such complaints; and (3) organizational features contributing to inertial tendencies or deafness. In the following sections, we discuss each of these themes, and then provide recommendations for avoiding the deaf-ear syndrome.

Inadequate Sexual Harassment Policies and Procedures

Individually, and in the aggregate, inadequate policies and procedures lay the groundwork for managerial inaction. In our interviews with EEOC attorneys, we identified three specific policy and procedure inadequacies associated with organizations that turn a deaf ear to sexual harassment complaints: poorly written policies or no policy at all; vague definitions of sexual harassment; and cumbersome reporting procedures.

Poorly written policies.

A surprising number of organizations have written harassment policies that our EEOC attorneys characterized as poorly articulated or inadequate in their coverage. Shortcomings in policies centered around the definition of sexual harassment and the guidelines for reporting harassment incidents. In several cases, employees seemed completely unaware of the existence of their organization's harassment policy. Featherlite Mfg., for example, stated its sexual harassment policy in a single paragraph embedded in a 50-page handbook "that no one was expected to read." In other organizations, the policies were written in "legalese" with no clarifying explanation. Still other organizations had no written sexual harassment policies at all. This was particularly the case for small enterprises. While it is true that federal EEOC laws only cover organizations with 15 or more employees, states are increasingly adopting laws requiring organizations of all sizes to develop written policies governing sexual harassment.

In the absence of any sexual harassment policies or in light of vague and poorly written policies, it was easy for organizations to overlook and ignore incidents of sexual harassment. Managers in a number of the cases examined appeared unsure how to interpret informal complaints and uncertain about what action to take. Consequently, the victims went to the EEOC with their concerns. The EEOC attorneys and the recent survey findings of Peirce, Rosen, and Hiller[14] indicate that, in the absence of written guidelines, victims of sexual harassment see no mechanisms for registering complaints and have little expectation that their complaints will be redressed. When the victims eventually determine that the situation is intolerable, they frequently seek out the EEOC to file formal charges.

Vague definitions of sexual harassment.

As our discussions with the EEOC attorneys revealed, many organizations do little to educate their managers on the definition of sexual harassment. And managers are not alone in their confusion regarding which behaviors constitute harassing behavior. The recent debate over incidents involving a six-year-old in North Carolina and a seven-year-old in Queens, New York, who were suspended for unsolicited demonstrations of affection to their classmates mirror the difficulties many institutions experience in defining sexual harassment.[15] While the EEOC provides some clarity in their "Guidelines on Discrimination Because of Sex," (see Figure 1 for more details), the EEOC attorneys interviewed emphasized that organizations have a difficult time defining a hostile environment for their employees.[16]

Hostile environment sexual harassment is complex and frequently misunderstood. It encompasses unwelcome sexual advances, requests for sexual favors, and other verbal or physical conduct of a sexual nature. Interpretation of this language has been expanded in numerous cases to include: unwelcome sexual banter, referral to women in demeaning terms such as "babe," or the display of sexually explicit materials such as cartoons, calendars, and photographs. It is evident from our discussions with the EEOC attorneys that managers frequently ignore, misinterpret, or underestimate the factors that contribute to a hostile work

Figure 1

Quid Pro Quo

Encompasses all situations in which submission to sexually harassing conduct is made a term or condition of employment, or in which submission to or rejection of sexually harassing conduct is used as the basis for employment decisions affecting the individual who is the target of such conduct. In Henson vs. City of Dundee the court stated four elements that a plaintiff must prove to establish a case of quid pro quo sexual harassment:

1. *That he or she belongs to a protected group;*
2. *That he or she was subject to unwelcome sexual harassment;*
3. *That the harassment complained of was based on sex; and*
4. *That the employee's reaction to harassment complained of affected tangible aspects of the employee's compensation, terms, conditions, or privileges of employment.*

Hostile Environment

Unwelcome and demeaning sexually related behavior that creates an intimidating, hostile, and offensive work environment. The plaintiff need not show some tangible job detriment in addition to the hostile work environment created by sexual harassment. Although not every instance or condition of work environment harassment gives rise to a sex discrimination claim, a plaintiff who can prove a number of elements can establish a claim. The five elements are similar to those for quid pro quo:

1. *The employee belongs to a protected group under Title VII of the 1964 Civil Rights Act;*
2. *The employee was subject to unwelcome sexual harassment;*
3. *The harassment complained of was based on sex;*
4. *The harassment complained of affected a term, condition, or privilege of employment; and*
5. *The employer knew, or should have known, of the harassment in question and failed to take prompt remedial action.*

---

environment, and are therefore often unable to identify and respond to various legitimate charges as forms of sexual harassment.

In a number of the cases discussed with the EEOC litigators, it was evident that managers did not think they were guilty of sexual harassment because they mistakenly believed that sexual attraction was a necessary component of the legal definition of hostile environment sexual harassment. For example, in a case brought against Noon's R.V., women complained that their supervisors would walk behind them making barking and howling sounds. During the EEOC investigation, one of the harassers denied that he ever engaged in sexual harassment as alleged because he considered the plaintiffs to be "dogs." As one of the EEOC attorneys commented in this instance, "[The harassers] were operating on this faulty logic that it can't be sexual harassment if there isn't some kind of sexual attraction. It might be sex-based, but if they don't feel attraction, they don't feel they are guilty."

Another vivid example of sexual harassment based on a hostile work environment was found in the Sears case. A Sears manager had the habit of inviting female subordinates into his office to view his vacation photographs—close-ups of women's bottoms and breasts taken at a beach. When the HR executive at Sears was deposed during the EEOC investigation, he questioned whether merely having employees view "vacation photos" could constitute sexual harassment. In this case, even the most senior HR executive failed to understand the impact of such an invitation. Subordinates would perceive such a request as a mandate or, at the very least, a request that they would be reluctant to turn down. As one EEOC attorney noted, abuse of power in such a fashion is not tolerated under harassment laws.

Our interviews further disclosed that difficulty arises when management fails to take steps to draw a line between joking and sexual harassment. As noted by our EEOC attorneys, in blue-collar settings where jobs can be routine and stressful, managers often permit horseplay to relieve tension. However, managers and employees often cannot distinguish between acceptable behavior and that which has crossed over the line into harassing behavior. Such was the case at Featherlite Mfg., where horseplay turned into crude and vulgar behavior directed at the women employees. Complaints went unheeded by management and tensions mounted, resulting in an EEOC filing. Knowing when the line has been crossed is particularly important given research evidence that men and women perceive and classify sexual behavior in very different ways. In a study of over 2,000 managers, male and female respondents had little difficulty agreeing that blatant behaviors such as pinching and patting constituted sexual harassment. However, females also perceived more subtle behaviors, such as innuendo, sexual joking, and leering as harassment, while male respondents did not.[17] In the absence of clear guidelines and examples of acceptable and unacceptable behavior, it is evident that organizations risk creating hostile work environments and leave themselves vulnerable to sexual harassment charges. Because Featherlite had not taken the time to draft an adequate policy defining sexual harassment, it landed in court and the plaintiffs were awarded significant amounts for the horseplay.

Cumbersome reporting procedures.

In a surprising number of EEOC cases, defendants disclaimed liability on the grounds that the incident had not been properly reported through the system set up by management. In other examples, the reporting procedure was ineffective or unclear. When the formal reporting procedures are ambiguous, victims become confused on how to proceed, management feels justified in ignoring or deferring investigation of the incident, and the problem escalates. At New York Carpet World, the victim reported a sales manager to another supervisor for making sexual comments to her after she had requested several times that he stop. She was told to keep notes on the manager's actions. When the comments escalated to physical harassment, the victim quit and reported the incidents directly to headquarters. And when the victim finally brought the case to the attention of the EEOC upon headquarters' failure to act, New York Carpet World executives denied liability for their inaction, stating that she had not followed proper procedure and had reported the incidents to the wrong person. What the EEOC (and ultimately the jury) found dubious about this particular line of defense was that both the victim and the supervisor to whom she reported the harassment believed that she was following proper channels. In still other cases discussed with the EEOC attorneys, managers who received sexual harassment complaints were uncertain how to proceed. Their employers failed to provide them with the necessary training on how to investigate harassment charges. Uncertain in their roles, many failed to take any action. As indicated in their depositions later, the managers were as confused and frustrated as the victims. As one EEOC attorney commented: "They do not know what to do with the information. This may be a result of a weak policy or no training on what the policy means. They may have it on paper, but it is not alive to them."

Obviously, policies requiring a victim to report incidents of sexual harassment to an immediate supervisor are unworkable when the supervisor is also the harasser. In several of the cases we examined, the harassers were the owners or related to the owners of the enterprise and the sole managers in the company. Under these circumstances, the victims could see no channel for registering a legitimate complaint. Clearly, giving the victim no place to voice her complaint internally compels her to go outside the organization to the EEOC.

Managerial Reactions and Rationalizations

While inadequate policies and procedures frustrate efforts to redress sexual harassment complaints, even organizations with relatively well-developed policies are not likely to respond effectively if their managers react defensively or rationalize away charges of sexual harassment. The case examples cited by the EEOC attorneys illustrate a number of reactions that contribute to organizational inaction in addressing reports of sexual harassment: denying the claims; blaming the victim; minimizing the seriousness of the offense; protecting a valued employee; ignoring a chronic harasser; or retaliating against the victim.

These six reactions parallel closely those that characterize the narcissist, a personality type in modern psychoanalysis as well as a recently identified managerial and organizational profile in the organizational behavior literature.[18] In relating narcissism to managers and to organizations, Brown defines narcissistic individuals as those who need to maintain a positive self-image and engage in "ego-defensive" behavior to preserve their self-esteem. He further describes narcissists in terms of six broad behavioral/psychological indicators: (1) denial, (2) rationalization, (3) self-aggrandizement, (4) attributional egoism, (5) sense of entitlement, and (6) anxiety.[19] As stated by Brown, "Individuals engage in these behaviors unselfconsciously, rather than for the benefit of an intended audience. . . ."[20] The reactions identified by EEOC attorneys parallel Brown's framework, and support his thesis that narcissistic individuals and organizations are hampered by a distorted view of negative situations because of the need to engage in ego-defensive behavior to preserve organizational (and individual) self-esteem.

Denying the harassment claims.

Denial is a well-known defense mechanism, as well as an indicator of narcissism. As noted by Staw, McKechnie, and Puffer[21] narcissistic personalities deny or conceal disagreeable facts from themselves and from others in a self-deceptive effort to maintain their self-esteem. Because harassment complaints are sensitive, highly personalized disputes, they often trigger psychological defense mechanisms.

From our EEOC interview data and our observations about Astra, it appears that organizations run by strong and egotistical people often demonstrate denial as a response to sexual harassment complaints. The founders, owners, or managers become defensive in the face of any information that might prove damaging to the reputations of their companies. They often refuse to accept that the reported incidents constitute sexual harassment. In many instances, they argue that what was called harassment was actually consensual activity between the parties involved, and often defend the character of the accused. They go to great lengths to deny that anyone in their organizations would be guilty of sexual harassment.

For example, the owner of New York Carpet World was indignant when one of his employees was accused of sexual harassment. He perceived the claim as a personal accusation and an attack on his own character. Instead of investigating the case, his reaction led him to a position of total denial. He became incapable of objectively dealing with the harassment or the harassed. Similarly, in the case of Noon's R.V., the owners of the company, a father and his two sons, were personally offended that a government agency, the EEOC, would dare tell them how to manage their business. Incensed, they disputed the claims vigorously.

Denial and defensiveness on the part of owners, founders, and organizational leaders preclude full investigation of harassment complaints. Disgruntled victims of harassment see no alternative but to take their cases to the courts and to the media, often resulting in negative publicity for the company. Recently, Mitsubishi management was publicly castigated for its absolute denial of sexual harassment at the Normal, Illinois plant in the face of what appears to be clear and substantiated allegations brought by the EEOC. The announcement that Mitsubishi had agreed to settle the claims led to equally large headlines.

Blaming the victim.

A common response of managers in companies that turn a deaf ear to sexual harassment complaints is the attitude that the employee brought it on herself or was no good to begin with. This perception parallels the attributional egotism ego-defensive mechanism identified in the narcissist literature. According to this characteristic, narcissists attribute favorable traits and outcomes to themselves, and negative attributes and outcomes to others. They tend to offer explanations for events that are self-serving and that distort the actual facts of the situation. Thus, the narcissistic owner/manager is unable to perceive that his managers are at fault in a dispute with workers, but is quick to attribute negative characteristics to those accusing his managers of misconduct. For example, in the Featherlite case, the owners hired investigators to probe into the sex lives of the two victims, revealing disparaging information. The owners attempted to portray the victims as "tramps" and inferred that any charge of sexual harassment at work was brought on by actions of the women themselves. These tactics are generally not allowed in court and often backfire by making the organization appear vindictive and unsympathetic to women's concerns. In the New York Carpet World case, the company argued that the victim of harassment had suffered spousal abuse and many other misfortunes, implying that she could not distinguish between her personal problems and her treatment on the job.

In other instances, managers have alleged that employees who bring charges of sexual harassment are seeking revenge against employers for poor performance reviews, once again demonstrating a belief that the lower-level employees are at fault, and not the manager or employee accused of harassment—a form of attributional egotism. In the Sears case, the manager who showed female employees suggestive photographs argued that their complaints were made in retaliation for marginal performance evaluations and for having to work for a demanding supervisor. Blaming the victim provides the organization with yet another reason for inaction.

Minimizing the seriousness of the offense.

Our EEOC interviews revealed that managers often trivialize or make light of sexual harassment complaints, and victims are typically perceived as weak and lacking a sense of humor. This response is also characteristic of the narcissistic manager who, according to Brown, "attempts to justify or find reasons for unacceptable behavior."[22] Once individuals establish in their own minds that the complaints are unjustified or lack substance, they feel no compulsion to conduct a follow-up investigation. However, when employees feel that the seriousness of their complaints is minimized, they respond to managerial apathy by seeking outside remedies. In the case of Holk Development, the owner was accused of harassing one of his female employees at a construction site. While he admitted making sexual comments and repeated invitations to go to the beach for the weekend, he defended himself by asserting that the woman was "making too big a deal out of it." In the Noon's R.V. case, one female employee reported to the manager that a male coworker kept asking her to have sex with him. Instead of investigating her complaint, the manager responded by saying, "Don't worry, you don't have to have sex with him, you have to have sex with me." In both cases, managers engaged in narcissistic behavior: in the former, the manager was defending his own behavior; in the latter, the manager was justifying that of his favored employee.

When managers convince themselves that the incident is trivial, they are practicing a form of self-deception that unreasonably leads them to believe the victim will accept their judgment and withdraw the complaint. This is seldom the case.

Research on organizational justice suggests that feelings of injustice are exacerbated when employees are treated in an insensitive or inconsiderate manner during the course of an organizational procedure, such as filing a grievance.[23] Often it is not simply an unsatisfactory outcome, such as not acting on a complaint, that motivates employees to seek redress, but the feeling of unjust treatment. In cases where a victim's concerns are minimized, the employee feels discounted, concludes that the organization is indifferent, and seeks out the EEOC.

Protecting valued employees.

Another typical reaction of managers in deaf ear organizations, according to our EEOC attorneys, is to ignore or excuse the behavior of high-ranking executives. At Astra, everyone at the firm knew Bildman's reputation and 17-year history of harassing women associates, but most overlooked it, knowing also of his status and record as a successful executive.

When an organization like Astra allows key employees to go unpunished for sexual harassment, a subtle complicity evolves among the other employees. Because of Bildman's position, long history, and financial success at Astra, he was perceived by other employees as being above the law. As one female manager told a new Astra employee who complained of sexual harassment, "That's the way it is at Astra, and you had better get used to it." For many years, Bildman was perceived as untouchable, and women who had complaints were paid off to keep quiet, or simply left. Further, when the chief officer in an organization engages in such unethical behavior, others in the organization perceive this as "implicit sanctioning"[24] of such behavior and feel less constrained themselves. Clearly this was the case at Astra where a number of managers felt license to follow Lars Bildman's example and engage in sexual harassment.

In a similar situation, the accusations of a career army officer, Sergeant Major Brenda Hoster, against Sergeant Major Gene McKinney, were ignored, and Hoster opted to end her career in the Army over the issue. The reaction that high-ranking individuals are untouchable is highlighted in the remarks of Sergeant Major Hoster: "It seems like people in a higher position and at a different level are exempt from those kinds of things. . . . I just don't understand why he [McKinney] gets a different system of justice."[25] Hoster decided to disclose the alleged harassment only when McKinney was placed on a panel to study sex abuse in the Army. The perception by lower-level employees that status protects certain high-level managers from sanction contributes to disillusionment and an underlying sense of unfairness that erodes worker loyalty.

Many lower-level managers do not wish to make waves or bring bad news to the attention of top officials. At the Baker and McKenzie law firm,[26] a highly successful and long-term partner, Martin Greenstein, who was accused of harassing his secretary, had a long record of harassing female employees. He was reputed to be a rainmaker, a lawyer who attracts business for the firm, and managers found ways to overlook his behavior and silence his accusers. In this particular case, however, the strategy backfired when the disgruntled victim sought redress by going to the EEOC. She was eventually awarded $7 million (later reduced to $3 million) by the court, and the law firm has appealed the decision. The jury openly stated that they recommended a significant award not only because of the egregious conduct of the law partner, but also based on evidence that the firm consistently overlooked his harassing behavior for many years.

Ignoring an habitual harasser.

Our EEOC attorneys reported that in several cases, managers discounted sexual harassment complaints based on the fact that the victim received fair warning about the harasser's propensity for misconduct. In one case, managers had warned a new female employee that she might be the target of advances from an employee named Dave. When she later registered a sexual harassment complaint, management replied, "Oh, that's just the way Dave is." The implication was clear—forewarned should be forearmed.

A warning conveyed to victims is an inappropriate way to handle, or perhaps forestall, a complaint, and it provides damning evidence that the organization was aware of an employee's harassing tendencies. Yet, this line of defense is offered in a surprising number of instances, according to EEOC attorneys. The "that's Dave" type of employee is particularly dangerous to firms in the sexual harassment arena because he typically believes he is above the rules of society and may insist that there is nothing wrong with his behavior.[27] Once again, the organization and its members are engaging in self-deception by rationalizing that because "that's Dave," the behavior can be overlooked, thus implicitly condoning Dave's behavior.

Retaliation against the victim.

Worse than organizational inaction is the possibility that an organization will take strong retaliatory action against the alleged victim. Retaliation against victims of sexual harassment parallels reactions to employees who blow the whistle against their organizations for other misdeeds. While retaliation against employees who charge sexual harassment is clearly illegal and grounds for strong organizational sanctions, it is an all too common managerial response. Court awards, however, run high where retaliation is proven. The California Supreme Court in 1992 awarded a former manager for Sentry Insurance Co. $1.34 million dollars after she was fired for supporting a coworker's claim of sexual harassment.[28]

News coverage of the sexual harassment scandal at Astra revealed that many women who complained about sexual harassment were either fired or silenced with compensation. At Astra, women who saw the fate of others and wanted to keep their jobs quickly learned to keep quiet about the harassment incidents. In the Lamplight case, several women complained internally about a hostile work environment created by their male coworkers' sexual references. Following the complaint, the owner confronted the complainants and harangued them for disloyalty. The women sued for retaliation and ultimately won a settlement against the firm. Threats of retaliation create a culture of fear and intimidation in the short run. In the long run, companies most likely will find themselves entangled in costly litigation. The notion of entitlement set forth by Brown (1997) illustrates how a manager might develop an exaggerated sense of rightness around his behavior or that of his favored employee and lead to retaliation against victims who raise complaints of harassment.

Features of Organizations Prone to Inaction

Relying solely on media accounts of sexual harassment cases may lead to an incomplete picture of the kinds of organizations vulnerable to sexual harassment litigation. Typically, only high profile cases of large, well-known companies make it into the newspaper headlines. Including the perspective of experienced EEOC attorneys provides important new insights that broaden our understanding of organizational vulnerability to the deaf ear syndrome. While it was easy to identify a consistent pattern of managerial behaviors associated with organizational inaction, characteristics of organizations were not as easy to categorize. The EEOC interview data revealed a number of different organizational features associated with organizational inaction and suggests that any one of these might place an organization at risk for deaf ear syndrome.

Family-owned businesses.

A disproportionate number of the defendant firms mentioned by the EEOC attorneys were family-owned businesses. The founders were self-made men, typically well up in years, who expressed great pride in the organizations they had built. They held paternalistic attitudes toward their employees. These self-made men in many cases conveyed a macho attitude toward their businesses and toward female employees. In the example of Noon's R.V., the owner had a reputation of running the company "like a plantation." He hired young, attractive women. These employees were constantly subjected to harassment and even groping. When suit was brought by the EEOC for sexual harassment, the owner responded that it was his company, and he could do what he pleased on his own turf. In many of these family-run or entrepreneurial companies there is a perception that the owner has a "no-whining" policy. Sexual harassment complaints are not viewed as legitimate, but as an annoyance or even disloyalty.

Small firms with minimal human resource functions.

Some of the example firms discussed by the EEOC attorneys were small, with poorly developed HR functions, and often with no clear policy on sexual harassment. Three of the companies reviewed had no written sexual harassment policy at all. In the case of Jim Dalley & Associates, a small real estate firm, the owner was the harasser. The victim claimed that there was no policy or procedure within the organization to pursue her complaint. It is possible that owners of small firms have only a limited understanding of federal employment regulations. Unlike worker's compensation, taxes, or wage and hour laws, there are no annual reporting procedures related to sexual harassment. Further, in reading the headlines, small businesses may perceive sexual harassment as a big firm problem and not one that concerns them.

Rural locations.

Companies located in rural areas frequently represent the only employment alternative for many workers. Because their employees are highly dependent on the company and have few options, the organizations appear to feel little pressure to respond to sexual harassment complaints. When one of the women in the Featherlite case reported repeated incidents of sexual harassment, she was told by a supervisor, "You're getting a man's wages, you should be happy. There's not a lot of work out there." Employees who are in tight financial straits and have few employment alternatives may be very reluctant to complain. Companies in rural locations or company towns may develop a false sense of immunity from charges of sexual harassment.

Male bastions.

Organizations that are slow to react to charges of sexual harassment are usually found in typically male-dominated blue-collar industries such as manufacturing and construction. In such industries where women have only recently gained entry, men have resisted changing their work culture, which historically focused on women as sex objects rather than coworkers.

One vivid example of resistance was illustrated by the reaction of male cadets to the admission of women at the Citadel. Within three months of their admission, two female candidates filed charges of sexual harassment.[29] The U.S. Army also has had its share of sexual harassment charges. Four drill instructors, a captain, and 15 others were accused of sexual harassment at an army training center in Maryland. Following the incident, the army received over 7,000 complaints on a special hotline.[30]

Male bastions are also found in white-collar environments. In the corporate world, women have lodged sexual harassment complaints against, among others, the investment firm Smith Barney. One woman who complained repeatedly of sexual harassment was told that she had to live with the intimidation of her boss. In the male bastion organizations, women are sometimes scorned and resented. Their complaints are perceived as a sign of weakness. Under these conditions, resentful male managers find it easy to ignore their harassment charges.

Sex-role spillover is often cited to explain sexual harassing behavior.[31] Men are more accustomed to treating women as wives and lovers than as coworkers. Many find it difficult to shift gears when they encounter women in their work environment. According to sex-role spillover theory, men attempt to secure their dominant roles by emphasizing the "womanness" of their female coworkers and subordinates. Sex-role spillover is greatly exacerbated when the gender composition in an organization is highly skewed. However, some evidence suggests that sex-role spillover even occurs, although to a lesser degree, in organizations where the gender composition is more balanced.[32]

Decentralized branches or franchises.

Large organizations often have difficulty controlling managers in branch offices, franchises, and local outlets. While the company headquarters may have well-developed policies and procedures governing sexual harassment, implementation and enforcement of the policies at outposts are left to local managers and franchisees. When problems of harassment occur, the organization denies responsibility and lays the blame at the feet of the local office or franchise. For example, Sears retail stores appear to operate with a high degree of autonomy. When a Sears manager was accused of sexual harassment, headquarters was quick to deny corporate responsibility, stating that the harassing manager was a renegade and that his harassing behavior should not be attributed to the home office. Ironically, Sears had just invested in a comprehensive sexual harassment awareness training program following the loss of a class action sexual harassment lawsuit.

When sexual harassment incidents are viewed as local problems or isolated events, human resource management professionals at headquarters may be very slow to respond. In such cases, authorities at headquarters often shift the responsibility for investigating the issue back to the local unit. However, managers at the local level may lack the expertise, experience, and resources to respond effectively. From the victim's perspective, the organization appears uninterested, and the problem remains unresolved. It should be noted that this line of defense is increasingly unsuccessful.

Cultural differences in multinational companies.

International organizations doing business in the United States frequently have problems complying with sexual harassment policies. When international executives who have been socialized in other cultures assume leadership positions in the United States, they often encounter difficulty understanding and complying with U.S. anti-discrimination laws. The accusations of sexual harassment at both Mitsubishi and Astra illustrate the problems encountered by internationally based companies in their U.S. operations.[33] At Astra, CEO Lars Bildman, a Swede, never comprehended the importance of American sexual harassment laws. At Mitsubishi, the Japanese owners greatly underestimated the public relations problems created by their failure to respond to charges of sexual harassment in their Illinois assembly plant. This miscalculation led to the threat of a national boycott.[34] In both the Astra and Mitsubishi cases, behaviors that may have been socially acceptable and legal in other countries were unacceptable and illegal in the United States. Failure to recognize and respond effectively proved costly and damaging to the reputations of each of these organizations with international roots.

In the case of Cafe Vienna, one of our case studies, the Austrian owner was constantly flirting with his female employees. He failed to recognize that behaviors that may have been acceptable in his home country were considered sexual harassment in the United States. United States sensitivity and attention to sexual harassment is often seen as overly legalistic by people from other cultures. Indeed, countries such as Belgium, Austria, Italy, and Japan have no sexual harassment laws on the books, and others like China have laws with very light penalties.[35] Consequently, managers from these countries have a whole new set of norms to learn about male/female interaction in the workplace.

Avoiding the Deaf Ear Syndrome: Increasing Corporate Responsiveness to Sexual Harassment

Organizations that fail to respond promptly to charges of sexual harassment run the risk of damaged employee morale, lost productivity, costly lawsuits, and public relations nightmares. Our discussions with EEOC attorneys and a review of current and recent lawsuits reveal some of the factors that contribute to organizational inaction. Certainly, an awareness of these factors is the first step in creating a work environment that is compatible with employee concerns about sexual harassment. However, an important second step is to learn from organizations that have handled sexual harassment complaints promptly and have effectively created harassment-free work environments. Many of these organizations have earned reputations as the "best companies for women."[36] Based on best practices from responsive companies and advice from EEOC attorneys and organizational consultants we offer a set of recommendations to lower the risk of deaf ear syndrome.[37]

Examine the characteristics of deaf ear organizations.

Although sexual harassment can occur in any organization, the features that we have identified may make an organization particularly vulnerable to organizational inaction and ultimately place it at a higher risk for sexual harassment litigation and negative publicity. Accordingly, managers in organizations that match any of our descriptions of deaf ear characteristics need to be particularly vigilant.

A number of experts suggest conducting in-house studies to identify sexual harassment issues in order to design policies and interventions. When HBO first began addressing the company's sexist atmosphere, a senior manager held dinners with small groups of female employees to assess their experiences. He later implemented company-wide training based on what he had learned.[38]

Foster management support and education.

Clearly, allegations of sexual harassment contribute to an emotionally charged corporate environment often resulting in defensiveness, denial, and rationalizations on the part of those designated to enforce the policies. As a result, managers who should be actively investigating and resolving complaints may lack the motivation and commitment to carry out their responsibilities. Overcoming managerial resistance to enforcing sexual harassment policies requires a comprehensive educational effort.

Top managers must realize that they set the standards of conduct through their behavior. Merck, for example, has developed an innovative sexual harassment training program that has been duplicated by scores of other companies. It was first implemented with 500 senior managers, who then became trainers for all Merck employees.[39] Similarly, Ernst & Young recently trained all 20,000 of its employees, renewing its commitment to a harassment-free work environment. In addition, E. I. DuPont de Nemours & Co. has 100 facilitators in the company whose job it is to meet with employees who want to talk about their sexual harassment concerns and support those employees if they want to go to their managers to formally report problems.[40] These successful organizations demonstrate that effective training can increase managers' ability to respond sensitively and respectfully.

Through workshops, simulations, and group discussions, managers can clarify for themselves what constitutes sexual harassment, broaden their understanding of the issues from the victim's perspective, confront the emotionalism surrounding harassment complaints, and work through the steps necessary to resolve complaints. A critical component of education is to help managers overcome the tendency to avoid, deny, blame and retaliate against victims rather than respond to their claims. Understanding that these are typical, yet ineffective, responses may be the first line of defense against them.

Stay vigilant.

Organizations are seldom successful in claiming that they were unaware of a hostile environment.[41] According to EEOC guidelines and case law, companies are held accountable for the actions of their employees and are responsible for knowing the climate in their organization. Managers should monitor the work environment for any displays of a sexual nature in offices, cubicles, and other work spaces, such as inappropriate posters, calendars, or magazines. They should also pay attention to general verbal exchanges where the content is sexual in nature or potentially harassing in nature. All managers must act to eliminate factors that contribute to a hostile work environment. Ideally, any employee, regardless of rank, should be able to monitor behavior and intervene to correct problems.

Progressive companies periodically review their sexual harassment policies and make any necessary adjustments. CBS, Fidelity Bank, and Time periodically reissue their strongly worded sexual harassment policies and their sanctions against such behavior.[42]

Take immediate action.

The most important lesson that organizations can learn from our findings is to act immediately on a complaint of sexual harassment. Swift action not only serves both the victim and harasser fairly, but also encourages the victim to report internally, instead of going to the EEOC to find an ear for her concerns. As one of the EEOC attorneys stated, "Worse than having no sexual harassment policy is a policy that is not followed. It's merely window dressing. You wind up with destroyed morale when people who come forward are ignored, ridiculed, retaliated against, or nothing happens to the harasser."

Many organizations identified as best places for women have reputations for dealing swiftly and severely with harassers. Several of these companies have even found that the organizational lore that springs up around swift action often keeps harassment in check. At General Mills, word quickly spread through the grapevine that a high-ranking manager had been fired for sexual harassment. Would-be harassers were deterred from future incidents and women felt assured that their complaints would be taken seriously.[43] AT&T recently won a case at the district and appellate court levels primarily because it handled the case "promptly and took appropriate remedial action."[44]

Create a state-of-the-art policy.

In a surprising number of organizations, sexual harassment policies are poorly articulated, inaccessible, or nonexistent. Drawing on the support of HR management professionals and legal experts, such organizations can conduct benchmark studies to identify model policies and procedures. Organizations such as Avon, Price Waterhouse, and Ernst & Young are regarded as having strongly worded, no-nonsense policies. Using such models as guides, organizations can then develop a customized set of policies and procedures to fit their own unique circumstances. The need to define sexual harassment in the policy in non-legalese is paramount. Examples should be given of various behaviors that have been identified by the courts as sexual harassment, particularly in the area of hostile environment harassment. This conveys a clearer picture to male employees of what constitutes harassment, and identifies for the female employees what activities they do not have to tolerate in the workplace.

Sanctions should also be clearly delineated. A company's written policy provides an important opportunity to spell out top management's conviction that sexual harassment will not be tolerated at any level in the organization. For example, Corning Inc.'s policy tells employees that "sexual harassment will not be tolerated in any form, whether committed by supervisors, other employees, or nonemployees. Any individual found violating this policy can be subject to disciplinary action up to and including termination, and possibly prosecution by the victim."[45]

Establish clear reporting procedures.

Even in those organizations that have sexual harassment policies in place, cumbersome reporting channels and ineffective investigative procedures hampered resolution of complaints. In a 1997 article involving a study of 1,500 women in administrative, managerial, and professional positions,

Peirce, Rosen, and Hiller outline a set of "user-friendly" policies—policies that are perceived by employees as leading to a responsive and fair resolution of harassment.[46] Key features of user-friendly policies include clear procedures for filing complaints, mechanisms to ensure rapid investigation by impartial managers, and provisions for protecting the privacy of both accusers and accused.

E. I. DuPont de Nemours & Co. addressed access and confidentiality issues by implementing a hotline that any employee can call 24 hours a day, 365 days a year.[47] Federal Express handles sexual harassment complaints through the Guaranteed Fair Treatment (GFT) program that has been cited as one of the top grievance procedures in the country. GFT provides a due process procedure for sexual harassment and other types of complaints that may ultimately be heard by the CEO, chief operating officer, and the chief personnel officer.[48] Responsive organizations are generally characterized by visible top management commitment and comprehensive education programs, periodic review, and continuous monitoring of the organizational environment, thorough and timely action against complaints, and unambiguous policies with clear reporting structures.

In summary, based on interviews with EEOC lawyers and an examination of cases reported in the media, we have identified some of the dynamics underlying the deaf ear syndrome—the inaction or complacency of organizations in the face of charges of sexual harassment. We have also documented the human, financial, and reputational costs to organizations that fall victim to the deaf ear syndrome. Finally, we have presented a list of best practices demonstrated by companies that have earned reputations for doing the right thing when it comes to sexual harassment. At a time when the labor force is increasingly diverse and employee lawsuits are increasingly commonplace, organizations cannot afford to turn a deaf ear to allegations of sexual harassment.

Notes

1. *New York Times*. 1997. "Top Enlisted Man in the Army Stands Accused of Sexual Assault." 4 Feb: A1.
2. *Wall Street Journal*. 1996. "EEOC Sues Mitsubishi Unit for Harassment." 10 April: A1.
3. *Business Week*. 1996. "Abuse of Power: The Astonishing Tale of Sexual Harassment at Astra USA." 13 May: 86–98.
4. *Wall Street Journal*. 1996. "Wall Street Fails to Stem Rising Claims of Sex Harassment and Discrimination." 26 May: C1.
5. *U.S. Army*. 1996. "Army Investigates Allegations of Sexual Misconduct and Rape in Training Command." 7 November: No. 96-78 (News Release).

6. *U.S. Equal Employment Opportunity Commission.* 1995. "EEOC Settles Sexual Harassment Suit Against Del Laboratories." 3 August. (News Release; Available by telephoning (212) 748-8406.)

7. *San Francisco Chronicle.* 1996. "Chevron Suit a Big Test on Gender Bias: Corporate America Watching Closely." 14 Oct: A1; and *New York Times.* 1998. "$34 Million Dollars Settles Suit for Women at Auto Plant." 12 June: A1.

8. *Washington Post National Weekly Edition.* 1997. "Confronting Hard-Core Harassers." 27 January: 6–9.

9. *EEOC Sexual Harassment Statistics for Fiscal Year 1990–Fiscal Year 1996.* This report can be obtained from the EEOC by writing the EEOC at 1801 L Street, N. W., Washington, D. C. 20507 or faxing a request to (202) 663-4912.

10. Terpstra, D. E. and Baker, D. D. 1992. "Outcomes of Federal Court Decisions on Sexual Harassment." *Academy of Management Journal* 35: 181–90.

11. *Working Woman.* 1988. December.

12. Crull, P. 1982. "Stress Effects of Sexual Harassment on the Job: Implications for Counseling." *American Journal of Orthopsychiatry* 52: 539–44.

13. For more details regarding these cases see the following legal documents: *EEOC vs. Sears, Roebuck & Co.*, Eastern District of Wisconsin, 94-C-0753; *EEOC vs. New York World*, 3: 94-CV-398MU; *EEOC vs. Total Systems*, 4: 96-CV-147; *EEOC vs. Lamplight Farms Inc.*, Eastern District of Wisconsin, 94-C-0548; *EEOC vs. Jim Dalley & Assoc.*, 1: 95 CV-2806; *EEOC vs. Noon Construction and Development Inc. D/B/A Noon's RV Center*, District of Minnesota, 3d. Division, 3-94-1590; *EEOC Plaintiff & Gina Taylor and Deann Shane Plaintiff Interveners vs. Featherlite Mfg. Inc.*, Northern District of Iowa, Eastern Division, 93C-2074; *EEOC vs. Cafe Vienna*, Eastern District of Wisconsin, 94-C-0925.

14. Peirce, E., B. Rosen, and T. B. Hiller. 1996. "Breaking the Silence: Creating User-Friendly Sexual Harassment Policies." *The Employee Rights and Responsibilities Journal.* 1997 10 (3): 225–42.

15. *New York Times.* 1996. "Harassment in 2nd Grade? Queens Kisser Is Pardoned." 3 Oct: B1.

16. Under the EEOC *Guidelines on Discrimination Because of Sex*, 29 C.F.R. &1604.119(a), harassment on the basis of sex is a violation of Section 703 of Title VII, 42 U.S.C. & 2000e-2.

17. Gutek, B. A., B. Morasch, and A. G. Cohen. 1983. "Interpreting Social Sexual Behavior in a Work Setting." *Journal of Vocational Behavior* 22: 30–48.

18. Brown, A. D. 1997. "Narcissism, Identity, and Legitimacy." *Academy of Management Review* 22: 643–98.

19. *Ibid.*, 467–68.

20. *Ibid.*, 645.

21. Staw, B. M., P. I. McKechnie, and S. M. Puffer. 1983. "Justification of Organizational Performance." *Administrative Science Quarterly* 28: 582–600.

22. Brown, *op. cit.*, 646.

23. Bies, R. J., and J. S. Moag. 1986. "Interactional Justice: Communication Criteria of Fairness." In *Research on Negotiation in Organizations*, edited by R. J. Lewicki, B. H. Sheppard, and M. H. Bazerman, 43–55. Greenwich, CT: JAI Press.

24. Gellerman, S. W. 1989. "Managing Ethics from the Top Down." *Sloan Management Review* (Winter): 73–79.

25. *New York Times.* 1997. 4 February.

26. *Sun-Sentinel.* 1996. "Sex Claims Nothing to Ignore: $7 Million Harassment Verdict a Costly Lesson." 12 December: 1D.

27. Some research on personality disorders suggests that many perpetrators of sexual harassment have narcissistic personalities. Narcissists often view their employees and coworkers as naive and incompetent. They often exploit others because they believe they are entitled to have whatever they want and often have a lack of empathy for other people. See McDonald, J. J., Jr., and P. R. Lees-Haley. 1996. "Personality Disorders in the Workplace: How They May Contribute to Claims of Employment Law Violations." *Employee Relations Law Journal* 22: 57–81.

28. Murphy, B S., W. E. Barlow, and D. D. Hatch. 1992. "Limits on Wrongful Discharge Damages: Manager's Newfront." *Personnel Journal* 71: 19.

29. CNN. 1996. "Army Widens Sexual Harassment Investigation." 11 November. [Online article]. http://www.cnn.com/US/9611/11/army.sex.2/index.html.

30. *USA Today.* 1996. "Bias Lawsuit Spotlights Brokerages." 16 November: 6B.

31. See the following articles for a more detailed discussion of sex-role spillover and the impact on the work environment. Gutek, B. A., and B. Morasch. 1982. "Sex Ratios, Sex-Role Spillover, and Sexual Harassment of Women at Work." *Journal of Social Issues* 36: 55–74; Tangri, S. S., M. R. Burt, and L. B. Johnson. 1982. "Sexual Harassment at Work: Three Explanatory Models." *Journal of Social Issues* 38: 33–54.

32. Kanter, R. M. 1977. "Some Effects of Proportions in Group Life: Skewed Sex Ratios and Response to Token Women." *American Journal of Sociology* 2: 965–90.

33. *Wall Street Journal.* 1996. "Sexual-Harassment Cases Trip up Foreign Companies." 9 May: B3.

34. *USA Today.* 1996. "Jackson, NOW Protest Mitsubishi." 8 May: 18.

35. Webb, S. L. 1994. *Shockwaves: The Global Impact of Sexual Harassment.* New York: MasterMedia Ltd.

36. See *BusinessWeek.* 1997. "Breaking Through." 17 February; *BusinessWeek.* 1990. "BusinessWeek's Best Companies for Women." 6 August; Zeitz, B., and L. Dusky. 1988. *The Best Companies for Women.* New York: Simon and Schuster.

37. A number of resources are available to assist both small and large organizations in preventing and resolving sexual harassment issues. For assistance, see Levy, A. C., and M. A. Paludi. 1997. *Workplace Sexual Harassment.* Upper Saddle River, NJ: Prentice-Hall; Petrocelli, W., and B. K. Repa. *Sexual Harassment on the Job.* Berkeley: Nolo Press; Wagner, E. J. 1992. *Sexual Harassment in the Workplace.* New York: AMACOM; Bravo, E., and E. Cassedy. 1992. *The 9 to 5 Guide to Combating Sexual Harassment.* New York: John Wiley & Sons.

38. Zeitz and Dusky. *op. cit.*

39. Zeitz and Dusky, *op. cit.*

40. Laabs, J. J., and M. Haight. 1995. "What to Do When Sexual Harassment Comes Calling." *Personnel Journal* 74: 42–49.

41. Webb, *op. cit.* The recommendations in this section are based on the work of Seattle-based sexual harassment expert Susan Webb.

42. Zeitz and Dusky, *op. cit.*

43. Zeitz and Dusky, *op. cit.*

44. Aalberts, R. J., and L. H. Seidman. 1996. "Sexual-Harassment Policies for the Workplace: A Tale of Two Companies." *Cornell Hotel & Restaurant Administration Quarterly* 37: 76–86.

45. Laabs and Haight, *op. cit.*

46. Peirce, Rosen, and Hiller, *op. cit.*

47. Laabs and Haight, *op. cit.*

48. Zeitz and Dusky, *op. cit.*

Annotated Bibliography

Decker, P. 1997. "Sexual Harassment in Health Care: A Major Productivity Problem." *Health Care Supervisor* 16 (1): 1–14. An illuminating discussion of the issue in terms of its financial implications.

Gibson, V. 1993. "Beyond Legal Compliance: What's Next?" *HR Focus* 70 (7): 17. A crisp outline of the relevance of sexual harassment to compliance and to organizational ethics.

Laabs, J., and M. Haight. "What to Do When Sexual Harassment Comes Calling." *Personnel Journal* 74 (1): 42–49. A practical discussion of managerial measures for dealing with sexual harassment.

Lee, R. "The Legal Evolution of Sexual Harassment." *Public Administration Review* 45 (4): 357–67. An excellent presentation of legal dimensions of the issue.

Levy, A., and M. Paludi. 1997. *Workplace Sexual Harassment.* Upper Saddle River, NJ: Prentice-Hall. A basic primer on the nature of the sexual harassment problem.

Stockdale, M. (ed.). 1996. *Sexual Harassment in the Workplace.* Thousand Oaks, CA: Sage. An up-to-date compendium of perspectives on the sexual harassment issue.

7

SUBSTANCE ABUSE IN THE ETHICS FRAMEWORK

S UBSTANCE ABUSE in organizations has become a national
organizational reality with heavy financial and ethical implications.
The U. S. Department of Health and Human Services estimates
the annual organizational cost from accidents, medical claims, and lost
productivity related to substance abuse in America at $140 billion![1]
In healthcare the phenomenon is aggravated by two factors: one, the
broad presence of controlled substances as part of the enterprise of
healthcare delivery; two, the direct consequences of abuse by providers
on the health and well-being of patients. Because of this the ethical
obligations of healthcare organizations in the substance abuse area
are considerable. Therefore, what are the salient aspects of the issue
and what can healthcare organizations do to address it ethically? The
anchoring case and reading that follow probe these focal questions.

CASE STUDY

Case Seven: And the Wisdom to Know the Difference

St. Serena's has, in recent years, experienced more than its share of
substance abuse incidents, some of which involved harm to patients
resulting in financial settlements. As a result, the corporation established
an employee assistance program (EAP) and incorporated policies of the
Federal Drug-Free Workplace Act of 1988 in the organization's code

of conduct. Specifically, the St. Serena's code of conduct includes the following provisions:

> *Section I.10: The St. Serena's corporation does not tolerate the use of illegal drugs or the abuse of legal drugs or alcohol by its employees. To protect the health and welfare of all patients and staff we have adopted the following policy:*
>
> (a) *The possession, use, sale, or purchase of illegal drugs or substances, or the abuse or misuse of legal drugs or alcohol on any corporate premises or anywhere while performing official services or business is subject to disciplinary action, up to and including termination.*
>
> (b) *Any employee under the influence of illegal drugs or alcohol while on St. Serena's premises, or anywhere while performing official services or business, is subject to disciplinary action, up to and including termination.*
>
> (c) *A medical screening for drugs may be a condition of employment; further, employees performing jobs involving patient or staff safety concerns may be notified by management that mandatory periodic or random testing for drug use will be conducted. Confirmed positive test results are grounds for disciplinary action up to and including termination or denial of employment. Employees may also be required to submit to a test when reasonable suspicion of substance abuse exists. Refusal to submit to a requested test will be grounds for unconditional termination of employment. Any employee wishing confidential assistance with a personal alcohol or drug problem is encouraged to contact the corporation's employee assistance program.*

As we have already discussed, the code of ethics also includes the provision of Section II: "*Every employee has the obligation to report promptly any suspected violation of the corporate code of conduct to their supervisor or divisional compliance coordinator.*"

Lawrence Lundy has been a division director at St. Serena's for three years. A loyal and respected member of the St. Serena's management team, he has twice in the past year requested random drug tests for employees in his division. He is also a member of the corporate compliance committee. Lawrence's best friend is "Eagle" Ed—the nickname coming from Ed's low-handicap golf game, which has produced more than a few two-under-par holes. Ed joined St. Serena's at the same time as Lawrence—ten years ago—and is also a division director. The two friends not only play golf together regularly but their families often share vacations.

Ed has always enjoyed the "19th" hole after a round on the links, but during the past year Lawrence has noticed increasingly erratic behavior from Ed and now suspects that his friend may have a drinking problem. Once or twice Lawrence has even noticed the scent of alcohol on Ed's breath at work. Yesterday, with some hesitation, Lawrence confronted

Ed. His friend at first denied any problem, but after lengthy discussion agreed to seek some help. He begged Lawrence not to report him lest his promising career at St. Serena's be jeopardized. "You know how these supposedly confidential matters somehow become known. I'll be blackballed and you know it. I'll go to AA on my own. I promise I'll get sober. Please, Larry, don't report me!"

When Lawrence suggested the EAP program at St. Serena's, Ed further resisted: "Yeah, sure. You saw what happened to Caroline last year. I'll get help from AA." (Caroline Walsh, a rising manager at St. Serena's, had gone to EAP with a drug problem. Six months later—when she was apparently clean of drugs—she was passed over for a promotion that most believed she would get.)

Questions for Discussion:

1. What should Lawrence do? What is he likely to do? Why?
2. Distinguish the formal organizational realities at St. Serena's from the informal factors that bear on the situation.
3. Organizationally, is St. Serena's ethically well-structured for dealing with substance abuse? Is there anything else the corporation could do to ensure compliance with standards such as the Federal Drug-Free Workplace Act?
4. Do personal relationships—with the emotions that are usually involved—pose an organizational-ethics challenge to management? Do they make a difference? Should they make a difference? Do you have any ideas or wisdom on how such a challenge can be addressed by the organization?
5. If the case involved physicians—one doctor noticing another doctor apparently drinking at work—instead of managers, would the ethical reasoning be any different given the traditional "white coat of silence" often associated with doctors? What if the people involved were a senior executive and the senior executive's friend? Does there tend to be a "white collar of silence?" How can an organization deal with this informal reality given the compliance context?
6. Should healthcare facilities such as St. Serena's require drug testing? Is such testing ethically fair to the vast majority of employees? Does it raise any privacy concerns like those addressed in Chapter five?

COMMENTARY

Lawrence is surely in a difficult personal position; he is also in a tough organizational position. He undoubtedly has strong feelings about his friend that prompt him to respond to Ed's call for loyalty and protection. As a member of the compliance committee as well as an actual implementer of drug testing, he also knows from experience the importance of the code's provisions. Existentially, the code might seem like mere ink on paper, while Ed is clearly flesh and blood. In this context is Lawrence likely to honor the corporate code and organizational well-being, report his friend, and say something like "It's for your own good, Ed"; or is he more likely to respond to his friend's plea, not report him, and instead perhaps go with him to AA and monitor his progress? Do organizational realities at St. Serena's do enough to help Lawrence meet his ethical obligations, or do they rather impede him from doing so? St. Serena's has spent significant time and money developing its code and compliance effort, but Ed is a good guy with a promising career. Once again, we can seek some clarity by thinking about the concepts behind the issues.

Individual Versus Organizational Ethics

Is this a matter of Lawrence summoning the moral fiber to do his professional duty, or is it a matter of the organization establishing a setting that requires, encourages, and facilitates ethical behavior by all employees? Is it a bit of both?

Lawrence has a clear emotional sense of the importance of his friend Ed, his loyalty to Ed and Ed's economic well-being. In this specific and personal situation (as opposed to generally) does Lawrence have an equally clear perspective on the importance of the organization, his commitment to its rules, and St. Serena's well-being? Ed has made clear the informal cost (to his career advancement) if Lawrence were to comply with the code provisions; has the organization made clear the cost to the organization of substance abuse? Has St. Serena's failed to equip and support Lawrence for dealing with this situation? Has the organization made it difficult for Lawrence to exercise his individual sense of ethical obligation? The concepts of formal and informal organization will address this question.

Formal Versus Informal Organization

St. Serena's has developed what appears to be an excellent structural response to the substance abuse reality. The organization has a strong clear code,[2] has a compliance program in place, conducts random drug testing, and has established a working EAP. Formally, the system seems to be supportive of staff like Lawrence and Ed. Informally, however, the organization undermines the ethical responsibility it claims the staff should exercise. Although EAP matters are officially absolutely

Figure 7.1 Organizational Lens for Substance Abuse

	Corporate	Group	Individual
Formal	Code	Compliance Committee	Addictions
	EAP	Drug Tests	Committee Member
Informal	Grapevine	Referents	Fears
	Attitudes	Friendships	Loyalties
	Incentives	Cliques	Beliefs

confidential, the unofficial grapevine proved not to be confidential in the Caroline Walsh episode. Does St. Serena's need to fix this reality? Additionally, although St. Serena's formally encourages substance abuse recovery and provides help in the form of EAP, does St. Serena's provide negative cultural incentives? Is there a subtle but real attitude such that people like Caroline (and Ed) are viewed in a different light? Are these negative organizational incentives at the heart of the case? Are there persistent organizational beliefs such as "once an abuser always an abuser"? Is this what St. Serena's needs to address if it is to avoid compliance complications?

Figure 7.1 condenses this kind of analysis.

Moral Approbation

Recall the concept of moral approbation introduced in Chapter three. We can reflect on the Lawrence and Ed situation as a question of whether Lawrence should and will continue to confront Ed and others individually, and whether he should and is likely to confront them organizationally as the code requires. The concept, as developed by Jones and Ryan,[3] emphasizes the role of "referent groups" in organizational behavior, suggesting that compliance with formal policies is significantly determined by the nature of referent groups. Using this notion, we would want to know Lawrence's referent groups and what these groups encourage. For example, do the division directors expect Lawrence to protect them or to report them? Do they constitute a referent group for Lawrence? Are there social groups and cliques—like golf foursomes—that include Lawrence, Ed, and others? Do such cliques act as referent groups and would they criticize or praise Lawrence were he to report Ed in compliance with the code? Has St. Serena's taken steps to develop the compliance committee into a referent group to support staff when in positions such as that which Lawrence is experiencing? As we noted in Chapter three's case involving Charley and Mike, a key organizational determinant of what St. Serena's staff will do in matters of compliance is the value system of the referent groups. If Lawrence's referent groups value loyalty to colleagues more than integrity of the code of the conduct it is much less likely that Lawrence will conform with code provisions.

Before-During-After

Once again, the simple before-during-after concept can be a helpful looking glass for organizational analysis. In the case of substance abuse, St. Serena's has done a lot in the before area. It has planned for dealing with the issue through clear policies and an EAP program.

In the during area, the organization has a drug testing system for monitoring compliance, but might it need more monitoring mechanisms? For example, does the corporation provide training regularly to familiarize staff with symptoms of substance abuse and to enable staff to discuss cases like the one that Lawrence is facing? In the after arena, does St. Serena's evaluate things like code provisions, the reported incidents of substance abuse, and reward systems? Are reporters of substance abuse being promoted or neutralized, applauded or ostracized? Rewards systems may be running counter to the desired compliance behavior. Such possibilities need to be addressed.

Notes

1. *Indiana Post Tribune.* 1998. 30 October: B5.
2. We might contend that the code—under compliance pressure—has too strong a reporting provision. The American College of Healthcare Executives, for example, recommends that healthcare executives report suspected impairment only "should the colleague refuse to seek professional assistance and should the state of impairment persist." Such a code provision by St. Serena's might well ease Lawrence's predicament. See ACHE Ethical Policy Statement. 1995. "Impaired Healthcare Executives." March.
3. Jones, T., and L. Ryan. 1998. "The Effect of Moral Forces on Individual Morality." *Business Ethics Quarterly* 8 (3): 431–40.

READING

Practical discussions of the drug abuse issue in the healthcare field have been remarkably few. The following piece from a health management journal offers a realistic perspective on the nature of the problem and on approaches to dealing with it. The authors present the current perspective of healthcare administrators gleaned from a survey. They suggest that the problem is a major one and that the ethics of dealing with it are complex. On the one hand, an organizational ethics obligation clearly exists to protect patients from treatment by providers under the influence of drugs. On the other hand, how far can an organization ethically go in dealing with its employees on the matter? Is random drug testing ethical? What is the ethical thing to do when an employee is discovered with a drug problem? Turner, Meredith, and Toma limit their analysis to formal structural organizational responses—such as policies, procedures, and EAPs. We might also consider the informal organization implications of their discussion. With regard to St. Serena's, what might the authors suggest given the Lawrence and Ed episode? How might Lawrence benefit from their ideas?

The Issue of Substance Abuse in the Healthcare Industry: A Preliminary Survey of Managerial Thinking

John R. Turner, Mary Meredith, and Alfred Toma[*]

Abstract

Substance abuse in the workplace has been a growing concern in recent years, and ways to detect employees and applicants who use drugs have been the subject of much debate. In this article, the results of a survey on the attitudes of medical practice human resource managers on drug testing of both employees and applicants are given. For this study, 273 human resource managers were sent questionnaires detailing various attitude statements and were asked for their level of agreement. Categories of questions included the administrators' general philosophy of drug testing, their attitudes toward the organizational impact of drug testing, their attitudes toward the implementation of drug testing, and their attitudes toward specific issues pertinent to drug testing in medical groups.

All types of management in today's organizations are confronted with a serious and challenging problem relating to substance abuse. Drug

Reprinted with permission from the Medical Group Management Association, 104 Inverness Terrace East, Englewood, CO 80112-5306; (303) 799-1111. Copyright 1996. Medical Group Management Journal 43 (1): 48, 50–52, 54, 56–60, 64. John R. Turner is professor of management at University of Southwestern Louisiana. Mary Meredith is associate professor of management at University of Southwestern Louisiana. Alfred Toma is adjunct associate professor of management at University of Southwestern Louisiana.

usage by current and potential employees is a salient management issue. "There are no longer any safe sectors from which to draw drug-free employees" (Carroll 1992).

Substance abuse is not a problem confined to certain socioeconomic groups or constrained by demographic factors. Moreover, the implications of substance abuse for management have become monumental in monetary costs and in pervasiveness. The statistics reflect the extent and scope of this problem:

- Nearly 70 percent of current users of illicit drugs are employed.
- The U.S. Chamber of Commerce estimates drug abuse costs U.S. businesses $75 billion a year ($640 per employee).
- Drug users are four times more likely to be involved in job-related deaths and 10 times more likely to be involved in employee theft (Sympson 1992).
- Use of alcohol or drugs is related to almost 40 percent of workplace injuries and nearly 50 percent of workplace deaths (Weber and Shea 1991).
- 76 percent of drug users are white (Zetlin 1991).
- Drug users have higher absenteeism and a higher incidence of involuntary turnover (Normand, Salyards, and Mahoney 1990).

Such statistical pictures seem to be both continuing and unfailingly negative. Moreover, the resulting costs from substance abuse, whether actual or projected potential liability, are sobering and must be considered by management.

How to effectively deal with the problem of substance abuse in the workplace is a complex and sensitive issue which management must address. Managers must formulate and administer effective policies and procedures to balance the demands of customers for quality services and products with the needs of employees and applicants for privacy and due process. And this balance must be achieved in ways that enable the organization to survive and grow. Some guidelines are evolving on what is allowable and what is not based on court decisions; but these guidelines are sometimes inconsistent and insufficient (Scott and Fisher 1990). Furthermore, some organizations have implemented special programs to deal with substance abuse and its effects although performance results of those programs are not readily available. Few such programs exist in the medical industry but do include the ones at Johns Hopkins (Scott and Fisher 1990; McCormick 1990) and in Chicago hospitals (Eubanks 1990). One particular need in the medical industry is empirical information relating to substance abuse. Various health professionals have stressed the need for this information (Scott and Fisher 1990), but little data have been reported. One study concluded that health professionals are 30 to 100 times more likely to participate in substance abuse than the general population (Brice 1990). Certainly "public safety" considerations are more critical in the health care industry than in many other industries.

There are no risk-free policies or procedures for dealing with the assiduous concerns over substance abuse. However, some results of existing organizational programs and some court decisions are available to assist organizations in dealing more effectively with substance abuse problems. In light of such a situation, an intriguing consideration is what management in the health care industry is thinking and doing. Hence the focus of this study is medical groups and their thoughts, policies, and procedures concerning substance abuse and testing for it. Specifically, the study aims to give insights into the status of substance abuse testing, as well as the reactions of managers in the areas of the general philosophy of drug testing, attitudes toward the organizational impacts of drug testing, attitudes toward the implementation of drug testing, and attitudes toward some specific issues pertinent to drug testing in medical groups.

The Study

The purpose of this study was twofold: (1) to assess the problem and status of substance abuse in medical groups throughout the United States, as perceived by medical group human resource managers; and (2) to examine the attitudes of those same administrators toward mandatory drug testing of medical groups' applicants and employees. Because human resource managers are instrumental in promulgating personnel policies, their perceptions and attitudes are reflected in the policies and attitudes of their employer(s). This study examined the ways medical groups prefer to deal with substance abuse in an attempt to provide medical group administrators with more information upon which to base decisions in this crucial area.

Study Methodology

A questionnaire comprised of 36 Likert-type statements using a five-point scale (1 = strongly agree, 2 = agree, 3 = neutral, 4 = disagree, 5 = strongly disagree) was developed and tested on seven medically affiliated human resource managers and three university professors whose primary teaching and research interests are in the area of human resource management. The comments from this small group were used to modify the instrument to secure clarity.

Thereafter, the instrument was mailed to a random sample of 273 medical group human resource managers throughout the United States. The sample was taken from the roster of the Human Resource Society of the Medical Group Management Association. There are certainly more medical groups than those listed in this roster, but this listing includes medical groups of all sizes (from five employees to more than 7,000, and from an average of 20 patients treated daily to more than 2,000) and would therefore appear to be a relatively representative body from which to sample. Fifty-six usable questionnaires were returned, for a response rate of 20.5 percent.

While this response rate might appear to be somewhat low on initial consideration, one should recall that only 273 instruments were mailed; also, a relatively good cross-section of medical groups from 25 states across the country is represented. The breakdown by geographic regions is as follows: West, 13 medical groups; Southwest, 5 medical groups; Midwest, 16 medical groups; South, 14 medical groups; and East Coast, 8 medical groups. These factors would seem to make the return rate more acceptable.

The following results and conclusions represent the findings from responses. The researchers considered addressing the problem of non-response bias, but because of the delicate nature of the subject matter (controlled substance/alcohol abuse and mandatory drug testing of medical group employees and applicants), and because respondents were assured of their anonymity, it was decided to keep respondents completely anonymous. To remain true to this guarantee, no procedures were established to determine which medical groups returned the questionnaire and which did not, thereby making a second mail follow-up impossible. Respondents were traceable only by state/region, as indicated above.

Findings

Before examining the responses of the human resource managers to the specific statements contained in the questionnaire, an important observation should be made. Only 20 percent of the employers represented in the survey have mandatory drug screening policies, and of that 20 percent, less than ten percent have policies requiring the screening of current employees. (As one might expect based on data available for other industries. Those medical groups treating more than 200 patients per day had significantly more mandatory drug screening programs than did those treating 200 or fewer patients per day. This is consistent with findings for other industries, where larger firms are more likely to have drug screening programs [Carraher, 1991]. However, unlike other industries, the number of full-time employees had no effect on drug-testing programs.) Because medical groups are generally regarded as being, at least in some way, responsible for the health and lives of others, these percentages would seem to be alarmingly low (Scott and Fisher 1990), especially when compared to American industry in general. According to the U.S. Drug Enforcement Administration, more than 30 percent of Fortune 500 companies screened job applicants or current employees for signs of illegal drug use (O'Boyle 1985). A survey by the Academy of Management found that 63 percent of responding employers had some form of drug testing, with the screening of job applicants being the most common technique (Weber and Shea 1991).

The same survey found that 85 percent of companies had some form of specific drug abuse policies (Zetlin 1991). These figures stress the need for medical group administrators to address the problem of substance abuse in their organizations.

Figure 1 presents the responses of the survey participants to 13 of the Likert-type statements contained in the questionnaire. These statements examined the medical group human resource managers' general philosophy regarding substance abuse throughout the country and explored their attitudes toward drug testing. The statements in Figure 1 and all subsequent tables are ranked with respect to their average (mean) level of agreement (1 = most agreement and 5 = least agreement) and are presented in that order.

Respondents agreed most with the statement that employers should not have to wait until an accident to require drug testing (statement 1 of Figure 1), and they disagreed most with the statement that testing should be required only after a work-related accident (statement 13 of Figure 1). The consistency of opinions on these two statements indicates that these human resource managers believe a program of preventive maintenance toward substance abuse should be followed (i.e., testing should be done before, not after, an accident occurs).

The second highest level of agreement was shown on the statement that drug testing is not an invasion of privacy. This is an issue which must be faced by each organization when it contemplates mandatory drug testing. While not completely silent, case law has not voiced many opinions on the subject in the courts yet; however, there is some indication that the general perception of the courts and arbitrators seems to lean toward the position that employees' civil rights do not extend to endangering the safety and welfare of others (Muczyk and Heshizer 1986; Scott and Fisher 1990). Apparently, the respondents herein feel the same way, since almost 64 percent believe that testing does not

Figure 1 Medical Group Human Resource Administrators' General Philosophy on Drug Testing

Statement	Mean*	Standard Deviation*	Percentage of Respondents at Each Level				
			Strongly Agree	Agree	Neutral	Disagree	Strongly Disagree
1. Employers should not have to wait until an accident occurs before requiring drug testing.	2.091	.845	21.8	54.5	18.2	3.6	1.9
2. In my opinion, drug testing is not an invasion of privacy.	2.382	1.147	16.4	47.3	14.5	14.5	7.3
3. Substance abuse has reached epidemic proportions in this country.	2.527	1.136	20.0	36.4	16.3	25.5	1.8
4. In my opinion, tests currently used to detect substance abuse yield valid and accurate results.	2.564	1.085	12.7	43.6	25.5	10.9	7.3
5. Mandatory drug testing of all applicants should be an integral part of the job application process.	2.786	1.358	23.2	19.6	26.8	16.1	14.3
6. I believe that legal opinions support mandatory drug testing for both job applicants and employees.	2.818	1.090	12.7	27.3	29.1	27.3	3.6
7. Mandatory drug testing suggests a lack of trust on the part of the employer.	3.545	1.184	5.4	14.5	25.5	29.1	25.5
8. Tests cannot determine what specific drugs have been taken.	3.704	.903	0.0	7.4	37.1	33.3	22.2
9. Mandatory drug testing will help dry up the supply of illegal drugs.	3.727	.971	1.8	9.1	25.5	41.8	21.8

continued

Figure 1 *continued*

Statement	Mean*	Standard Deviation*	Percentage of Respondents at Each Level				
			Strongly Agree	Agree	Neutral	Disagree	Strongly Disagree
10. Drug testing is unfair because it subjects the innocent as well as the guilty to intrusive searches.	3.745	.947	3.5	7.3	16.4	56.4	16.4
11. Mandatory drug testing should be required of job applicants but not employees.	3.836	.958	3.6	7.1	10.6	57.1	19.6
12. Drug testing should be strictly voluntary.	3.927	.920	1.7	5.5	18.2	47.3	27.3
13. Employers should require drug testing only after a work-related accident.	4.036	1.245	3.6	23.6	25.5	18.2	29.1

*1 = Strongly Agree; 2 = Agree; 3 = Neutral; 4 = Disagree; 5 = Strongly Disagree.

invade privacy, even though only about 40 percent feel that legal opinions support mandatory drug testing (statement 6 of Figure 1). An *Industry Week* survey reported 80.7 percent of the respondents believed that testing does not invade privacy; this represents an increase from 70 percent in an earlier survey (Verespej 1992). Perceptions of danger from impaired performance in a job have been found to predicate such beliefs about invasion/noninvasion of privacy (Murphy, Thornton, and Prue 1991). However, a note of caution is raised by a California case where it was held that a psychological test violated a job applicant's right to privacy (Meyers 1992).

The third highest level of agreement was with the statement that substance abuse has reached epidemic proportions in this country. Others who are experts in the field would agree, terming the epidemic as "underestimated" (Carroll 1992). According to one source, "Public and private efforts to eliminate, or even reduce the problem would seem to be important" (Muczyk and Heshizer 1986). However, when asked if mandatory drug testing programs would help dry up the supply of illegal drugs (statement 9 of Figure 1), more than 63 percent of the respondents disagreed. This disagreement should not be taken in a totally negative manner. The fact that these medical group human resource managers admit the seriousness and pervasiveness of the problem is a positive sign, and this may well be a first step toward the development of some type of resolution within their own respective organizations.

The fourth highest level of agreement was with the statement that current drug tests yield valid and accurate results (statement 4 of Figure 1), with more than 56 percent of the respondents exhibiting some level of agreement; this same perception was further documented with the level of disagreement shown with statement 8 of Figure 1, which stated that tests cannot determine which specific drugs have been taken (more than 55 percent disagreed). Again, probably the most important point to be learned from this response is that the fault does not lie with the tests themselves as much as with the fact that a small number of these respondents' organizations are conducting drug testing.

The next highest level of agreement was with the statement that drug testing should be an integral part of the job application process for all job applicants (statement 5 of Figure 1), with almost 43 percent of the respondents showing some level of agreement. This agreement, along with the high rate of disagreement with statement 11 of Figure 1 (more than 75 percent), which stated that tests should be for job applicants but not current employees, shows that the respondents believe that mandatory testing should generally be given to everyone, applicants and current employees alike. However, some experts have said that current employees have more protection against testing than applicants (Schein 1986), meaning that human resource administrators and others must exercise caution when developing drug testing policies for current employees. However, there is some evidence that caution should also be advised when testing job applicants. This is due to a California District Court of Appeals' rejection of the traditional "reasonableness" standard and application of a more stringent test in its finding that a psychological test violated privacy rights of a job applicant (Meyers 1992).

Further evidence that the respondents perceive a need for drug testing policies is indicated by their responses to statements 7, 10, and 12 of Figure 1. Almost 55 percent disagreed that testing suggests a lack of trust by the employer, while more than 70 percent disagreed that testing is unfair because it subjects the innocent as well as the guilty to the intrusive searches often associated with such tests, and almost 75 percent disagreed that testing should be strictly voluntary. Certainly, there may be some "administrator bias" in such findings, but such perceptions may have some basis in fact, since another study ("War on Drugs" 1986) showed that 72 percent of all full-time workers surveyed would volunteer for drug testing in 1986. In 1991, the percentage had

Figure 2 Medical Group Human Resource Administrators' Attitude Toward the Organizational Impact of Drug Testing

Statement	Mean*	Standard Deviation*	Percentage of Respondents at Each Level				
			Strongly Agree	Agree	Neutral	Disagree	Strongly Disagree
1. Mandatory drug testing of employees will have a significant impact on drug use in the workplace.	2.327	.862	32.7	52.7	5.5	3.6	5.5
1. Drug testing is primarily a means to ensure a safe work environment.	2.327	.944	12.7	58.2	16.4	9.1	3.6
3. As a result of drug testing in American industry, the number of job-related accidents is beginning to decrease.	2.964	.508	21.9	54.5	18.2	3.6	1.8
4. A policy of mandatory drug testing will result in fewer job applicants.	3.527	1.052	3.6	16.4	18.2	47.3	14.5
5. The implementation of a policy requiring mandatory drug testing causes employee morale to decline.	3.545*	1.015*	1.8	14.5	29.1	36.4	18.2

*1 = Strongly Agree; 2 = Agree; 3 = Neutral; 4 = Disagree; 5 = Strongly Disagree.

increased to 75 percent willing—another 17 percent would not refuse ("American Workers 'Just Say Yes'" 1991).

The five statements contained in Figure 2 focus on the respondents' attitudes regarding the organizational impact of mandatory drug-testing programs. Responses to the first three statements provide further evidence that these human resource managers have what could be interpreted as a positive view of mandatory drug testing for organizational members: A large majority (85.4 percent, 70.9 percent, and 76.4 percent, respectively) agreed that testing will impact drug use in the workplace (statement 1 of Figure 2), enhance safer working conditions (statement 2 of Figure 2), and is causing a decrease in the number of accidents on the job (statement 3 of Figure 2). (The means of the first two statements resulted in a tie.) Such opinions seem also to be held by executives in other industries, as research reveals that companies involved in drug testing range from IBM and Exxon to the U.S. Postal Service and the U.S. Department of Defense ("Difficulties Cited" 1986).

Successful results such as reduction in workers' compensation claims and in absenteeism have been experienced by organizations implementing programs to help prevent drug use (Staller 1991; Jaquette 1991; Intindola 1991). Other results cited are improvements in the quality of job applicants, employee morale, and job performance (Mazzuca 1990). Respondents' positive views of mandatory drug testing is further documented by the strong level of disagreement (61.8 and 54.6 percent, respectively) with statements 4 and 5 of Figure 2, that drug testing will result in fewer job applicants and will cause employee morale to decrease. Such results, should they occur, would be contradictory to the those just cited for other organizations which have drug-testing programs.

Figure 3 contains 11 statements concerning the respondents' attitudes toward the implementation of drug testing and drug-testing programs. The highest level of agreement (96.4 percent) was with the statement that employees should have written notice of rules pertaining to drug use on the job. This plan of putting company policies on drug use and abuse in writing, in the context of concern for job safety, is strongly recommended and is used by Fortune 500 companies with drug abuse policies ("Fortune 500 Firms" 1986). Moreover, a company's drug policy should be:

- simple (Evans 1992);
- clearly defined (Evans 1992; Mangan 1992);
- fair (Brookler 1992);
- explained in advance (Scott and Fisher 1990);
- related to job performance (Scott and Fisher 1990); and
- reviewed and updated regularly (Carroll 1992).

Further, 85.4 percent of the respondents agreed, at some level, that consent forms should be signed prior to any kind of drug test (statement 2 of Figure 3).

The most common and least expensive type of test is urinalysis, but it cannot always distinguish between cough syrups, decongestants, pain killers, and illegal drugs (Hoerr 1986). Moreover, the Center for Disease Control has stated that these tests can be inaccurate as much as 66 percent of the time ("Worker Drug Tests Spread" 1985). Such possibilities make the signing of a consent form prior to a test advisable. Since human resource administrators are often responsible for some degree of litigation related to such matters, it is understandable that they would strongly support thorough documentation before problems arise.

Figure 3 Medical Group Human Resource Administrators' Attitudes Toward Implementation of Drug Testing

Statement	Mean*	Standard Deviation*	Percentage of Respondents at Each Level				
			Strongly Agree	Agree	Neutral	Disagree	Strongly Disagree
1. Employees should be given a written notice of the rules governing drug use on the job.	1.491	.717	58.2	38.2	1.8	0.0	1.8
2. Job applicants should be required to sign a consent form prior to a urinalysis or blood test.	1.964	1.018	32.7	52.7	5.5	3.6	5.5
3. If mandatory drug testing is required of employees, the actual testing should be unannounced.	2.491	1.153	18.2	43.6	14.5	18.2	5.5
3. A system of progressive penalties should apply to substance abuse cases, just as it applies to other violations of workplace rules.	2.491	1.153	16.4	47.3	14.5	14.5	7.3
5. Employees should be screened for drug abuse only if there is reasonable cause to suspect drug use.	2.673	1.263	16.4	40.0	14.5	18.2	10.9
6. Employers should have the right to conduct workplace searches but right should not extend to personal searches of employees.	2.836	1.102	5.5	43.6	21.8	20.0	9.1
7. Employee Assistance Programs (EAPs) established to provide assistance to employees who have substance abuse problems should be voluntary.	2.855	1.208	10.9	40.0	9.1	32.7	7.3

continued

Figure 3 *continued*

			Percentage of Respondents at Each Level				
Statement	Mean*	Standard Deviation*	Strongly Agree	Agree	Neutral	Disagree	Strongly Disagree
8. Penalties for drug use on the job should range from moderate to severe, depending on the substance.	3.074	1.211	11.1	25.9	16.7	37.0	9.3
9. Employers should develop standards for acceptable alcohol and drug levels for their employees.	3.455	1.245	0.0	3.6	18.2	49.1	29.1
10. Penalties should be imposed against employees who use drugs only if the employer can show a relationship between drug use and adverse job behavior.	3.545	1.199	7.2	16.4	10.9	45.5	20.0
11. Termination is the best solution to problems involving substance abuse.	4.093	.784	0.0	5.6	9.3	55.6	29.6

*1 = Strongly Agree; 2 = Agree; 3 = Neutral; 4 = Disagree; 5 = Strongly Disagree.

In support of statement 12 of Figure 1, in which the respondents disagreed that testing should be strictly voluntary, more than 61 percent agreed with the first statement 3 of Figure 3 (there was a tie between the mean response of this and another statement in Figure 3), which said that testing should be unannounced. This again underscores respondents' feelings about the gravity of the problem and the desire to take serious and substantive steps to help reduce it, even though some would deem such steps uncalled for and too severe.

Most of the medical group human resource administrators (63.7 percent) favored a system of progressive penalties for violations of workplace rules governing substance abuse (the second statement 3 in this figure), but their attitudes were somewhat mixed concerning the severity of the penalties and the type of substance, as shown in statement 8 of Figure 3. More than 85 percent disagreed that termination is the best solution to drug abuse problems (statement 11 of Figure 3). This opinion is shared by many experts in the field; in fact, one expert says that employees should not be terminated on the basis of one positive test, and companies with good employee assistance programs (EAPs) should follow up with a more sophisticated test (Hoerr 1986; Scott and Fisher 1990). Employers seem to agree as more are offering EAPs as an alternative to dismissal (Weber and Shea 1991; Frieden 1991; Brice 1990). One survey in the health care area reported a general trend of providing EAPs for employees who want help and coming down hard on substance abusers who hide their problems (Brice 1990).

With respect to EAPs, more than 50 percent felt that such programs should be voluntary (statement 7 of Figure 3). This opinion appears to be consistent with current practice according to one expert, who said about half of all such programs were initiated by employees and the other half resulted from supervisory action (Hoffer 1986). EAPs are usually worthwhile if an organization can afford them; it has been reported that the recovery rate is between 35 percent and 60 percent of the treated employees, and a good EAP returns $4.23 for each dollar invested (Intindola 1991).

More than 56 percent of the respondents agreed that reasonable cause should precede screening for drugs (statement 5 of Figure 3), and almost 50 percent agreed that searches should not include personal searches of employees (statement 6 of Figure 3). These perceptions appear to be consistent with those relating to documentation. Reasonable cause is important, as evidenced in one case where the judge said that a company must have a "reasonable suspicion based on specific, objective facts" before demanding that a worker be tested (Muczyk and Heshizer 1986). There is, however, some precedent in court rulings that such considerations as public safety justify "suspicionless drug testing" (Scott and Fisher 1990). Interestingly enough, however, more than 65 percent of the respondents disagreed that there is a need to show a relationship between drug use and work performance before imposing penalties (statement 10 of Figure 3), a perception that is shared by some experts (Hamilton 1991) but not all (Anagarola 1985). Again, some considerations (for example, perceptions of danger) may render drug testing more acceptable to employees as well as to the judicial system (Murphy, Thornton, and Prue 1991).

More than 68 percent of the respondents did not feel that employers should be responsible for developing standards for acceptable alcohol and drug levels (statement 9 of Figure 3). Perhaps those who disagreed perceived their responsibility to be in the area of sound policy development after the acceptable levels have been exceeded.

Figure 4 includes five statements which focused specifically on medical group human resource managers' attitudes toward mandatory drug testing of medical group employees and job applicants. As shown in statement 1 of this table, more than 65 percent agreed that a higher degree of accountability should be in effect for those having responsibility for the health and lives of others. However, more than 55 percent of the respondents disagreed that mandatory drug screening in medical groups is more critical than in other types of organizations (statement 4 of Figure 4). A plausible explanation for this dichotomy in attitudes could be found in terms of how these administrators view the functions of a medical group; perhaps they see medical groups as being more diagnostic or prognostic than remedial in nature.

As shown in statement 2 of Figure 4, the respondents were relatively evenly divided as to their opinions about the number of abusers in their own organizations, with the largest single category percentage occurring in the "neutral" response. Apparently this uncertainty or denial that a problem exists is not unusual, as one study stated that many administrators in hospitals, for example, seemed to think that their organization had no problem (Cherskov 1987) and testing programs are very much the exception to the norm (Scott and Fisher 1990). Perhaps this attitude may partially explain some of the 20.5 percent response rate for this survey. Some of the medical group human resource administrators might not have responded to the questionnaire because they were unaware that problems existed, or they were unwilling to admit the existence of problems and thus felt no need to respond. In fact, pursuing this thought a step further, some might not have responded because they have drug or alcohol abuse problems.

More of the respondents agreed than disagreed (38.3 percent to 27.2 percent, respectively) that mandatory drug testing programs would lead to improved health care for patients, but the largest single-category percentage (34.5 percent) were somewhat neutral in their attitudes toward this statement. And more then 72 percent showed some level of disagreement with the statement that only those employees directly involved in patient care should be tested (statement 5 of Figure 4). This opinion may suggest that while respondents believe that drug abuse is a problem that permeates the entire organization, they have mixed feelings about the solution to the problem.

Summary and Conclusions

Drug and alcohol abuse in the workplace is a pervasive problem of enormous proportions and can be blamed, in many different types

Figure 4 Medical Group Human Resource Administrators' Attitude Toward Specific Issues Pertinent to Drug Testing in Medical Groups

Statement	Mean*	Standard Deviation*	Percentage of Respondents at Each Level				
			Strongly Agree	Agree	Neutral	Disagree	Strongly Disagree
1. People who hold the lives of others in their hands should be held to a stricter standard than other workers.	2.327	1.106	23.7	41.8	16.4	14.5	3.6
2. Substance abuse among employees at my medical group is limited to only a few individuals.	2.655	1.075	16.3	25.5	40.0	12.7	5.5
3. Mandatory drug testing will yield improved health care to patients.	2.964	1.105	5.5	32.8	34.5	14.5	12.7
4. Mandatory drug screening among medical group employees is more critical than for employees in other organizations because of the basic nature of their jobs.	3.309	1.184	10.9	14.5	18.2	45.5	10.9
5. Only those medical group employees (or applicants) directly involved in patient or employee morale should be subjected to mandatory drug testing.	3.855	1.061	3.7	9.1	14.5	43.6	29.1

*1 = Strongly Agree; 2 = Agree; 3 = Neutral; 4 = Disagree; 5 = Strongly Disagree.

of organizations, for accidents, poor job performance, employee theft, and many other undesirable work-related problems. Naturally, the cost associated with such problems causes prices of goods and services to rise, not to mention the cost of health care, creating additional economic burdens for consumers.

Unfortunately, substance abuse problems appear to be increasing rather than diminishing. The number of companies with some type of drug screening program is growing substantially. However, the results of this study show that for medical groups, the figures are essentially still quite low.

Nevertheless, the medical group human resource managers responding to this survey do show awareness and involvement. They realize that drug and alcohol abuse in the workplace is a serious and pervasive problem in this country, and they reveal positive attitudes toward the initiation of drug detection policies and procedures for their organizations. Hopefully, they are moving away from a "wait and see" attitude toward the implementation of policies concerning substance abuse as court decisions, once hazy in this area, begin to provide legal guidance. Further, these administrators do favor a non-voluntary drug testing program, and they believe that such a program can be implemented without a decline in employee morale or a loss of job applicants. Apparently they realize that they are employees themselves and they do not have to stand idly by while time, money, and productivity are being wasted.

Respondents favor workplace searches for illegal drugs, but not personal searches. They are also strongly in favor of sound written documentation for all employees. This shows concern about legality, but it could also be evidence of an underlying desire for fairness, especially when combined with their attitudes toward penalties for abusers. They favor a progressive penalty system ranging from moderate to severe, and do not view termination as the only solution. Also, they appear to have a favorable attitude toward voluntary EAPs.

Overall, these human resource managers believe that their organizations operate under a higher standard of accountability than other organizations, because of the nature of health care institutions, including "public safety" considerations. Therefore, mandatory drug testing policies are more critical, even though these managers do not feel that employers should actually develop standards for acceptable drug and alcohol levels. They do, however, feel that mandatory drug testing will yield better health care overall and if sound policies are established as to how to detect, penalize, and assist drug users and abusers, future and current employees will have a better understanding of the rules. These respondents seem to grasp the fact that if any organization condones (even covertly) its employees' drug problems, employees will be less willing to seek treatment and the company will continue to be exposed to negative consequences of substance abuse.

Because the respondents' attitudes appear to be in a positive mode for the implementation of drug testing policies, they should ensure that other managerial personnel at all levels in their organizations are trained to identify drug use symptoms. This is the most commonly used detection method (Cook and Wilson 1991). Upon detection of substance abuse symptoms, management should be aware that there are other, better solutions than humiliation, professional ostracism, and termination. Employers should have positive, supportive attitudes when dealing with errant employees. Based on the findings in this survey, such attitudes appear to exist. Now is the appropriate time for the successful initiation and implementation of drug-testing programs in the medical group sector of the healthcare industry.

References

"American Workers 'Just Say Yes' to Drug Testing." 1991. *Supervision*. (Aug): 12–13.

Anagarola, R.T. 1985. "Drug Testing in the Workplace: Is it Legal?" *Personnel Administrator* 30 (Sept): 79–88.

Brice, J. 1990. "Confronting Drug Abuse on the Job." *Healthcare Forum* 33 (1): 25–29.

Brookler, R. 1992. "Industry Standards in Workplace Testing." *Personnel Journal* 71 (Apr): 128–32.

Carraher, J. 1991. "Progress Report: Drug Tests." *Security* 28 (Oct): 40.

Carroll, C. R. 1992. "The Dilemma of Detoxing the Work Force." *Security Management* 36 (May): 54–56.

Cherskov, M. 1987. "Substance Abuse in the Workplace." *Hospitals* 1 (20 June): 72.

Cook, R. L., and J. H. Wilson. 1991. "U.S. Corporate Substance Abuse Policies: A Benchmark." *International Journal of Physical Distribution and Logistics Management* 21: 31–38.

"Difficulties Cited in Combating Employee Drug Abuse." 1986. *Journal of Accountancy* 162 (Oct): 52.

Eubanks, P. 1990. "Chicago Hospitals: No Drug Users Apply." *Hospitals* 64 (5 July): 79.

Evans, D. G. 1992. "A Dose of Drug Testing." *Security Management* 36 (May): 48–53.

"Fortune 500 Firms Use Urinalysis Tests to Stem Employee Drug Abuse." 1986. *Administrative Management* 47 (Jan): 12.

Frieden, J. 1991. "Drug Testing: Time Marches On." *Business and Health* 9 (June): 70–74.

Hamilton, J. O. 1991. "A Video Game that Tells if Employees Are Fit for Work." *BusinessWeek* (3 June): 36.

Hoerr, J. 1986. "The Drug War Will Be Won with Treatment, Not Tests." *BusinessWeek* 13 (Oct): 52.

Hoffer, W. 1986. "Business' War on Drugs." *Nation's Business Review* 74 (Oct): 19–24.

Intindola, B. 1991. "EAPs Still Foreign to Many Small Businesses." *National Underwriter* 95 (6 May): 21.

Jaquette, L. 1991. "Red Lion Pleased with Drug Testing Program." *Hotel and Motel Management* 206 (25 Feb): 3, 36.

Mangan, D. 1992. "An Rx for Drug Abuse." *Small Business Reports* 17 (5): 28–38.

Mazzuca, L. 1990. "Employer Poll Finds 55% Test for Drugs, or Plan to." *Business Insurance* 24 (17 Sept): 3, 44.

McCormick, B. 1990. "Johns Hopkins Breaks Controversial New Ground in Drug Testing." *Trustee* 43 (July): 16–17.

Meyers, J. F. 1992. "Soroka v. Dayton Hudson Corp.—Is the Door Closing on Pre-Employment Testing of Applicants?" *Employee Relations Law Journal* 17 (Spring): 645–53.

Muczyk. J. P., and B. P. Heshizer. 1986. "Managing in an Era of Substance Abuse." *Personnel Administrator* 39 (Aug): 91–96.

Murphy, K. R., G. C. Thornton, and K. Prue. 1991. "Influence of Job Characteristics on the Acceptability of Employee Drug Testing." *Journal of Applied Psychology* 76 (June): 447–53.

Normand, J., S. D. Salyards, and J. J. Mahoney. 1990. "An Evaluation of Pre-Employment Drug Testing." *Journal of Applied Psychology* 75 (Dec): 629–39.

O'Boyle, T. F. 1985. "More Firms Require Employee Drug Tests." *Wall Street Journal* 8 August: 6.

Schein, D. D. 1986. "The Work Environment: How to Prepare a Company on Substance Abuse Control." *Personnel Journal* 65 (1): 30–38.

Scott, M., and K. S. Fisher. 1990. "The Evolving Legal Context for Drug Testing Programs." *Anesthesiology* 73 (Nov): 1022–27.

Staller, W. H. 1991. "Sobering up for Success." *Security Management* 35 (Sept): 127–28.

Sympson, R. M. 1992. "Busted." *Restaurant Business* 91 (1 May): 90–102.

Verespej, M. A. 1992. "Drug Users—Not Testing—Anger Workers." *Industry Week* 241 (17 Feb): 33–34.

"War on Drugs." 1986. *Fortune* (29 Sept): 8.

Weber, K. A., and R. E. Shea. 1991. "Drug Testing: The Necessary Evil." *Bobbin* 12 (Aug): 98–102.

"Worker Drug Tests Spread Despite Deep Controversy." 1985. *Money* (Oct): 13.

Zetlin, M. 1991. "Corporate America Declares War on Drugs." *Personnel* 68 (Aug): 1, 8.

Annotated Bibliography

Brice, J. 1990. "Confronting Drug Abuse on the Job." *Healthcare Forum* 33 (1): 25–29. A crisp introduction to the substance abuse problem in healthcare organizations.

Cherskov, M. 1987. "Substance Abuse in the Workplace." *Hospitals* 1 (20 June): 72. Provides a sound insight to the nature of the problem.

Mangan, D. 1992. "An Rx for Drug Abuse." *Small Business Reports* 17 (5): 28–38. Among the better discussions of managerial approaches for dealing with the drug abuse reality.

Schein, D. D. 1986. "The Work Environment: How to Prepare a Company on Substance Abuse Control." *Personnel Journal* 65 (1): 30–38. An excellent primer on organizational aspects of the substance abuse problem.

8

THE ETHICS OF DIVERSITY

DIVERSITY IN healthcare organizations has become one of the "in" topics in recent years. Many, including the authors of the readings attached to this chapter, have touted diversity as a key to future organizational competitiveness in the healthcare industry. Diversity has also become a controversial issue because of its often-perceived relationship to reverse discrimination, affirmative action, quotas, and equal opportunity. Moreover, a recent study found that, good intentions notwithstanding, the field of healthcare administration is far short of diversity expectations.[1] A definition of the diversity issue and its ramifications for organizational ethics is discussed in this chapter.

CASE STUDY

Case Eight: A Rainbow Coalition

St. Serena's serves an exceptionally diverse clientele, and strives through a vigorous equal opportunity and affirmative action program, to build and maintain a correspondingly diverse workforce. Further, it has incorporated into its code of conduct provisions that emphasize its organizational commitment to diversity in every dimension. For example, Section I.9 of the code states:

> *Federal, state, and local laws, rules, and regulations require that the corporation provide equal opportunity to every applicant and employee who is qualified to*

perform the requirements of the job. It is the corporation's policy to do this, regardless of the individual's race, color, religion, sex, national origin, age, physical or mental disability/handicap, marital status, sexual orientation, alienage or citizenship, or status as a Vietnam era veteran or disabled veteran. St. Serena's is also committed to providing reasonable accommodations for its disabled employees and applicants. Equal employment opportunities are provided in all aspects of the employment relationship, including recruitment, hiring, work assignment, promotion, transfer, termination, salary and benefits administration, and selection for training.

In addition, Section I.9.b(ii) of the code stipulates that *"the corporation will not initiate, sponsor, or participate in any events that require the use of facilities, such as social or sports clubs, that are known to have exclusionary membership policies."* And, of course, Section II of the code relates to compliance with diversity-related issues: Every employee *"has the obligation to report promptly any suspected violation of the corporate code of conduct to their supervisor or divisional compliance coordinator."* Recently, St. Serena's chief executive officer, Samantha Savage, made it a corporate priority to attract major industry to subscribe to St. Serena's extensive healthcare services. Several of the largest prospects were well-known for their commitment to diversity in business relationships, so Samantha naturally made a point of ensuring that, in all promotional activities for attracting these prospective clients, the management team from St. Serena's would include a rainbow of representation. In several instances she specifically directed that junior executives of certain racial, ethnic, and gender characteristics be selected for important meetings, even when other managers were more technically qualified for the matters under discussion. Because these promotional activities provided career-enhancing experience and exposure to those attending, executives not selected to be part of the team lost significant personal opportunities.

Related to this diversity emphasis, Sandy Simpson, manager of employment in the human relations department, has been experiencing more than the normal challenges of her job. In addition to its commitment to affirmative action and diversity, St. Serena's has also emphasized internal promotion over hiring from the outside. Filling vacancies is a joint decision between department heads and Sandy; department heads tend to stress technically needed skills and departmental interests, and Sandy stresses corporate policies (such as diversity) and institutional needs.

The recent search to fill the supervisory position in the clinical chemistry lab illustrates Sandy's challenges.

Two internal and one external candidates applied. Keneta is a young African American woman with three years' experience in the lab and outstanding technical skills but limited leadership and interpersonal skills. She has been working to develop those skills with little active support from her department head. She has also experienced a personality conflict with the department head's administrative assistant, a person with whom the lab supervisor works closely.

Kimberly is a young white woman with one year experience in the lab. Her technical skills are satisfactory, but her interpersonal skills are outstanding. She is liked by everyone. She is also a very good friend of Keneta.

The department head, an energetic, white, male physician, contacted an external candidate (a white male) whom he believes has the experience needed to take over the supervisory position immediately. He feels that neither of the internal candidates is ready for the management position and that, were either of them to be promoted, he would need to spend a lot of time and effort to develop them into an effective supervisor.

Sandy was caught between the corporation's emphasis on diversity, the department head's need for competence, and the reality of interpersonal problems involving Keneta—all in the context of a diversity priority and equal opportunity and affirmative action rules.

Last week, Dr. Max Smart, the director of pathology, was confronted with another diversity issue. His father-in-law finally had invited him for lunch and golf at the prestigious Gent Golf Club at which he holds a membership. The club is among the most highly rated golf courses in America and is also one of the most exclusionary. Not only do no women nor minorities hold membership in the club, but women are even prohibited as guests in the "Polar Bar" social area. Dr. Smart enjoyed a fantastic lunch in the bar area, but while there he noticed St. Serena's vice president of finance, Hank Hyde, on the practice putting green. Hank was a golfing guest that day of Dan Dapper, the CEO of a major client of St. Serena's. They were apparently discussing details of their business relationship while enjoying a round of golf. Hank nodded at Dr. Smart and he was reminded of Hank's reputation as one of the most avid golfers on St. Serena's staff but as a highly successful executive as well.

Questions for Discussion:

1. Is Samantha acting in an ethical manner by selecting participants primarily on the basis of race and gender? Is it ethical for a corporation to prioritize diversity over technical merit?

2. What is Sandy's ethical obligation? What is she likely to do? Is the organization—in its formal and informal realities—helping or hindering her in doing her job ethically?

3. What should Dr. Smart do? Why? What is he likely to do? Is it ethical for him to be at the Gent Golf Club? What about Hank?
4. Identify the structural and cultural aspects of St. Serena's that pertain to the diversity issue.

COMMENTARY

A lot is certainly going on at St. Serena's. The organization's aggressive strategic alignment efforts and its progressive diversity policy are at the forefront of healthcare management. But does the case suggest that a few compliance and ethics matters may reveal an "Achilles's heal" for this thriving organization? We again return to concepts to assist our analysis.

Equal Opportunity, Affirmative Action, and Diversity

First, let's clarify terms under discussion. Three notions—equal opportunity, affirmative action, and diversity—are historically connected and conceptually progressive.

Equal opportunity.

Equal opportunity was first on the scene, resulting largely from civil rights developments of the 1950s and early 1960s. Conceptually equal opportunity is a policy, an ideal, or a goal that says anyone can apply and be fairly considered. As more a passive than an active notion, it simply opens the door wide, but does nothing to show people where the door is, how to get to the door, or how to get through it. St. Serena's has the open door of an equal opportunity policy.

Affirmative action.

Affirmative action, on the other hand, is an active notion. Resulting from the realization in the late 1960s and 1970s that equal opportunity was not producing statistically equal results, affirmative action involves tangible efforts to help people get to and through the open door of equal opportunity—especially people who have been unfamiliar with the location and intricacies of the door. The notion is analogous to athletic opportunity: I may be the best ball player in town, but if I don't know where the stadium is, have no transportation to get there, or cannot find the entrance ramp, I will not have the opportunity to show what I can do on the level playing field. Equal opportunity merely says that anyone can compete to play the game. Affirmative action says a good team manager does not sit back and wait for the phone to ring; a good manager actively recruits the best prospects and develops them into star players. A good manager goes out and looks for the best, tells them where the game is, and provides transportation to get there and, if necessary, an escort to find the entrance. Once there the player may need coaching about the rules of the league and other aspects of the game, but an affirmatively active manager brings the natural skills into the arena lest they lie undiscovered across town.

Notice that, conceptually, affirmative action has nothing to do with quotas: A good team manager seeks the best prowess—not a demographic mix—rather than just waiting for that prowess to appear. A good team manager recruits the best players, but not just from familiar environs; he or she recruits everywhere. Once the recruits are found and given the chance, those with the best athletic prowess play, regardless of how they got in the door, and those with less prowess do not make the team. But everyone has the chance to "try-out."

In practice, then, affirmative action programs consist of three tangible elements:

1. Ongoing study of the representation of minorities in each major job classification to determine the situation compared with what would be expected given the availability of qualified applicants in the recruitment area. St. Serena's does this.

2. Development of a plan of goals and action with timetables for addressing any discerned imbalance. Bad management cops out here by turning to easy quotas instead of making the more difficult creative efforts to attract and groom *qualified* minorities. A focus on numerical "quotas" instead of on expansion of the pool of qualified minority candidates is a corruption of the affirmative action notion. Affirmative action requires that preference be given to minorities only when they are equally qualified with non-minority candidates.[2] St. Serena's does this.

3. Appointment of an affirmative action officer to implement the action plan in a "good faith" effort. St. Serena's has such an affirmative action program and has, in fact, attracted qualified candidates for most job classifications, but managerial positions are an exception.

Diversity.

Whereas equal opportunity opens the door and affirmative action gets minorities to and through the door, diversity involves what happens next. Once minorities are selected, an organization's level of diversity is

Figure 8.1 The Historical Context of Diversity

indicated by whether the minorities truly become a part of the organization or are treated as just window dressing; are appreciated for who they are and what they can do, or for the demographic characteristic they bring into the organization; or—continuing the athletics analogy—are just bench-warmers or actually get to play. Whereas equal opportunity relates to basic civil rights, and affirmative action to recruitment, hiring, and promotion efforts, diversity goes a step further. Equal opportunity is about access; affirmative action is about assistance in getting access; diversity is about appreciation once access is gained. Figure 8.1 depicts the progression in this, a matter of attitudes and relationships.[3]

Diversity highlights the value that demographic differences contribute to organizational performance; it therefore suggests that an actual qualification for certain jobs could be particular racial, ethnic, gender, or age experience. In healthcare, for example, if many people in the community served are of Asian background, the diversity concept would suggest that to be qualified providers need a sense of Asian culture as well as technical skills. The concept also suggests that in a culturally diverse community—such as that which St. Serena's serves—any healthcare organization might need the perspective of certain demographic experience in any high-level decision-making processes.

Is this what St. Serena's is doing? Do its stated policies prioritizing diversity stem from an attitude that cultural diversity brings the insights and wisdom necessary for St. Serena's to meet its healthcare mission? Does CEO Samantha mandate diverse representation on management teams because of a belief that culturally diverse perspectives produce better healthcare services? Or, does St. Serena's emphasize diversity without really believing that the backgrounds and perspectives from, for example, different ethnicities, races, genders, and ages, are as important as technical skills? Does St. Serena's emphasize diversity more for "show" because it helps marketing in certain communities? Does Samantha insist on diverse representation on the management teams because she correctly believes it will look good to prospective clients or because she believes those different backgrounds are needed to reach a level of competence?

Just as quotas are a corruption of the affirmative action concept, so too is "show" a corruption of the diversity concept.[4] Fred Miller's notion of "inclusion"—discussed in his article attached to this chapter—as key to true diversity elaborates on these distinctions that are important in understanding the ethics of diversity.

Formal and Informal Realities

We can evaluate the St. Serena's scenario by limning structural and cultural aspects of the situations described. Formally, the system looks pretty impressive. The code and policies sound good, an affirmative action program is in place, and management appears to be considerably involved in the diversity effort. What does not appear in the case is any mention of diversity training, although perhaps the corporation does provide it. On the negative side, the neglect of a fundamental aspect of affirmative action, that is, the provision of professional development resources (like coaching) to qualified candidates is distinct. Indeed, the department director over the clinical chemistry lab not only has not provided any assistance to Keneta but seems not even to be interested in her development. This lack of attention to a basic aspect of affirmative action is probably the reason for Sandy's ethical stress. Had Keneta been developed for a supervisory role, Sandy's hiring decision might be a slam dunk; Keneta's unattended deficiency makes the decision difficult. If this neglect of professional development and mentoring is an organizational, not just departmental, malady, we might well count this as a strike against St. Serena's organizational ethics. To tout an affirmative action and diversity program and then not provide the basic follow-up needed raises a question of ethical responsibility. Federal compliance investigators describe such action as a "pattern of indifference."

St. Serena's could, for example, not only give teeth to its diversity efforts by identifying and providing the managerial training needed by prospective culturally different candidates like Keneta, but it could embrace a policy similar to the Beth Israel Health Care System model of "special initiatives for understanding cultural traditions in order to improve patient care."[5] Beth Israel provides a day-long diversity work-shop for all new employees and conducts joint projects with community

Figure 8.2   A Lens to Diversity Analysis

	Corporate	Group	Individual
Formal			
Informal			

Hasidic, Chinese, and other ethnic groups. The system formally established an organizational goal to become "culturally proficient," meaning to hold cultural differences and diversity in the highest esteem.[6]

Informally, we might wonder about St. Serena's organizational attitudes, beliefs, and social groupings—the attitudes of Samantha and the rest of the staff toward diversity. We could reasonably wonder whether CEO Samantha views diversity with esteem or simply with a marketing myopia and whether the attitude of the rank and file at St. Serena's toward diversity is one of resentment and "reverse discrimination" or a bit more positive. That Hank conducts business discussions at an exclusionary golf club would suggest—perhaps erroneously given his golfing addiction—that diversity is merely given lip service at St. Serena's. We might ask Hank if he ever plays golf with women, African Americans, or Asians as part of his business discussions. If his, and other senior staff's, social groups tend to be parochial, that would be an informal sign inconsistent with the formally articulated commitment to diversity and another indication of the existence of a "pattern of indifference." As John Bruhn puts it, "An organization cannot be considered multi-cultural if it only tolerates diversity; it must value, promote, and proactively manage differences to minimize conflict and maximize the advantages of diversity."[7] Figure 8.2 can be used to capture these and other insights.

Values Emphasis

In Chapter two we suggested the notion of "values emphasis" as a key to understanding organizational ethics. The concept suggests that in organizational life values conflict and some values may be over-emphasized at the expense of others. The task of the organization is to be alert to such over emphasis, and a tangible quest for equal emphasis was suggested. The diversity issue brings out the problem. Representation can be emphasized over competence and fairness, and vice versa. The well-being of the whole can be emphasized over that of each individual. Legal compliance can be emphasized over individual dignity and well-being. Is Samantha emphasizing the economic interests of the organization over fairness to all employees? Is the department head emphasizing efficiency over responsiveness to employee needs? Is Sandy emphasizing diversity over competence? Is Hank emphasizing his own self-interest over compliance with the code's prohibition of exclusionary golf clubs? And, by the way, is Dr. Smart going to emphasize the code—with its requirement to report suspicions of violation—over his own welfare in the corporation and with his father-in-law?

The answers to these questions are largely a product of what the organization, in its formal and informal realities, emphasizes. Informally, Samantha may be seen as emphasizing economics over fairness and competence despite formal statements to the contrary. Should she clarify her values vocally? Similarly, Hank seems to be sending a clear though informal message that provisions in the formal code are not to be emphasized too much, especially when golf is involved. Should he be provided with an organizational opportunity for reflection?

Dignity Versus Denigration

A salient issue in the ethics of diversity matter is the treatment of people. Does the diversity effort at St. Serena's dignify its people or denigrate them? Theoretically, diversity efforts dignify minorities by giving respect and honor to their special characteristics. But diversity in practice can actually denigrate minorities by using them as symbols instead of as substance. Does Samantha respect the contribution that minority young executives can make to the management team or does she just use them for image purposes? The distinction can be subtle, as can be the ethics of the situation. Miller's insistence on "inclusion," discussed in the reading below, is really an insistence on dignity.

On the other hand, we could ask whether in the process of honoring, respecting, and dignifying the minority executives, the CEO denigrates others by cavalierly excluding them from the management teams despite their competence. Is the department head denigrating Keneta and Kimberly by not spending time with them to develop their skills? Is Hank denigrating all minorities by playing a round of golf at a club that excludes all but white males? Does St. Serena's dignify its staff and clients formally, but denigrate them informally? These are hard questions to ask, let alone ponder and answer. As Lakoff insightfully suggests: "To recognize that we are following set patterns, sometimes engaging in strategies to achieve something at the expense of someone else, is to be forced to see ourselves . . . in an ungenerous light."[8] Unwillingness to see ourselves in this way may be at the source of difficulties with diversity as well as with other compliance and organizational ethics standards.

Notes

1. Dolan, T. 1998. "Diversity in Healthcare Management." *Healthcare Executive* 13 (3): 7.
2. Office of Federal Contract Compliance Programs. 1984. "OFCCP Digest: A Digest of Cases Under the Office of Federal Contract Compliance Programs." [Online article.] http:/204.136.2/public/ofccp/refrnc/odigtc.htm.
3. See Cox, T. 1993. *Cultural Diversity in Organizations.* San Francisco: Berrett-Koehler.
4. See Fiol, C. 1994. "Consensus, Diversity and Learning in Organizations." *Organization Science* 5 (4): 403–20.
5. Adler, M. 1996. "The Beth Israel Health Care System Addresses the Challenge of Culture Diversity." *Journal of Nursing Administration* 26 (9): 3.
6. *Ibid.*, 26.
7. Bruhn, J. 1996. "Creating an Organizational Climate for Multiculturalism." *Health Care Supervisor* 14 (4): 12.
8. Lakoff, R. 1990. *Talking Power*, 2. New York: Basic Books.

READINGS

Although the advantages of workforce diversity and its management in healthcare have been widely promoted, the ethics of diversity have received little explicit literary attention. Implicit in the literature, however, has been the ethical question. The following two pieces are illustrative. The Wallace, Ermer, and Motshabi article provides a good overview of the diversity in healthcare concept, including statistics on progress and executives' attitudes toward it. They argue that diversity is a key to organizational competitiveness in the healthcare industry. Not discussed but implicit in their presentation are two ethical questions: (1) Are diversity management programs fair and ethical, or do they discriminate against traditional groups; and (2) Is diversity by itself ethical, or does diversity require more attention to the concept of "inclusion"? The latter concept is the key notion of the Miller article. Although he argues for inclusion on the basis of the advantages for organizational development, implicit in his analysis is the suggestion that diversity can be denigrating—and therefore unethical—if it merely requires the presence but not the full participation of minorities. Miller provides wonderful insight on how to do diversity ethically. Notice how he deals both with the formal and the informal realities of organizational life. St. Serena's would well benefit from the notions offered.

Managing Diversity:
A Senior Management Perspective

Paul E. Wallace, Jr., Charles M.
Ermer, and Dimakatso N. Motshabi*

Summary

Diversity and managing diverse workgroups have become strategic imperatives for many organizations. Corporations are developing programs and opportunities to increase the participation of their employees, especially those who have not been previously included in the mainstream of their organizations. Many healthcare institutions are also focusing on diversity management. This study was designed to examine the manner in which diversity management is perceived and implemented by hospital executives. To determine the perception of executives, a 16-item questionnaire was developed and distributed to hospital executives. The data showed that executives in urban teaching hospitals considered their workforce diverse, and many of these organizations had implemented diversity management programs in their facilities. Surprisingly, this study found that although most executives (68 percent) agreed they had a diverse workforce, less than one-third (30 percent) of these executives had specifically developed diversity management programs in their hospitals.

The debate regarding diversity and managing diversified workgroups has been a focus of discussion among business executives and managers for several years. Interest in diversity in the workplace was stimulated in the late 1980s and early 1990s by projections that the workforce was changing and that the number of women, ethnic minorities, and immigrants in the workforce would increase. Projected increases in nonwhites in the labor market has resulted in many organizations' developing diversity initiatives to assist managers and employees to function more effectively. In 1993, the American College of Healthcare Executives (ACHE) and the National Association of Health Services Executives (NAHSE) recommended that health care organizations review promotion and hiring practices to ensure access to employment opportunities for minorities (Dolan 1993).

Some organizations see managing diversity as a business imperative and have developed strategies to increase opportunities for ethnic

Reprinted with permission of the American College of Healthcare Executives from Hospital & Health Services Administration 1996. 41 (1): 91–104. Paul E. Wallace is executive director of Urban Medical Institute, Baltimore. Charles M. Ermer is associate professor at Howard University, Washington, D. C. Dimakatso N. Motshabi is research methodologist at Howard University, Washington, D. C.

minorities and women in their companies. Are health administrators preparing their workforces to ensure inclusion of all regardless of gender, ethnicity, or racial heritage? The focus of this article is to assess the perceptions of hospital executives regarding whether workforce diversity is seen as valuable to their organizations. A second element that will be examined is what characteristics, if any, differentiate the perceptions of respondents regarding the importance of diversity management or the benefits it may yield. These questions will be pursued in an effort to form a better understanding of the development of diversity and diversity management in hospitals.

Diversity in the Workforce

The concept of diversity has gained unprecedented attention in recent years. The Hudson Report suggested that women and ethnic minorities will become a major part of the workforce by the year 2000 and beyond, according to Denton (1992). If the demographics projected for the year 2000 are accurate, organizations that have aggressively hired, trained, and promoted women and minorities will succeed, according to Dreyfus (1990). Dreyfus reported that companies with diversity initiatives such as Hewlett-Packard, Procter & Gamble, and Goodyear positioned themselves to be competitive by addressing the needs of a diverse workforce (Dreyfus 1990). Leonard (1991) reported that diversity consultants worked with Boeing, Coca-Cola, Avon, and Corning to address diversity management needs in their organizations.

The discussion of diversity in the workplace has expanded to include the variety of differences among individuals or groups. In addition to differences related to age, race, gender, ethnicity, and physical ability, diversity has also come to include individuals or groups who differ according to sexual preferences, marital status, educational background, parental status, work experience, and income. According to Overmann (1991) managing diversity should include characteristics common to a culture, race, gender, age, or sexual preference.

Although diversity has been associated with Affirmative Action or EEO initiatives, many organizations see diversity as a business imperative (Thomas 1990). For example, Caudron (1990) and Weidenfeller (1992) reported on organizations that valued diversity among their employees and made diversity a part of the strategic objectives of the company. Personnel policies, management techniques, and supervisory methods needed to change to address the diverse workforce according to Allen (1991). Greenslade (1991) reported that managing diversity was an attempt to create a climate of acceptance of differences rather than merely to meet statistical goals. The literature shows that the non–healthcare industry has viewed managing diverse groups as important and has implemented programs to improve opportunities for members of minority and under-represented groups. The question becomes, What are hospitals doing to prepare to manage these diverse workgroups now, and what are the implications for the future?

Diversity in Health Care

Has the focus on diversity in health care evolved as it has in non–health care organizations? Cejka (1993) reported that health care organizations are responding to the upcoming changes in the workforces by planning to manage a diverse workforce. She indicated that the emphasis on patient-focused care and more integrated jobs places a high value on teamwork. Managers, supervisors, and executives must be trained to promote a more diverse organization to maintain their competitive positions. Wagner (1991) also reported that the health care workforce of the future will be impacted by diversity generated by foreign-born and foreign-educated physicians, clinical professionals trained outside of the United States, and unskilled and semiskilled service workers. It has been reported that the number of female physicians will increase to 26.3 percent of total physicians in the year 2010, as compared to 17.3 percent of total physicians recorded in 1990 (U.S. DHHS 1990). The literature on diversity in a health care environment is sparse. However, do health care executives feel there are benefits in managing diverse workforces? The answer to this question may provide some insight into how acceptance of diversity management is being viewed by health care executives.

The focus on diversity by a hospital may depend on numerous factors. For example, Muller and Haase (1994) reported on the experiences of health care providers in the Southwest regarding diversity. The investigators reported that the proportion of racioethnic minority employees in the health labor forces was lower than in the civilian labor force. Another study on minorities in health care found that blacks were more likely to be employed by institutions with 400 or more beds than in small hospitals (Dolan 1993). Have health care organizations embraced establishing diversity initiatives in their organization?

Benefits from Workplace Diversity

Managing the diverse workforce is not only important but can be critical to the success of an organization. Shea and Okada (1992) reported that diversity was an imperative in some companies because not only will the workforce be diverse, so will the customers served. Foster et al. (1988) stated that "diversity competence in tomorrow's supervisors and managers will mean the capacity to effectively monitor and motivate differences across race, gender, age, social attitudes, and lifestyles." These investigators believe that organizations that do not employ and develop people of different communities and countries are restricting their client and customer base. Eubanks (1990) reported that the challenge for hospitals in the future will be to attract and retain employees with diverse needs, values, expectations, assumptions, and languages. Williams (1992) also reported that to effectively serve their communities and remain competitive, hospitals and health care organizations must tap the intelligence, imagination, energy, and dedication of a heterogenous workforce.

Managing diversity is seen as a process of making employees aware of individual differences and involves training sessions, subordinates' feedback, performance appraisals, and reward systems.

Statement of the Problem

The management of health care organizations is becoming more difficult as executives realize they must respond to the changing diversity in the workforce. The skills and training required to manage the modern health care organization must include diversity management. Over the last few years, increased emphasis has been placed on diversity in the workplace. Thus, in view of the challenges that will face managers in the areas of "diversity," the perceptions of executives regarding this issue is critical. In order to assess the perception of this issue, the following questions must be addressed:

1. How do health care executives define the term diversity?
2. Do health care executives view diversity management as important in their organization?

Understanding how practitioners view diversity is important and could be valuable in understanding whether organizations can effectively manage in the future. The research questions proposed in this study are:

1. What are the perceptions of health care executives concerning diversity of their workforce?
2. What is the status of diversity management in health care organizations?

The purpose of this study is to determine the responses of health care executives regarding their perceptions of diversity in health care organizations.

Method

A survey document was prepared for distribution to the chief executive officer or president of all short-term acute care hospitals located in Delaware, Kentucky, Maryland, North Carolina, Virginia, West Virginia, and the District of Columbia. These hospitals were listed in the 1991 edition of the American Hospital Association's (AHA) *Guide to the Health Care Field* (1989) and represented AHA's Region Three. These 580 hospitals included teaching and community hospitals in urban, rural, and suburban areas. Hospitals in Region Three were selected to encourage participation and increase the return rate of the survey instrument. The survey instrument was mailed with a brief letter from the investigator outlining the importance of a survey on diversity.

Survey instrument.

A questionnaire was developed to assess the perceptions of hospital executives regarding diversity in their organizations. Prior to the distribution of the questionnaire, a panel of academicians was assembled to review the questionnaire for comprehensiveness and clarity. The professors were selected because of their knowledge of diversity and the problems encountered by managers in the work setting.

The questionnaire consisted of 16 items. Six items were structured to obtain background information on the respondent and the facility. The remaining ten items sought information regarding diversity programs and the executives' perceptions of this issue. Nine of the informational items used a Likert scale ranging from 1 to 5, with 1 representing "strongly disagree" and 5 representing "strongly agree." To encourage participation, respondents were allowed to remain anonymous.

Data analysis.

Using an SPSS computer software package, the data were analyzed using descriptive statistics, the Pearson chi-square to determine associations between variables, the Mann-Whitney U-test, and the Kruskal-Wallis analysis of variance (ANOVA) to determine group differences. A Logit regression analysis was computed to evaluate the relationship between variables and whether a hospital has a diversity program. A factor analysis was used to determine the relationship between respondents. A t-test was calculated between teaching and nonteaching organizations.

Limitations of the study.

There are certain limitations to this study that should be examined. For example, since only 35 percent of the surveys were returned, it is unknown as to whether the participants were representative of the

Table 1   Summary on the Demographic Profile of Respondents

Factor	Number	Percent
Type		
Community	102	51
Community-teaching	27	13
University-teaching	21	10
Other	52	26
Location		
Urban	38	19
Suburban	25	12
Rural	89	44
Other	50	25
Sponsorship		
Public	59	29
Private nonprofit	94	47
Private investor	21	10
Other	28	14
Size		
< 100 beds	67	33
100–350 beds	84	42
350–600 beds	32	16
600+ beds	16	8
Other	3	1

opinions regarding diversity of the majority of hospital executives. A second limitation is that follow-up studies were not possible because identifying information was not obtained from respondents nor were the surveys coded. Therefore, the individual or institutional backgrounds of respondents and nonrespondents were not available for further analysis.

Results

Thirty-five percent (202) of the 580 surveys were returned completed. An analysis of the demographic data in Table 1 shows that twice as many nonteaching community hospitals responded to the survey as teaching hospitals. A majority of the respondents were from rural hospitals, with urban hospitals providing the second largest number of respondents. Eighty-five percent of the respondents were either president/chief executive officers or senior vice presidents. Ten percent of the respondents were chief operation officers or assistant administrators and five percent were directors of human resources.

Under the sponsorship category, the largest number of responses were from private nonprofit hospitals, with public hospitals comprising

Table 2 Response to Survey

Description (in Brief)	Mode	Mean	Standard Deviation
1. Classify workforce diverse	4.0	3.73	1.11
2. Not as important as other industries*	1.0	1.94	1.05
3. Important for employees of different backgrounds	4.0	4.10	0.72
4. Important for employees of different income	4.0	4.05	0.62
5. Important because of community	4.0	3.89	0.98
6. Benefits patients	4.0	4.11	0.81
7. Benefits organization	4.0	4.24	0.72
8. Contributes to success	4.0	4.25	0.68
9. Positive effect on efficiency	4.0	3.99	0.75
10. Have a diversity program			Yes = 29%; No = 71%

Note: This is a negative statement, thus the scale is reversed with respect to the other questions.

almost one-third of the respondents. For size of facility, 75 percent of the respondents were hospitals with less than 350 beds.

Table 2 summarizes the responses of the executives regarding workforce diversity. Overall, the results show that the respondents agreed that their organization had a diverse workforce. In particular, the average responses were in the agreed range. This conclusion was further supported by the fact that 68 percent of the respondents either agreed or strongly agreed with the statement. Conversely, only 16 percent disagreed or strongly disagreed. The remaining questions dealt with the administrators' attitudes on the importance of diversity management and on the benefits of diversity management. Questions 2 through 5 probed the importance of diversity management in the health care field. These questions addressed the educational background of employees and the community the organization served. Questions 6 through 9 probed the perceived benefit to the organization of diversity management as it related to patients, the long-term success of the organization, as well as organizational efficiency. As can be seen in Table 2, the overall responses to these questions were favorable for both the importance and benefits of diversity management. Given the current focus on diversity management, this positive attitude might not be unexpected; however, what was surprising was that only 29 percent of the respondents indicated they had diversity programs in place at their institutions.

Diversity of the workforce.

While the respondents as a whole agreed that their workforces were diversified, further analysis of the data was completed to determine whether other differences existed. The categories used to explore other relationships were: size (number of beds), type (teaching and nonteaching), location (urban and rural), and sponsorship (public and private).

A Kruskal-Wallis test was performed for each of the demographic categories of type, sponsorship, location, and size. This ANOVA showed that when grouped by sponsorship no differences existed in the responses to the diversity of their workforce; the test statistic was 2.27 ($p = 0.3219$). When grouped by type, location, and size, differences in response to the diversity of the workforce were significant at the .05 levels (6.06 with a $p = 0.04840$; 15.23 with a $p = 0.0005$) and at the .01 level (16.13 with a $p = 0.00110$) for type, location, and size, respectively.

Since location and size presented such convincing cases for differences in responses to the question regarding the organization being perceived as diverse, a Logit regression analysis was performed to determine the interaction of variables such as type, location, size, and sponsorship.

A Logit regression analysis was performed to determine the effects of the relationships between respondents to the question of whether there was a diversity program in their organization. The result of the interaction of the variables' type, location, sponsorship, and size appear in Table 3. The findings indicate that chi-square model and improvement were significant at the .05 level. The cross-tabs are predictors at overall 78.39 percent. The most important variable in the equations was type followed by location and sponsorship. Size was not significant.

A multiple factor analysis was calculated to compare the impact of type, size, and sponsorship—the results appear in Table 4. The responses were placed into two categories, type (teaching and nonteaching) and were compared by the variables' location (urban versus rural); sizes (small—under 350 beds—and large—over 350 beds); and sponsorship (nonprofit and private). In all of the comparisons, except for the large and public hospitals, the differences in the percent responding "Yes" were significant. The results of this analysis suggested that hospitals with a diversity program favor urban over rural, teaching over nonteaching, larger over smaller, and public over private hospitals. Since the strongest difference in Yes/No response was seen in the demographic factor of type (teaching versus nonteaching), it is believed that this is the primary factor in differentiating between hospitals that have diversity programs and those that do not.

A factor analysis was computed to examine the relationship between the four importance (items 2 to 5 in Table 2) and four benefit items (items 6 to 9 in Table 2); the results appear in Table 5. The findings indicate that the four items under benefit and importance were highly correlated. The factor loading shows no differences between importance and benefit, while the correlation coefficients show significant correlations

Table 3 Results of Stepwise Logit Regression on Type, Location, Sponsor, and Size on Question Regarding Diversity Program

	Chi-Square	Degrees of Freedom	Significance
−2 LOG likelihood	101.263	112	.7575
Model chi-square	41.509	4	.0000
Improvement	41.509	4	.0000
Goodness of fit	118.589	112	.3170

Classification Table

	Predicted		
Observed	Yes	No	Percent Correct
Yes	21	12	60.00
No	11	71	86.59
Overall			78.63

Variables in the Equations

Variable	Value	Standard Error	Test Statistics	Degrees of Freedom	p Value	r-Value	EXP(B)
Type	−1.09	.563	3.710	1	.054	−.109	.338
Location	1.83	.600	9.243	1	.002	.225	6.202
Sponsor	1.73	.578	8.937	1	.003	.220	5.632
Size	−.42	.558	.554	1	.457	.000	.660
Constant	.56	.255	4.861	1	.028		

at the .01 level between nonteaching and teaching regarding having a diversity program. Since differences in responses exist between teaching and nonteaching institutions, a t-test was performed on the sum of each individual response to questions 7 through 9. The result of this test showed significant differences in the responses from the two groups. The teaching institutions averaged 30.13 out of a possible 40 and the nonteaching institutions averaged 27.91 out of a possible 40. The t-test showed that these differences in means were significant at the 0.001 level. The administrators of teaching hospitals were strongly in support of the importance and benefits of diversity management.

The executives in this study were asked whether they had diversity programs or efforts in effect at their organizations. Overall, 29 percent of the respondents indicated that they did have diversity programs or efforts in existence. Given the perceived level of diversity in the workforce, this number appeared to be rather low. It was also interesting

Table 4 Multiple-Factor Comparing Responses to the Question Regarding a Diversity Program

Demographic Factor	% Yes	Chi-Square	p Value	Degrees of Freedom
Location				
Urban		7.08	0.0078	1
Teaching	68			
Nonteaching	30			
Rural		6.62	0.0001	1
Teaching	40			
Nonteaching	10			
Size				
Small		15.90	0.0001	1
Teaching	56			
Nonteaching	13			
Large		2.29	0.0189	1
Teaching	62			
Nonteaching	33			
Sponsorship				
Public		5.51	0.0189	1
Teaching	70			
Nonteaching	33			
Private		13.01	0.0003	1
Teaching	47			
Nonteaching	10			

that teaching hospitals were more likely to have a diversity program and saw more benefits to having such an initiative than nonteaching hospitals.

Conclusions and Implications

The results of this study support that hospital executives perceive that urban/suburban hospitals have a more diverse workforce than rural hospitals. On the whole, executives in this study agreed that they had diversified workforces and that managing diversity was important. However, the finding in this study showed that hospitals with diversity management programs were primarily teaching facilities located in urban areas. The proportion of diversity programs was higher among teaching (60 percent) than nonteaching hospitals (15 percent). The reason for this difference appears to be that more executives in teaching hospitals believe that diversity management is important and that benefits exist if their diverse workforce is properly managed. A second unusual finding

Table 5 Results of Factor Loading and Correlations on Responses for Importance and Benefits of Diversity Management

Item Description	Factor 1	Factor 2
As other industries	.3666	.8619
For those of different backgrounds	.6641	.2871
For those of different income	.7621	.0769
Backgrounds of community	.6841	−.0491
Benefits patients in institution	.8256	−.1642
Benefits organization	.8746	−.1683
Contributes to success	.8802	−.2016
Improves efficiency	.7416	−.0962

Correlation Coefficients—Benefits Significant at the .01 Level			
	Benefit 1	Benefit 2	Benefit 3	Benefit 4
Importance 1	.238	.248	.198	.205
Importance 2	.395	.443	.468	.465
Importance 3	.543	.529	.597	.445
Importance 4	.498	.530	.556	.345

is that even though hospital executives reported that diversity management was important and would benefit their organizations, less than 30 percent had diversity programs in effect.

A majority of teaching hospitals and hospitals in urban areas in this study had diversity programs. These findings appear to agree with those of Geber (1990) that changing demographics have accelerated emphasis on managing diversity. Certainly, teaching hospitals, especially those in urban areas, attract a host of employees and patients with different ethnic, racial, and cultural backgrounds. Thus, it is understandable why many urban teaching hospitals had diversity programs. The hospital executives in these urban hospitals viewed diversity management issues differently from their counterparts in rural areas.

The executives in this study who had a diversity program strongly agreed that they had a diversified workforce. These hospitals were located primarily in urban areas. If hospitals in this study are similar to those in the general hospital industry, the low number having diversity programs suggests that diversity management may not be broadly supported in the health care industry. This raises the question, Are hospitals without diversity programs prepared to manage future workgroups? This question was raised in a report by Eubanks (1990) and in an editorial by Wallace (1994). If there is to be a shortage of competent workers in the future, how hospitals address diversity today may set the foundation for their future. It appears that public hospitals were more likely to have a diversity program than private for-profit hospitals. These findings were similar to those of Muller and Haase (1994), who reported that in some institutions public accountability was a factor that raised the issue of participation of individuals with diverse backgrounds. These investigators also found that state and federal institutions in the Southwest employed twice as many racial minorities as other health care organizations.

The questions that have not been answered by this study are: Why have some health care executives implemented diversity programs in their organizations? Are the hospitals that have placed these programs in effect on the forefront of human resource management for the year 2000 and beyond? Will these hospitals have a competitive edge in the future by being sensitive to diversity among their customers and work-force? Are organizations with diversity programs responding to some political or social pressures that mandated that minorities have greater participation in these organizations? As for those institutions that do not have diversity programs, will they lose the ability to attract talented individuals in the future to work in their organizations, especially at the senior management level? Muller and Haase (1994) concluded from their investigation that attempts to include people with different characteristics would become more important as the labor force becomes more heterogeneous.

The debate regarding the impact of diversity on the workforce will continue in both health care and the general business industry. Diversity is being advocated by some investigators as a key element that will make and keep their organizations competitive. Thus, if diversity can make a difference in how an organization functions, health care administrators may see utility in placing the management of a diverse workforce higher on their list of priorities. Hospital executives must consider what would happen if they are not able to attract administrators, physicians, and other clinical individuals to work in their organizations. The health care industry is in a state of transition, and organizations that effectively manage their diverse workgroups can have a competitive edge. Thus, executives who are considering strategies for the future should include managing their human resource needs as a priority.

Certainly having a diversity management initiative may not seem as critical or important to executives as preparing their organization for managed care, working out affiliation relationships with physicians and other hospitals, or controlling their cost and expenditures. However, what will happen as the pool of qualified individuals becomes smaller?

One of the challenges facing hospital executives today and in the future is maximizing their human resources. Successful organizations of the future may well be those that have placed diversity management high on their list of priorities. This study found executives in teaching hospitals with more than 350 beds, located in an urban area more likely to have a diversity management program in place than executives in other types of hospitals. Hospital executives who can manage diversified workgroups should benefit from the effective use of this vital organization resource. The competition in the health care industry has accelerated the restructuring or reengineering in many organizations. Thus, the question that hospital executives should ask themselves and their administrators is, Can effective reengineering occur and be successful if we do not recognize the diversity of our current and future workforces?

References

American Hospital Association. 1989. *Guide to the Health Care Field*. Chicago: AHA.

Allen, G. 1991. "Valuing Cultural Diversity: Industry Woos a New Work Force." *Communication World* 8 (May): 14–17.

Caudron, S. 1990. "Monsanto Responds to Diversity." *Personnel Journal* (Nov): 72–80.

Cejka, S. 1993. "The Changing Health Care Workforce: A Call for Managing Diversity." *Health Care Executive* 8 (Mar/Apr): 20–23.

Denton, W. 1992. "Workforce 2000." *Credit World* 81 (Sept/Oct): 14–18.

Dolan, T. 1993. "Appreciating Diversity." *Health Management Quarterly* 15 (4): 17–20.

Dreyfus, J. 1990. "Get Ready for the New Work Force." *Fortune* (23 April): 166–81.

Eubanks, P. 1990. "Workforce Diversity in Health Care: Managing the Melting Pot." *Hospitals* (20 June): 48–50.

Foster, B., G. Jackson, W. Cross, B. Jackson, and R. Hardiman. 1988. "Workforce Diversity and Business." *Training and Development Journal* 42 (Apr): 38–42.

Geber, B. 1990. "Managing Diversity." *Training* 27 (July): 23–30.

Greenslade, M. 1991. "Managing Diversity: Lessons from the United States." *Personnel Management* (Dec): 28–33.

Leonard, B. 1991. "Ways to Make Diversity Programs Work." *Human Resources Magazine* (Apr): 37–41.

Muller, R., and B. Haase. 1994. "Managing Diversity in Health Services Organizations." *Hospital & Health Services Administration* 39 (4): 415–34.

Overmann, S. 1991. "Managing the Diverse Work Force." *Human Resources Magazine* 36 (Apr): 32–36.

Shea, S., and R. Okada. 1992. "Benefiting from Workforce Diversity." *Health Care Forum Journal* (Jan/Feb): 23–26.

Thomas, R. 1990. "From Affirmative Action to Affirming Diversity." *Harvard Business Review* (Mar/Apr): 107–17.

Wagner, M. 1991. "Managing Diversity." *Modern Health Care* (31 Sept): 24–29.

Wallace, P. 1994. "Diversity: A Proactive or Reactive Response?" *Hospital & Health Services Administration* 39 (4): 413–14.

Weidenfeller, N. 1992. "Celebrating Diversity." *Public Utilities Fortnightly* 129 (15 June): 20–22.

Williams, J. 1992. "The New Workforce." *Health Care Forum Journal* (Jan/Feb): 15–17.

United States Department of Health and Human Services. 1990. *7th Report to the President and Congress on the Status of Health Personnel in the U.S.* Washington, D. C.: U.S. DHHS.

Strategic Culture Change: The Door to Achieving High Performance and Inclusion

Frederick A. Miller*

Abstract

Diversity is one of the most significant forces influencing organizational change in the 1990s. The number of diversity workshops, videos, journal articles, boardgames, handbooks, and CD-ROMs testifies to its significance. Many of these present diversity as a problem to overcome or manage. Few recognize diversity as a potential source of organizational effectiveness. This article presents diversity as a key resource to create a high-performing work culture that enables all members of the organization to do their best work. I share some of the lessons learned in over 25 years' experience consulting with public and private organizations in their quest to build inclusive, high-performing work environments. The article distinguishes between diversity and inclusion, describes a model for diagnosing an organization's culture, sets forth steps for implementing organizational change, and discusses the human resource professional's role. These concepts grew out of my work with organizations such as Mobil Corporation, Dun & Bradstreet, Apple Computer, and the Cities of Portland, Maine; Columbus, Indiana; and San Diego, California.

Inclusion¹ Broadens the Bandwidth

Diversity describes the make-up of a group. Inclusion describes which individuals are allowed to participate and are enabled to contribute fully in the group. In reality, diversity is an attribute of every group. People are unique individuals who belong to several different identity groups. There are wide ranges of differences among people who look, sound, act, and appear to think and feel alike.

* Reprinted with permission of the International Personnel Management Association from Public Personnel Management 1998. 27 (2): 151–60. Frederick A. Miller is president and CEO of the Kaleel Jamison Consulting Group, Troy, NY.

Among people who value sameness, diversity tends to mean visible differences. There is an assumption that differences ought to be suppressed, and therefore only people who cannot suppress their differences are really different. People who cannot look, dress, act, or communicate like the organization's norm are viewed as potential problems that must be managed.

Inclusion increases the total human energy available to the organization. When differences are regarded as valued resources, as in a truly inclusive environment, individual and group differences no longer need to be suppressed. Those who cannot fit into the monocultural model do not have to waste their energy trying to be what they cannot. People can bring far more of themselves to their jobs because they are required to suppress far less. An inclusive organizational culture enables contributions from a broader range of styles, perspectives, and skills, providing a greater range of available routes to success.

Achieving Inclusion Through Strategic Cultural Change

For an organization to succeed, it must find ways to maximize the contributions of all of its people. Many organizations are filled with barriers that prevent people from contributing all their skills, ideas, and energies to the organization's success.

Expressed in conscious and unconscious behaviors as well as routine practices, procedures, and bylaws, these barriers are often rooted in the very culture of an organization. Typically, they favor people who look and act like the leaders of the organization, and to those they favor, the barriers can be as invisible as air. But to those who confront them daily, these barriers can be demeaning, discouraging, and insurmountable.

The barriers can be as tangible as the stairways that block access to people in wheelchairs, or the sign that reads "MEN" on the door of the only bathroom on the executive floor. The barriers can also be subtle, such as not remembering one's ideas or name. The result is the loss of large numbers of people and their potential contributions.

Before an organization can expect to gain the full commitment and contribution of all its people, these exclusive barriers must be recognized and removed. Removing the barriers cannot be accomplished by a multicultural awareness workshop, an ethnic foods week, or a valuing diversity initiative. Building an inclusive organization requires a serious commitment to fundamental change in the structures, behaviors, operating procedures, human resources systems, formal and informal reward systems, leadership practices, competency requirements, and culture of the organization.

Implementing Organization Change

Changing an organizational culture requires powerful motivators. Getting the entire organization to move in a new direction, and continue moving, requires a carefully considered strategy. While every organization is and must be treated as a unique entity, the following five steps form a good starting point for building an effective and sustainable organizational culture change strategy.

1. Identify the organizational imperative.

The first step in changing an organization is to provide it with a compelling reason to change; establish the organizational imperative for inclusion. It is important that the people of the organization understand the inter-relationship of an inclusion effort and the organization's ability to achieve its mission and future success.

2. Build a core of advocates for change.

Reinforce existing resources for change instead of attacking areas of resistance. Start by identifying leaders from all levels of the organization who already hold inclusive values—a diverse group of pioneers, top management, and other members of the original culture. Help strengthen their commitment and competencies for supporting change throughout the organization through coaching, education, networking, and mentoring efforts.

3. Build on the successes of pockets of readiness.

Establish groups or teams that are committed to the change, equip them with the skills and resources that they need to work together, and let them prove that the change works. Their successes will then be the standard others will want to emulate, and they can become a core of internal change agents as well as role models. Offer examples of success. Don't try to fix or change people.

4. Coach the leaders.

The skills for building inclusion require learning and practice. To assist leaders and managers in leading the change, they need skilled, experienced people to support and coach them. Internal and external change agents can facilitate this process.

5. Change the system.

Edgar Schein defined culture as a pattern of basic group assumptions that has worked well enough to be considered valid and, therefore, is taught to new members as the correct way to perceive, think, and feel.[2] These established rules, procedures, rewards, and other components of the internal organizational environment determine the outcomes of a change process. Root out the structures that perpetuate the old culture. Remove the barriers that prevent people from doing their best work. Establish new norms, values, practices, and policies that support inclusion and high performance.

The Organizational Imperative for Inclusion

For an organization to leverage diversity in the service of achieving its strategic goals and objectives, it must start by establishing a clear and direct vision of why a more inclusive work culture and a more diverse workforce are required to achieve those goals and objectives. It must be clear to all why change is imperative for their success and the organization's survival. Change that does not serve the overall mission of the organization is unlikely to sustain widespread support. Initiatives undertaken because they are "the right thing to do" tend to lose momentum in the face of more pressing, bottom-line business matters or shifts in the political winds.

The organizational culture change must serve the organization's present and/or future self-interest. For the change effort to be successful, there must be widespread understanding of the need for change and of the bottom-line benefits to be gained from the change effort. It must be clear to all concerned that the change is vital to the success of the organization and to the well-being of every member. Self-interest is a powerful motivator.

A key part of any change strategy is to clearly identify and communicate the rationale behind the change effort to the entire organization. In articulating this organizational imperative for culture change, most organizations find that the pressures for and benefits of the change fall into three major areas: competitive marketplace issues, workforce issues, and community and societal issues.

Competitive marketplace issues involve:

- Connecting with diverse customers, locally and globally;
- Partnering effectively with an increasingly diverse spectrum of suppliers and strategic business allies;
- Responding quickly and decisively to challenges and opportunities; and
- Positioning products and marketing strategies for different cultures and market niches.

Workforce issues include:

- Productivity;
- Internal partnership and teamwork skills;
- Continuity and quality of customer service;

- Retention of irreplaceable skills and knowledge;
- Training and recruitment costs; and
- Value of innovation.

Community and societal issues involve:

- Ensuring continuity of workforce and markets;
- Social and environmental responsibility;
- Regulatory and legal compliance;
- Work-family-life balance; and
- Creating a community environment that is supportive of the organizational infrastructure, attitude, and politics.

The Path from Exclusive "Club" to Inclusive Organization

The organizational imperative for change makes clear why the reasons for change are necessary. Bringing about the desired change is another major challenge. A crucial requirement for designing an effective culture change strategy is a baseline diagnosis of the existing culture—a clear determination of where the organization is along the path from exclusive, monocultural "club" to inclusive, diverse organization.

The Myth of the Monocultural Advantage

In many ways, monocultural groups are still seen as the ideal for productivity. In some work situations, they may be the best way to solve a problem when it is narrow and requires specialization. But many of today's problems are webs of complexity with numerous angles that must be explored.

Monocultural values tend to discourage people from suggesting change or questioning the status quo. Over time, monocultural teams lack the creativity and ability to change when necessary to achieve the continuous improvement required to fit today's high performance standards.

Difference as an Asset

With an increasing diversity of consumers, stakeholders, and potential partners, organizations need a diverse and inclusive membership to provide the necessary range of talents, communication skills, problem solving styles, perspectives, and cultural awareness they require to succeed. Faced with this broad vision and an expanding range of skills, organizations are beginning to identify diversity as a potential asset and are making inclusion of differences a part of their culture and success. Most organizations, however, require a fundamental culture change to value difference as an asset, or to see the benefit in truly including unique individuals and members of different identity groups.

Tailoring Change Initiatives to Organizations on "The Path"

The following section describes the various stages organizations undergo moving from exclusivity to inclusion and discusses methods to tailor change initiatives in each stage.[3]

Diagnosis: Exclusive club.

Organizations in this stage actively or passively pursue monocultural norms and values, and are open only to those who are willing and able to fit in.

Intervention Strategy: Where there is little or no tolerance for differences, recruitment is too often an exercise in hiring people just like everybody else. These organizations are better served with internal programs for their current people to widen the bandwidth of acceptable behavior. Before they attempt to include new people, they must find value in including the differences of the people who are already there.[4]

Diagnosis: Symbolic difference organization.

Members of this organization tolerate differences in appearance but not in behavior and are often self-described as "bias-free" or "blind to differences." Pioneers from different identity groups are often called "tokens" in these organizations.

Intervention Strategy: Effective interventions for organizations in this phase support the organization's pioneers and minimize their isolation while educating the wider organization about obstacles that limit or prevent the full contribution of all people. Gathering committed individuals, including champions from the original culture as well as new-culture pioneers, into organizationally sanctioned networks can provide needed support as well as build "pockets of readiness" that can help move the organization to the next stage.[5]

Diagnosis: Critical mass.

In this stage organizations have a growing core of people who are different from the founding culture and growing support for a diverse, inclusive culture. This is a key transition point: The old rules no longer work, but the new rules have not all been created. At this stage many organizations turn back, stop where they are, bring in a different consulting team, or try a different "initiative of the month."

Intervention Strategy: Leadership education, training, and support are critical at this stage. Coaching and skill enhancement of the organization's leaders and champions for change are important. It is crucial for leaders to establish, communicate, and model how the mission, vision, and values of the organization are served by building inclusion and leveraging diversity.

Diagnosis: Acceptance.

People in organizations at this stage are recognized, multi-dimensional, unique, and belong to several identity groups. The imperative for building inclusion and leveraging diversity is apparent. The organization experiences the payoff on a daily basis in loyalty, productivity, and performance.

Intervention Strategy: Organizational leaders, change agents, and members implement strategies to:

1. Redefine competence and provide education to impart and improve competencies required for forming effective cross-cultural, cross-gender, and cross-organizational partnerships and teams;
2. Establish informal mentoring and partnering opportunities to support people living in the new culture;
3. Redefine success (and who can be successful) to include sustainable benefit for a broader group of stakeholders; and
4. Change organizational structures, policies, and practices to enable the new culture.

Diagnosis: Inclusive organization.

The inclusive culture actively includes and utilizes the full range of perspectives, opinions, and skills offered by different individuals, identity groups, and functional specialties. Members of these organizations are committed to and geared for constant change, continuous improvement, a search for breadth of vision, and constantly widening their bandwidth of human resources and potential. They are eager to gain from the synergy that can be tapped when these differences are brought together.

Intervention Strategy: Effort should be made to study and replicate successful practices and procedures and to ensure that they are used throughout the organization. These should include approaches such as:

1. Training in and encouraging the use of clear, direct, authentic communication;

2. Training in recognizing and engaging in conflict as a creative, problem solving process to ensure diverse perspectives are represented in management; and ensuring that processes are in place to ensure diverse perspectives;

3. Challenging and supporting each individual, partnership, team, and group to continuously learn, grow, develop new skills, and behave inclusively;

4. Finding new ways to maximize each person's ability to contribute and add value;

5. Expanding the boundaries of the organization's efforts to include stockholders, communities, customers, and suppliers; and

6. Constantly searching for new ways to reward courage and participation.

The path to continuous improvement also requires new skills and competencies:

- Treat people and their differences as an asset.
- Create the safety required for honest communication, informed dialogue, conflict engagement, risk-taking, and learning.
- Celebrate constant change as the path to continuous improvement and sustainable success.
- Purposefully engage in conflicts and actively explore differences to produce better solutions to problems, not expecting total harmony and perfect agreement.

Action is Required to Sustain the Effort

Continuous improvement can only be achieved by a constant effort to expand the vision and skills available to the organization. In that sense, the quest to leverage diversity in an inclusive organization is a quest for continuous improvement.

The continuing need for new viewpoints creates a challenge. Over time, even teams that are diverse in terms of ethnicity, gender, and race tend to develop a unified point of view. They can develop a closeness that seems like exclusivity; they can become so comfortable with their existing diversity that it seems like assimilation. They can become too agreeable, lacking a constant questioning of what is and, therefore, limit their vision of what can be.

In order to remain on a path of continuous improvement, diverse teams need to be proactive in recruiting new team members who can bring new viewpoints, talents, and disagreements to the team. Without "fresh eyes," no team or organization can be high-performing, inclusive, and sustainable in the long term.

To provide the ongoing expansion of perspectives required for continuous improvement, organizations must continually expand the limits of inclusion. They must constantly seek out, connect with, and change the team and organizational culture to be inclusive of "new" dimensions of difference: gays and lesbians; people with disabilities; people of different generations, educational backgrounds, family situations, nationalities, and language groups; and other dimensions of difference. Human resource (HR) professionals can facilitate this process.

The Role of HR Professionals

An essential role for HR in a culture change effort is assisting organizational leaders to realize that people are their most important resource. To create a sustainable, high-performing work culture, the people of the organization must be treated as valuable resources who are essential for the continuing success of the organization. Barriers to their full involvement and contribution must be identified, removed, and replaced with inclusive norms and values that allow all people to do their best work. People must be equipped with skills for partnering across differences and working in inclusive teams to achieve the organization's strategic objectives and mission. They must be supported and rewarded for bringing their full range of talents and energies to their work.

HR professionals' tools for helping to bring about this culture change include training, coaching, mentoring, modeling, monitoring, and measuring. Following are some key strategies for HR in building an organizational culture that supports high performance and inclusion.

1. Partner with senior managers of other departments and functions to facilitate alignment and focus on the organization's mission, vision, desired culture, and strategic plan. This includes providing training, coaching, and consultation to line managers and staff and modeling inclusive behaviors and skills for high performance.

2. Ensure that the organization's infrastructure enables all its people to perform at their maximum ability by addressing questions such as:

    • Does the organizational structure enable people to work to their potential?

    • Do people receive the information and management they need to do their best work?

- Are people being developed on a path of continuous skill improvement so their performance today will be even better tomorrow?

3. Develop and implement measurement systems that reward people for behaving in ways that support the organization.
4. Review and revise incentive and compensation programs, and discard outmoded personnel evaluation processes.
5. Integrate inclusive people-policies and practices into the organization's everyday activities, and make sure they are tied to the bottom line—the organization's ability to accomplish its mission and goals.

In many organizations, HR is relegated to technical roles and un-involved in the strategic business objectives of the organization. By assuming its rightful place in the organization, HR can play a key role in establishing the organizational imperative for valuing people and enabling their best work through the creation of a high-performing and inclusive work culture.

EEO? AA? Diversity? Inclusion: They're Not the Same

EEO.

Laws which collectively prohibit discrimination on the basis of sex, color, race, religion, national origin, age, or physical ability.

Affirmative action.

Positive steps to reduce underrepresentation in situations where a pattern of past discrimination has occurred.

Diversity.

The acknowledgment of the differences among people.

Inclusion.

Different voices are sought out and utilized as opportunities for added value. Different perspectives and frames of reference offer competitive advantages in teamwork, service delivery, product quality, and work output.

Notes

1. The Kaleel Jamison Consulting Group began using the concept of "inclusion" in 1990, in part because it more fully described our goal for strategic culture change, and in part to differentiate between true culture change and a mere change in head count.

2. Schein, E. H. 1985. *Organizational Culture and Leadership*, 9. San Francisco: Jossey-Bass.

3. The path from monocultural club to inclusive organization was excerpted from "Cultural Diversity as a Developmental Process" by Katz, J. H. and F. A. Miller. 1995. *Annual*, vol. 2, 267–78. San Diego, CA: J. Pfeiffer.

4. Katz, J. H., and F. A. Miller. 1998. "Between Monoculturalism and Multiculturalism: Traps Awaiting the Organization." *OD Practitioner* 20 (3): 1–5.

5. Miller, F. A. 1988. "Moving a Team to Multiculturalism." In *Team Building: Blueprints for Productivity and Satisfaction*. NTL Institute and San Diego University Associates, Inc.

Annotated Bibliography

Bruhn, A. 1996. "Creating an Organizational Climate for Multiculturalism. *Health Care Supervisor* 14 (4): 11–18. The most managerially practical article on diversity in print.

Capowski, G. 1996. "Managing Diversity." *Management Review* 17 (2): 234–39. A good introductory brief on the subject.

Cox, T. 1993. *Cultural Diversity in Organizations*. San Francisco: Berret-Koehler. Among the best primers on diversity.

Fiol, C. 1994. "Consensus, Diversity, and Learning in Organizations." *Organization Science* 5 (4): 403–20. An outstanding presentation of an enlightened approach to the issue of diversity.

Institute for Corporate Diversity. 1996. *Diversity in Corporate America*. Minneapolis: ICD. An excellent resource from an organization of which managers should be aware.

Loden, M. 1996. *Implementing Diversity*. New York: Irwin. A useful guide for managers seeking diversity strategies.

Stephenson, K. 1994. "Diversity: A Managerial Paradox." *Clinical Sociology Review* 12 (2): 189–205. Offers a helpful perspective on the nature of the diversity issue.

9

HEALTHCARE ORGANIZATIONAL ETHICS REVISITED

W E HAVE reflected on eight cases with the help of numerous concepts and readings; let us now conclude by again asking, What is healthcare organizational ethics in the compliance context and how does a healthcare organization do it? What final insights can we glean from the previous discussions as well as from the following case and suggested reading?

CASE STUDY

Case Nine: What's Good for the Goose

Dr. Max Smart was, of course, smart enough not to report vice president Hank despite the code's formal admonition to do so. The more effective admonition, it seems, was the informal norm to avoid any organizational wrath that might fall on his promising career were he to suggest that a respected and powerful executive had broken the code. During his two years at St. Serena's Dr. Smart had seen a "whistle-blower" ostracized after reporting suspected code violations by senior executives. St. Serena's had not rewarded the reporting staff member; instead she was challenged with intense questioning. No action was taken against the executives reported. Dr. Smart knew that he did not need such a hassle; he had worked hard to get where he was and his family had made sacrifices along the way.

What Dr. Smart did do was make an inquiry to the newly established organizational ethics committee at St. Serena's: Was it proper for himself, he asked, in view of Section I.9.b of the code, to lunch at an exclusionary club with a family member who has no connection to St. Serena's? He shrewdly suspected that, in addressing the inquiry, the question of episodes like Hank playing golf with a St. Serena's business associate at the club would likely be raised, but in an anonymous and much less threatening way. If the committee then published its analysis and used the matter in training sessions, word would likely get to Hank and others and code compliance would eventually result.

Remember Sandy, the director of employment from Chapter eight? She also ended up trying to find a way around a difficult situation. In a compromise with the department head who initially had insisted on hiring the white male candidate, Sandy arranged for Kimberly to be promoted, believing the "personality conflict" involving Keneta would be too disruptive. In the process she obtained a commitment from the department head and others to provide professional development training and mentoring to Keneta (and to others) so that her interpersonal skills would be improved when the next supervisory position became available.

Compliance committee member Lawrence did accompany his friend Ed to AA meetings and monitored his sobriety. Convinced that Ed was right about the grapevine in and out of EAP and the organizational attitude toward recovering substance abusers, Lawrence did not—contrary to Section II of the code—report his friend. What he did do was submit an agenda item for the next compliance committee meeting. The item requested a discussion of the variance between St. Serena's code requirement of reporting suspected substance abuse and the policy recommended by the American College of Healthcare Executives.

St. Serena's nursing home administrator, Andrew Able—whom we met in Chapter two, did give private-pay patient Mrs. Livingston priority when the next bed became available. He also formed a task force to design a strategy for bringing the facility's private-pay census up to the norm for nursing homes in the region. He reasoned that if he could establish a competitively "level playing field," then St. Serena's admissions policy could be more realistically implemented.

The task force's work included travel to nursing homes in other parts of the country that had successfully developed an appropriate mix of private-pay and Medicaid residents. One member of the task force, Faith Furie, regularly traveled in her capacity as a strategic planning and marketing coordinator for St. Serena's. When the financial management consulting firm mentioned in case two came to St. Serena's, it had instituted—as part of the effort to bring more discipline to cost-containment processes at St. Serena's—a new travel policy that limits lodging and meal reimbursements to maximums that sometimes do not cover Faith's actual out-of-pocket expenses. This occurred only occasionally when she traveled to large cities and chose to stay at more expensive hotels for security reasons. (A year ago she was mugged while staying at a cheaper hotel.) Outraged by what she viewed as the consultant's arrogant and unrealistic measures, Faith (and apparently other colleagues) has adopted a routine of "padding" her expense report with small taxicab items that, in line with the policy, do not require receipts. The bogus taxi items cover the difference between actual hotel expenses and the reimbursement maximum.

Faith is a rising star in the healthcare management field. Extremely conscientious and hard working, she takes pride in her productivity, integrity, and performance. Largely because of her conscientiousness the travel expense limitation irritates her. "Don't they trust me to use good sense!" she wonders. And, because of the mugging incident, she has deep feelings about the issue: "It's not fair that we should have to foot the bill when our work takes us to more expensive cities and we are trying to be productive," she has said to a colleague. "It's not safe at those hotels that are within the reimbursement rate, and my anxiety there affects my productivity." In finding their way around the limitation she and her colleagues meticulously ensure—perhaps owing to their sense of integrity—that their reimbursement claims total exactly their actual costs and no more. Probably because the dollar amount is very small, no one has yet been questioned about their expense reports.

Questions for Discussion:

1. Have Max, Sandy, Lawrence, and Andrew met their ethical obligations? Are they "in compliance"? What about Faith?
2. Are these members of the St. Serena's family bad people or good people? Why do you think they are they taking the actions described?
3. What formal structural realities affected their actions? What informal cultural realities at Serena's affected their actions?
4. Does St. Serena's organizationally encourage and facilitate compliance and ethical behavior, or does it impede and discourage compliance and ethical behavior? If the former, specify how. If the latter, explain why.
5. What can St. Serena's do to develop an organizational ethics initiative that better promotes compliance and ethical behavior?

COMMENTARY

We have come to know a bit about the St. Serena's Healthcare Corporation and its struggle with compliance and organizational ethics. What does this situation suggest about managerial approaches to the field of healthcare organizational ethics?

The Nature of Organizational Ethics

Throughout our visit to St. Serena's we have encountered good people in ethically awkward organizational situations, most of which appear to be more of the humdrum than headline variety. This journey has suggested that organizational ethics may be about good people facing bad circumstances in the routine of an organizational setting. Could organizational ethics, fundamentally, be about establishing formal and informal realities within organizations such that good people routinely find themselves in ethically supportive organizational situations? Could organizational ethics be what organizations actually do—structurally and culturally—to facilitate or impede staff compliance with rules and regulations *as well as with* less codifiable principles and values?

Through the cases and commentary we have argued that organizational ethics is decisively not about preaching but about proaction, and not about platitudes but about practical mechanisms. Clearly "compliance" has much to do with this, but, although we began our discussion with the title "Organizational Ethics in the Compliance Context," we might conclude with the contention that organizational ethics is rather the context for compliance, and that organizational ethics provides the foundation and insight to effectively and wisely guide compliance initiatives. Let us reflect more deeply on this notion by drawing on the St. Serena's experience with which we have become familiar.

Three basic categories of realities appear with regard to the ethics of organizations. First, realities exist that facilitate and encourage compliant and ethical behavior. At St. Serena's we have identified many of these realities. In the formal dimension its comprehensive code of conduct, the policy statements such as those at the nursing home, the top-level involvement of the CEO, the compliance program, and the orientation training enforce compliant behavior. For Dr. Smart these realities included the ethics committee with its deliberation, publishing, and training components; for Lawrence the compliance committee and its meeting structure as well as the ACHE policy guideline encouraged compliance, as did the drug-testing program and the EAP unit. Andrew's compliance was facilitated by the policy statement, the task force,

Figure 9.1 Formal Organizational Ethics Mechanisms

Corporate	*Group*	*Individual*

Code of Conduct
Compliance Program
EAP Unit
Reporting Hotline
Training Program
Joint Commission
   Standards
Ethics Committee
CEO Involvement
	Compliance
	   Committee
	Unit Policies
	Task Force
	Drug Testing
	Group Training
		Training
		Compliance
		Attendance
		Coordinator
		Diversity
		Ethics Officer

Figure 9.2 Informal Organizational Ethics Realities

Corporate	*Group*	*Individual*
JCAHO Presence CEO Attitude	Referent Groups Social Groups	Beliefs Feelings

and structured plan process. We have seen many structural mechanisms at St. Serena's that are supportive of organizational ethics. Figure 9.1 lists some of them. Organizational ethics has a lot to do with developing and maintaining such ethically supportive mechanisms at corporate, group, and individual levels.

In the informal dimension the Joint Commission presence, corporate attitudes and beliefs, various referent groups, and individual moral codes and feelings encourage ethical behavior. The Joint Commission was there for Nancy and others; the attitude of CEO Samantha seems to have been mostly supportive; undoubtedly Andrew had a referent group that helped him think of the task force and plan idea; Sandy's belief in fairness probably prompted her professional development insistence; and Faith and her colleagues seem to have strong moral codes that could be used. Figure 9.2 illustrates the kinds of realities involved. Organizational ethics has a lot to do with developing these kinds of informal supports of ethical behavior and compliance at all three levels.

Second, organizational realities exist that impede and discourage compliant and ethical behavior. We have seen many examples at

Figure 9.3 Formal Impediments to Organizational Ethics

Corporate	*Group*	*Individual*
Rigid Policies Fuzzy Policies Hierarchical Directives	Inadequate Procedures	Limited Training

St. Serena's. In the formal dimension Andrew Brien's insights—reprinted in Chapter two—illuminate the debilatating rigidity of some code provisions, and at St. Serena's we have observed inconsistent hierarchical directives and deficient procedural mechanisms as well as limited training. In Case three, did Frank and Mike run up against unreasonably inflexible code provisions about personal use of corporate computers and reporting violations? Did overly rigid rules cause Lawrence and Faith to be in awkward situations? On the other hand, one could argue that Roger was in the basketball ticket situation because the code provision on gifts was insufficiently rigid in not prohibiting all gifts regardless of value. In case two, executive vice president Lance's directive to Andrew about Mrs. Livingston was inconsistent with corporate policies and caused the difficulty. Did inadequate affirmative action procedures put Sandy in her awkward situation? If provision had been made for routine professional development of minority candidates like Keneta, perhaps the dilemma would not have emerged. Similarly, the consultant's failure to provide for reasonable exceptions to the travel policy could be viewed as unfairly putting Faith and other staff in an awkward spot. And failure to provide for formal training on information privacy undoubtedly contributed to the messy scenario involving Joseph Coughlan in case five. Figure 9.3 provides a lens for this kind of analysis. Organizational ethics has a lot to do with identifying and removing such structural impediments to ethical behavior.

In the informal dimension we have encountered numerous impediments to organizational ethics at St. Serena's. Grapevines, role models, norms, and reward systems as well as attitudes, peer pressure, referent groups, and personal feelings all affected good people in different cases. The grapevine reality impinged on Lawrence and Ed's situation, as did the negative role modeling of vice president Lance and director Mary in case six. The corporate "attitude" expressed by vice president Vinny in case one and Lance in case two, conflicted with official statements causing the anxiety experienced by Inga and Andrew. Was it a "referent

Figure 9.4 Informal Impediments to Organizational Ethics

Corporate	*Group*	*Individual*
Grapevines	Referents	Feelings
Attitudes	Peer Pressure	Loyalties
Sanctions		
Role Models		
Norms		
Beliefs		

group" effect that geared Charley's behavior in case three? Was any manager attuned to the understandable feelings that staff like Faith faced with the travel constraints? How about the subtle sanctions that Dr. Smart knew were associated with reporting senior executives, and the similarly subtle sanctions that affected Ed's plea to Lawrence? Informal realities can be powerful influences on compliance and organizational ethics. Figure 9.4 indicates some aspects. Organizational ethics has a lot to do with identifying and removing the cultural realities that negatively affect ethical behavior in the organization.

In this informal dimension we should note the interconnectedness of realities. For example, the "norm" against Dr. Smart reporting Hank is reinforced by the "model" of previous whistle-blowers being ostracized, which produces the "belief" in Dr. Smart and others that the same sanctions will happen again, which then leads to noncompliance with the code provision about reporting. The task of organizational ethics, of course, is to create norms, models, and beliefs that lead to compliance rather than noncompliance.

Third, there is the reality of organizational ethics voids, that is, areas in which no organizational encouragement or discouragement exists, neither facilitating mechanisms nor impediments to compliant and ethical behavior. Perhaps this "void" phenomenon was at the core of the Joe Coughlan situation in case five. The aides probably had little notion of any ethical dimension to their reading the chart and referring to Mr. Coughlan as "senile." Because they lacked training on information privacy, the statement was probably ethically neutral to them. Similarly, data-entry clerks may have no sense of an ethical dimension for information timeliness and accuracy. No impediments exist to encourage clerks to pay more attention. Government inspectors tend to describe these kinds of situations as "patterns of indifference." The void exists, and the resulting treatment of Mr. Coughlan raises ethical questions about the organization. Organizational ethics has a lot to do with identifying such voids and filling them in both formal and informal ways so that good people are less likely to end up doing some bad things.

Values Emphasis

Throughout our stay at St. Serena's we have encountered more than occasional overemphasis of some values and underemphasis of others. This notion of "values emphasis" was introduced in Chapter two. We observed that conflicting values is a routine reality in healthcare and that the typical organizational response emphasizes certain values in some cases and different values in other cases. St. Serena's would seem to bear out this contention. In case one Vinny and Inga emphasized compliance with Joint Commission standards and de-emphasized honesty; Nancy, on the other hand, seemed ready to emphasize honesty over corporate well-being. In case two, Lance clearly emphasized economic values and down-played fairness when he encouraged that the nursing home favor the private-pay patient.

In case three Mike emphasized rules over relationships when the situation involved Clare, but then reversed his stance when his friend Frank was involved, just as Lawrence seemed to emphasize rules in his unit but relationships when Ed's behavior came into question. And so on. Case-specific values emphasis seems to be a reality. As suggested in Chapter two, organizational ethics has something to do with structurally and culturally promoting equal values emphasis at all times. Andrew attempts this in his response to case two, Sandy seeks it in case eight, and the lack of some values balance between economic efficiency and individual responsiveness seems to be behind Faith's response in case nine.

Raymond Andrews has addressed this reality with a specific focus on the values emphasis of boards of trustees of healthcare organizations. "Many trustees see their role as protecting their institution's finances, first and foremost," he argues, and this inevitably sends "subtle messages that mislead workers as to priorities or practices expected of them."[1] Was this the factor behind the behavior of Vinny and Inga and Lance—clear signals from St. Serena's board that economic considerations are to be emphasized above all else? Does organization ethics have something to do with developing equal values emphasis from the top down, inclusive of the board? Coming from another perspective, the American Academy of Arts and Sciences responds affirmatively. In seeking an equal emphasis on patient values and economic values, the Academy's first principle for healthcare ethics states: "The care of the individual patients must be at the center of healthcare systems, *but must be balanced* by maintenance of the collective health of groups and communities" (emphasis mine).[2]

Organizational efforts at developing an equal values emphasis inevitably confront what I have elsewhere[3] called the "either-or ethics syndrome." In the hectic routine of daily healthcare delivery, organizations typically are captured by an either-or perspective such that vice presidents see things as either private-payors first or economic disaster; compliance coordinators see things as either report all suspicions or be noncompliant; and patient advocates see things as either provide the service or be unethical. As John LaPuma puts it, typically "to ethics committee members 'managed care ethics' is an oxymoron—managed care cares about profits, not ethics."[4] Organizational ethics, I believe, has a lot to do with surrender of this either-or syndrome and the embracing of the "win-win" paradigm in which organizations seek a values balance in their structural and cultural efforts at compliance and ethics.

Good Ethics as Good Business

In the reading that follows, Harvard Business School professor Lynn Sharp Paine contends that good organizational ethics is simply a matter of good business; organizational ethics is basically about doing business successfully. She echos the views of theoreticians like Hosmer[5] and practitioners like Kotter and Heskett.[6] Harrington has found corporate CEOs concurring.[7] American Medical Association research sustains the contention; it concludes that the more productive physicians are those with relational skills, not just clinical talent.[8]

Of course, recent compliance enforcement experience makes the observation somewhat obvious: The high financial fines being imposed for failure to be in compliance and to demonstrate organizational ethics development affect the bottom line in practical business ways. But beyond that successful business—whether it be healthcare or other industries—depends in large part on development and nurturing of relationships, which in turn depends on the conveyance of respect and honor to clients, employees, and business partners. Garfield holds to this view,[9] Kelly's interviews sustain it,[10] and Conger and Kanungo's studies support it.[11] Organizational ethics in healthcare has a lot to do with structurally and culturally developing behavior that respects and honors human dignity, which in turn contributes to business success.

Dignity Versus Denigration

In the final analysis, our excursion through St. Serena's strongly suggests that organizational ethics is about developing and maintaining formal and informal organizational realities that promote the recognition of the human dignity of clients, staff, and partners, and that eradicate all forms of denigration, subtle as well as blatant. Compliance mechanisms fundamentally seek to ensure that people are not mistreated: that they are neither lied to, abused, dealt with unfairly, endangered, nor defrauded. Beyond that, organizational ethics mechanisms fundamentally seek to ensure that people are respected and honored in all circumstances.

When we look at St. Serena's through this conceptual lens we might see that:

- Case one is fundamentally about Joint Commission people being denigrated through the elaborate deception process;
- Case two is about elderly people being treated unfairly through a short-circuited admissions process;
- Case three is about employees being treated unfairly through an inconsistent reporting process;
- Case four is about a business partner being treated unfairly because of a loophole in entertainment policy;
- Case five is about a patient being denigrated by a sloppy information management process;
- Case six is about female employees being dishonored by a corrupted attitude system;
- Case seven is about preventing harm to clients and maintaining the dignity of employees through a substance abuse detection process;
- Case eight is about majority and minority groups being honored and respected through a diversity policy; and
- Case nine is about managers being lied to through a travel reimbursement scheme and employees being denigrated through a myopic travel policy.

In all cases the notion of dignity is a core issue. Organizational ethics, consistent with Paine's analysis below, is what organizations do to institutionalize and inculturate—in the routine of healthcare delivery—an awareness and behavioral appreciation of the dignity of all people involved with the organization.

Actually doing "organizational ethics" involves giving practical rigor to the otherwise platitudinal notion. Jostein Gaarder in his wonderful best-seller *Sophie's World*[12] summarizes the history of philosophy as an effort to rescue humankind from the trivialities of everyday existence so that we can see the wonder of it all. As a platitude, organizational ethics could similarly be described as an organizational effort to rescue its staff from the routine of everyday healthcare delivery so that staff can better see the wonder of human dignity in all clients, patients, and partners. As a practical matter, organizational ethics could be described as a package of tangible formal and informal mechanisms—employed before, during, and after the daily routine—that make it more difficult for organizational members to miss the point of the platitude.

Notes

1. Andrews, R. 1998. "When Good People Do Bad Things." *Trustee* 51 (2): 27.
2. American Academy of Arts and Sciences. "Ethical Principles for Health Care Systems," quoted in Kavanaugh, J. 1998. "Ethical Commitments in Health Care Systems." *America* 179 (14): 20.
3. Worthley, J. 1997. *The Ethics of the Ordinary in Healthcare*, 282. Chicago: Health Administration Press.
4. LaPuma, J. 1998. "Is Medical Ethics the Same as Corporate Compliance?" *Managed Care* 7 (8): 46.
5. Hosmer, L. 1995. "Trust: The Connecting Link Between Organizational Theory and Philosophical Ethics." *Academy of Management Review* 22 (2): 400.
6. Kotter, J., and J. Heskett. 1992. *Corporate Culture and Performance*. New York: Free Press.
7. Harrington, S. 1991. "What Corporate America Is Teaching About Ethics." *Academy of Management Executives* 5 (1): 21–30.
8. Levinson, W., D. Roter, J. Mullooly, V. Dull, and R. Frankel. 1997. "Physician-Patient Communication: The Relationship with Malpractice Claims Among Primary Care Physicians and Surgeons." *Journal of the American Medical Association* 277 (7): 553–59.
9. Garfield, C. 1992. *Second to None: How Our Smartest Companies Put People First.* Homewood, IL: Irwin.
10. Kelly, C. 1988. *The Destructive Achiever*. Reading, MA: Addison-Wesley.
11. Conger, J., and R. Kanungo. 1988. "The Empowerment Process." *Academy of Management Review* 13 (3): 471–82.
12. Gaarder, J. 1997. *Sophie's World*. New York: Berkley.

READING

We conclude with one of the finest "ethics in the compliance context" pieces in print. Published by the management profession's premier business journal, this article convincingly demonstrates the wisdom of the "good ethics is good business" adage. Lynn Sharp Paine brings together many of the concepts we have probed in this book. Her discussion of three organizational experiences with the ethics challenge illustrates the practical relationship between the formal and informal realities of organizations, particularly the role of structural incentives in generating attitudes and patterns of behavior. Her analysis is particularly good at clarifying the "self-interest versus covenantal approach" concept and in demonstrating the concept's practical significance in developing a highly ethical and compliant organization. Nurturing respect for people and for relationships with employees, clients, and regulators seems to be the key to effectively meeting the challenge of organizational ethics in the compliance context. As Paine puts it, "Organizational ethics helps define what a company is and what it stands for." Her analysis of St. Serena's would be illuminating.

Managing for Organizational Integrity

Lynn Sharp Paine[*]

Many managers think of ethics as a question of personal scruples, a confidential matter between individuals and their consciences. These executives are quick to describe any wrongdoing as an isolated incident, the work of a rogue employee.

The thought that the company could bear any responsibility for an individual's misdeeds never enters their minds. Ethics, after all, has nothing to do with management.

In fact, ethics has everything to do with management. Rarely do the character flaws of a lone actor fully explain corporate misconduct. More typically, unethical business practice involves the tacit, if not explicit, cooperation of others and reflects the values, attitudes, beliefs, language, and behavioral patterns that define an organization's operating culture. Ethics, then, is as much an organizational as a personal issue. Managers who fail to provide proper leadership and to institute systems that facilitate ethical conduct share responsibility with those who conceive, execute, and knowingly benefit from corporate misdeeds.

Managers must acknowledge their role in shaping organizational ethics and seize this opportunity to create a climate that can strengthen the relationships and reputations on which their companies' success depends. Executives who ignore ethics run the risk of personal and corporate liability in today's increasingly tough legal environment. In addition, they deprive their organizations of the benefits available under new federal guidelines for sentencing organizations convicted of wrongdoing. These sentencing guidelines recognize for the first time

* Reprinted by permission of Harvard Business Review. 1994. (Mar/Apr): 106–17. Copyright 1994 by the President and Fellows of Harvard College; all rights reserved. Lynn Sharp Paine is associate professor at Harvard Business School.

the organizational and managerial roots of unlawful conduct and base fines partly on the extent to which companies have taken steps to prevent that misconduct.

Prompted by the prospect of leniency, many companies are rushing to implement compliance-based ethics programs. Designed by corporate counsel, the goal of these programs is to prevent, detect, and punish legal violations. But organizational ethics means more than avoiding illegal practice; and providing employees with a rule book will do little to address the problems underlying unlawful conduct. To foster a climate that encourages exemplary behavior, corporations need a comprehensive approach that goes beyond the often punitive legal compliance stance.

An integrity-based approach to ethics management combines a concern for the law with an emphasis on managerial responsibility for ethical behavior. Though integrity strategies may vary in design and scope, all strive to define companies' guiding values, aspirations, and patterns of thought and conduct. When integrated into the day-to-day operations of an organization, such strategies can help prevent damaging ethical lapses while tapping into powerful human impulses for moral thought and action. Then an ethical framework becomes no longer a burdensome constraint within which companies must operate, but the governing ethos of an organization.

How Organizations Shape Individuals' Behavior

The once familiar picture of ethics as individualistic, unchanging, and impervious to organizational influences has not stood up to scrutiny in recent years. Sears Auto Centers' and Beech-Nut Nutrition Corporation's experiences illustrate the role organizations play in shaping individuals' behavior—and how even sound moral fiber can fray when stretched too thin.

In 1992, Sears, Roebuck & Company was inundated with complaints about its automotive service business. Consumers and attorneys general in more than 40 states had accused the company of misleading customers and selling them unnecessary parts and services, from brake jobs to front-end alignments. It would be a mistake, however, to see this situation exclusively in terms of any one individual's moral failings. Nor did management set out to defraud Sears customers. Instead, a number of organizational factors contributed to the problematic sales practices.

In the face of declining revenues, shrinking market share, and an increasingly competitive market for undercar services, Sears management attempted to spur the performance of its auto centers by introducing new goals and incentives for employees. The company increased minimum work quotas and introduced productivity incentives for mechanics. The automotive service advisers were given product-specific sales quotas—sell so many springs, shock absorbers, alignments, or brake jobs per shift—and paid a commission based on sales. According to advisers, failure to meet quotas could lead to a transfer or a reduction in work hours. Some employees spoke of the "pressure, pressure, pressure" to bring in sales.

Under this new set of organizational pressures and incentives, with few options for meeting their sales goals legitimately, some employees' judgment understandably suffered. Management's failure to clarify the line between unnecessary service and legitimate preventive maintenance, coupled with consumer ignorance, left employees to chart their own courses through a vast gray area, subject to a wide range of interpretations. Without active management support for ethical practice and mechanisms to detect and check questionable sales methods and poor work, it is not surprising that some employees may have reacted to contextual forces by resorting to exaggeration, carelessness, or even misrepresentation.

Shortly after the allegations against Sears became public, CEO Edward Brennan acknowledged management's responsibility for putting in place compensation and goal-setting systems that "created an environment in which mistakes did occur." Although the company denied any intent to deceive consumers, senior executives eliminated commissions for service advisers and discontinued sales quotas for specific parts. They also instituted a system of unannounced shopping audits and made plans to expand the internal monitoring of service. In settling the pending lawsuits, Sears offered coupons to customers who had bought certain auto services between 1990 and 1992. The total cost of the settlement, including potential customer refunds, was an estimated $60 million.

Contextual forces can also influence the behavior of top management, as a former CEO of Beech-Nut Nutrition Corporation discovered. In the early 1980s, only two years after joining the company, the CEO found evidence suggesting that the apple juice concentrate, supplied by the company's vendors for use in Beech-Nut's "100 percent pure" apple juice, contained nothing more than sugar water and chemicals. The CEO could have destroyed the bogus inventory and withdrawn the juice from grocers' shelves, but he was under extraordinary pressure to turn the ailing company around. Eliminating the inventory would have killed any hope of turning even the meager $700,000 profit promised to Beech-Nut's then-parent, Nestlé.

A number of people in the corporation, it turned out, had doubted the purity of the juice for several years before the CEO arrived. But the 25 percent price advantage offered by the supplier of the bogus concentrate allowed the operations head to meet cost-control goals. Furthermore, the company lacked an effective quality control system, and a conclusive lab test for juice purity did not yet exist. When a member of the research department voiced concerns about the juice to operating management, he was accused of not being a team player and of acting like "Chicken Little." His judgment, his supervisor wrote in an annual performance review, was "colored by naivete and impractical ideals." No one else seemed to have considered the company's obligations to its customers or to have thought about the potential harm of disclosure. No one considered the fact that the sale of adulterated or misbranded juice is a legal offense, putting the company and its top management at risk of criminal liability.

An FDA investigation taught Beech-Nut the hard way. In 1987, the company pleaded guilty to selling adulterated and misbranded juice. Two years and two criminal trials later, the CEO pleaded guilty to ten counts of mislabeling. The total cost to the company—including fines, legal expenses, and lost sales—was an estimated $25 million.

Such errors of judgment rarely reflect an organizational culture and management philosophy that sets out to harm or deceive. More often, they reveal a culture that is insensitive or indifferent to ethical considerations or one that lacks effective organizational systems. By the same token, exemplary conduct usually reflects an organizational culture and philosophy that are infused with a sense of responsibility.

For example, Johnson & Johnson's handling of the Tylenol crisis is sometimes attributed to the singular personality of then-CEO James Burke. However, the decision to do a nationwide recall of Tylenol capsules in order to avoid further loss of life from product tampering was in reality not one decision but thousands of decisions made by individuals at all levels of the organization. The "Tylenol decision," then, is best understood not as an isolated incident, the achievement of a lone individual, but as the reflection of an organization's culture. Without a shared set of values and guiding principles deeply ingrained throughout the organization, it is doubtful that Johnson & Johnson's response would have been as rapid, cohesive, and ethically sound.

Many people resist acknowledging the influence of organizational factors on individual behavior—especially on misconduct—for fear of diluting people's sense of personal moral responsibility. But this fear is based on a false dichotomy between holding individual transgressors accountable and holding "the system" accountable. Acknowledging the importance of organizational context need not imply exculpating individual wrongdoers. To understand all is not to forgive all.

The Limits of a Legal Compliance Program

The consequences of an ethical lapse can be serious and far-reaching. Organizations can quickly become entangled in an all-consuming web of legal proceedings. The risk of litigation and liability has increased in the past decade as lawmakers have legislated new civil and criminal offenses, stepped up penalties, and improved support for law enforcement. Equally—if not more—important is the damage an ethical lapse can do to an organization's reputation and relationships. Both Sears and Beech-Nut, for instance, struggled to regain consumer trust and market share long after legal proceedings had ended.

As more managers have become alerted to the importance of organizational ethics, many have asked their lawyers to develop corporate ethics programs to detect and prevent violations of the law. The 1991 Federal Sentencing Guidelines offer a compelling rationale. Sanctions such as fines and probation for organizations convicted of wrongdoing can vary dramatically depending both on the degree of management cooperation in reporting and investigating corporate misdeeds and on whether or not the company has implemented a legal compliance program. (See the insert "Corporate Fines Under the Federal Sentencing Guidelines.")

Such programs tend to emphasize the prevention of unlawful conduct, primarily by increasing surveillance and control and by imposing penalties for wrongdoers. While plans vary, the basic framework is outlined in the sentencing guidelines. Managers must establish compliance standards and procedures; designate high-level personnel to oversee compliance; avoid delegating discretionary authority to those likely to act unlawfully; effectively communicate the company's standards and procedures through training or publications; take reasonable steps to achieve compliance through audits, monitoring processes, and a system for employees to report criminal misconduct without fear of retribution; consistently enforce standards through appropriate disciplinary measures; respond appropriately when offenses are detected; and, finally, take reasonable steps to prevent the occurrence of similar offenses in the future.

There is no question of the necessity of a sound, well-articulated strategy for legal compliance in an organization. After all, employees can be frustrated and frightened by the complexity of today's legal environment. And even managers who claim to use the law as a guide

Corporate Fines Under the Federal Sentencing Guidelines

What size fine is a corporation likely to pay if convicted of a crime? It depends on a number of factors, some of which are beyond a CEO's control, such as the existence of a prior record of similar misconduct. But it also depends on more controllable factors. The most important of these are reporting and accepting responsibility for the crime, cooperating with authorities, and having an effective program in place to prevent and detect unlawful behavior.

The following example, based on a case studied by the United States Sentencing Commission, shows how the 1991 Federal Sentencing Guidelines have affected overall fine levels and how managers' actions influence organizational fines.

Acme Corporation was charged and convicted of mail fraud. The company systematically charged customers who damaged rented automobiles more than the actual cost of repairs. Acme also billed some customers for the cost of repairs to vehicles for which they were not responsible. Prior to the criminal adjudication, Acme paid $13.7 million in restitution to the customers who had been overcharged.

Deciding before the enactment of the sentencing guidelines, the judge in the criminal case imposed a fine of $6.85 million, roughly half the pecuniary loss suffered by Acme's customers. Under the sentencing guidelines, however, the results could have been dramatically different. Acme could have been fined anywhere from 5 percent to 200 percent of the loss suffered by customers, depending on whether or not it had an effective program to prevent and detect violations of law and on whether or not it reported the crime, cooperated with authorities, and accepted responsibility for the unlawful conduct. If a high-ranking official at Acme were found to have been involved, the maximum fine could have been as large as $54,800,000, or four times the loss to Acme customers. The following chart shows a possible range of fines for each situation:

What Fine Can Acme Expect?

	Maximum	Minimum
Program, reporting, cooperation, responsibility	$2,740,000	$685,000
Program only	10,960,000	5,480,000
No program, no reporting, no cooperation, no responsibility	27,400,000	13,700,000
No program, no reporting, no cooperation, no responsibility, involvement of high-level personnel	54,800,000	27,400,000

Based on Case No.: 88-266, United States Sentencing Commission, *Supplementary Report on Sentencing Guidelines for Organizations.*

to ethical behavior often lack more than a rudimentary understanding of complex legal issues.

Managers would be mistaken, however, to regard legal compliance as an adequate means for addressing the full range of ethical issues that arise every day. "If it's legal, it's ethical," is a frequently heard slogan. But conduct that is lawful may be highly problematic from an ethical point of view. Consider the sale in some countries of hazardous products without appropriate warnings or the purchase of goods from suppliers who operate inhumane sweatshops in developing countries. Companies engaged in international business often discover that conduct that infringes on recognized standards of human rights and decency is legally permissible in some jurisdictions.

Legal clearance does not certify the absence of ethical problems in the United States either, as a 1991 case at Salomon Brothers illustrates. Four top-level executives failed to take appropriate action when learning of unlawful activities on the government trading desk. Company lawyers found no law obligating the executives to disclose the improprieties. Nevertheless, the executives' delay in disclosing and failure to reveal their prior knowledge prompted a serious crisis of confidence among employees, creditors, shareholders, and customers. The executives were forced to resign, having lost the moral authority to lead. Their ethical lapse compounded the trading desk's legal offenses, and the company ended up suffering losses—including legal costs, increased funding costs, and lost business—estimated at nearly $1 billion.

A compliance approach to ethics also overemphasizes the threat of detection and punishment in order to channel behavior in lawful directions. The underlying model for this approach is deterrence theory, which envisions people as rational maximizers of self-interest, responsive to the personal costs and benefits of their choices, yet indifferent to the moral legitimacy of those choices. But a recent study reported in *Why People Obey the Law* by Tom R. Tyler shows that obedience to the law is strongly influenced by a belief in its legitimacy and its moral correctness. People generally feel that they have a strong obligation to obey the law. Education about the legal standards and a supportive environment may be all that's required to insure compliance.

Discipline is, of course, a necessary part of any ethical system. Justified penalties for the infringement of legitimate norms are fair and appropriate. Some people do need the threat of sanctions. However, an overemphasis on potential sanctions can be superfluous and even counter productive. Employees may rebel against programs that stress penalties, particularly if they are designed and imposed without employee involvement or if the standards are vague or unrealistic.

Management may talk of mutual trust when unveiling a compliance plan, but employees often receive the message as a warning from on high. Indeed, the more skeptical among them may view compliance programs as nothing more than liability insurance for senior management. This is not an unreasonable conclusion, considering that compliance programs rarely address the root causes of misconduct.

Even in the best cases, legal compliance is unlikely to unleash much moral imagination or commitment. The law does not generally seek to inspire human excellence or distinction. It is no guide for exemplary behavior—or even good practice. Those managers who define ethics as legal compliance are implicitly endorsing a code of moral mediocrity for their organizations. As Richard Breeden, former chairman of the Securities and Exchange Commission, noted, "It is not an adequate ethical standard to aspire to get through the day without being indicted."

Integrity as a Governing Ethic

A strategy based on integrity holds organizations to a more robust standard. While compliance is rooted in avoiding legal sanctions, organizational integrity is based on the concept of self-governance in accordance with a set of guiding principles. From the perspective of integrity, the task of ethics management is to define and give life to an organization's guiding values, to create an environment that supports ethically sound behavior, and to instill a sense of shared accountability among employees. The need to obey the law is viewed as a positive aspect of organizational life, rather than an unwelcome constraint imposed by external authorities.

An integrity strategy is characterized by a conception of ethics as a driving force of an enterprise. Ethical values shape the search for opportunities, the design of organizational systems, and the decision-making process used by individuals and groups. They provide a common frame of reference and serve as a unifying force across different functions, lines of business, and employee groups. Organizational ethics helps define what a company is and what it stands for.

Many integrity initiatives have structural features common to compliance-based initiatives: a code of conduct, training in relevant areas of law, mechanisms for reporting and investigating potential misconduct, and audits and controls to ensure that laws and company standards are being met. In addition, if suitably designed, an integrity-based initiative can establish a foundation for seeking the legal benefits that are available under the sentencing guidelines should criminal wrong-doing occur. (See the insert "The Hallmarks of an Effective Integrity Strategy.")

The Hallmarks of an Effective Integrity Strategy

There is no one right integrity strategy. Factors such as management personality, company history, culture, lines of business, and industry regulations must be taken into account when shaping an appropriate set of values and designing an implementation program. Still, several features are common to efforts that have achieved some success:

- *The guiding values and commitments make sense and are clearly communicated.* They reflect important organizational obligations and widely shared aspirations that appeal to the organization's members. Employees at all levels take them seriously, feel comfortable discussing them, and have a concrete understanding of their practical importance. This does not signal the absence of ambiguity and conflict but a willingness to seek solutions compatible with the framework of values.

- *Company leaders are personally committed, credible, and willing to take action on the values they espouse.* They are not mere mouthpieces. They are willing to scrutinize their own decisions. Consistency on the part of leadership is key. Waffling on values will lead to employee cynicism and a rejection of the program. At the same time, managers must assume responsibility for making tough calls when ethical obligations conflict.

- *The espoused values are integrated into the normal channels of management decision making and are reflected in the organization's critical activities*: the development of plans, the setting of goals, the search for opportunities, the allocation of resources, the gathering and communication of information, the measurement of performance, and the promotion and advancement of personnel.

- *The company's systems and structures support and reinforce its values.* Information systems, for example, are designed to provide timely and accurate information. Reporting relationships are structured to build in checks and balances to promote objective judgment. Performance appraisal is sensitive to means as well as ends.

- *Managers throughout the company have the decision-making skills, knowledge, and competencies needed to make ethically sound decisions on a day-to-day basis.* Ethical thinking and awareness must be part of every managers' mental equipment. Ethics education is usually part of the process.

Success in creating a climate for responsible and ethically sound behavior requires continuing effort and a considerable investment of time and resources. A glossy code of conduct, a high-ranking ethics officer, a training program, an annual ethics audit—these trappings of an ethics program do not necessarily add up to a responsible, law-abiding organization whose espoused values match its actions. A formal ethics program can serve as a catalyst and a support system, but organizational integrity depends on the integration of the company's values into its driving systems.

But an integrity strategy is broader, deeper, and more demanding than a legal compliance initiative. Broader in that it seeks to enable responsible conduct. Deeper in that it cuts to the ethos and operating systems of the organization and its members, their guiding values, and patterns of thought and action. And more demanding in that it requires an active effort to define the responsibilities and aspirations that constitute an organization's ethical compass. Above all, organizational ethics is seen as the work of management. Corporate counsel may play a role in the design and implementation of integrity strategies, but managers at all levels and across all functions are involved in the process. (See the chart "Strategies for Ethics Management.")

During the past decade, a number of companies have undertaken integrity initiatives. They vary according to the ethical values focused on and the implementation approaches used. Some companies focus on the core values of integrity that reflect basic social obligations, such as respect for the rights of others, honesty, fair dealing, and obedience to the law. Other companies emphasize aspirations—values that are ethically desirable but not necessarily morally obligatory—such as good service to customers, a commitment to diversity, and involvement in the community.

When it comes to implementation, some companies begin with behavior. Following Aristotle's view that one becomes courageous by acting as a courageous person, such companies develop codes of conduct specifying appropriate behavior, along with a system of incentives, audits, and controls. Other companies focus less on specific actions and more on developing attitudes, decision-making processes, and ways of thinking that reflect their values. The assumption is that personal commitment and appropriate decision processes will lead to right action.

Martin Marietta, NovaCare, and Wetherill Associates have implemented and lived with quite different integrity strategies. In each case, management has found that the initiative has made important and often unexpected contributions to competitiveness, work environment, and key relationships on which the company depends.

Martin Marietta: Emphasizing core values.

Martin Marietta Corporation, the U.S. aerospace and defense contractor, opted for an integrity-based ethics program in 1985. At the time, the defense industry was under attack for fraud and mismanagement, and Martin Marietta was under investigation for improper travel billings. Managers knew they needed a better form of self-governance but were skeptical that an ethics program could influence behavior. "Back then people asked, 'Do you really need an ethics program to be ethical?'"

Strategies for Ethics Management

Characteristics of Compliance Strategy

Ethos	Conformity with externally imposed standards
Objective	Prevent criminal misconduct
Leadership	Lawyer driven
Methods	Education, reduced discretion, auditing and controls, penalties
Behavioral Assumptions	Autonomous beings guided by material self-interest

Characteristics of Integrity Strategy

Ethos	Self-governance according to chosen standards
Objective	Enable responsible conduct
Leadership	Management driven with aid of lawyers, HR, others
Methods	Education, leadership, accountability, organizational systems and decision processes, auditing and controls, penalties
Behavioral Assumptions	Social beings guided by material self-interest, values, ideals, peers

Implementation of Compliance Strategy

Standards	Criminal and regulatory law
Staffing	Lawyers
Activities	Develop compliance standards Train and communicate Handle reports of misconduct Conduct investigations Oversee compliance audits Enforce standards
Education	Compliance standards and system

Implementation of Integrity Strategy

Standards	Company values and aspirations Social obligations, including law
Staffing	Executives and managers with lawyers, others
Activities	Lead development of company values and standards Train and communicate Integrate into company systems Provide guidance and consultation Assess values performance Identify and resolve problems Oversee compliance activities
Education	Decision making and values Compliance standards and system

recalls current President Thomas Young. "Ethics was something personal. Either you had it, or you didn't."

The corporate general counsel played a pivotal role in promoting the program, and legal compliance was a critical objective. But it was conceived of and implemented from the start as a company-wide management initiative aimed at creating and maintaining a "do-it-right" climate. In its original conception, the program emphasized core values, such as honesty and fair play. Over time, it expanded to encompass quality and environmental responsibility as well.

Today the initiative consists of a code of conduct, an ethics training program, and procedures for reporting and investigating ethical concerns within the company. It also includes a system for disclosing violations of federal procurement law to the government. A corporate ethics office manages the program, and ethics representatives are stationed at major facilities. An ethics steering committee, made up of Martin Marietta's president, senior executives, and two rotating members selected from field operations, oversees the ethics office. The audit and ethics committee of the board of directors oversees the steering committee.

The ethics office is responsible for responding to questions and concerns from the company employees. Its network of representatives serves as a sounding board, a source of guidance, and a channel for raising a range of issues, from allegations of wrongdoing to complaints about poor management, unfair supervision, and company policies and practices. Martin Marietta's ethics network, which accepts anonymous complaints, logged over 9,000 calls in 1991, when the company had about 60,000 employees. In 1992, it investigated 684 cases. The ethics office also works closely with the human resources, legal, audit, communications, and security functions to respond to employee concerns.

Shortly after establishing the program, the company began its first round of ethics training for the entire workforce, starting with the CEO and senior executives. Now in its third round, training for senior executives focuses on decision making, the challenges of balancing multiple responsibilities, and compliance with laws and regulations critical to the company. The incentive compensation plan for executives makes responsibility for promoting ethical conduct an explicit requirement for reward eligibility and requires that business and personal goals be achieved in accordance with the company's policy on ethics. Ethical conduct and support for the ethics program are also criteria in regular performance reviews.

Today top-level managers say the ethics program has helped the company avoid serious problems and become more responsive to its more than 90,000 employees. The ethics network, which tracks the number and types of cases and complaints, has served as an early warning system for poor management, quality and safety defects, racial and gender discrimination, environmental concerns, inaccurate and false records, and personnel grievances regarding salaries, promotions, and layoffs. By providing an alternative channel for raising such concerns, Martin Marietta is able to take corrective action more quickly and with a lot less pain. In many cases, potentially embarrassing problems have been identified and dealt with before becoming a management crisis, a lawsuit, or a criminal investigation. Among employees who brought complaints in 1993, 75 percent were satisfied with the results.

Company executives are also convinced that the program has helped reduce the incidence of misconduct. When allegations of misconduct do surface, the company says it deals with them more openly. On several occasions, for instance, Martin Marietta has voluntarily disclosed and made restitution to the government for misconduct involving potential violations of federal procurement laws. In addition, when an employee alleged that the company had retaliated against him for voicing safety concerns about his plant on CBS news, top management commissioned an investigation by an outside law firm. Although failing to support the allegations, the investigation found that employees at the plant feared retaliation when raising health, safety, or environmental complaints. The company redoubled its efforts to identify and discipline those employees taking retaliatory action and stressed the desirability of an open work environment in its ethics training and company communications.

Although the ethics program helps Martin Marietta avoid certain types of litigation, it has occasionally led to other kinds of legal action. In a few cases, employees dismissed for violating the code of ethics sued Martin Marietta, arguing that the company had violated its own code by imposing unfair and excessive discipline.

Still, the company believes that its attention to ethics has been worth it. The ethics program has led to better relationships with the government, as well as to new business opportunities. Along with prices and technology, Martin Marietta's record of integrity, quality, and reliability of estimates plays a role in the awarding of defense contracts, which account for some 75 percent of the company's revenues. Executives believe that the reputation they've earned through their ethics program has helped them build trust with government auditors, as well. By opening up communications, the company has reduced the time spent on redundant audits.

The program has also helped change employees' perceptions and priorities. Some managers compare their new ways of thinking about ethics to the way they understand quality. They consider more carefully how situations will be perceived by others, the possible long-term consequences of short-term thinking, and the need for continuous improvement. CEO Norman Augustine notes, "Ten years ago, people would have said that there were no ethical issues in business. Today employees think their number-one objective is to be thought of as decent people doing quality work."

NovaCare: Building shared aspirations.

NovaCare Inc., one of the largest providers of rehabilitation services to nursing homes and hospitals in the United States, has oriented its ethics effort toward building a common core of shared aspirations. But in 1988, when the company was called InSpeech, the only sentiment shared was mutual mistrust.

Senior executives built the company from a series of aggressive acquisitions over a brief period of time to take advantage of the expanding market for therapeutic services. However, in 1988, the viability of the company was in question. Turnover among its frontline employees—the clinicians and therapists who care for patients in nursing homes and hospitals—escalated to 57 percent per year. The company's inability to retain therapists caused customers to defect and the stock price to languish in an extended slump.

After months of soul-searching, InSpeech executives realized that the turnover rate was a symptom of a more basic problem: the lack of a common set of values and aspirations. There was, as one executive put it, a "huge disconnect" between the values of the therapists and clinicians and those of the managers who ran the company. The therapists and clinicians evaluated the company's success in terms of its delivery of high-quality health care. InSpeech management, led by executives with financial services and venture capital backgrounds, measured the company's worth exclusively in terms of financial success. Management's single-minded emphasis on increasing hours of reimbursable care turned clinicians off. They took management's performance orientation for indifference to patient care and left the company in droves.

CEO John Foster recognized the need for a common frame of reference and a common language to unify the diverse groups. So he brought in consultants to conduct interviews and focus groups with the company health care professionals, managers, and customers. Based on the results, an employee task force drafted a proposed vision statement for the company, and another 250 employees suggested revisions. Then Foster and several senior managers developed a succinct statement of the company's guiding purpose and fundamental beliefs that could be used as a framework for making decisions and setting goals, policies, and practices.

Unlike a code of conduct, which articulates specific behavioral standards, the statement of vision, purposes, and beliefs lays out in very simple terms the company's central purpose and core values. The purpose—meeting the rehabilitation needs of patients through clinical leadership—is supported by four key beliefs: respect for the individual, service to the customer, pursuit of excellence, and commitment to personal integrity. Each value is discussed with examples of how it is manifested in the day-to-day activities and policies of the company, such as how to measure the quality of care.

To support the newly defined values, the company changed its name to NovaCare and introduced a number of structural and operational changes. Field managers and clinicians were given greater decision-making authority; clinicians were provided with additional resources to assist in the delivery of effective therapy; and a new management structure integrated the various therapies offered by the company. The hiring of new corporate personnel with health care backgrounds reinforced the company's new clinical focus.

The introduction of the vision, purpose, and beliefs met with varied reactions from employees, ranging from cool skepticism to open enthusiasm. One employee remembered thinking the talk about values "much ado about nothing." Another recalled, "It was really wonderful. It gave us a goal that everyone aspired to, no matter what their place in the company." At first, some were baffled about how the vision, purpose, and beliefs were to be used. But, over time, managers became more adept at explaining and using them as a guide. When a customer tried to hire away a valued employee, for example, managers considered raiding the customer's company for employees. After reviewing the beliefs, the managers abandoned the idea.

NovaCare managers acknowledge and company surveys indicate that there is plenty of room for improvement. While the values are used as a firm reference point for decision making and evaluation in some areas of the company, they are still viewed with reservation in others. Some managers do not "walk the talk," employees complain. And recently acquired companies have yet to be fully integrated into the program. Nevertheless, many NovaCare employees say the values initiative played a critical role in the company's 1990 turnaround.

The values reorientation also helped the company deal with its most serious problem: turnover among health care providers. In 1990, the turnover rate stood at 32 percent, still above target but a significant improvement over the 1988 rate of 57 percent. By 1993, turnover had dropped to 27 percent. Moreover, recruiting new clinicians became easier. Barely able to hire 25 new clinicians each month in 1988, the company added 776 in 1990 and 2,546 in 1993. Indeed, one employee who left during the 1988 turmoil said that her decision to return in 1990 hinged on the company's adoption of the vision, purpose, and beliefs.

Wetherill Associates: Defining right action.

Wetherill Associates, Inc.—a small, privately held supplier of electrical parts to the automotive market—has neither a conventional code of conduct nor a statement of values. Instead, WAI has a Quality Assurance Manual—a combination of philosophy text, conduct guide, technical manual, and company profile—that describes the company's commitment to honesty and its guiding principle of right action.

WAI doesn't have a corporate ethics officer who reports to top management, because at WAI, the company's corporate ethics officer is top management. Marie Bothe, WAI's chief executive officer, sees her main function as keeping the 350-employee company on the path of right action and looking for opportunities to help the community. She delegates the "technical" aspects of the business—marketing, finance, personnel, operations—to other members of the organization.

Right action, the basis for all of WAI's decisions, is a well-developed approach that challenges most conventional management thinking. The company explicitly rejects the usual conceptual boundaries that separate morality and self-interest. Instead, they define right behavior as logically, expediently, and morally right. Managers teach employees to look at the needs of the customers, suppliers, and the community—in addition to those of the company and its employees—when making decisions.

WAI also has a unique approach to competition. One employee explains, "We are not 'in competition' with anybody. We just do what we have to do to serve the customer." Indeed, when occasionally unable to fill orders, WAI salespeople refer customers to competitors. Artificial incentives, such as sales contests, are never used to spur individual performance. Nor are sales results used in determining compensation. Instead, the focus is on teamwork and customer service. Managers tell all new recruits that absolute honesty, mutual courtesy, and respect are standard operating procedure.

Newcomers generally react positively to company philosophy, but not all are prepared for such a radical departure from the practices they have known elsewhere. Recalling her initial interview, one recruit described her response to being told that lying was not allowed, "What do you mean? No lying? I'm a buyer. I lie for a living!" Today she is persuaded that the policy makes sound business sense. WAI is known for informing suppliers of overshipments as well as undershipments and for scrupulous honesty in the sale of parts, even when deception cannot be readily detected.

Since its entry into the distribution business 13 years ago, WAI has seen its revenues climb steadily from just under $1 million to nearly $98 million in 1993, and this in an industry with little growth. Once seen as an upstart beset by naysayers and industry skeptics, WAI is now credited with entering and professionalizing an industry in which kickbacks, bribes, and "gratuities" were commonplace. Employees—equal numbers of men and women ranging in age from 17 to 92—praise the work environment as both productive and supportive.

WAI's approach could be difficult to introduce in a larger, more traditional organizations. WAI is a small company founded by 34 people who shared a belief in right action; its ethical values were naturally built into the organization from the start. Those values are so deeply ingrained in the company's culture and operating systems that they have been largely self-sustaining. Still, the company has developed its own training program and takes special care to hire people willing to support right action. Ethics and job skills are considered equally important in determining an individual's competence and suitability for employment. For WAI, the challenge will be to sustain its vision as the company grows and taps into markets overseas.

At WAI, as at Martin Marietta and NovaCare, a management-led commitment to ethical values has contributed to competitiveness, positive workforce morale, as well as solid sustainable relationships with the company's key constituencies. In the end, creating a climate that encourages exemplary conduct may be the best way to discourage damaging misconduct. Only in such an environment do rogues really act alone.

Annotated Bibliography

Bok, S. 1979. *Lying*. New York: Vintage. A sensational and popular reflection on the "seemingly trivial" routine of everyday matters, including a chapter on healthcare.

Kelly, C. 1988. *The Destructive Achiever*. Reading, MA: Addison-Wesley. A penetrating analysis of managerial responses to the human dignity notion.

Luthringer, G. 1991. "The Ethics of Ordinary Time." *Nutrition in Clinical Practice* 6 (3): 99–105. A terrific portrayal of the ethical dimension of everyday healthcare routines.

Nash, L. 1990. *Good Intentions Aside*. Boston: Harvard Business School. Among the better practical discourses on the nature of organizational ethics.

AMERICAN COLLEGE OF HEALTHCARE EXECUTIVES CODE OF ETHICS*[1]

PREFACE

The *Code of Ethics* is administered by the Ethics Committee, which is appointed by the Board of Governors upon nomination by the Chairman. It is composed of at least nine Fellows of the College, each of whom serves a three-year term on a staggered basis, with three members retiring each year.

The Ethics Committee shall:

- Review and evaluate annually the *Code of Ethics*, and make any necessary recommendations for updating the *Code*.
- Review and recommend action to the Board of Governors on allegations brought forth regarding breaches of the *Code of Ethics*.
- Develop ethical policy statements to serve as guidelines of ethical conduct for healthcare executives and their professional relationships.
- Prepare an annual report of observations, accomplishments, and recommendations to the Board of Governors, and such other periodic reports as required.

*As amended by the Council of Regents at its annual meeting on August 22, 1995.
Reprinted with permission of the American College of Healthcare Executives.

The Ethics Committee invokes the *Code of Ethics* under authority of the ACHE *Bylaws*, Article II, Membership, Section 6, Resignation and Termination of Membership; Transfer to Inactive Status, subsection (b), as follows:

> Membership may be terminated or rendered inactive by action of the Board of Governors as a result of violation of the *Code of Ethics*; nonconformity with the *Bylaws* or *Regulations Governing Admission, Advancement, Recertification, and Reappointment*; conviction of a felony; or conviction of a crime of moral turpitude or a crime relating to the healthcare management profession. No such termination of membership or imposition of inactive status shall be effected without affording a reasonable opportunity for the member to consider the charges and to appear in his or her own defense before the Board of Governors or its designated hearing committee, as outlined in the "Grievance Procedure," Appendix I of the College's *Code of Ethics*.

PREAMBLE

The purpose of the *Code of Ethics* of the American College of Healthcare Executives is to serve as a guide to conduct for members. It contains standards of ethical behavior for healthcare executives in their professional relationships. These relationships include members of the healthcare executive's organization and other organizations.

Also included are patients or others served, colleagues, the community, and society as a whole. The *Code of Ethics* also incorporates standards of ethical behavior governing personal behavior, particularly when that conduct directly relates to the role and identity of the healthcare executive.

The fundamental objectives of the healthcare management profession are to enhance overall quality of life, dignity, and well-being of every individual needing healthcare services; and to create a more equitable, accessible, effective, and efficient healthcare system.

Healthcare executives have an obligation to act in ways that will merit the trust, confidence, and respect of healthcare professionals and the general public. Therefore, healthcare executives should lead lives that embody an exemplary system of values and ethics.

In fulfilling their commitments and obligations to patients or others served, healthcare executives function as moral advocates. Since every management decision affects the health and well-being of both individuals and communities, healthcare executives must carefully evaluate the possible outcomes of their decisions. In organizations that deliver healthcare services, they must work to safeguard and foster the rights, interests, and prerogatives of patients or others served. The role of moral advocate requires that healthcare executives speak out and take actions necessary to promote such rights, interests, and prerogatives if they are threatened.

I. THE HEALTHCARE EXECUTIVE'S RESPONSIBILITIES TO THE PROFESSION OF HEALTHCARE MANAGEMENT

The healthcare executive shall:

- A. Uphold the values, ethics, and mission of the healthcare management profession;
- B. Conduct all personal and professional activities with honesty, integrity, respect, fairness, and good faith in a manner that will reflect well upon the profession;
- C. Comply with all laws pertaining to healthcare management in the jurisdictions in which the healthcare executive is located, or conducts professional activities;
- D. Maintain competence and proficiency in healthcare management by implementing a personal program of assessment and continuing professional education;
- E. Avoid the exploitation of professional relationships for personal gain;
- F. Use this *Code* to further the interests of the profession and not for selfish reasons;
- G. Respect professional confidences;
- H. Enhance the dignity and image of the healthcare management profession through positive public information programs; and
- I. Refrain from participating in any activity that demeans the credibility and dignity of the healthcare management profession.

II. THE HEALTHCARE EXECUTIVE'S RESPONSIBILITIES TO PATIENTS OR OTHERS SERVED, TO THE ORGANIZATION, AND TO EMPLOYEES

A. RESPONSIBILITIES TO PATIENTS OR OTHERS SERVED

The healthcare executive shall, within the scope of his or her authority:

1. Work to ensure the existence of a process to evaluate the quality of care or service rendered;
2. Avoid practicing or facilitating discrimination and institute safeguards to prevent discriminatory organizational practices;
3. Work to ensure the existence of a process that will advise patients or others served of the rights, opportunities, responsibilities, and risks regarding available healthcare services;
4. Work to provide a process that ensures the autonomy and self-determination of patients or others served; and
5. Work to ensure the existence of procedures that will safeguard the confidentiality and privacy of patients or others served.

B. RESPONSIBILITIES TO THE ORGANIZATION

The healthcare executive shall, within the scope of his or her authority:

1. Provide healthcare services consistent with available resources and work to ensure the existence of a resource allocation process that considers ethical ramifications;
2. Conduct both competitive and cooperative activities in ways that improve community healthcare services;
3. Lead the organization in the use and improvement of standards of management and sound business practices;
4. Respect the customs and practices of patients or others served, consistent with the organization's philosophy; and
5. Be truthful in all forms of professional and organizational communication, and avoid disseminating information that is false, misleading, or deceptive.

C. RESPONSIBILITIES TO EMPLOYEES

Healthcare executives have an ethical and professional obligation to employees of the organizations they manage that encompasses but is not limited to:

1. Working to create a working environment conducive for underscoring ethical employee conduct and behavior;
2. Working to ensure that individuals may freely express ethical concerns and providing mechanisms for discussing and addressing such concerns;
3. Working to ensure a working environment that is free from harassment, sexual and other; coercion of any kind, especially to

perform illegal or unethical acts; and discrimination on the basis of race, creed, color, sex, ethnic origin, age, or disability;

4. Working to ensure a working environment that is conducive to proper utilization of employees' skills and abilities;

5. Paying particular attention to the employee's work environment and job safety; and

6. Working to establish appropriate grievance and appeals mechanisms.

III. CONFLICTS OF INTEREST

A conflict of interest may be only a matter of degree, but exists when the healthcare executive:

A. Acts to benefit directly or indirectly by using authority or inside information, or allows a friend, relative, or associate to benefit from such authority or information.

B. Uses authority or information to make a decision to intentionally affect the organization in an adverse manner.

The healthcare executive shall:

A. Conduct all personal and professional relationships in such a way that all those affected are assured that management decisions are made in the best interests of the organization and the individuals served by it;

B. Disclose to the appropriate authority any direct or indirect financial or personal interests that pose potential or actual conflicts of interest;

C. Accept no gifts or benefits offered with the express or implied expectation of influencing a management decision; and

D. Inform the appropriate authority and other involved parties of potential or actual conflicts of interest related to appointments or elections to boards or committees inside or outside the healthcare executive's organization.

IV. THE HEALTHCARE EXECUTIVE'S RESPONSIBILITIES TO COMMUNITY AND SOCIETY

The healthcare executive shall:

A. Work to identify and meet the healthcare needs of the community;

    B. Work to ensure that all people have reasonable access to healthcare services;

    C. Participate in public dialogue on healthcare policy issues and advocate solutions that will improve health status and promote quality healthcare;

    D. Consider the short-term and long-term impact of management decisions on both the community and on society; and

    E. Provide prospective consumers with adequate and accurate information, enabling them to make enlightened judgments and decisions regarding services.

V. THE HEALTHCARE EXECUTIVE'S RESPONSIBILITY TO REPORT VIOLATIONS OF THE CODE

A member of the College who has reasonable grounds to believe that another member has violated this *Code* has a duty to communicate such facts to the Ethics Committee.

APPENDIX I

AMERICAN COLLEGE OF HEALTHCARE EXECUTIVES GRIEVANCE PROCEDURE

1. In order to be processed by the College, a complaint must be filed in writing to the Ethics Committee of the College within three years of the date of discovery of the alleged violation, and the Committee has the responsibility to look into incidents brought to its attention regardless of the informality of the information, provided the information can be documented or supported or may be a matter of public record. The three-year period within which a complaint must be filed shall temporarily cease to run during intervals when the accused member is in inactive status, or when the accused member resigns from the College.

2. The Committee chairman initially will determine whether the complaint falls within the purview of the Ethics Committee and whether immediate investigation is necessary. However, all letters of complaint that are filed with the Ethics Committee will appear

on the agenda of the next committee meeting. The Ethics Committee shall have the final discretion to determine whether a complaint falls within the purview of the Ethics Committee.

3. If a grievance proceeding is initiated by the Ethics Committee:
   a. Specifics of the complaint will be sent to the respondent by certified mail. In such mailing, committee staff will inform the respondent that the grievance proceeding has been initiated, and that the respondent may respond directly to the Ethics Committee; the respondent also will be asked to cooperate with the Regent investigating the complaint.
   b. The Ethics Committee shall refer the matter to the appropriate Regent who is deemed best able to investigate the alleged infraction. The Regent shall make inquiry into the matter, and in the process the respondent shall be given an opportunity to be heard.
   c. Upon completion of the inquiry, the Regent shall present a complete report and recommended disposition of the matter in writing to the Ethics Committee. Absent unusual circumstances, the Regent is expected to complete his or her report and recommended disposition, and provide them to the Committee, within 60 days.

4. Upon the Committee's receipt of the Regent's report and recommended disposition, the Committee shall review them and make its written recommendation to the Board of Governors as to what action shall be taken and the reason or reasons therefor. A copy of the Committee's recommended decision along with the Regent's report and recommended disposition to the Board will be mailed to the respondent by certified mail. In such mailing, the respondent will be notified that within 30 days after his or her receipt of the Ethics Committee's recommended decision, the respondent may file a written appeal of the recommended decision with the Board of Governors.

5. Any written appeal submitted by the respondent must be received by the Board of Governors within 30 days after the recommended decision of the Ethics Committee is received by the respondent. The Board of Governors shall not take action on the Ethics Committee's recommended decision until the 30-day appeal period has elapsed. If no appeal to the Board of Governors is filed in a timely fashion, the Board shall review the recommended decision and determine action to be taken.

6. If an appeal to the Board of Governors is timely filed, the College Chairman shall appoint an ad hoc committee consisting of three Fellows to hear the matter. At least 30 days' notice of the formation of this committee, and of the hearing date, time, and place, with an opportunity for representation, shall be mailed to the respondent. Reasonable requests for postponement shall be given consideration.

7. This ad hoc committee shall give the respondent adequate opportunity to present his or her case at the hearing, including the opportunity to submit a written statement and other documents deemed relevant by the respondent, and to be represented if so desired. Within a reasonable period of time following the hearing, the ad hoc committee shall write a detailed report with recommendations to the Board of Governors.

8. The Board of Governors shall decide what action to take after reviewing the report of the ad hoc committee. The Board shall provide the respondent with a copy of its decision. The decision of the Board of Governors shall be final. The Board of Governors shall have the authority to accept or reject any of the findings or recommended decisions of the Regent, the Ethics Committee, or the ad hoc committee, and to order whatever level of discipline it feels is justified.

9. At each level of the grievance proceeding, the Board of Governors shall have the sole discretion to notify or contact the complainant relating to the grievance proceeding; provided, however, that the complainant shall be notified as to whether the complaint was reviewed by the Ethics Committee and whether the Ethics Committee or the Board of Governors has taken final action with respect to the complaint.

10. No individual shall serve on the ad hoc committee described above, or otherwise participate in these grievance proceedings on behalf of the College, if he or she is in direct economic competition with the respondent or otherwise has a financial conflict of interest in the matter, unless such conflict is disclosed to and waived in writing by the respondent.

11. All information obtained, reviewed, discussed, and otherwise used or developed in a grievance proceeding that is not otherwise publicly known, publicly available, or part of the public domain is considered to be privileged and strictly confidential information of the College, and is not to be disclosed to anyone outside of the grievance proceeding except as determined by the Board of

Reprinted with permission of the American College of Healthcare Executives.

Governors or as required by law; provided, however, that an individual's membership status is not confidential and may be made available to the public upon request.

APPENDIX II

ETHICS COMMITTEE ACTION

Once the grievance proceeding has been initiated, the Ethics Committee may take any of the following actions based upon its findings:

1. Determine the grievance complaint to be invalid.
2. Dismiss the grievance complaint.
3. Recommend censure.
4. Recommend transfer to inactive status for a specified minimum period of time.
5. Recommend expulsion.

Note

1. Appendices I and II, entitled "American College of Healthcare Executives Grievance Procedure" and "Ethics Committee Action," respectively, are a material part of this *Code of Ethics* and are incorporated herein by reference.

AMERICAN HEALTHCARE ASSOCIATION
ETHICAL CONDUCT OF HEALTH CARE INSTITUTIONS

INTRODUCTION

Health care institutions, by virtue of their roles as health care providers, employers, and community health resources, have special responsibilities for ethical conduct and practices. Their broad range of patient care, education, public health, social service, and business functions is essential to the health and well-being of their communities. In general, the public expects that they will conduct themselves in an ethical manner that emphasizes a basic community service orientation.

This management advisory is intended to assist members of the American Hospital Association to better define the ethical aspects and implications of institutional policies and practicies. It is offered with the understanding that individual decisions seldom reflect an absolute ethical right or wrong, and that each institution's leadership in making policy and decisions must take into account the needs and values of the institution, its medical community, and employees and those of individual patients, their families, and the community as a whole.

The governing board of the institution is responsible for establishing and periodically evaluating the ethical standards that guide institutional

---

practices. The chief executive officer is responsible for assuring that hospital medical staff, employees, and volunteers and auxilians understand and adhere to these standards and for promoting an environment sensitive to differing values and conducive to ethical behavior.

This management advisory examines the hospital's ethical responsibilities to its community and patients as well as those deriving from its organizational roles as employer and a business entity. Although some responsibilities also may be included in legal and accreditation requirements, it should be remembered that legal, accreditation, and ethical obligations often overlap and that ethical obligations often extend beyond legal and accreditation requirements.

COMMUNITY ROLE

- Health care institutions should be concerned with the overall health status of their communities while continuing to provide direct patient services. This principle requires them to communicate and work with other health care and social agencies to improve the availability and provision of health promotion and education and services as well as patient care and to take a leadership role in enhancing public health and continuity of care in the community.
- Health care institutions are responsible for fair and effective use of available health care delivery resources to promote access to comprehensive and affordable health care services of high quality. This responsibility extends beyond the resources of the given institution to include efforts to coordinate with other health care providers and to share in community solutions for providing care for the medically indigent and others.
- All health care institutions have community service responsibilities which may include care for the poor and the uninsured, provision of needed services, and education and various programs designed to meet the specific needs of their communities. Not-for-profit institutions, in consideration of their community service origins, Hill-Burton obligations, and tax status, should be particularly sensitive to the importance of providing and designing services for their communities.
- Health care institutions, being dependent upon community confidence and support, are accountable to the public, and therefore their communications and disclosure of information

and data related to the institution should be clear, accurate, and sufficiently complete to assure that it is not misleading. Such disclosure should be aimed primarily at better public understanding of health issues, the services available to prevent and treat illness, and patients' rights and responsibilities relating to health care decisions.

- As health care institutions operate in an increasingly competitive environment, they should consider the overall welfare of their communities and their own missions in determining their activities, service mixes, and business ventures and conduct their business activities in an ethical manner.

PATIENT CARE

- Health care institutions are responsible for assuring that the care provided to each patient is appropriate and of the highest quality they are able to provide. Health care institutions should establish and follow procedures to verify the credentials of physicians and other health professionals, assess and improve quality of care, and review appropriateness of utilization.
- Health care institutions should have policies and practices that support the process of informed consent for diagnostic and therapeutic procedures and that respect and promote the patient's responsibility for decision making.
- Health care institutions are responsible for assuring confidentiality of patient-specific information. They are responsible for providing safeguards to prevent unauthorized release of information and establishing procedures for authorizing release of data.
- Health care institutions should assure that the psychological, social, spiritual, and physical needs and cultural beliefs and practices of patients and families are recognized and should promote employee and medical staff sensitivity to the full range of such needs and practices.
- Health care institutions should assure respect for and reasonable accommodation of individual religious and social beliefs and customs of patients whenever possible.
- Health care institutions should have specific mechanisms or procedures to resolve conflicting values and ethical dilemmas

among patients, their families, medical staff, employees, the institution, and the community.

ORGANIZATIONAL CONDUCT

- The policies and practices of health care institutions should respect the professional ethical codes and responsibilities of their employees and medical staff members and be sensitive to institutional decisions that employees might interpret as compromising their ability to provide high-quality health care.
- Health care institutions should have policies and practices that provide for equitably administered employee policies and practices.
- To the extent possible and consistent with the ethical commitments of the institution, health care institutions should accommodate the desires of employees and medical staff to embody religious and moral values in their professional activities.
- Health care institutions should have written policies on conflict of interest that apply to officers, governing board members, physicians, and others who make or influence decisions for or on behalf of the institution. These policies should recognize that individuals in decision-making or administrative positions often have duality of interests that may not ordinarily present conflicts. But they should provide mechanisms for identifying and addressing conflicts when they do exist.
- Health care institutions should communicate their mission, values, and priorities to the employees and volunteers, whose patient care and service activities are the most visible embodiment of the institution's ethical commitments and values.

AHA RESOURCES

This management advisory identifies the major areas affecting the ethical conduct of health care institutions. It would be impossible for one advisory document to detail all of the factors and issues relating to each area. Additional information and guidance is available in the following AHA management advisories:

A Patient's Bill of Rights
Advertising
Discharge Planning
Disclosure of Financial and Operating Information
Disclosure of Medical Record Information
Establishment of an Employee Grievance Procedure
Ethics Committees
Imperatives of Hospital Leadership
Quality Management
Resolution of Conflicts of Interest
The Patient's Choice of Treatment Options
Verifying Physician Credentials
Verifying Credentials of Medical Students and Residents

The following AHA publications may also be useful:

Values in Conflict: Resolving Ethical Issues in Hospital Care (AHA #025002)

Effective DNR Policies: Development, Revision, and Implementation (AHA #058750)

INDEX

A

B

ABOUT THE AUTHOR

An educator and public service professional with extensive experience in healthcare, higher education, government, and ministry, John Abbott Worthley holds professorships in the United States and Asia. He was dean of the Center for Public Affairs at Briarcliff College and program director at an international research unit of the State University of New York. In 1980 John Worthley went to Seton Hall University as director of the Graduate Public Management Program. He became a deputy chancellor and the University Professor of Public Administration and headed task forces that designed new administrative and academic structures for the New Jersey institution. In recent years he has served as visiting professor at the University of International Business and Economics in Beijing, Indiana University, the University of Illinois at Chicago, Russell Sage College, the Shanghai Foreign Trade Institute, and the Chinese University of Hong Kong.

Author of seven books, his prolific writings on various aspects of public service management and policy span nearly three decades. He has been principal ethics consultant to the New York state government, and has lectured on the subject in settings that range from Mother Teresa's headquarters in Calcutta to the United Nations European center in Geneva. Known in healthcare circles as the author of *Managing Computers in Healthcare* (Health Administration Press) and codeveloper of a special learning series for the American College of Healthcare Executives, he recently authored the acclaimed *Ethics of the Ordinary in Healthcare* (Health Administration Press). His considerable healthcare consulting includes work with hospitals, with state and local government health departments, with hospice and home care agencies, and with health-related corporations.

Dr. Worthley is a retired Navy commander and has been active in politics and pastoral work. A graduate of the College of the Holy Cross, he holds master's degrees in foreign affairs from the University of Virginia and in theology from the Seton Hall Seminary as well as a management doctorate from the State University of New York at Albany. He is 55 years of age and a low-handicap golfer—the pursuit of which has provided considerable experience with ethical issues.